MW00651737

murach's
OS/390 and
z/OS JCL

Raul Menendez

Doug Lowe

MIKE MURACH & ASSOCIATES, INC.

2560 West Shaw Lane, Suite 101 • Fresno, CA 93711-2765

Author:	Raul Menendez
Editor:	Judy Taylor
Cover design:	Zylka Design
Production:	Tom Murach

Thanks to Mike Andrews of Data Dallas Corporation for his technical assistance.

Books in the Murach series

Murach's OS/390 and z/OS JCL

Murach's Structured COBOL

Murach's CICS for the COBOL Programmer

Murach's Beginning Java 2

Murach's Beginning Visual Basic .NET

Other books for OS/390 and z/OS programmers

MVS TSO, Parts 1 & 2

VSAM: AMS and Application Programming

DB2 for the COBOL Programmer, Parts 1 & 2

© 2002, Mike Murach & Associates, Inc.
All rights reserved.

Printed in the United States of America

10 9 8 7 6 5 4 3 2 1
ISBN: 1-890774-14-6

Contents

Expanded contents

Chapter 7   How to manage tape data sets

Chapter 8   How to manage SYSOUT data sets

Introduction

OS/390 is the operating system that is used on most IBM mainframes. These are the powerful computers that handle thousands of users every day in large companies throughout the world. z/OS is the latest version of OS/390, and it runs on IBM's z/900 servers. These are the latest IBM mainframes that can also be used as servers for Internet applications. Because IBM mainframes process more transactions than all of the other platforms combined, you can be sure that OS/390 and z/OS will be around for many years to come.

Job Control Language, or JCL, is the language that controls OS/390 and z/OS. So if you're working as a programmer or operator on a mainframe that runs one of these operating systems, you need to know JCL. Although programmers often get by with minimal JCL skills, the best programmers develop a solid set of JCL skills because it helps them get more done in less time.

The intent of this book, of course, is to teach you JCL. If you're completely new to it, this book will start you from the beginning. And if you already have some JCL experience, it will raise you to a new level of mastery. Along the way, you'll learn how to use many of the facilities of OS/390 and z/OS including ISPF, Access Method Services, utility programs, the sort/merge utility, TSO, CLIST, REXX, and UNIX System Services. When you finish this book, you'll have a rich view of what OS/390 and z/OS can do, and you'll know how to take advantage of those capabilities in your own jobs.

7 ways this book helps you learn faster and better

- If you're new to IBM mainframes, the three chapters in section 1 introduce you to mainframe components and processing, OS/390, z/OS, and ISPF. This is the introduction that every new mainframer needs because no other platform is like a mainframe.

- If you're new to JCL, chapter 4 teaches you a subset of JCL that will get you started right. Then, you can build on that subset in the five chapters that complete section 2. When you finish this section, you'll have better JCL skills than most long-time professional programmers.

- After you complete the first two sections of this book, you can read sections 3, 4, and 5 in whatever sequence you prefer. You can also read the chapters in sections 3 and 5 in whatever sequence you prefer. That's because these sections and chapters are designed as independent modules. We refer to this as "modular organization," and it lets you get the training you need when you need it.

- Throughout the book, hundreds of examples show you the right way to code JCL for specific operations. Whether you're a beginner or a professional, these examples clarify the critical decisions that you have to make and help you avoid the errors that cause your jobs to fail.

- Besides showing you *how* to code the JCL for an operation, this book gives you the background you need for knowing *why* you should code it that way. That gives you a measure of confidence and competence that many experienced mainframers lack.

- All of the information in this book is presented in "paired pages" with the essential syntax, guidelines, and coding examples on the right and the perspective and extra explanation on the left. This lets you learn faster by reading less...and it's an important feature of all our recent books.

- After you use this book for training, the examples, paired pages, and modular organization make this book the best on-the-job reference you'll ever use. Just find the paired pages that present the skill you're looking for, and you're on your way. You usually don't even have to read the left page of the pair.

Who this book is for

If you're a programmer trainee, this book represents the fastest and best way to get started with OS/390 or z/OS JCL. By the time you complete the first nine chapters of the book, you'll have most of the knowledge and skills that you need for programming. Then, you can build on those skills whenever you need to. When you start working with VSAM files, for example, you can read the three chapters in section 4. And to learn more about using the IBM procedures for compiling and testing programs, you can read chapter 17.

If you're an experienced programmer, this is also a book you should have on your desk because it will help you enhance your JCL skills whenever you need to. If, for example, you need to work with generation data groups, chapter 12 shows you how. If you want to generate a test file by using the IEBDG utility, chapter 18 shows you how. And if you are called upon to work with UNIX files on your mainframe, chapter 21 shows you how. At some point, in fact, you should take the time to page through this entire book so you can get a complete view of the facilities that OS/390 and z/OS offer.

Finally, if you're an operator or an operator trainee, we don't know of a better way to get the JCL training that you need than using this book. Of course, there's more to being an operator than knowing JCL. But this book will give you the JCL background that every operator needs, and it will be the first reference that you turn to when JCL problems arise.

Support materials for trainers and instructors

If you're a trainer or instructor who would like to use this book as the basis for a course, we offer an Instructor's Guide on CD that includes a complete set of instructional materials. These include PowerPoint slides for classroom presentations, short-answer tests and test answers, and student exercises and solutions.

To download a sample of this Guide and to find out how to get the complete Guide, please go to our web site at www.murach.com and click on the "Instructor Info" button. Or, if you prefer, you can call Karen at 1-800-221-5528 or e-mail karen@murach.com.

Please let us know how this book works for you

Since the first edition of our JCL book came out in 1980, more than 165,000 programmers have learned JCL from it. Now, we think the improvements to this latest edition, both in the content itself and in the way it's organized into paired pages, are going to make training and reference easier than ever before.

If you have any comments about this book, we would enjoy hearing from you. We would especially like to know if this book has lived up to your expectations. To reply, you can e-mail us at murachbooks@murach.com or send your comments to our street address.

Thanks for buying this book. Thanks for reading it. And good luck with your work on your OS/390 or z/OS system.

Raul Menendez
Author

Mike Murach
Publisher

Section 1

The IBM mainframe environment

Before you can learn how to code JCL for the OS/390 and z/OS operating systems, you need to understand something about the IBM mainframe environment in which they operate. So the three chapters in this section give you the background you need.

Chapter 1 is a general introduction to mainframe processing that describes the typical components of an IBM system. After this overview, chapter 2 gives you more specifics about OS/390 and z/OS so you have some idea of how they manage the processing on today's IBM mainframes. And chapter 3 teaches you how to use ISPF, an interactive facility, to create OS/390 and z/OS jobs and submit them for processing.

Some of the material in this section may be review for you, depending on your background. As a result, if you have mainframe experience, I suggest you review the outline at the beginning of each chapter and then page through the figures to get a better idea of the content. That will help you decide whether you want to study the chapter in depth, skim it, or skip it entirely.

1

An introduction to IBM mainframe systems

The purpose of this chapter is to give you an overview of IBM mainframe systems by presenting both their hardware components and the operating systems that control their processing. Although many of these concepts may be familiar to you from your PC experience, IBM has a lot of specialized vocabulary that you need to be familiar with, so you'll be introduced to that. In addition, you'll begin to get some idea of the heavy-duty processing that the mainframe allows for and the complexity that's involved in handling thousands of users at a time.

If you already have IBM mainframe experience, you can just skim through this chapter to find any details that you aren't already familiar with. You may be especially interested in learning something about IBM's new zSeries of processors and the z/OS operating system designed to run on them.

IBM mainframe processors

The central component of an IBM mainframe computer system is the *processor*, just as it is on a PC. The IBM mainframe operating systems you'll learn about in this book, OS/390 and z/OS, run on processors that are members of the System/390 and zSeries families, a group of processors that have evolved over a period of almost 40 years. Although today's systems are much more complex and powerful than the systems available only a few years ago, you'll soon discover that IBM has maintained a high degree of compatibility between all of its processors over the years.

The basic architecture of a processor

Figure 1-1 gives a general view of the three subcomponents that make up a typical IBM mainframe processor: the CPU, main storage, and channels. In fact, these same components apply to all mainframe processors from the systems of the 1960's through to today's mainframes. However, the arrangements of these components are more complex in processors with greater processing power.

The *central processing unit*, or *CPU*, contains the circuitry needed to execute program instructions that manipulate data stored in *main storage*, or *main memory*. Although not shown in this figure, most processors use a special-purpose, high-speed memory buffer called a *cache* that operates between the CPU and main memory. This relatively small amount of storage operates at speeds even faster than the storage in main memory, so the overall speed of the processor is increased. Special circuitry constantly monitors accesses to main memory and keeps the most frequently accessed sections in the cache.

Today, most mainframe systems are *multiprocessor systems* with two or more CPUs that can share access to main memory. Multiprocessing provides two benefits. First, the overall instruction processing rate of the system is increased because two or more processors are available to execute program instructions. Second, the system's availability is increased because if one of the processors fails, the others can take over its work.

Regardless of the number of CPUs available, today's System/390 and zSeries processors can be logically divided to give the appearance of multiple computers on a single hardware configuration. This logical partitioning is handled by a facility called the *Processor Resource/Systems Manager* (*PR/SM*), which allows a single server to be divided into as many as 15 *logical partitions* (*LPARs*).

The third subcomponent of the processor consists of *channels* that provide fiber optic paths between the processor and *input/output devices* (*I/O devices*), like printers or terminals. Each channel can connect to devices called *control units* that in turn connect to multiple I/O devices. The channels execute instructions that control the operation of the I/O devices attached to them, freeing up the processor to execute other instructions so that overall system performance is improved. Although eight channels are shown in this figure, the actual number varies from processor to processor.

The basic processor architecture for IBM mainframe systems

Processor

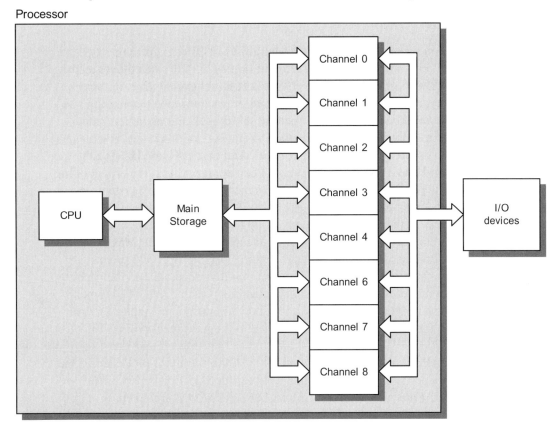

Description

- In general, the subcomponents that make up a *processor* have remained stable on all IBM mainframe systems from the 1960's System/360 to today's zSeries servers.
- The *central processing unit*, or *CPU*, contains the circuitry needed to execute program instructions that manipulate data stored in *main storage*.
- The *cache* is a high-speed memory buffer that operates between the CPU and main storage. The most frequently accessed sections of memory are kept in the cache to speed up processing.
- *Channels* (also referred to as *ESCON channels*) connect the processor to *input/output devices*, thus providing access to communication networks and stored data. The number of channels available varies from processor to processor.
- *Multiprocessor systems* are processors that have more than one CPU sharing access to main memory. Multiprocessing can increase the overall instruction processing rate of a system. It can also increase a system's availability because if one CPU fails, another can take over its work.
- *PR/SM* is a facility that's used to divide a processor into *logical partitions* (*LPARs*), each of which appears to be a separate system.

Figure 1-1   The basic architecture of an IBM mainframe processor

The history of the System 360/370 family of processors

To give you some perspective on the longevity of IBM mainframe systems, figure 1-2 includes a timeline of the different processors introduced over a span of 40 years. IBM introduced its first system processors even earlier, in the 1950's. However, these processors were based on vacuum tube technology and were typically designed to address a specific set of applications rather than a more general, multipurpose environment.

The System/360, or S/360, processors released in 1964 were IBM's first attempt to standardize mainframe systems. Their design was so forward-looking that many of the architectural principles introduced in these early systems are still used in today's processors.

The success of the S/360 system gave way to the next big step in mainframe processor development. In 1970, IBM introduced the first of what was to be a long family of System/370, or S/370, processors. Originally, S/370 processors were based on 24-bit technology. That meant that the processor had the capacity to address the highest number of memory locations possible in a 24-bit binary numbering system (you'll learn more about how this works in chapter 2). Over time the need for greater memory capacity led to the introduction of 31-bit S/370 processors.

In 1990, IBM introduced the System/390 (S/390) family of processors. One of the major benefits S/390 systems had over earlier S/370 systems was the introduction of *Enterprise Systems Connection*, or *ESCON*, architecture. ESCON uses fiber optic cables to connect I/O devices to the processor over long distances. Before ESCON, I/O devices were connected to channels using heavy copper cables that could be no longer than 400 feet. ESCON extended that limit to anywhere from 3km to 60km away from the processor unit. In addition, ESCON allows for information to flow at a higher speed between the devices and the channel subsystem on the processor.

In October of 2000, IBM announced the availability of their newest line of processors. The zSeries line is designed to address the growing dominance of mainframe systems in e-business. The *z/Architecture* that these processors are based on is perhaps one of the most significant changes in system architecture since the introduction of the System/360. That's because zSeries processors use a 64-bit addressing technology rather than the 31-bit addressing technology found on S/390 systems. This 64-bit architecture allows the processor to achieve an unprecedented level of memory addressing. For example, a 31-bit S/390 processor can access up to 2GB (gigabytes) of memory per application, whereas a z900 processor can theoretically address up to 16EB (exabytes) of memory…about 8 billion times as much! But for practical reasons, memory addressability on most z900 servers is currently limited to 64GB.

Incidentally, IBM has recently started referring to their mainframe computers as *mainframe servers*, a term that helps associate their mainframe processors with e-business strategy. This book will use the terms *server* and *mainframe computer* interchangeably.

IBM processor history

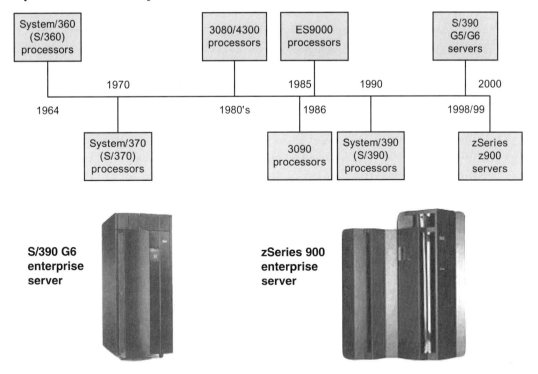

S/390 G6 enterprise server

zSeries 900 enterprise server

Description

- IBM introduced its first system processors in the 1950's. Then, in 1964, it introduced the System/360 family of processors that provides the foundation for all subsequent systems.

- Aside from greater performance, one of the major advantages offered by S/390 systems over earlier processors was the introduction of *ESCON* architecture. ESCON uses fiber optic cables to connect I/O devices to the processor over long distances. It also allows for a higher-speed information flow between the I/O devices and the channel subsystem on the processor.

- The *z/Architecture* found on IBM's zSeries processors is perhaps the largest change in system architecture since the introduction of the S/360 system. That's because it uses a 64-bit addressing technology rather than the 31-bit addressing technology found on S/390s and earlier systems. This allows for an unprecedented level of memory addressing.

- In a 31-bit environment, S/390 systems are capable of addressing up to 2 gigabytes (GB) of main storage. In a 64-bit environment, the addressing range can theoretically reach up to 16 exabytes (EB). However, current z900 server models are limited to 64GB of addressable main storage.

- When talking about computer capacity, some units of measure you'll commonly hear are *megabyte* or *MB* (about a million bytes), *gigabyte* or *GB* (about a billion bytes), *terabyte* or *TB* (about a trillion bytes), and *exabyte* or *EB* (about a million terabytes).

Figure 1-2   The history of the System 360/370 family of processors

Input/output devices for IBM mainframes

As an applications programmer, you need to know something about the input/output devices that connect to a processor to provide it with input, output, primary storage, and secondary storage. Figure 1-3 shows some of the typical devices you'll find attached to an S/390 or z900 server. Although this doesn't include all of the types of devices that can attach to mainframes, it does include the ones you're likely to use most as you run your programs. In fact, this book has whole chapters devoted to the information you need to provide to your system to ensure that your programs run the way you want them to using the I/O devices shown in this figure.

Devices that store data that a mainframe server can later retrieve and process are essential to any system. Most systems use direct access storage devices, or DASD, to directly and rapidly access large quantities of data. Multiple DASD units can typically be classified as a system's primary storage devices. Secondary storage devices such as tape drives and optical disk drives store information that is seldom used and takes much longer to retrieve.

Interactive devices such as display terminals allow users to interact directly with the mainframe server. A user can enter information into an application, issues commands to the server, and access information stored on storage devices through terminals. On the other hand, output devices like printers produce hardcopy versions of data processed by a mainframe server.

An overview of the types of I/O devices that connect to mainframe servers

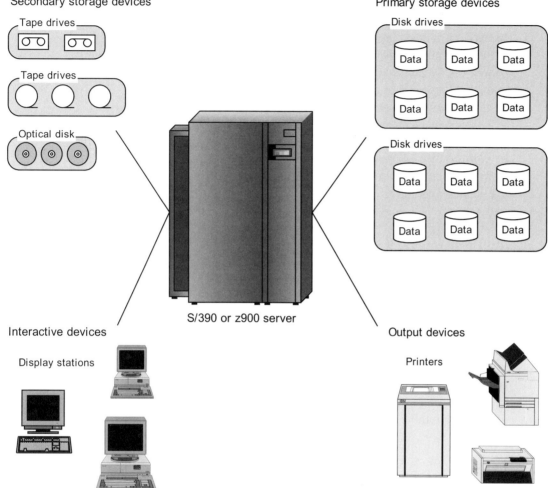

Figure 1-3   Input/output devices on a mainframe system

Description

- In order for a mainframe computer to be useful, it must be attached to several different types of input/output (I/O) devices.

- Direct access storage devices, or DASD, allow direct and rapid access to large quantities of data.

- Tape drives write and retrieve data from magnetic tape sources such as tape cartridges and traditional reel-to-reel tapes.

- Large quantities of reference material can also be stored in an optical disk format similar to a CD-ROM.

- Display stations provide the means for a user to communicate with and review information on a mainframe server.

- Printers produce hardcopy versions of data processed by a mainframe server.

Terminal display devices

The *3270 display station* (or *terminal*) has been the standard workstation for IBM mainframe computers since 1971. The 3270 information display system includes terminals (display stations), printers, and controllers. As figure 1-4 shows, the terminals access the mainframe through IBM 3174 controllers, which can provide for anywhere from 32 to 64 terminals. As a result, a large system consists of many of these controllers.

Although 3270 terminals were common in the 1980's and early 1990's, you won't find too many mainframe shops using them any more. Today, *3270 emulation software* makes it possible for personal computers (PCs) to be used as 3270 terminals. That way, you not only have access to the mainframe and its applications but also to PC applications like word processing and spreadsheet software.

In this figure, you can see that there are several ways to connect PCs with 3270 emulation software to the mainframe server. One way is through a *local area network* (*LAN*) or a *wide area network* (*WAN*). Another way is through the Internet or an intranet. Whichever way is used, the 3270 emulation software interprets data streams sent from the mainframe and constructs a 3270 screen display on a PC's monitor, usually in a window.

IBM offers several different types of 3270 emulation software. Of particular interest is a Java-enabled 3270 emulator that can be used through a web browser. However, you can also purchase 3270 emulators from other third-party companies. For example, to test the examples in this book, I used a *Telnet* (*TN3270*) *emulator* called *EXTRA! for Windows 98* to access a mainframe system at a remote site over the Internet.

Terminal display devices

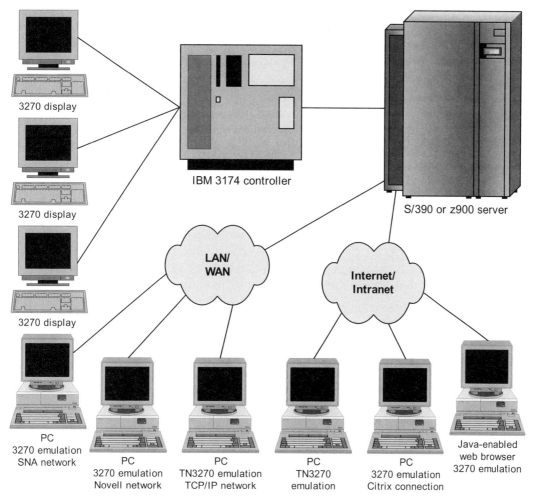

Figure 1-4   Terminal display devices

Description

- The 3270 family of terminal display devices has been the standard for IBM mainframe computers since 1971. Although 3270s can be connected to a mainframe directly, they're usually connected remotely via a 3174 controller.

- Today, the typical user connects to the mainframe via a PC running some form of *3270 emulation software*. This software interprets 3270 data streams sent through a network and constructs a 3270 display screen, usually in a window on the PC's desktop.

- The type of PC emulation you use depends on how you connect to the mainframe. In general, though, they all function the same way.

- In a *local area network* (*LAN*) or a *wide area network* (*WAN*), several emulation software programs are available depending on whether you are connected to an SNA, Novell, or TCP/IP network.

- In an Internet or intranet environment, you can use a *Telnet* (TN3270) based emulator, connect to a Citrix server that in turn connects to the mainframe, or use a Java-enabled web browser to display a 3270 screen.

Printer devices

Most mainframe systems use a variety of printer devices to produce reports, forms, and many other types of hardcopy output. Printer technology has evolved over the years and so have the uses for printers in large systems. In the 1960's and early 1970's, printed reports were the primary way of obtaining information stored on a mainframe. Today though, when you can view output on a terminal screen, printers are typically used to print smaller summary reports, invoices, and other types of specialized documents. Although countless types of printers can work with S/390 and zSeries servers, all generally fall into one of the three categories shown in figure 1-5: line printers, character printers, and page printers.

Line printers, or *impact printers*, produce printed output by striking an image of the characters to be printed on a ribbon. The ribbon, in turn, transfers ink to the paper. The paper varies in size and is usually tractor-fed. Line printers are among the oldest type of printers used in a mainframe environment. Sizewise, they tend to be larger than most other types of printers. That's because a metal belt engraved with the character set spins at a high speed within the printer. When the desired character on the spinning belt aligns with the correct position on the paper, an impression is made. This allows line printers to print fast. In fact, some line printers are capable of producing up to 1400 lines per minute (lpm). Line printers are primarily used today to print information on special forms like checks and other preprinted forms.

Character printers, sometimes called *dot-matrix printers*, create character images by causing a series of small pins on the print head to strike a ribbon. The ribbon, in turn, transfers ink to the paper. Like line printers, character printers can handle paper of various sizes, but the paper is usually tractor-fed. Traditionally, large installations would have at least one character printer in every department. They were typically used to print out customer information and multi-form reports, and occasionally, system messages were broadcast through them. Today, you'll still find character printers in some companies. In fact, a variation of the character printer can be found at most banks. They're the small printers that are often used to print out a transaction receipt.

Page printers, more commonly known as *laser printers*, produce one page of output at a time, typically on 8 ½ x 11 paper. This type of printer is by far the most popular and varies in size from desktop models to full duplex printers capable of printing up to 1002 *ipm* or *impressions per minute* (an impression is one page). Page printers are primarily used to print out reports but can also be used to print forms on preprinted and plain paper. For the latter, the laser printer uses an image of what the form should look like and merges it with the data for an individual form before it prints it out. Some laser printers can even produce the magnetic MICR lines found at the bottom of most checks.

The three categories of printers in an IBM mainframe system

Page printers (laser printers)
Uses: Reports, forms, checks with MICR lines

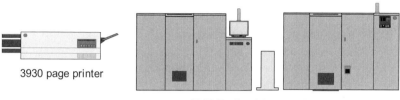

3930 page printer

3900 Duplex Advanced Functioning
Printing System

3130 Advanced Function
printer

Line printers (impact printers)
Uses: Reports, preprinted forms, checks

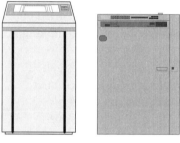

Character printers (dot-matrix printers)
Uses: Single-page reports, multi-part forms

4230 matrix printer   4247 multi-form printer

4245 line printer   6262 impact printer

Description

- *Page printers*, or *laser printers*, produce one page at a time on individual sheets of paper typically 8 ½ x 11 in size. These printers vary in size from desktop models to full duplex printers capable of printing up to 1002 ipm (impressions per minute) or pages per minute.

- *Line printers*, or *impact printers*, produce printed output by striking an image of the characters to be printed against a ribbon, which in turn transfers ink to the paper. The paper can vary in size and is usually tractor-fed. Some line printers can print up to 1400 lines per minute (lpm).

- *Character printers*, or *dot-matrix printers*, create character images by causing a series of small pins in the print head to strike a ribbon, which in turn transfers ink to the paper. Like line printers, the paper can vary in size and is usually tractor-fed. Character printers are slower than line printers, with some models capable of producing only 300 to 600 characters per second (cps).

Figure 1-5   Printer devices

Direct access storage devices

The official IBM term for a disk drive is *direct access storage device*, or *DASD*. Because DASDs allow direct and rapid access to large quantities of data, they are a key component of mainframe systems. They're used not only to store user programs and data but also to store programs and data for operating system functions, as you'll see later in this chapter.

The diagram in figure 1-6 shows how DASD units are accessed by the mainframe. First, the S/390 or z900 server is connected to a 3990 storage controller through a series of ESCON channel connections. The 3990 controller, in turn, connects to one or several RAMAC DASD array units. It also provides high-speed *cache storage* that improves the retrieval speed of the disk data that's accessed most frequently.

A RAMAC DASD array houses several individual disk drives, each of which reads and writes data on a *disk pack* (also called a *volume*). A disk pack is a stack of metal platters coated with a metal oxide material. Data is recorded on each side of the platter. Some RAMAC DASD arrays have the ability to hold up to 1.6TB (terabytes) of information.

Data is recorded on the surfaces of a disk pack in concentric circles called *tracks*. When a disk drive is in operation, the disks rotate at a high speed on a spindle. To read or write data on a disk, an *access mechanism*, or *actuator*, moves the *read/write heads* to the appropriate track. As you can see in this figure, the actuator has one read/write head for each recording surface on the volume. That way, when the actuator moves, all of the read/write heads move together so that they're positioned on the same track on each surface. If, for example, the actuator moves the heads from track 200 to track 300, all of the heads move to track 300.

The tracks that are positioned under the heads of the actuator at any one time can be thought of as a *cylinder*. As a result, there are as many cylinders in a volume as there are tracks on one of the recording surfaces. So a volume that has 19 surfaces, each with 808 tracks, has 808 cylinders, each with 19 tracks.

Direct access storage devices

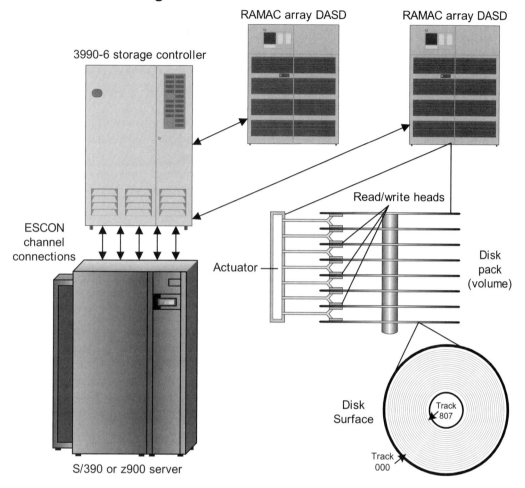

Description

- The official IBM term for a disk drive is *direct access storage device*, or *DASD*. DASD units allow a mainframe server direct and rapid access to large quantities of data.

- A DASD reads and writes data on a *disk pack*, or *volume*, which consists of a stack of metal disks coated with a metal oxide material. Data is recorded on both sides of each disk by read and write heads attached to an *access mechanism*, or *actuator*.

- Data is recorded on each surface in concentric circles called *tracks*. The tracks that are positioned under the heads of the actuator at one time make up a *cylinder*.

- DASD devices are attached in groups called *DASD arrays*. There are several types and models of RAMAC DASD arrays available, with some capable of holding up to 1.6TB (terabytes) of data.

- The 3990 storage controller manages the flow of information between the DASD devices and the S/390 or z900 server by providing high-speed *cache storage* for the data that's accessed most frequently. Then, when that data is referenced, it can be read directly from the cache, which is faster than accessing the actual DASD unit it's stored on.

Figure 1-6   Direct access storage devices

Magnetic tape and optical disk storage devices

Figure 1-7 shows some other devices used by a mainframe system to store data. *Magnetic tapes* are primarily used to back up or archive information that is normally kept on DASD. And *optical disks* are an efficient and cost-effective way to store information that is traditionally kept on paper or microfiche.

A tape drive reads and writes data on a magnetic tape that's a continuous strip of plastic coated on one side with a metal oxide. Originally, most tape drives processed tape wrapped around an open reel much like an old-fashioned reel-to-reel tape recorder. Although *reel-to-reel tape* is still used today by some installations or for some applications, newer tape drive systems (like the *3590 tape subsystem*) process tape that's sealed within a tape cartridge. *Tape cartridges* have higher capacities than tape reels, are more durable, and process information faster.

A serious drawback of tape processing is that it must be sequential. In other words, to read the 50,000[th] record on a tape, the first 49,999 records must be read first. As you can imagine, tape processing is therefore ill-suited for the processing requirements of most systems today. Still, tape is an excellent, and in fact, a primary way to back up information that must be retained but isn't accessed regularly. Tape is also the principal way to exchange large quantities of data between organizations and systems.

In the late 1980's and early 1990's, IBM introduced the first of a series of optical disk drives for mainframe systems. Many envisioned that with the introduction of optical disk media, the potential for a "paperless" office would someday be realized. Although the paperless office has never materialized, optical disk storage is an excellent way to store information, particularly older information kept on paper and microfiche. Optical disk media have made it possible for many companies to free thousands of square feet of office and warehouse space that would normally be reserved for paper file storage.

An optical disk drive, like a CD-ROM drive on a PC, uses light from a laser to read and write information on an optical disk. These optical disks and the drive that reads and writes them are stored in a device that is typically referred to as an *optical disk library*, or *jukebox*. The term "jukebox" originates from the fact that the optical disks are stored in slots that are retrieved by a robotic arm and placed in a drive reader.

Most optical drives provide support for *Write-Once, Read-Many (WORM)* 5.25-inch, 5.2GB optical media disks. An advantage to WORM storage is that the data written to the disk is permanent. That means that unlike DASD or tape, once a portion of an optical disk is written to, it can never be overwritten or erased. Because of this, WORM storage is a good choice for companies that have to store a large quantity of information for legal reasons.

Magnetic tape and optical disk storage devices

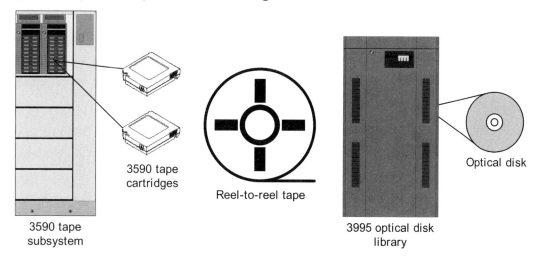

3590 tape
cartridges

Reel-to-reel tape

Optical disk

3590 tape
subsystem

3995 optical disk
library

Description

- *Magnetic tapes* are primarily used to back up information from DASD and to store older archived information.

- Tape processing can only be used to store and retrieve sequential data. As a result, tapes are ill-suited for applications that require direct access to stored data.

- Although *reel-to-reel tapes* were once predominantly used, today it is more common to use *tape cartridges* like those in a 3590 tape subsystem. Tape cartridges can store more information, are more durable, and process information much faster.

- Information that is infrequently used or traditionally stored on paper or microfiche can be stored instead on *optical disks*. An optical disk drive, like a CD-ROM drive on a PC, uses light from a laser to read and write information on an optical disk.

- Most optical drives provide *WORM* (*Write-Once, Read-Many*) support, which produces an unalterable copy of the data onto a 5.25-inch, 5.2GB optical media disk.

- Optical storage library systems store optical disks in slots that are retrieved by robotic arms and placed in a drive reader. Some system models have a capacity of up to 1.34TB.

Figure 1-7   Magnetic tape and optical disk storage devices

The basic characteristics of a mainframe operating system

As you know from working with PC operating systems like Windows, an *operating system* is a set of programs that controls the operation of the computer. Mainframe operating systems like *OS/390* and *z/OS* have to control the resources that are available to hundreds or thousands of users at a time as they run application and system-level programs, so these systems and their supporting software are incredibly complex. In fact, mainframe installations cannot function without a full-time staff of *systems programmers* who work to keep the operating system and related system software in shape.

As an applications programmer, you'll have a better sense of how your programs are being processed if you're aware of five basic characteristics of mainframe operating systems: virtual storage, multiprogramming, spooling, batch processing, and time sharing. Many of these characteristics can also be found in PC operating systems, although usually not at the same level of sophistication as they're found on the mainframe.

Virtual storage

On most computer systems, the processor's main storage is among the most valuable of the system's resources. As a result, mainframe operating systems provide facilities that make the best use of the available main storage. Among the most basic of these services is virtual storage.

Virtual storage is a technique that lets a large amount of main storage be simulated by a processor that actually has a smaller amount of *real storage*. For example, a processor that has 256 MB of real storage might use virtual storage to simulate 512 MB of main storage. To do this, the computer uses disk storage as an extension of real storage, as illustrated in the diagram in figure 1-8. The key here is that only the program instruction that's currently executing and the data it accesses need to be in real storage. Other data and instructions can be placed temporarily on disk storage and recalled into main storage when needed.

Although the details of how virtual storage is implemented vary from one operating system to another, the basic concept is the same. In chapter 2, you'll learn how virtual storage is implemented under OS/390 and z/OS.

Multiprogramming

Another feature common to all mainframe operating systems is multiprogramming. *Multiprogramming* simply means that the computer lets more than one program execute at the same time. Actually, that's misleading because at any given moment, only one program can have control of the CPU. Nevertheless, a multiprogramming system *appears* to execute more than one program at the same time. For example, in figure 1-8, programs A, B, and C all appear to be executing, but only program A is being processed by the CPU.

An overview of virtual storage and multiprogramming

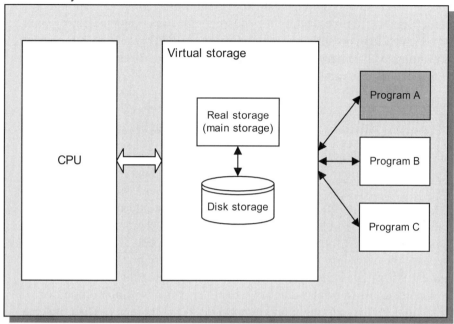

Mainframe system

Virtual storage

- *Virtual storage* is a technique that lets a large amount of main storage be simulated by a processor that actually has a smaller amount of main, or *real*, storage.

- The processor creates virtual storage by using disk storage to simulate and extend real storage.

- Although the current program instruction being executed and any data it requires have to be in real storage, other data and instructions can be placed in virtual storage and re-called into real storage when needed.

Multiprogramming

- *Multiprogramming* allows more than one program to be executed by the processor at the same time.

- Many programs spend a large percentage of their time idle waiting for I/O operations to complete. With multiprocessing, the system can move on to the next program and use its CPU time more effectively.

Figure 1-8   Virtual storage and multiprogramming

The key to understanding multiprogramming is to realize that some processing operations, like reading data from an input device, take much longer than others. As a result, most programs that run on mainframe computers are idle a large percentage of the time waiting for I/O operations to complete. If programs were run one at a time on a mainframe computer, the CPU would spend most of its time waiting. Multiprogramming simply reclaims the CPU during these idle periods to let other programs execute.

Spooling

A significant problem that must be overcome by multiprogramming systems is sharing access to input and output devices among the programs that execute together. For example, if two programs executing at the same time try to write output to a printer, the output from both programs will be intermixed in the printout. One way to avoid this problem is to give one of the programs complete control of the printer. Unfortunately, that defeats the purpose of multiprogramming because the other program will have to wait until the printer is available.

Figure 1-9 illustrates how *spooling* is used by the operating system to provide shared access to printer devices. Spooling manages printer output for the applications by intercepting it and directing it to a disk device. Then, when a program is finished, the operating system collects its spooled print output and directs it to the printer. In a multiprogramming environment, each program's spooled output is stored separately on disk so that it can be printed separately.

Another benefit of spooling results from the fact that disk devices are much faster than printers. As a result, programs that produce spooled print output can execute faster than programs that access printers directly. The operating system component that actually prints the spooled output is multiprogrammed along with the application programs so that the printer is kept as busy as possible. But the application programs themselves aren't slowed down by the relatively slow operation of the printer.

How the operating system spools output from application programs

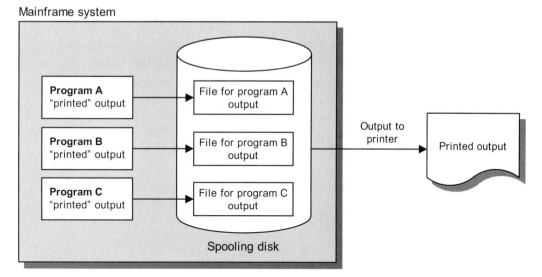

Description

- *Spooling* manages printer output for applications by intercepting the output that's directed to a printer and directing it to disk instead. Then, when the program is finished, the operating system collects the spooled output and sends it to the printer.

- In a multiprogramming environment, each program's spooled output is stored separately on disk so it can be printed separately.

- Since spooling print output to disk is faster than actually printing the output, programs finish faster and therefore free up the processor for other activities.

- The operating system program that handles spooling is multiprogrammed just as the application programs are.

Figure 1-9   Spooling

Batch processing

If you ever used a PC back in the days of the DOS operating system, you're probably familiar with the concept of batch files. Batch files contain a series of commands that are processed together as a batch. Today, PC operating systems like Windows XP have virtually eliminated the need for batch files. On a mainframe computer, however, *batch processing* is the norm and has been for decades. In fact, the term originates from the early days when punched cards were used for processing. You would put a "batch" of cards in a box that were then fed into the processor.

When batch processing is used, work is processed in units called *jobs*. A job may cause one or more programs to be executed in sequence. For example, a single job can invoke the programs necessary to update a file of employee records, print a report listing employee information, and produce payroll checks.

Job Control Language, or *JCL*, describes a job to the system by providing information that identifies the programs to be executed and the data to be processed. JCL is a complex language that consists of several types of state-ments with dozens of different specifications. This book will teach you how to code JCL statements to create jobs that can run on an OS/390 or z/OS system.

To manage all of the jobs that are executed, the system's *job scheduler* processes each job in an orderly fashion. When a user submits a job to the system, that job is added to a list of other jobs that are waiting to be executed. As the processor becomes available, the job scheduling portion of the operating system selects the next job to be executed from this list.

The diagram in figure 1-10 illustrates how the job scheduler receives and processes jobs submitted to the system. As you can see, the job scheduler makes decisions about which jobs to execute next. In the diagram, job 2 is chosen and sent to the processor. The job scheduler will next choose either job 1 or job 3. In other words, jobs aren't necessarily executed in the order in which they're submitted. Instead, jobs with higher priorities can be given preference over jobs with lower priorities.

How batch processing works

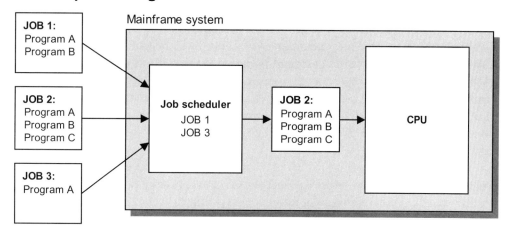

Description

- *Batch processing* is used to execute one or more programs in a specified sequence with no further interaction by a user.

- Batch work is processed in units called *jobs*. Each job can contain one or more programs to be executed.

- *Job Control Language*, or *JCL*, describes a job by providing information that identifies the programs to be executed and the data to be processed.

- A system's *job scheduler* controls the execution of all jobs submitted for processing, deciding which job should be executed next based on JCL specifications and system settings.

Figure 1-10   Batch processing

Time sharing

In a *time sharing* system, each user has access to the system through a terminal device, as shown in the diagram in figure 1-11. Instead of submitting jobs that are scheduled for later execution as in batch processing, the user enters commands that are processed immediately. As a result, time sharing is sometimes called *interactive* or *online processing* because it lets users interact directly with the computer. For technical reasons, time sharing is also sometimes called *foreground processing*, while batch processing is called *background processing*.

Because of time sharing, mainframe computer systems have two faces: batch job processing and online processing. In practice, you need to be familiar with both techniques of using your computer system. In fact, as a programmer, you'll use time sharing facilities to create, maintain, and store JCL statements and programs so they can be processed as jobs in batch mode. (You'll learn more about this in chapter 3.)

One other thing to note in this figure is that the operating system allows more than one user at a time to access the same software in a time sharing environment, as long as the software is written for shared access. Here, then, users 1 and 2 are using the same program to enter orders. Meanwhile, users 3 and 4 could be using the same systems software to do program-development tasks. What's interesting is that the systems programs that control hundreds or thousands of time sharing users at a time are themselves running as individual batch programs. So again, the batch and time sharing aspects of a mainframe system are tightly integrated.

Multiple users in a time sharing environment

Mainframe system

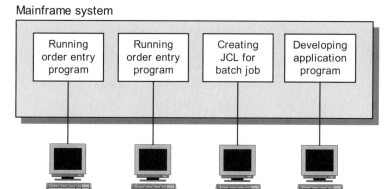

Description

- In a *time sharing* system, multiple users interact with the computer at the same time.

- In contrast to batch processing, each user in a time sharing environment accesses the system through a terminal device using commands that are processed immediately. As a result, time sharing is often called *online* or *interactive processing*.

- Time sharing also allows users to share access to the same application or systems programs (assuming, of course, that the programs are written for shared access).

- The systems programs that control time sharing are themselves running as batch jobs in the multiprogramming environment.

Figure 1-11   Time sharing

Operating systems for IBM mainframes

Now that you're familiar with some basic features of a mainframe operating system, you're ready to learn more about the systems available on an IBM mainframe today, especially OS/390 and z/OS. As you'll see, IBM has continually enhanced its operating systems over the years to make effective use of ever more powerful hardware and to meet increased processing demands.

The OS family of operating systems

Figure 1-12 give you a timeline of the evolution of the OS/390 and z/OS operating systems. Starting in 1964, the original OS for System/360 processors was introduced. After that, successive enhancements were applied in order to accommodate the growing demand for processing. In the late 1960's and early 1970's, there were two versions of the OS in widespread use, *OS/MFT* and *OS/MVT*, that differed in the way they handled multiprogramming. Under MFT, the size of each storage area used to execute jobs remained constant, as did the number of jobs that could be multiprogrammed. In contrast, MVT allocated storage to each program as it entered the system according to its needs and the current demands on the system.

Perhaps the most significant enhancement occurred in 1974 with the introduction of *MVS*. That's because MVS was the first operating system to offer *multiple virtual storage*, which allowed each process or job to have its own virtual storage address space. You'll learn more about how this works in chapter 2.

MVS continued to evolve over the years, with subsequent releases continuing though to MVS/ESA version 5 in 1994. In 1995, IBM decided to repackage MVS and bundle many of the separate but required products needed to operate an S/390 system into one package called OS/390. Then in 2001, a 64-bit version of OS/390 was introduced called z/OS. MVS is still the core of these newer operating systems, though, so all of the JCL you'll learn in this book applies directly to the MVS processes within. For the sake of clarity (and to save some space), I'll simply use the term *OS/390* to refer to MVS, OS/390, and z/OS throughout this book.

Other IBM mainframe operating systems

Figure 1-12 also gives you a brief description of the other operating systems that are available today on IBM mainframes. *DOS*, which stands for *Disk Operating System*, was first released in the 1960's and was originally designed for small System/360 configurations that had limited processing requirements (it's not related at all to PC-based DOS). Over the years, DOS has evolved significantly to the point that it bears little resemblance to the original version. Today, DOS is commonly called *DOS/VSE* or *VSE/ESA*. VSE stands for *Virtual Storage Extended*, which is a particular way virtual storage is handled.

The evolution of the OS/390 and z/OS operating systems

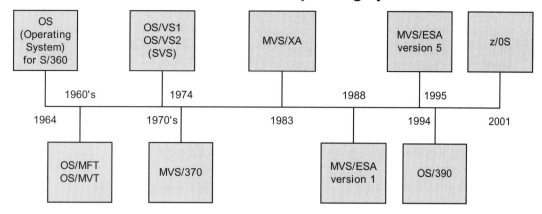

3 other IBM operating systems

The DOS/VSE operating system

- *DOS*, or *Disk Operating System*, was released in the 1960's and was designed to run on smaller systems.

- DOS today is commonly called *DOS/VSE* or *VSE/ESA*. VSE stands for *Virtual Storage Extended*, which refers to the particular way virtual storage is handled.

The VM operating system

- *VM*, or *Virtual Machine*, originated in 1972 and is usually found today on smaller systems. It enables the simulation of more than one computer system on a single mainframe, with each virtual machine running under its own operating system.

- The latest VM operating system, z/VM, was announced in October 2000. Like its z/OS counterpart, it takes advantage of many of the capabilities of a z900 server.

The Linux operating system

- *Linux* is a UNIX-like operating system developed by Linus Torvalds, after whom it is named.

- In 1999, IBM released the source code that supported the open systems Linux operating system on the S/390 series of servers.

- In 2001, IBM released the Linux operating system on the zSeries servers.

Description

- The *MVS*, or *Multiple Virtual Storage*, operating system makes up the core of today's OS/390 and z/OS operating systems. Because you're most likely to be using OS/390 at this point, I'll refer to all MVS processes as OS/390 processes throughout this book.

- Although the JCL facilities you'll learn how to use in this book apply most directly to OS/390 and z/OS, the basic forms of JCL statements haven't changed much since the original OS was introduced in the mid-1960s.

Figure 1-12   An overview of IBM mainframe operating systems

The *VM* operating system, which stands for *Virtual Machine*, uses a variety of techniques including virtual storage and multiprogramming to simulate more than one computer system on a single hardware configuration. Each simulated virtual machine needs its own operating system apart from VM, however. Sometimes CMS, an interactive operating system that works only under VM, is used, but versions of VSE or MVS can also be used as guest operating systems. That means that under VM, a single hardware configuration can run both VSE and MVS.

In 1999, IBM released the source code that supported the open systems *Linux* operating system on the S/390 series of servers. Linux is a UNIX-like operating system that is exceptionally efficient at handling a large load of e-business transactions. Then, in 2001, IBM released a version of Linux for zSeries servers.

Features of the OS/390 and z/OS operating systems

As I mentioned earlier, OS/390 transformed MVS into a server operating system by combining more than 30 separate products into the MVS environment. This simplified the installation process and provided for closer, more efficient integration among the once separate services. Some of these base services are listed in figure 1-13. First and foremost is the *Base Control Program*, or *BCP*, which is in essence MVS. It provides all of the essential operating services for OS/390 and z/OS. In addition to the base services, IBM offers optional services for OS/390 that can be purchased separately.

The z/OS operating system was announced at the same time as the zSeries line of processors. It's essentially a follow-up version of OS/390 designed to run in the new z/Architecture 64-bit mode. Actually z/OS version 1, release 1 can be considered in many ways to be the same as OS/390 release 2, version 10. However, the newest release of z/OS (release 2) has been enhanced with the features that are listed in this figure.

As an applications programmer, you don't have to worry about the particulars of each operating system in any more detail. In fact, this figure probably gives you more detail than you'll ever need! Most of the JCL features you'll learn about in this book will work in any version of the OS your installation happens to have. If there are any differences in how a statement is handled between OS/390 and z/OS, they'll be mentioned.

A partial listing of the base services offered by OS/390 and z/OS

- Base Control Program (BCP or MVS)
- Workload Manager (WLM)
- Systems Management Services
- Application Enablement Services
- OS/390 UNIX System Services
- Distributed computing services
- Communication Server
- LAN Services Network Computing Services
- Network File System (NFS)
- Softcopy Services

New features in z/OS version 1, release 2

- HiperSockets
- TCP/IP Networking enhancements
- Internet and Intranet Security enhancements
- Distributed Print
- New File System and C++ compiler
- Intelligent Resource Director (IRD)

Description

- OS/390 transformed MVS into a server operating system by combining more than 30 products that were separate in the MVS environment. Besides providing for features that are required in today's servers, this packaging of components was designed to simplify system installation and to enable the products to work together more efficiently.
- Besides the base services that are included with OS/390, IBM also offers optional features that are separately priced.
- The z/OS operating system is a follow-up version of OS/390 designed to run in 64-bit mode on zSeries servers and in 31-bit mode on S/390 G5/G6 servers.
- z/OS version 1, release 1 is the same product as OS/390 version 2, release 10. In contrast, z/OS version 1, release 2 includes the additional features listed above.

Figure 1-13   The OS/390 and z/OS operating systems

Perspective

The purpose of this chapter has been to orient you to the world of IBM mainframe processing. Although the information presented here is not integral to your ultimate understanding of JCL, it does serve to give you a broad perspective of the types of processors you may encounter and the processes involved in mainframe computing. In the next chapter, you'll learn about the operating system in more depth as you see how it manages virtual storage as well as how it processes data and application programs. At that point, you'll be in a good position to understand how the JCL you code affects the processing and the use of system resources on your mainframe system.

Terms that you need to be familiar with

The terms that follow are those that are most critical to your understanding of OS/390 and z/OS JCL. A number of other terms have been presented in this chapter, however, and you're likely to hear them used in your conversations with application programmers, systems programmers, and operators.

processor	line (impact) printer	real storage
CPU	character (dot-matrix) printer	multiprogramming
main storage	page (laser) printer	spooling
cache	direct access storage device	batch processing
multiprocessor system	DASD	job
channel	disk pack	Job Control Language
input/output device	volume	JCL
I/O device	track	job scheduler
z/Architecture	cylinder	time sharing
mainframe server	magnetic tape	interactive processing
megabyte (MB)	reel-to-reel tape	online processing
gigabyte (GB)	tape cartridge	foreground processing
terabyte (TB)	operating system	background processing
exabyte (EB)	OS/390	MVS
3270 display station	z/OS	multiple virtual storage
terminal	systems programmer	
3270 emulation software	virtual storage	

2

OS/390 and z/OS concepts and terms

Now that you know about the basic features that are common to IBM mainframe operating systems, this chapter will tell you more about the specific capabilities and functions of OS/390 and z/OS. Since these operating systems are so large and complex, we'll concentrate on the aspects that relate to batch processing and data and job management because these affect your understanding of JCL the most. As I said at the end of the last chapter, I'll use the term *OS/390* to apply to both systems except when a feature relates specifically to z/OS.

Virtual storage and multiprogramming concepts

As you learned in chapter 1, OS/390 relies on virtual storage and multiprogramming to help maximize its efficiency as it handles multiple processes and users at a time. With virtual storage, the system can simulate a large amount of main storage by treating DASD storage as an extension of real storage. With multiprogramming, two or more programs can use the processor at the same time because of the disparity of execution time between I/O operations and CPU operations (while one program waits for an I/O operation to finish, the processor can execute the instructions for another program). Now, you're ready to learn more about how virtual storage and multiprogramming work together under OS/390, a relationship that's based on the use of address spaces.

Address spaces

The diagram in figure 2-1 illustrates the concept of main storage in more detail than you saw in chapter 1. Main storage consists of millions of individual storage locations, each of which can store one character, or byte, of information. To refer to a particular location, you use an *address* that indicates the storage location's offset from the beginning of memory. The first byte of storage is at address 0, the second byte is at address 1, and so on.

An *address space* is simply the complete range of addresses (that is, the number of storage locations) that can be accessed by the computer. The maximum size of a computer's address space is limited by the number of digits that can be used to represent an address. To illustrate, suppose a computer records its address using six decimal digits. Such a computer could access storage with addresses from 0 to 999,999, so the address space could contain a maximum of one million bytes of storage.

Computers actually record their addresses using binary digits rather than decimal digits, and the original System/370 processors used 24-bit binary numbers to represent addresses (a bit is a binary digit, as you'll see in more detail later in this chapter). Since the largest number that can be represented in 24 bits is about 16 million, an address space on a System/370 couldn't contain more than 16MB (megabytes) of storage. On the other hand, S/390 processors use a 31-bit binary number to represent addresses, so an address space can contain up to 2GB (gigabtyes) of storage.

With the introduction of z/Series server architecture and its 64-bit numbering scheme, the addressability of an address space is now enormous. In fact, you could theoretically address up to 16EB (exabytes) of storage. But for practical reasons, the largest z/900 server to date is capable of addressing only up to 64GB.

Address spaces

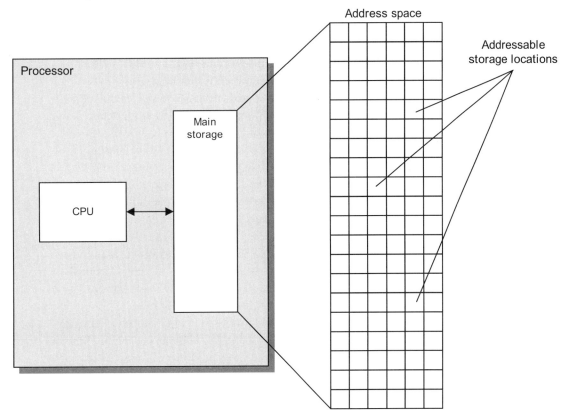

Description

- A processor's main storage consists of millions of individual storage locations, each capable of storing one byte of information.

- To refer to a particular location, you use an *address* that indicates the storage location's offset from the beginning of memory.

- An *address space* is the complete range of addresses that can be accessed by the processor.

- The maximum size of a computer's address space is limited by the number of digits that can be used to represent an address.

- Originally, System/370 processors used a 24-bit binary numbering scheme to represent addresses. That meant that an address space in main storage could only contain 16MB of addressable storage.

- S/390 system architecture uses a 31-bit binary numbering scheme. That means that the address space on those processors can be up to 2GB.

- z/Series server architecture uses a 64-bit binary numbering scheme. Theoretically, that allows an address space to be up to 16EB in size. Currently, though, the largest z900 server has an address space of 64GB.

Figure 2-1   Address spaces

Multiple virtual storage and paging

In earlier IBM operating systems, virtual storage was simply used to simulate additional real storage. However, starting with MVS, the operating system began to use a technique called *multiple virtual storage* to simulate entire address spaces, each of which is independent of the others.

This concept is illustrated in figure 2-2. Here, you can see that real and DASD storage, along with a S/390 buffer area called expanded storage, are used in combination to simulate several virtual storage address spaces. In this example, four address spaces each provide an entire 2GB range of addresses. To refer to a particular byte of virtual storage, the system needs to know both the address for the specific byte and the address space to which the address applies.

To handle multiprogramming, OS/390 assigns an individual address space to each background job or user logged into the system. However, even though the system can support all these address spaces at the same time, the CPU can access only one at a time. So when the CPU is accessing instructions and data from a particular address space, that address space is said to be in control of the CPU. To pass control from one job or user to another, then, OS/390 simply passes control of the CPU to the next job's or user's address space.

Theoretically, the total amount of virtual storage that can be simulated using multiple virtual storage is almost limitless because OS/390 can create an almost unlimited number of address spaces. However, the size of an address (31 bits or 64 bits) still limits the size of each individual address space. And various factors such as the speed of the processor and the amount of real storage installed effectively limit the number of address spaces that can be simulated.

Even with these limits, though, the amount of real storage present on a particular processor is almost always going to be less than the amount of virtual storage that's currently being accessed. To allow the portions of each virtual address space that are needed for immediate processing to be present in real storage, OS/390 uses a technique called *paging*.

If you look at this figure again, you'll see how this works. OS/390 divides virtual storage into 4K sections called *pages*. Data is transferred between real and DASD storage one page at a time. As a result, real storage is divided into 4K sections called *page frames*, each of which can hold one page of virtual storage. Similarly, the DASD area used for virtual storage, called a *page data set*, is divided into 4K *page slots*, each of which holds one page of virtual storage.

When a program refers to a storage location that isn't in real storage, a *page fault* occurs. When that happens, OS/390 locates the page that contains the needed data on DASD and transfers it into real storage. That operation is called a *page-in*. In some cases, the new page can overlay data in a real storage page frame. In other cases, data in a page frame has to be moved to a page data set to make room for the new page. That's called a *page-out*.

At any given moment, real storage contains pages from more than one address space, as shown by the shading in this figure. To keep track of what pages are in real storage, OS/390 maintains tables that can't be paged out of real storage.

The concept of multiple virtual storage

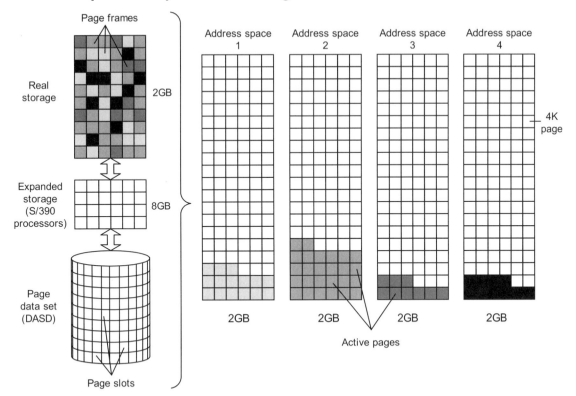

Description

- Virtual storage allows a processor to appear to have more real storage than it actually does by treating DASD as an extension of real storage.

- On an OS/390 system, *multiple virtual storage* (MVS) goes one step further by using expanded storage (a buffer area) and DASD to simulate several independent address spaces.

- To refer to a byte of virtual storage under OS/390, you need to know (1) the address of the byte and (2) the address space to which the address applies.

- OS/390 divides virtual storage into 4K sections called *pages*. *Page frames* in real storage can each hold one page of virtual storage. Similarly, the DASD area used for virtual storage (a *page data set*) holds pages in *page slots*.

- When data in a page slot is transferred to a page frame in real storage, the operation is called a *page-in*. When data is moved from a page frame to a page slot, it's called a *page-out*. At any moment, real storage contains pages from more than one address space.

- *Expanded storage* acts as a large buffer between real storage and page data sets to improve the efficiency of virtual storage operations. The maximum amount of expanded storage on S/390 servers is 8GB. On z/Series servers, expanded storage has been incorporated into real storage.

- OS/390 uses multiple virtual storage to handle multiprogramming by assigning each background job or time sharing user its own address space.

Figure 2-2   Multiple virtual storage and paging

The *expanded storage* I mentioned earlier is a special type of memory used on S/390 processors to improve the efficiency of paging. It acts as a large buffer between real storage and the page data sets so when paging occurs, it can be done at CPU speeds rather than at DASD speeds. The amount of expanded storage on most S/390 processors is about 8GB. On z/Series servers, the need for expanded storage has been eliminated, with the extra storage being incorporated into real storage instead.

How address spaces are swapped

Depending on the amount of real and expanded storage a system has and the types of jobs it's processing, OS/390 can efficiently multiprogram only a certain number of jobs at once. So the system uses a process called *swapping* to periodically transfer entire address spaces in and out of virtual storage as needed. When an address space is *swapped out*, its critical pages (the ones that contain the tables that keep track of the location of each virtual storage page for the address space) are written to a special data set called a *swap data set*. Later, when the system can accommodate the job again, the address space is *swapped in* so it can be processed again.

Figure 2-3 includes a diagram that shows how swapping works. Here, four address spaces are swapped in (the shading indicates the address space that's currently in control of the CPU). The four additional address spaces that are swapped out can't compete for virtual storage or the CPU until they're swapped in.

You can think of swapping as the same thing as paging, only at a higher level. Instead of moving small 4K pieces of virtual storage in and out of real storage, swapping effectively moves entire address spaces in and out of virtual storage.

Whether or not a program in an address space is subject to paging and swapping depends on whether it runs in *real mode* or *virtual mode*. Paging and swapping operate only for programs that run in virtual mode. Programs that run in real mode, like those that stay *resident* in real storage all the time, aren't paged or swapped. Instead, they stay in real storage until they finish processing. For example, the parts of the operating system that are responsible for managing virtual storage must run in real mode. Most programs, however, run in virtual mode.

Address space swapping under OS/390

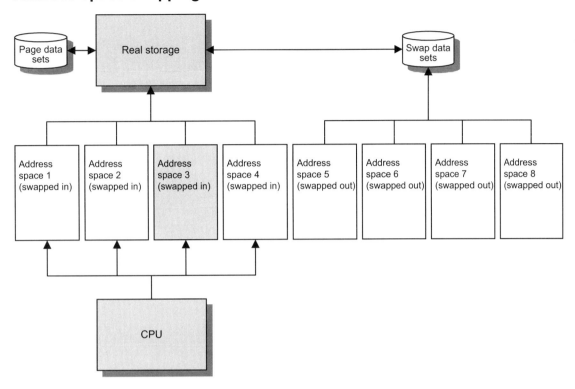

Description

- OS/390 can efficiently process only a certain number of jobs at once, depending on the amount of real storage available and the types of jobs being executed. So it uses a process called *swapping* to transfer entire address spaces in and out of virtual storage as needed.

- When an address space is *swapped out*, its critical pages are written to a special data set called a *swap data set*.

- When the processor can accommodate the job again, its address space is *swapped in* so it can continue to process.

- Some programs (like parts of the operating system itself) need to run in *real mode* rather than *virtual mode*. Programs running in real mode are not subject to paging or swapping processes. Instead, they stay in real storage until they finish processing.

- Programs that must remain in real storage all the time are considered to be *resident* in real storage.

Figure 2-3   How address spaces are swapped

How address spaces are organized

Once you understand how each job or user on an OS/390 system executes in a separate address space, you're ready to learn how the data within an address space is organized. One thing to keep in mind right from the start is that some of the storage in an address space is required for various components of the operating system, some is required by the program or programs run by the job or user, and some is simply left unallocated.

If you look at figure 2-4, you can see that an address space is divided into four basic areas: the private area, the common area, the extended common area, and the extended private area. The extended areas are separated from the primary areas at the 16MB level. IBM had to do this to provide compatibility for software written for 24-bit systems. Software written for 31-bit and 64-bit systems can access the areas both below and above the 16MB line, while software written for 24-bit systems can access only the areas below it.

The *common area* and *extended common area* are the portions of the address space that contain operating system programs and data. These areas are shared by all of the address spaces on the system. In other words, these areas are the same for each address space.

The OS/390 nucleus and extended nucleus control the operation of virtual storage paging and swapping, among other things. Notice how the nucleus occupies the highest locations of storage below the 16MB line while the extended nucleus occupies the lowest locations above 16MB. This ensures that both will occupy a continuous range of addresses. Because these areas must stay resident at all times, they operate in real mode.

Both common areas also contain additional components of the operating system. The *system queue area*, or *SQA*, contains important system tables and data areas that are used by programs residing in the nucleus. Like the nucleus, the SQA can only operate in real mode. The *common service area*, or *CSA*, contains information that's similar to information in the SQA but doesn't have to be fixed in real storage. And the *pageable link pack area*, or *PLPA*, contains operating system programs that don't have to be fixed in real storage. The PLPA can also contain programs that are heavily used by the system.

The *private area* and *extended private area* contain data that's unique for each address space. The *system region* is an area of storage used by operating system programs that provide services for user programs running in the private area. The *local system queue area*, or *LSQA*, contains tables used to control the private area, including the tables needed to manage the private area's virtual storage. The *scheduler work area*, or *SWA*, contains tables used to manage the execution of jobs and programs within the private area. And the *subpool 229/ 230* contains additional system information.

The rest of the private areas, which comprise most of the address space, are either unallocated or allocated to a *user region*. It's in the user region that your program or programs actually execute. The size of the user region varies depending on the amount of storage required by the program being executed.

A virtual storage address space

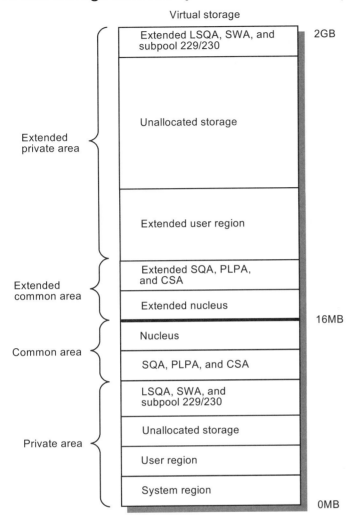

Figure 2-4   How address spaces are organized

Description

- Address spaces are divided into two basic areas: the *private area* and the *common area*.

- To provide compatibility for software written for 24-bit systems, 31-bit and 64-bit processors and their operating systems include special provisions for the first 16MB of address space memory. As a result, the private and common areas each have two sections. The section below the16MB line of memory is for 24-bit processing, while the *extended* area above it allows a system to reap the benefits of 31-bit and 64-bit processing.

- The common area contains the OS/390 nucleus as well as other operating system data.

- The private area contains data that's unique to each user's address space, including the program that's being executed.

Dataspaces and hiperspaces

Although each job or user is assigned its own address space, OS/390 also provides a way to allocate one or more additional address spaces that can be used to hold large amounts of data. Depending on the requirements of the application, these additional address spaces can be one of two types: *dataspaces* or *hiperspaces*.

One difference between dataspaces and hiperspaces is how their contents are managed. The contents of dataspaces are managed directly by user-written programs, while the contents of hiperspaces are managed by OS/390 and are made available to application programs in 4KB blocks. Another difference is that dataspaces can only contain data whereas hiperspaces can contain both data and programs.

On an S/390 system, a third difference between the two is where they reside. Dataspaces reside in normal virtual storage and are subject to paging and swapping operations. By contrast, hiperspaces reside in expanded storage and are never brought into real storage. Thus, hiperspaces provide a unique way to take advantage of expanded storage. (Since expanded storage doesn't exist on the zSeries processors, hiperspaces reside in real storage, just as dataspaces do.)

The diagram in figure 2-5 illustrates how both dataspaces and hiperspaces interact with virtual storage on a System/390. As you can see, when dataspaces are allocated, they receive the same amount of memory allocation as a normal address space. On the other hand, since hiperspaces are allocated in expanded memory, their memory allocations can vary.

A feature called *hiperbatch* uses hiperspaces to improve the performance of certain types of batch jobs. To do that, hiperbatch copies entire data sets into hiperspace where they can be accessed concurrently by several batch jobs. Once a hiperbatch environment is set up (a job that's done by the systems programming staff), application programs can access the data in a hiperspace as if the data were stored in an ordinary DASD data set. In other words, hiperbatch doesn't affect how you code your application programs or the JCL that's used to run them.

How an address space accesses dataspace data and hiperspace data on an S/390 system

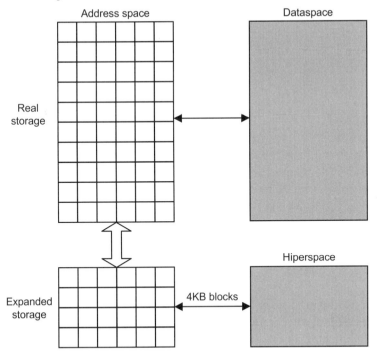

Description

- OS/390 lets a job or user create one or more additional address spaces that can be used to hold large amounts of data. These additional address spaces can be one of two types: *dataspaces* or *hiperspaces*.

- Dataspaces can only contain data, and their contents are managed directly by user-written programs. They reside in normal virtual storage and are subject to paging and swapping operations.

- Hiperspaces can contain both data and programs. Their contents are managed by the operating system and are made available to application programs in 4KB units. On S/390 systems, hiperspaces reside only in expanded memory and are never brought into real storage. On zSeries systems, hiperspaces reside only in real storage.

- Hiperspaces are used by a feature called *hiperbatch* to improve the performance of certain types of batch jobs. To do this, entire data sets are copied into a hiperspace where they can be accessed concurrently by several batch jobs.

Figure 2-5   Dataspaces and hiperspaces

How OS/390 manages data

OS/390 provides a variety of facilities that let you manage data that resides on tape, DASD, and other I/O devices. In IBM literature, a collection of related data that is managed as a unit is referred to as a *data set*, and you'll see the letters *DS* in many of the acronyms for data management features and in JCL statements. A data set is the same as a *file*, though, so the two terms are used interchangeably in this book.

Within a data set, data is organized into smaller units called *records*, which can be processed individually by application programs. Records can be stored in groups called *blocks*, with the *blocking factor* for the file indicating how many records are in each block. Blocking saves on the number of I/O operations needed to read or write a file because the system can access a whole block at a time instead of having to read or write each record individually. As you'll see, OS/390 is aware of all these factors as it manages data.

Data set labels and names

When a data set is stored on disk or tape, OS/390 normally identifies it with special records called *labels*. To access a data set identified by labels, you supply information in JCL statements that OS/390 compares with the label information. That way, you can be sure that the correct data is processed.

Figure 2-6 shows a simplified example of labels on a DASD unit. To start, the DASD volume contains a *volume label*, often called a *VOL1 label*, that has two important functions. First, it identifies the volume by providing a *volume serial number*, or *vol-ser*. Every DASD volume must a have a unique six-character vol-ser. Second, it contains the disk address of the VTOC.

The *VTOC*, or *Volume Table of Contents*, is a special file that contains file labels called *Data Set Control Blocks* or *DSCBs* for all the data sets on the volume. One DSCB describes the VTOC itself, while others describe user data sets by supplying the data set's name, DASD location, and other characteristics. This figure includes the rules for forming an OS/390 data set name. In general, data set names are divided into *qualifiers* separated by periods that allow you to more easily identify the function or purpose of the file.

Space is allocated to DASD files in areas called *extents*, each consisting of one or more adjacent tracks. When a file is initially created, one extent, called the *primary extent*, is allocated to it. As additional records are written to the file, however, that extent might not be large enough. So OS/390 tries to automatically allocate additional extents, called *secondary extents*, for the file. Depending on the number of secondary extents, two or more DSCBs may be needed to identify a file, as shown in the labels for FILE-B in this figure. DSCBs are also used to identify the *free extents* on a volume, the areas that aren't currently allocated.

Beyond its name and location, the information in a file's DSCB depends on the file type. For non-VSAM files, the DSCB contains information on the file's characteristics, such as its organization, the size of its blocks and records, and so on. Normally, this information is obtained from JCL specifications when the file is

How DASD labels identify files on a disk volume

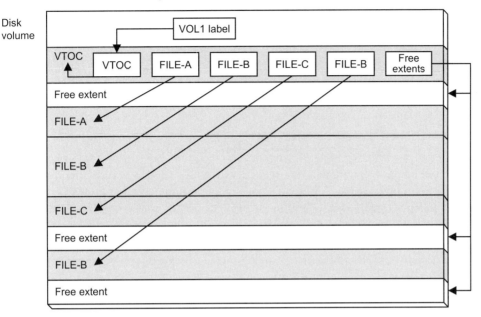

Rules for forming data set names

Length	1 to 44 characters (standard)
	1 to 35 characters (generation data group; see chapter 12)
	Only first 17 characters are used for tape data sets
Characters	Alphanumeric (A-Z, 0-9)
	National (@,#, and $)
	Period (.)
Qualifiers	Data set names with more than 8 characters must be broken into *qualifiers* that each contain between 1 and 8 characters. Separate qualifiers from one another with periods. The periods are counted in the overall length of the data set name.
First character	The first character of each qualifier must be a letter or national character.
Last character	The last character of a data set name should not be a period.

A valid data set name

`AR.TRANS.Y2001`

Description

- OS/390 identifies data sets stored on DASD with special records called *labels*.

- All DASD volumes contain a *volume label*, or *VOL1 label*, that identifies the *volume serial number* (*vol-ser*) as well as the disk address for the *VTOC*.

- The VTOC (*Volume Table of Contents*) contains labels called *Data Set Control Blocks*, or *DSCBs*, that provide information about all the data sets and available space on the volume. The DSCB for a data set includes the data set's name and location.

- Labels are optional on tape volumes but most use standard labels. You'll learn more about tape labels in chapter 7.

Figure 2-6   Data set labels and names

created, although it can also come from the application program that creates it or from the system itself. In contrast, the file characteristics for VSAM files are recorded in a catalog instead of in the VTOC, as you'll see in a minute.

Unlike DASD volumes, labels are optional on tape volumes. Most tapes have *standard labels* that conform to OS/390 conventions, but a tape can also have *non-standard labels* or no labels at all. Since tapes are used less often than DASD, tape labels will be described along with tape processing in chapter 7.

How data sets are organized

Within a data set, data can be organized in one of several ways depending on how it will be processed. The types of organization you can choose from vary depending on whether you're dealing with non-VSAM or VSAM files.

For non-VSAM files, OS/390 provides four basic ways of organizing data: sequential, indexed sequential, direct, and partitioned. In practice, though, the only two you'll use today are sequential and partitioned (which is covered in the next topic).

When *sequential organization* is used, records are stored one after another in consecutive sequence. Sometimes, a data element within each record contains a value that's used for sequencing. For example, the first table in figure 2-7 shows a simple employee file in sequence by employee number.

A sequential file can reside on just about any I/O device that can be attached to an OS/390 system. In fact, sequential organization is the only file organization allowed on tape drives and printers because, by nature, they require data to be processed in sequential order. As for DASD files, sequential organization is appropriate when the file records don't have to be retrieved randomly. In that case, it's a good choice because access from one record to the next is fast. However, since the records have to be processed one at a time from the beginning, it can take awhile to get to a particular record.

To solve this problem, you usually use a VSAM data set with *key-sequenced organization*. A *key-sequenced data set* (or *KSDS*) is set up so that records can be accessed both sequentially and *randomly*. To do that, the file is written on DASD in sequence by a *key* field, but it also includes an *index* that relates the key field values to the locations of their corresponding data records. The second table in this figure illustrates how the employee file would appear with key-sequenced organization using employee number as the key value. To find a particular record, the system looks up its employee number in the index and retrieves it immediately, without having to read the records that precede it.

When it comes to file handling, this book will focus on sequential, key-sequenced, and partitioned data sets. However, just so you're familiar with the other terms you may hear, an *indexed sequential* file is similar to a KSDS. Indexed organization is less efficient than key-sequenced, however, which is why you seldom see indexed files anymore. In a file with *direct organization*, each record can be accessed at random, but you have to know a record's disk location to access it. Because of the complexities involved in calculating disk addresses, direct files are hardly ever used.

A file with sequential organization by employee number

Disk location	Social Security number	First name	Middle initial	Last name	Employee number
1	498-27-6117	Thomas	T	Bluestone	01003
2	213-64-9290	William	J	Collins	01054
3	279-00-1210	Constance	M	Harris	01702
4	499-35-5079	Ronald		Garcia	02145
5	334-96-8721	Marie	L	Abbott	02181

A file with VSAM key-sequenced organization, indexed by employee number

Index component

Employee number	Disk location
01003	1
01054	2
01702	3
02145	4
02181	5

Data component

Disk location	Social Security number	First name	Middle initial	Last name	Employee number
1	498-27-6117	Thomas	T	Bluestone	01003
2	213-64-9290	William	J	Collins	01054
3	279-00-1210	Constance	M	Harris	01702
4	499-35-5079	Ronald		Garcia	02145
5	334-96-8721	Marie	L	Abbott	02181

Non-VSAM data set organization

- There are four basic ways of organizing data that's stored in non-VSAM data sets: *sequential, indexed sequential, direct,* or *partitioned organization* (partitioned organization is discussed in the next topic). The two that are used today are sequential and partitioned organization.

- In a file that has sequential organization, the records are stored one after the other in consecutive disk locations. This type of file is also called a *sequential file.*

- To retrieve records from a sequential file, you must read them sequentially by disk location. This type of record retrieval is referred to as *sequential access.*

VSAM data set organization

- VSAM files have three basic types of organization. There are *entry-sequenced data sets (ESDS), key-sequenced data sets (KSDS),* and *relative-record data sets (RRDS).* Today, most VSAM files are key-sequenced.

- A key-sequenced data set consists of two parts: an *index component* and a *data component.* Within the index component, each entry contains a *key* field value and the location of the corresponding record in the data component of the file.

- You can retrieve records from a KSDS either sequentially or *randomly* (directly) by their key values.

- You'll learn more about VSAM file organization in chapter 14.

Figure 2-7   How data sets are organized

For VSAM files, there are two other types of organization available. *Entry-sequenced data sets (ESDS)* are similar to sequential files, but they're less flexible and harder to use. Finally, *relative-record data sets (RRDS)* are similar to direct files and involve the same type of programming overhead, so they're seldom used.

How partitioned data sets work

In addition to the file organizations already described, OS/390 provides support for non-VSAM data sets with *partitioned organization*. A *partitioned data set*, also called a *PDS* or *library*, is similar to a sequential file except that the data contained within it is divided into groups of records called *members*. Each member can be treated as a separate sequential file, or the entire library can be processed as a unit.

The diagram in figure 2-8 illustrates a typical use for a PDS library. Here, the data set named MM01.TEST.COBOL has three individual members, each containing COBOL source code. To keep track of the members in a PDS, the system stores each member's name in a *directory*. New members can be created and saved to the PDS or deleted from the PDS without disturbing any of the other members.

In addition to source code, PDS libraries can be used to store JCL, subroutines, data, and compiled application programs ready for execution. In fact, as you'll see at the end of this chapter, OS/390 uses PDS data sets to store important system components in what are called *system libraries*.

Partitioned data set extended, or *PDSE*, libraries offer some advantages over normal PDS libraries. But in order to use them, an optional OS/390 feature called the *Storage Management Subsystem*, or *SMS*, is required. You'll learn more about SMS and PDSE libraries in chapter 13.

A partitioned data set with three members

Data set name: MM01.TEST.COBOL

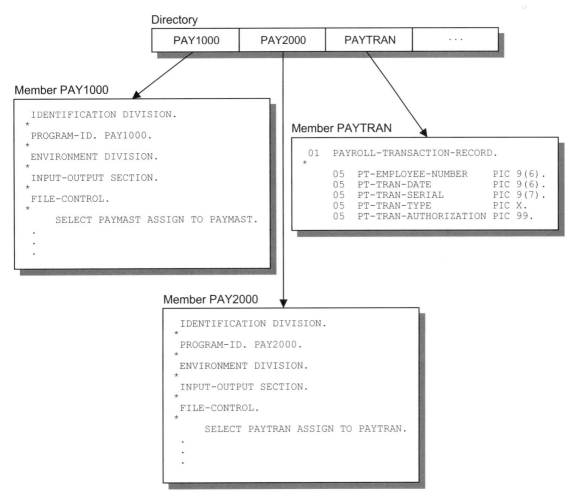

Description

- A *partitioned data set*, or *library*, consists of one or more *members*, each of which can be processed as if it were a separate sequential file.

- There are two types of partitioned data set organization: standard *PDS* and *PDSE* (*partitioned data set extended*). PDS libraries are the most common. You'll learn more about PDSE libraries in chapter 13.

- To keep track of members in a PDS, each member's name is stored in a *directory*.

- Members of a PDS are usually processed individually, but the entire library can also be processed as a unit.

- PDS libraries are widely used by OS/390 to store operating system information, as well as by programmers to store programs in various stages of development. JCL code is also stored in members of a PDS library.

Figure 2-8   How partitioned data sets work

The catalog facility

To keep track of the hundreds of DASD volumes and thousands of data sets found in a typical mainframe installation, OS/390 provides a comprehensive *catalog facility* that records the location of files. That means that when you want to access a file, you don't have to know the volume serial number of the volume that contains the file. The system can look it up in the catalog for you.

Figure 2-9 shows the two types of catalogs available: *master catalogs* and *user catalogs*. Each system has just one master catalog along with an unlimited number of user catalogs. The master catalog contains entries that identify (1) system data sets that are used by the operating system and (2) user catalogs. User catalogs, on the other hand, contain entries that identify user data sets. Today, both types of catalogs are commonly created using the *Integrated Catalog Facility*, or *ICF*, format, although other formats have been used in the past.

All VSAM files *must* be cataloged in the master or user catalog. That's because the catalog entry for a VSAM file contains not just information that locates the file, but information that specifies the file's characteristics as well. For non-VSAM files, this information is stored in the data set labels in the VTOC, so they don't have to be cataloged. Still, cataloging a non-VSAM file makes the file easier to locate later on because you don't have to keep track of its volume serial number, so it's common to catalog new non-VSAM data sets.

When a new data set is created, the first qualifier in the data set name (the *high-level qualifier*) is normally used to indicate the catalog in which the file is defined. For example, a data set named MMA2.CUSTOMER.MASTER would be cataloged in the user catalog indicated by MMA2.

In some cases, the high-level qualifier and the user catalog name are the same. More often, though, the high-level qualifier is an *alias* of the actual name. For example, suppose MMA2 is an alias assigned to a catalog named VCAT.MPS800. In that case, a data set named MMA2.CUSTOMER.MASTER would be cataloged in VCAT.MPS800. By using aliases, files with different high-level qualifiers can be cataloged in the same user catalog.

The relationships among the master catalog, user catalogs, and data sets

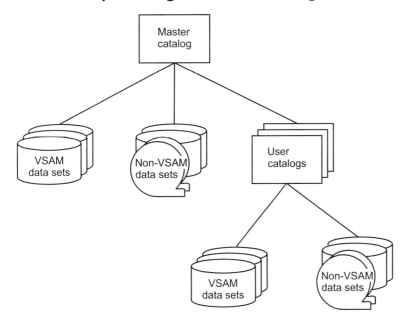

Description

- OS/390 provides a *catalog facility* that records the locations of files so that you don't have to know the volume serial number for the volume that contains the file you want. Most catalogs are created using the *ICF (Integrated Catalog Facility)* format.

- There are two types of catalogs: *master catalogs* and *user catalogs*. Typically, a system has just one master catalog and an unlimited number of user catalogs.

- The master catalog contains entries that identify system data sets and user catalogs.

- User catalogs contain entries that identify user data sets.

- VSAM files *must* be cataloged. That's because, in addition to containing information that locates the file, the catalog also includes information that specifies the VSAM file's characteristics (like record size).

- Since the characteristics of non-VSAM files are stored in data set labels in the VTOC, these files don't have to be cataloged. However, we recommend that you do catalog any data set you create.

- The *high-level qualifier* in a data set name often indicates the user catalog in which the data set is cataloged.

- User catalogs typically have several *aliases*. That way, files with different high-level qualifiers can be cataloged in the same user catalog.

Figure 2-9   The catalog facility

Binary, hex, and EBCDIC notation

On disk, tape, or internal storage, the byte is the measuring unit that's used. For instance, we say that a disk volume can hold 80 gigabytes of data or that an address space is assigned 2 gigabytes of virtual storage. But what can a byte hold?

As figure 2-10 explains, a byte consists of eight *binary digits*, or *bits*, that can be turned on or off (1 or 0). Since there can be 256 different combinations of on and off bits, a single byte can represent up to 256 different characters. These include both uppercase and lowercase letters, the digits 0-9, and special characters.

Since binary characters are difficult to work with, you usually use *hexadecimal*, or *hex*, *codes* as shorthand for binary codes. For instance, as this figure shows, D4 is the hex code for binary 11010100. Here, one hex digit replaces four binary digits as shown by the conversion chart in this figure.

On IBM mainframes, EBCDIC (usually pronounced EB-suh-dik) is used to represent the 256 characters that can be stored in a byte. In this figure, you can see the hexadecimal codes for some of the common characters in the EBCDIC *character set*. For instance, hex 40 is a space, hex C1 is the letter A, and hex F3 is the digit 3.

Most of the debugging features on an OS/390 system represent fields in hex, so it's important that you become familiar with some of the most common codes. For instance, it helps to know that hex 40 is one space, that the digits 0-9 are represented by the hex codes F0 through F9, and that the uppercase letters are represented by hex codes C1 through C9, D1 through D9, and E2 through E9.

The hex codes for the EBCDIC character set also represent the *collating sequence* for the computer. This is the sequence in which the characters will be sorted. As you would guess, the characters are sorted in sequence by their hex codes. Thus, the space (hex 40) comes before the letter S (hex E2), which comes before the number 1 (hex F1).

Although EBCDIC code is used by IBM mainframes, PCs and most midrange computers use *ASCII* (pronounced AS-key) code to represent the characters that can be stored in a byte. That means that data that originates on PCs and midrange computers has to be converted to EBCDIC before it can be used on a mainframe. Fortunately, there are OS/390 facilities that make this conversion automatic.

However, since the collating sequences for EBCDIC and ASCII are slightly different, the sort sequence of a file is changed during a conversion if the field that determines the sequence contains both letters and digits. This means that a file may need to be sorted again after its data has been converted.

The eight bits in the binary code for the letter M

```
1101 0100
```

The hex code for the letter M

```
D4
```

A binary-to-hexadecimal conversion chart

Binary	Hex	Binary	Hex	Binary	Hex	Binary	Hex
0000	0	0100	4	1000	8	1100	C
0001	1	0101	5	1001	9	1101	D
0010	2	0110	6	1010	A	1110	E
0011	3	0111	7	1011	B	1111	F

The EBCDIC codes for some common alphanumeric characters

Character	Hex	Character	Hex	Character	Hex	Character	Hex	Character	Hex
space	40							0	F0
.	4B	A	C1	J	D1			1	F1
(	4D	B	C2	K	D2	S	E2	2	F2
+	4E	C	C3	L	D3	T	E3	3	F3
&	50	D	C4	M	D4	U	E4	4	F4
$	5B	E	C5	N	D5	V	E5	5	F5
*	5C	F	C6	O	D6	W	E6	6	F6
)	5D	G	C7	P	D7	X	E7	7	F7
;	5E	H	C8	Q	D8	Y	E8	8	F8
-	60	I	C9	R	D9	Z	E9	9	F9

Description

- A byte of internal or disk storage consists of eight *binary digits*, or *bits*, that can be either on (1) or off (0). The first four bits are the *zone bits*; the last four are the *digit bits*.

- The *hexadecimal*, or *hex*, numbering system has 16 digits: 0, 1, 2, 3, 4, 5, 6, 7, 8, 9, A, B, C, D, E, and F. With this notation, you can use one hex digit to represent the zone bits in a byte, and one to represent the digit bits. Hex notation is used by the debugging features on IBM systems to display the contents of fields.

- Because eight bits can be turned on or off in 256 different combinations, one byte of storage can be used to represent 256 different characters. On an IBM mainframe, the code that's used to represent these characters is *EBCDIC* (Extended Binary Coded Decimal Interchange Code). The 256 characters make up the *character set*.

- Although IBM mainframes use EBCDIC, most other computers use *ASCII* (American Standard Code for Information Interchange). So when data is transferred to or from the mainframe, the code has to be converted from ASCII to EBCDIC or vice versa.

- The codes that are used for a character set also represent the *collating sequence* for the computer. In EBCDIC, the special characters come before the letters, which come before the numbers. But in ASCII, the numbers come after the special characters but before the letters.

Figure 2-10   Binary, hex, and EBCDIC notation

How OS/390 processes data sets

Now that you know about the basic techniques OS/390 uses to store data sets, you're ready to see what happens when user jobs and application programs process those data sets. In general, there are three phases the system goes through in processing a data set: allocation, processing, and deallocation.

How data sets are allocated

When you request access to an existing data set, OS/390 uses information that you provide in your JCL along with information in the data set label and catalog to locate the data set. Similarly, if you're creating a new data set, OS/390 uses the information you provide to locate and set aside space for the data set. The process of locating a new or existing data set and preparing the system control blocks needed to use the data set is called *allocation*.

Under OS/390, there are three levels involved in allocating a data set, as shown in figure 2-11. First, a *unit* (device) is selected and allocated, then a volume is allocated, and finally, a data set on that volume is allocated.

You can request the unit you want OS/390 to allocate by specifying the three-digit hexadecimal address of the device, by using an IBM-supplied *generic name* for the device, or by specifying a *group name*. Although specifying a device address is the most direct method, it's seldom used because it's difficult and cumbersome. On the other hand, using a generic name, like 3350 or 3380, to identify a device allows OS/390 to select a unit from all of the devices of that particular type on the system.

But the best way to allocate a unit is to specify a group name, sometimes called an *esoteric name*. Then, OS/390 can choose any unit that's included in the group. Each installation creates its own group names and associates specific devices with them. For example, almost all OS/390 shops define a group named SYSDA, which identifies the DASD devices available for general use. Similarly, most shops define a group named TAPE for all of the installation's tape drives. You'll need to check to see what other group names are available in your shop.

When it comes to volume allocation, there are two ways to request a volume. If you use a *specific volume request*, you identify a particular volume by specifying its vol-ser or letting OS/390 obtain the volume identification from a catalog. If you use a *non-specific volume request*, you don't specify a vol-ser. Instead, you let OS/390 select the volume to be used for a new data set (non-specific volume requests aren't valid for existing data sets).

Once the unit and volume for an existing data set are allocated, the data set's file labels are read to ensure that the requested data set actually exists. For a new data set, file labels are created and, if the data set is to reside on DASD, space is allocated and the VTOC is updated to indicate the allocation.

For non-VSAM files, the file's *disposition* (coded in the JCL) affects the allocation by telling the system whether the file already exists or is being created. In addition, for an existing file, the disposition indicates whether the file can be shared by other jobs.

The three levels of data set allocation

Level 1: Unit allocation

- When you request a data set, OS/390 determines which *unit*, or device, the data set resides on or will reside on. Then the unit is allocated to your job.

- Although you can request a device by its unique three-digit hexadecimal address, you're more likely to specify a generic name or group name. Both indicate that you're requesting one of a group of devices rather than a particular device.

- A *generic name* is an IBM-supplied name that indicates a device type, like 3380 for a 3380 disk drive. Then, any device of that particular type can be used for the data set.

- A *group name*, sometimes called an *esoteric name*, is the most flexible way to allocate units. Each installation creates its own group names and associates specific devices with each name.

- Most installations define a group name of SYSDA to identify the DASD devices available for general use. Another common group name is TAPE, which identifies the installation's tape drives.

Level 2: Volume allocation

- In a *specific volume request*, you identify a particular volume to be allocated for a new or existing file by specifying the volume serial number (vol-ser*)*. If an existing file is cataloged, you can let OS/390 retrieve the vol-ser from the catalog.

- In a *non-specific volume request*, you don't specify a vol-ser. Instead, you let OS/390 select the volume on which the new data set will be created. Non-specific volume requests aren't valid for existing data sets.

Level 3: Data set allocation

- Once unit and volume information are obtained for an existing data set, the data set's labels are read to ensure that the requested data set exists.

- For new data sets, file labels are created, space for the data set is allocated, and the VTOC is updated to indicate the allocation.

Description

- If an existing data set is cataloged, the system uses the catalog entry to retrieve the information it needs to *allocate* the data set.

- If a data set isn't cataloged or if you're creating a new data set, you need to provide the system with information about the data set's location and size before it can be allocated.

- To tell the system whether the file already exists or whether it's being created, you specify the file's *disposition* in the JCL for the job. For existing files, the disposition also indicates whether the file can be shared by other jobs or is allocated for exclusive use.

Figure 2-11   How data sets are allocated

How data sets are processed and deallocated

Once a data set is allocated, an application program can process it as shown in the diagram in figure 2-12. As you can see, a special operating system facility called an *access method* serves as an interface between a program and the physical operations of the storage devices. When you code an I/O instruction in a program, you're actually invoking an access method, which in turn issues the proper I/O instructions to access the I/O device.

There are two commonly used access methods: *QSAM* and *VSAM*. QSAM is used for sequential files or members of a partitioned data set, while VSAM provides access method support for its key-sequenced, entry-sequenced, and relative-record data sets. There are also some older access methods that may still be in use by your system, including BDAM, BISAM, and QISAM.

Before a program can issue I/O instructions, it must issue an OPEN instruction to establish a connection between a program, a data set, and an appropriate access method. For non-VSAM files, that connection is made through a *data control block*, or *DCB*. For VSAM files, an *access method control block*, or *ACB*, has a similar function. Both the DCB and ACB are tables in storage that contain vital information about the status of a data set as it's processed. The main purpose of OPEN processing is to initialize the DCB or ACB. Once the data set is opened, the DCB/ACB information comes from one of three sources: the data set's label or catalog entry, the JCL, or the program itself.

When you open a data set, you can use any of several *open modes*. In *input mode*, records can be read but not written to the data set. In *output mode*, records can be written but not read. And in *I/O mode*, records can be both read and written.

Depending on the open mode, there are four types of I/O operations you can issue in a program. You can read a record, write a record, update (or rewrite) a record, and delete a record. The access method handles any blocking and deblocking of the records as they are written and read and maintains other elements of a data set's structure, such as the index of a VSAM key-sequenced data set.

When a program is finished processing a data set, it issues a CLOSE instruction to disconnect itself from the file. If a file is not properly closed, you may not be able to open it the next time you need to process it.

You don't have to do anything explicitly to *deallocate* a file. That's because each file is automatically deallocated when a job is finished with it. However, be aware that the file's disposition indicates what OS/390 does with a non-VSAM file when it's deallocated. To be specific, the disposition determines whether a file should be kept, cataloged, or deleted.

How data sets are processed

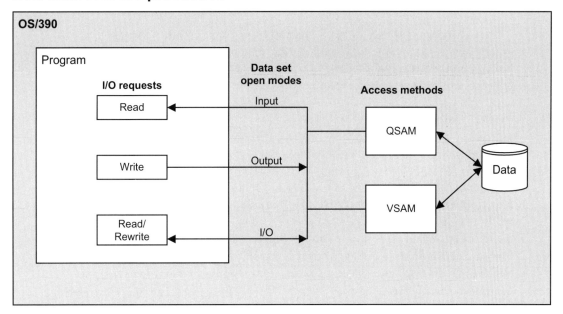

Description

- An *access method* is an interface between an application program and the physical operations of I/O devices. Two of the most common access methods are *QSAM* and *VSAM*.

- For sequential files or members of a partitioned data set, QSAM (Queued Sequential Access Method) is used.

- VSAM provides support for its key-sequenced, entry-sequenced, and relative-record data sets.

- Before a program can issue any I/O requests to a file, it must issue an OPEN instruction. There are three *open modes* you can use: *input mode*, *output mode*, and *I/O mode*.

- In input mode, records can only be read from an existing data set. In output mode, records can only be written to a new or existing data set. And in I/O mode, records can be read, written, updated, and deleted.

- When a program is finished processing a data set, it issues a CLOSE instruction to disconnect itself from the file.

- A data set is automatically *deallocated* once a job is finished with it. At that point, its disposition in the JCL indicates whether it should be kept, entered into the master catalog or user catalog, or deleted.

Figure 2-12   How data sets are processed and deallocated

How OS/390 manages user jobs

To work most effectively with OS/390 and its job control language, it's critical to have an understanding of the facilities that manage job execution. So the topics that follow describe the basic elements of OS/390 *job management*.

Jobs, job control language, and JES

As I mentioned in chapter 1, a *job* is the execution of one or more related programs in sequence. Each program to be executed is called a *job step*. For example, suppose you want to process a job that executes two programs: the first sorts a customer file into customer name sequence, and the second prints a report that lists customers by name. That's a two-step job because two programs are required. When you submit a job to be processed by OS/390, the job is treated as a whole. It begins with the execution of the first program and continues until the last program has finished executing, unless an unforeseen error condition occurs.

Job Control Language, or *JCL*, is a set of control statements that provide the specifications necessary to process a job, and the series of JCL statements that make up a job is typically called a *job stream*. Obviously, the purpose of this book is to teach you JCL, so you'll learn about it in depth in later chapters. For now, though, I want you to know about three basic JCL statements that are present in every job: JOB, EXEC, and DD.

The first statement of any job is a JOB statement. It provides information that identifies the job, such as the job's name and your name. For each job step in the job, an EXEC statement indicates the name of the program to be executed. Following an EXEC statement, a DD statement is normally required for every file that's processed by the program.

To give you an idea of what a job looks like, figure 2-13 includes a simple one-step job that prints a sales report from a customer master file. As you can see, the first statement is a JOB statement that gives the name of the job (MM01RN), the processing account number (36512), my user name (R Menendez), and my user-id (MM01). Then, an EXEC statement specifies that the program for this job's only step is named RPT3000.

Three DD statements are used in this job. The first one, CUSTMAST, identifies the existing customer master file on DASD. The high-level qualifier in its data set name shows that it's defined in the MM01 catalog. In addition, its disposition is SHR, meaning that other programs can share access to the file while this job is executing. The other two files, SALESRPT and ERRLST, are both output files and include the specification SYSOUT=A, which tells OS/390 to direct the output to a printer.

The three basic JCL statements that are present in every job

JOB	Provides information that identifies the job.
EXEC	Indicates the name of the program to be executed.
DD	Identifies a file to be processed by the program.

JCL statements for a job that posts transactions to a customer master file

```
//MM01RN    JOB   (36512),'R MENENDEZ',NOTIFY=MM01
//RPTRUN    EXEC  PGM=RPT3000
//CUSTMAST  DD    DSNAME=MM01.CUSTOMER.MASTER,DISP=SHR
//SALESRPT  DD    SYSOUT=A
//ERRLIST   DD    SYSOUT=A
```

How JES2 and JES3 process jobs

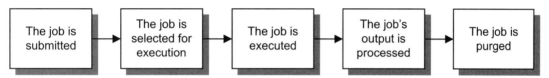

Description

- A *job* is the execution of one or more related programs in sequence. Each individual program executed in a job is called a *job step*.

- *Job Control Language*, or *JCL*, is a set of control statements that provide the specifications necessary to process a job. The series of statements that makes up a job is often called a *job stream*.

- To process a job, a *Job Entry Subsystem*, or *JES*, is used. It keeps track of jobs that enter the system, presents them to OS/390 for processing, and sends their spooled output to the correct destination.

- There are two versions of JES available under OS/390: *JES2* and *JES3*. Since JES2 and JES3 are incompatible with one another, your shop should have only one or the other installed.

Figure 2-13   Jobs, job control language, and JES

How a job is entered into the system

In the early days of System/360-370 processing, the phrase "entering a job into the system" meant that a system operator took a deck of cards containing a job's JCL and data, placed them into a card reader, and pressed the reader's "start" button. Today, a programmer enters JCL code and data into a display terminal, and the resulting job stream is stored in a file on a DASD unit. However, the job isn't entered into the system yet because JES2/JES3 isn't aware of it.

To enter, or *submit*, the job into the system, the programmer or system operator issues a SUBMIT (SUB) command. That causes JES2/JES3 to read the job stream from the DASD file and copy it to a *job queue*, which is a part of a special DASD file called the *JES spool*. Because this process is essentially the same as when card readers were used, the JES component that processes the input job stream is called an *internal reader*.

How a job is scheduled for execution

OS/390 doesn't necessarily process jobs in the order in which they are submitted. Instead, JES examines the jobs in the job queue and selects the most important jobs for execution first.

JES uses *job class* and *job priority* to classify a job's importance, both of which can be specified in the job's JCL. Of the two, job class is more significant. Then, if two or more jobs of the same class arc waiting to execute, the JES scheduler selects the one with the higher priority. As you can see in figure 2-14, job classes are assigned based on the processing characteristics of a job. Although this figure lists common job class assignments, keep in mind that each installation can make up its own class assignments, so the job classes at your installation may be different.

At this point, it's not essential that you understand the details of how jobs are selected for execution. But I do want you to know about a special type of program called an *initiator*, because that knowledge will help you understand not only job scheduling, but multiprogramming as well. An initiator is a program that runs in the system region of an address space that's eligible for batch processing. It examines that JES spool, selects an appropriate job for execution, executes the job in its address space, and returns to the JES spool for another job. Each initiator can run only one program at a time, so the number of initiators running on a system reflects the number of programs being multiprogrammed.

Each initiator has one or more job classes associated with it. It selects jobs only from those classes and executes them based on their priorities. As a result, an installation can control how many jobs of each class can be executed simultaneously, and in what combinations. To illustrate, this figure shows the job classes associated with four initiators. Because there's only one initiator associated with class A, only one class A job can execute at a time.

Typical job class assignments

Job class	Characteristics
A	The job will execute within 15 minutes of submission.
B	The job will execute within 30 minutes of submission.
C	The job will execute within 1 hour of submission.
D	The job will execute overnight.
H	The job is held until released by an operator.
L	The job will execute within 15 minutes of submission but each step is limited to 1 minute of execution time.

An example of how job classes are assigned to initiators

Initiator	Eligible job classes
1	A
2	B,C,D,H,L
3	B,C
4	C

How a job is entered into the system

- Jobs are created by entering JCL commands into a display terminal. Then, the jobs are stored in files on DASD.

- To enter, or *submit*, the job into the system, the terminal user issues a SUBMIT, or SUB, command. That causes JES2 or JES3 to read the job stream from the DASD file and copy it to the *job queue* on the *JES spool*.

How a job is scheduled for execution

- OS/390 doesn't necessarily process jobs in the order in which they are submitted. Instead, JES examines the jobs in the job queue and prioritizes the work, selecting the most important jobs to be executed first.

- *Job class* and *priority* are two characteristics that JES uses to classify a job's importance. Both can be specified in a job's JCL, with job class being more important than job priority.

- Each job class is represented by a single alphanumeric character and is assigned based on the processing characteristics of the job. Class assignments vary from shop to shop.

- An *initiator* is a program that runs in the system region of an address space that's eligible for batch job processing. Each initiator can handle one job at a time.

- The initiator examines the JES spool, selects an appropriate job for execution, executes the job in its address space, and returns to the JES spool for another job.

- Each initiator has one or more job classes associated with it and can execute jobs only from those classes. Within a job class, initiators select jobs based on their priorities, executing higher-priority jobs first.

Figure 2-14   How a job is entered into the system and scheduled for execution

How a job is executed

Figure 2-15 shows how a job is executed once an initiator has selected it for execution. As you can see, the initiator and several other OS/390 programs run in the system region. The first thing an initiator does after it selects a job for execution is invoke a program called the *interpreter*. The interpreter's job is to examine the job information passed to it by JES and create a series of control blocks in the scheduler work area (SWA), a part of the address space's private area. Among other things, these control blocks describe all of the data sets the job needs.

After the interpreter creates the SWA control blocks, the initiator goes through three phases for each step in the job. First, it invokes *allocation routines* that analyze the SWA control blocks to see what resources (units, volumes, and data sets) the job step needs. If the resources are available, they're allocated so the job step can process them. Next, the initiator builds a user region where the user program can execute, loads the program into the region, and transfers control to it. As the user program executes, it uses the control blocks for the resources allocated to it. When the program is completed, the initiator invokes the *unallocation routines* that release any resources used by the job step.

As a user program executes, it can retrieve data that was included as part of the job stream and stored in the JES spool. Input data processed in this way is called *SYSIN data* or *instream data*. The user program treats the data as if it were read from a card reader. Similarly, the user program can produce output data that's stored in the JES spool. The program treats this data, called *SYSOUT data*, as if it were written to a printer. SYSOUT data is held in a *SYSOUT queue* until it can be processed by JES2/JES3.

How a job is executed once an initiator has selected it for execution

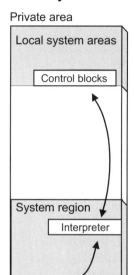
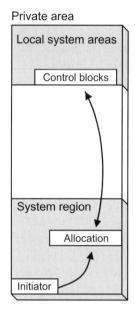
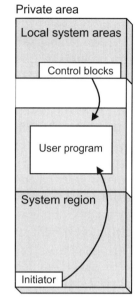
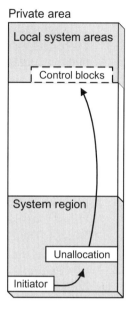

After the initiator selects a job for execution, it invokes the interpreter, which builds the required control blocks in the address space's SWA.

For each job step, the initiator invokes allocation routines to allocate the units, volumes, and data sets required by the job step.

After the job step's resources have been allocated, the initiator creates a user region, loads the user program into it, and transfers control to the user program.

When the user program completes, the initiator invokes unallocation routines to deallocate the resources used by the job step. Then, if the job has more steps, the initiator repeats the allocation-execution-unallocation process.

SYSIN and SYSOUT data

- As a user program executes, it can retrieve data that was included as part of the job stream and stored in the JES spool. Input data processed in this way is called *SYSIN data* or *instream data*.

- A user program can also produce output data that's stored in the JES spool. The program treats this data, called *SYSOUT data*, as if it were written to a printer. SYSOUT data is held in a *SYSOUT queue* until it can be processed by JES2 or JES3.

Figure 2-15   How a job is executed

How a job's output is processed

Figure 2-16 lists the four types of SYSOUT data sets typically produced by a job. The first three are common to all jobs. They include the JES message log that lists the messages produced by JES2 or JES3 during job execution, the JCL listing that's simply a listing of the JCL submitted, and the system message log that lists any messages produced by OS/390 as the job was executed. Additionally, any number of SYSOUT data sets can be produced by the programs executed in the job. Of course, the information in these SYSOUT data sets varies according to the requirements of the programs that produce them.

Like jobs, SYSOUT data sets are each assigned an *output class* that determines how the output will be handled. An output class usually indicates which printer or printers can be used to print the output. In some cases, however, an output class specifies that the output not be printed. Instead, it's held in the SYSOUT queue indefinitely until it's released for printing or deleted (usually, the reason for holding output is so that the data can be viewed from a display terminal rather than printed). Common output classes are A for standard printer output, B for special printer output, and X for held output.

A single job can produce SYSOUT data using more than one output class. For example, you might specify that the job message output be produced using class A. Similarly, you might specify class A for output produced by one or more of your programs. Then, all of that class A output is gathered together and printed as a unit. However, you might specify class D for some of your job's spooled output. Then, the class D output will be treated separately from the class A output.

JES lets you control how SYSOUT data is handled in other ways besides specifying output classes. For example, you can specify that output be routed to a specific printer, that two or more copies of the output be produced, or that the output be printed on special forms rather than on standard paper. Throughout this book, you'll learn about various ways of handling SYSOUT data.

How a job is purged

After a job's output has been processed, the job is purged from the system. That means that the JES spool space the job used is freed so it can be used by other jobs. In addition, any JES control blocks associated with the job are deleted. Once a job has been purged, JES no longer knows of its existence. To process the job again, you must submit the job again.

The SYSOUT data sets produced by most jobs

SYSOUT data set	Description
JESMSGLG	The JES message log is a listing of messages produced by JES2 or JES3 as the job was executed.
JESJCL	The JES JCL listing is a listing of the JCL processed by the job.
JESYSMSG	The system message log is a collection of messages produced by OS/390 as the job was executed.
Program SYSOUT data	SYSOUT data produced by a program executed in the job. The number of program SYSOUT data sets produced depends on the types of programs executed by the job and their output requirements.

Typical output class assignments

Output class	Type of output
A	Standard printer output, usually routed to one of the installation's high-speed printers and printed on standard computer paper.
B	Special printer output.
X	Held output that stays on the SYSOUT queue until it's released for printing or deleted.

Description

- Each job that is processed by JES produces a series of SYSOUT data sets. The first three listed above consist of system messages and job documentation. Any additional data sets are typically produced by the programs executed in the job.

- Each SYSOUT data set is assigned an *output class* that determines how the output will be handled. In most cases, the output class determines which printer or printers can be used to print the output.

- A single job can produce SYSOUT data using more than one output class. In fact, you can specify a separate output class for each SYSOUT data set produced by the job.

- You can handle SYSOUT data in other ways besides using output classes. For example, you can specify a particular printer to use, the number of copies to print, or any special forms that the SYSOUT data should be printed on.

- After a job's output has been processed, the job is purged from the system. That means that the JES spool space the job used is freed and any JES control blocks associated with the job are deleted.

Figure 2-16   How a job's output is processed and how a job is purged

Key components in an OS/390 environment

Now that you've been introduced to some of the basic features of OS/390, you're going to learn about some of the additional subsystems and facilities that the operating system has to offer. You'll also learn about two important activities that are required to establish a working OS/390 system: system generation and system initialization.

OS/390 subsystems and facilities

So far, I've discussed the facilities that are a direct part of the OS/390 operating system or its job entry subsystems, JES2 and JES3. However, a complete production OS/390 environment contains a variety of other software products, some of which come bundled with OS/390 and others that can be purchased separately. Figure 2-17 lists some of the most common ones you're likely to find at your installation.

Some of the products listed in this figure are considered to be subsystems. Strictly speaking, a *subsystem* is a software product that operates in its own address space under the control of OS/390. What it does within the address space, however, is of no concern to OS/390. In fact, a subsystem may provide services that duplicate services provided by the operating system. For example, the *primary subsystem* at every OS/390 installation is the Job Entry Subsystem. JES2 and JES3 both run in their own address space, and they provide services that are normally associated with an operating system: job management and spooling.

To be honest, though, the distinction between subsystems and other OS/390 facilities is more technical than practical. Some of the products listed in this figure aren't subsystems, but they provide important services and have as broad a scope as a subsystem.

A partial list of products commonly found in an OS/390 environment

Product	Description
TSO/E	*TSO/E* (Time Sharing Option/Extended) is a subsystem that lets terminal users invoke system facilities interactively. Each TSO/E user is given a unique address space and can allocate data sets and invoke programs just as a batch job can. You'll learn more about TSO/E in chapter 20.
ISPF	*ISPF* (Interactive System Productivity Facility) runs as part of TSO/E and takes advantage of the full-screen capabilities of display terminals. You'll learn how to use ISPF to create and submit jobs and view job output in chapter 3.
VTAM	*VTAM* (Virtual Telecommunications Access Method) is actually part of a comprehensive telecommunications product called *SNA* (System Network Architecture). VTAM can provide centralized control over all of the terminal devices attached to the system.
CICS	*CICS* (Customer Information Control System) makes it possible for the system to run interactive application programs written in COBOL, PL/I, assembler language, C, C++, or Java. CICS runs in its own address space and provides multiprogramming capabilities within that address space.
DB2	*DB2* (Database 2) is a database management system. It manages relational databases that can be accessed using *SQL* (Structured Query Language).
RACF	*RACF* (Resource Access Control Facility) identifies both users and system resources such as data sets. It ensures that a user has the correct authority to access system resources and facilities.
SMS	*SMS* (Storage Management Subsystem) is an automated storage management system that removes many of the manual procedures associated with managing data sets, such as deciding on volume usage or determining when a data set can be deleted. You'll learn more about SMS in chapter 13.
UNIX System Services	*UNIX System Services* allow OS/390 to run UNIX applications and process files from UNIX systems. You'll learn more about UNIX System Services in chapter 21.
WLM	*WLM* (Workload Manager) allows you to define performance goals and assign an importance to each goal. It monitors system processes such as batch jobs and online transactions and decides how much of the system's resources, such as CPU and storage, should be given to each process.
Websphere	*Websphere* is a Java-based application server designed to enable e-business transactions. It supports servlets, JavaServer Pages (JSPs), and Enterprise JavaBeans (EJBs).
Utility programs	The operating system provides a set of general-purpose *utility programs* to perform such functions as copying files and sorting file records. When you invoke a utility program, you can supply parameters to control the exact processing it does. You'll learn more about utility programs in chapters 18 and 19.

Figure 2-17   OS/390 subsystems and facilities

System generation, initialization, and libraries

System generation and initialization are activities that are required to establish a working OS/390 or z/OS system. *System generation* (often called *sysgen*) is the process of creating an OS/390 system, and *system initialization* is the process of starting a previously generated OS/390 system. Both system generation and initialization are the responsibility of the systems programming staff, so you don't have to worry about the overwhelming details of these activities. Still, you'll better understand OS/390 if you have a basic idea of how system generation and initialization work.

When an installation purchases OS/390, IBM sends the basic components that make up the operating system on a series of tapes, called *distribution libraries*. System generation, which is only a part of the overall process of installing OS/390 from the distribution libraries, selects and assembles the various components an installation needs to create a working operating system. To control sysgen, a systems programmer codes special macro instructions that specify how the OS/390 components from the distribution libraries should be put together.

The result of sysgen is a series of system libraries that contain various components that make up the operating system. Figure 2-18 lists some of these libraries. These, along with other files, make up the *system data sets* that are required for OS/390 to operate properly. Notice how the name of each begins with SYS1, the standard identifier for a system data set.

Once the operating system has been generated, it can be used to the control the operation of the computer system. To begin a system initialization, the system operator uses the system console to start an *Initial Program Load*, or *IPL*. That causes the computer system to clear its real storage and begin the process of loading OS/390 into storage from the system libraries. During system initialization, many options can be selected to affect how OS/390 will operate. In fact, systems programmers and operators have more control over OS/390 at initialization time than they do during sysgen. Initialization options can either be manually entered by the operator or come from the system library named SYS1.PARMLIB.

System initialization is a complicated process that won't be discussed in more detail in this book. Just realize that when system initialization is complete, OS/390 is ready to process your work. Realize, too, that the system may occasionally need to be powered down or reinitialized, in which case the system operator goes through the IPL process again.

System generation

- *System generation (sysgen)* is the process of creating the OS/390 system.
- IBM sends an installation the basic components that make up OS/390 on a series of tapes called *distribution libraries*. System generation selects and assembles the various components an installation needs to create a working operating system.
- To control system generation, a systems programmer codes special macro instructions that specify how the components from the distribution libraries should be put together.
- The output from sysgen is a series of system libraries that contain, among other things, the executable code that makes up the operating system.

System initialization

- *System initialization* is the process of starting a previously generated OS/390 system, either immediately after sysgen or when the system has to be reinitialized due to system maintenance or a system error. It's similar to booting up a PC, though far more complex.
- To begin a system initialization, the system operator uses the system console to start an *Initial Program Load*, or *IPL*. That causes the system to clear its real storage and begin the process of loading the operating system into storage from the system libraries.

System libraries

Data set	Description
SYS1.NUCLEUS	Contains, among other things, the OS/390 nucleus program. The members of this library are created during sysgen. When the system is initialized, the members are brought into real main storage and control is given to the nucleus.
SYS1.PARMLIB	Contains several options OS/390 is to use when the system is initialized. Most of the options included in this library are coded by the systems programmers at your installation.
SYS1.LINKLIB	Contains executable programs that are either a part of the operating system or are written by users.
SYS1.LPALIB	Contains executable programs that are part of the *link pack area* (*LPA*). Heavily used portions of the operating system, such as access methods, are usually placed in this library.
SYS1.MACLIB	Contains the assembler macro instructions that are used for sysgen as well as other instructions that provide a standard interface for the operating system's facilities such as access methods.
SYS1.PROCLIB	Contains standardized JCL statements called procedures that can be used by the jobs that invoke them. You'll learn about procedures and the SYS1.PROCLIB in chapter 9.
SYS1.CMDLIB	Contains the program modules that implement the various TSO/E commands you enter from a TSO terminal.
SYS1.LOGREC	Contains information about hardware problems.

Figure 2-18   System generation, initialization, and libraries

Perspective

The goal of this chapter has been to help you understand what's going on behind the scenes as you use JCL to submit jobs for processing. Although this is more than you need to know, it will help you code your JCL more effectively. Remember that the system programmers deal with most of the complexities of OS/390 or z/OS so the application programmers don't have to.

Now, if you understand that each job or user operates in its own address space, if you're familiar with the techniques OS/390 uses for data management and job management, and if you have a sense of the components that make up a complete OS/390 environment, you're ready to go on. Then, as you learn to use JCL, many of the concepts and terms that you've been introduced to in this chapter will become clearer. Before you learn JCL, though, chapter 3 will teach you how to use ISPF to create and submit jobs and to review their output.

Terms that you need to be familiar with

Although this chapter has presented many other terms, the ones that follow are the most critical to your understanding of OS/390 and z/OS JCL.

address	KSDS	DCB
address space	index	access method control block
multiple virtual storage	key	ACB
paging	partitioned data set	deallocation
swapping	PDS	job management
real mode	library	job
virtual mode	member	job step
resident program	system library	Job Control Language
user region	directory	JCL
data set	catalog facility	job stream
file	master catalog	Job Entry Subsystem
record	user catalog	JES2 or JES3
block	high-level qualifier	submit a job
blocking factor	alias	job queue
label	byte	JES spool
volume label	bit	job class
volume serial number	hexadecimal code	job priority
VTOC	EBCDIC	SYSIN data
Data Set Control Block	character set	SYSOUT data
DSCB	ASCII	output class
qualifier	allocation	subsystem
extent	unit	system generation
sequential organization	disposition	system initialization
sequential file	access method	Initial Program Load
sequential access	QSAM	IPL
random access	VSAM	
key-sequenced data set	data control block	

3

How to use ISPF to work with JCL

In chapter 2, you learned that TSO/E is an OS/390 component that lets terminal users interact with the OS/390 system. ISPF, which runs under the control of TSO/E, provides a powerful and comprehensive program development environment that includes a full-screen text editor and facilities to manage background job processing. In this chapter, you'll learn how to use the ISPF editor to create and maintain job streams. You'll also learn how to submit jobs for execution, monitor their progress, and display their output using ISPF-related tools.

The ISPF user interface

You need to have some basic skills for working with ISPF before you can use it to create and execute JCL jobs. As a result, the topics that follow acquaint you with the look and feel of ISPF and teach you how to navigate through it so you can start to take advantage of the functions it provides.

How to access and terminate ISPF

To access ISPF, three things must always happen. You must establish a session between your terminal and TSO/E; you must identify yourself to TSO/E; and you must start ISPF. In most shops, you can enter a single LOGON command that both connects and identifies you to TSO/E. In some shops, this will also start ISPF, but if it doesn't, you can usually just enter the command, ISPF. As you can tell, though, the access procedure varies from one installation to another, so check to find out the exact procedure to follow in your shop.

Once you've accessed ISPF, you'll see a Primary Option Menu like the one shown in figure 3-1. Since an OS/390 shop can customize this menu in various ways, the screen on your system may look slightly different, but that shouldn't confuse you. Although this menu includes a number of helpful program-development options, you'll learn about only three of them in this chapter: the Edit option, the SDSF option, and the Outlist utility (which is found under the Utilities option). Once you know how to use a few ISPF options, however, you'll find it's easy to use new ones on your own.

To terminate ISPF when you're done using it, you select option X from the Primary Option Menu. Depending on your installation's setup, this may also log you off of TSO/E. If it doesn't, simply enter LOGOFF from the TSO/E screen.

The format of ISPF panels

The format of all ISPF display screens, or *panels*, is similar to the one in figure 3-1. At the top of the screen is a line that displays the panel's name and, when appropriate, a brief message on the righthand side. The next line is used to enter commands to be processed by ISPF. At the bottom of the screen, a couple of lines list the functions of the PF keys that can be used from that screen. Then, the bulk of the screen displays menu choices (as in this example), data, or information you need to use ISPF features.

It's also common for the panel title line to be preceded by a line with an action bar, which is a menu bar that gives you access to various ISPF options. In this figure, the Primary Option Menu has been customized so it doesn't include an action bar, but you'll see how to use one later in this chapter.

ISPF is designed to run on a 3270 display terminal or a PC that emulates one. More than likely, you're using a PC that's running a third-party emulator program like EXTRA! for Windows 98, the program that's used in this book. If so, you need to become acquainted with the keyboard layout that your emulator

The ISPF Primary Option Menu

Panel title

Command entry

Menu options

PF key functions

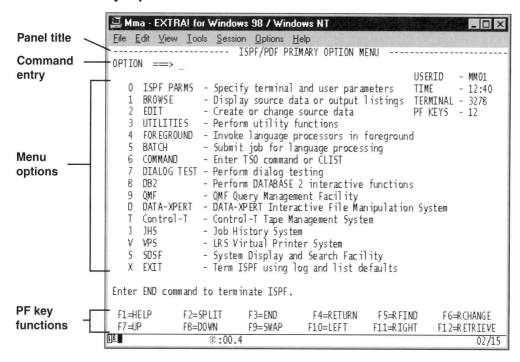

```
Mma - EXTRA! for Windows 98 / Windows NT                    _ □ ×
File  Edit  View  Tools  Session  Options  Help
------------------------ ISPF/PDF PRIMARY OPTION MENU -----------------------
OPTION ===> _

                                                      USERID   - MM01
     0  ISPF PARMS  - Specify terminal and user parameters   TIME     - 12:40
     1  BROWSE      - Display source data or output listings  TERMINAL - 3278
     2  EDIT        - Create or change source data            PF KEYS  - 12
     3  UTILITIES   - Perform utility functions
     4  FOREGROUND  - Invoke language processors in foreground
     5  BATCH       - Submit job for language processing
     6  COMMAND     - Enter TSO command or CLIST
     7  DIALOG TEST - Perform dialog testing
     8  DB2         - Perform DATABASE 2 interactive functions
     9  QMF         - QMF Query Management Facility
     D  DATA-XPERT  - DATA-XPERT Interactive File Manipulation System
     T  Control-T   - Control-T Tape Management System
     J  JHS         - Job History System
     V  VPS         - LRS Virtual Printer System
     S  SDSF        - System Display and Search Facility
     X  EXIT        - Term ISPF using log and list defaults

Enter END command to terminate ISPF.

F1=HELP      F2=SPLIT     F3=END      F4=RETURN    F5=RFIND     F6=RCHANGE
F7=UP        F8=DOWN      F9=SWAP     F10=LEFT     F11=RIGHT    F12=RETRIEVE
                    :00.4                                        02/15
```

Description

- If the Primary Option Menu isn't displayed when you log on to TSO/E, you can usually display it by entering ISPF at the TSO/E ready prompt. Check with your system administrator for the exact procedure at your shop.

- The format for all ISPF screens, called *panels*, is similar. A line at the top displays the panel's name and, if needed, a brief message on the righthand side. The next line is used to enter commands or options processed by ISPF. The bottom two lines display the PF key functions that apply to the panel. And the rest of the screen is used to display menu options or data.

- The panel title line is often preceded by an action bar, which provides drop-down menu access to ISPF options (see figure 3-3 for details).

- ISPF typically operates on a 3270 display terminal or a PC emulating one. Since ISPF is keystroke-based, check the keystroke assignments in any 3270 emulator software you're using. For example, you may have to use a key other than the Enter key to enter commands.

- Although not widely used, a *GUI* (*graphical user interface*) version of ISPF is also available. It does as much of its processing as possible on a PC and connects to the mainframe to send and receive information.

- To terminate ISPF, you select X from the Primary Option Menu.

Figure 3-1   How to access and terminate ISPF

uses because you depend on keystrokes to navigate in ISPF. For example, some emulators designate the PC's Enter key as a carriage return and use the right-sided CTRL key as the Enter or Send key because that more closely resembles the layout of a 3270 keyboard. If your system's set up like that, you'll have to enter the correct keystroke when this chapter tells you to press the Enter key.

IBM also offers a *GUI (graphical user interface)* version of ISPF designed to work on a PC running Windows or OS/2. Besides displaying a friendlier and more contemporary graphical interface, the GUI version of ISPF does as much processing as possible on the PC's CPU with only occasional transfers of information to and from the mainframe host. It also gives you the added flexibility of using the PC's mouse to select options, press buttons, and access pull-down menus. Unfortunately, this version of ISPF hasn't really caught on, so I'll be presenting ISPF in its standard format in this book.

How to navigate in ISPF

Navigating through the ISPF panels is easy. To select a menu option, you simply enter the option's number or letter in the command area. For example, to select the Edit option from the Primary Option Menu, you enter 2. When you press the Enter key, ISPF displays the first panel of the edit function. Likewise, when you're using a panel that's not a menu, you can enter commands to execute specific functions, like copying or saving information.

Many of the options on the Primary Option Menu lead to additional menus. For instance, if you select option 3 (Utilities), the next panel that's displayed is another menu showing utility programs. You can easily bypass the second menu screen, however, by specifying both options at the Primary Option Menu, using a period (.) to separate them. On the other hand, suppose you're already in one ISPF function, and you want to select an entirely different function. In that case, you can bypass the Primary Option Menu and go directly to the new function by inserting an equals sign (=) before the desired option. The first four examples at the top of figure 3-2 show you how these navigation techniques work.

ISPF also allows you to stack commands on the command line by separating each command with a semicolon (;), which implies that the Enter key is pressed. ISPF will then execute each command in order. If you enter a semicolon without a command, ISPF proceeds as if you'd pressed the Enter key without changing any of the values in the current panel. Although this approach is illustrated by the last example in this figure, it probably won't make much sense to you until you know more about ISPF and have experimented with commands on your own. For now, then, just be aware that you can stack commands if you want to.

As you navigate through ISPF, you'll find that the same character may be used for different commands depending on which panel you're in. For instance, if you look again at the examples in figure 3-2, you'll see that *S* invokes the SDSF menu in the fourth example, while it selects (displays) a PDS member in the last example.

Commonly used navigation techniques

Command	Starting panel	Effect of command
3	Primary Option Menu	→ Utility Selection panel
3.8	Primary Option Menu	→ Utility Selection panel → Outlist Utility panel
=2	Current panel	→ Primary Option Menu → Edit Entry panel
=S.H	Current panel	→ Primary Option Menu → SDSF Menu → Held output queue
2;;S MM01A1	Primary Option Menu	→ Edit Entry panel → PDS listing → Select member MM01A1

Commonly used PF keys

PF key	Command	Meaning
PF1/13	Help	Displays the online tutorial or additional information on an error message.
PF2/14	Split	Splits the screen into two separate screens divided by a horizontal line. It can also be used to change the position of the screen split.
PF3/15	End	Returns to the previous panel.
PF4/16	Return	Returns directly to the Primary Option Menu.
PF7/19	Up	Scrolls the display up.
PF8/20	Down	Scrolls the display down.
PF10/22	Left	Scrolls the display to the left.
PF11/23	Right	Scrolls the display to the right.

Description

- To select a menu option from the Primary Option Menu, enter the option's number or letter in the command entry area (Option ===>) and then press Enter.

- You can bypass intermediate ISPF panels and go directly to a desired function by typing a series of menu options separated by periods (.).

- To go from one ISPF option to another without returning to the Primary Option Menu, enter an equals sign (=) followed by the option or options desired. The equals sign indicates that the first option is from the Primary Option Menu, not from the panel currently displayed.

- You can also stack commands on the command prompt by separating them with a semicolon (;). The semicolon implies that the Enter key has been pressed, so its use allows you to perform several commands at once. If a semicolon isn't preceded by a command, the effect is the same as pressing the Enter key without changing any of the values on the screen.

- You can control certain ISPF functions using program function (PF) keys like those shown above.

Figure 3-2   How to navigate and use PF keys in ISPF

Besides entering commands in the command area, you can control certain ISPF functions using the program function (PF) keys. In figure 3-2, you can see the default meanings of the more commonly used PF keys in ISPF. These defaults may be changed at your installation, though, so be sure to find out what function each key performs on your system.

Most of these PF key functions are self-explanatory. However, note the difference between the PF3/15 key, or End key, and the PF4/16 key, or Return key. Although both keys terminate the current ISPF function, PF3/15 returns to the previous panel while PF4/16 returns directly to the Primary Option Menu.

How to use the action bar in ISPF

As I mentioned earlier, many screens start with an *action bar* that provides yet another way to navigate through ISPF. Instead of having to return to the Primary Option Menu whenever you're unsure of how to get to another ISPF option, you can simply access some of the more popular options from the action bar. Figure 3-3 shows you what the action bar looks like in an ISPF edit panel. As you use ISPF, you'll notice that the items listed in the action bar vary according to which panel you're on.

To select an item from the action bar, you need to position the cursor over the desired item and press Enter. You can do this in one of three ways. One way is to use the arrow keys on your keyboard. Another way is to type the command ACTIONS on the command line and press Enter. This places the cursor on the first item of the action bar. The third way is to press the PF10 key to move the cursor to the first item of the action bar. Be aware, though, that the PF10 key isn't assigned this function on all screens. For example, on this editing screen, you can see that the PF10 key is used to scroll to the left instead.

Once you've selected an action bar item, a pull-down menu is displayed like the one for the Utilities item in this figure. You can then select a menu item by typing its number in the entry field provided or by moving the cursor to the item and pressing Enter. If you want to cancel a pull-down menu without making a selection, simply press the PF12 key.

One of the advantages of using the action bar is that it provides for *com mand nesting*. This is a relatively new ISPF feature that allows you to suspend one activity while you work on another. For example, suppose that you're creating a JCL job stream in an edit panel when you realize that you have to allocate a new data set. In this case, you could use the action bar to navigate directly to the data set allocation panel (option 2 on the Utilities pull-down menu), allocate your data set, and then press PF3 to return to the edit panel and pick up where you left off.

An ISPF panel with an action bar

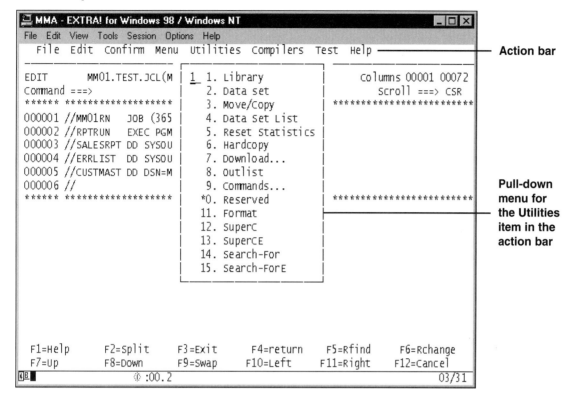

Action bar

Pull-down menu for the Utilities item in the action bar

Description

- *Action bars* appear at the top of most ISPF screens. They provide an additional way to navigate through ISPF panels.

- To select an item from the action bar, you position the cursor over the desired item and press Enter. You can move the cursor to the action bar by using the arrow keys on your keyboard, by typing the command ACTIONS on the command line and pressing Enter, or, on some screens, by pressing PF10.

- A pull-down menu appears when an action bar item is selected. The items within the pull-down menu can be selected either by typing the item number in the space provided or by moving the cursor to the item and pressing Enter.

- To cancel a pull-down menu without making a selection, press PF12 (Cancel).

- *Command nesting* allows you to suspend your current activity while you perform a new one. To do this, you must choose a new activity or function with the action bar. Once you've finished the new activity and press PF3, ISPF returns you directly to the activity you suspended earlier.

Figure 3-3   How to use the action bar in ISPF

How to use the ISPF editor

The *ISPF editor* lets you enter data and store it in a partitioned data set member. It also lets you retrieve a member and make changes to it. As a result, you'll use the ISPF editor to create and update JCL job streams and programs. Although the ISPF editor provides many advanced features, this chapter focuses on how to get started using it and some of its more commonly used features. Before you use the editor to create JCL, though, you have to have a partitioned data set in which to store your JCL job streams.

How to create a partitioned data set to store JCL members

Figure 3-4 describes how you use the ISPF Data Set Utility panel to allocate a new partitioned data set (or library). Under ISPF, the name you give to a library typically consists of three qualifiers as shown in the panels in this figure. When the full name is used, the qualifiers are separated by periods, as shown in the second panel.

The high-level qualifier (the first qualifier) identifies the project and is typically your TSO/E user-id. In this example, the high-level qualifier is MM01. The second qualifier is the group name. This is usually a name you make up to identify the contents of the data set. In this example, the group name is TEST, which indicates that the library will contain job streams used in developing new applications. The third qualifier is the type, which indicates the type of data the library contains, as shown by the chart in this figure. For a library that will contain job streams, you typically use JCL as the type. (Another type, CNTL, predates the JCL type, so you may also see it used.)

When you create a partitioned data set as shown in this figure, the attributes on the Allocate New Data Set panel default to the attributes for the last data set you created. If that's not what you want, you need to change them. In particular, you want to be sure that you specify the right amount of space for the data set. You also want to be sure that you specify the right number of directory blocks and that you enter PDS for the data set name type so that a partitioned data set is created rather than a sequential data set. For more information on the appropriate attributes, see your system administrator.

The panels for creating a partitioned data set

Access from the ISPF Primary Option Menu: 3 (Utilities) → 2 (Data Set)

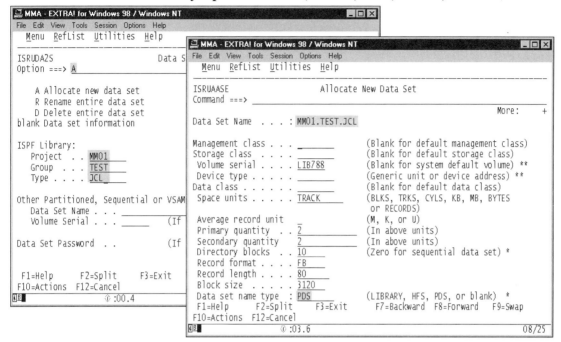

Common library types

Type	Meaning
ASM	Assembler language source code
CLIST	Command procedure containing TSO/E commands
COBOL	COBOL source code
DATA	Data repository
JCL	Job stream containing JCL statements
PROCLIB	Cataloged procedures containing JCL statements

Description

- Under ISPF, a partitioned data set (or library) name consists of three qualifiers: a project-id, which is usually your TSO/E user-id; a group name that can be any name you want; and a type that indicates the kind of data that's stored in the PDS members.

- As with any data set name, each qualifier in an ISPF library name can be a maximum of 8 characters and the entire data set name, including the periods between qualifiers, can be a maximum of 44 characters.

- To allocate a new partitioned data set in which to store JCL members, you can use the Data Set Utility panel shown above. To do that, enter A in the command area; enter the Project, Group, and Type components of the library name; and press Enter. Then, enter the appropriate information on the Allocate New Data Set panel (check with your system administrator for details), and press Enter.

Figure 3-4   How to create a partitioned data set to store JCL members

How to start an edit session

To access the ISPF editor, you select 2 from the Primary Option Menu, and ISPF responds by displaying the Edit Entry Panel shown in figure 3-5. Here, you enter the name of the library and member you want to edit. If the member already exists, ISPF displays the data it contains in the primary edit panel shown in the next figure. If you enter the name of a new member, the data portion of the edit panel will be empty so you can create the new member from scratch.

In the last topic, you learned that the type you specify for an ISPF library identifies the type of data the library contains. When you edit a library member, the editor uses the type to determine the *edit profile* for the member. If a library has the type JCL, for example, the editor uses the JCL profile for its members. This profile specifies, among other things, that the member contains 80-character, fixed-length records and that automatic recovery is on in the event your ISPF session is terminated before you have a chance to save your work. Although the editor provides a number of commands that you can use to change the profile settings, you don't usually need to do that.

The Edit Entry panel

Access from the ISPF Primary Option Menu: 2 (Edit)

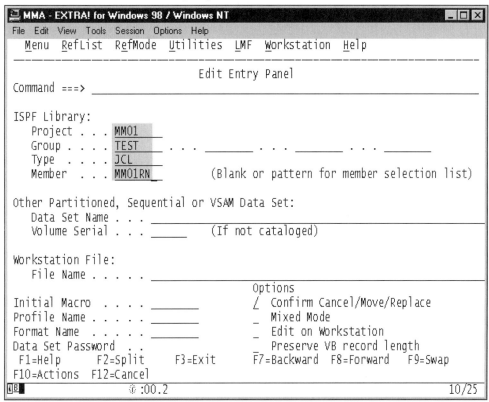

Description

- To edit a member of a partitioned data set, enter the names of the library and member in the Edit Entry panel and press Enter.

- If the member you specify already exists, its contents are displayed in the edit data display shown in the next figure. If the member doesn't exist, the edit data display is blank.

- The library type determines the *edit profile* ISPF uses for each member in the library. The edit profile contains settings such as the number of columns in the editing area, the type of line numbering that's used, the tab settings, and whether recovery mode is on or off.

Figure 3-5   How to start an edit session

How to work in the primary edit panel

Figure 3-6 shows the *primary edit panel* that's displayed once you've specified the library member you want to work on. This panel consists of three distinct areas. The top two lines of the panel form the *heading area* where you can enter *primary commands* that invoke various editing functions. The six leftmost columns of lines 3 through 24 form the *line command area* where you can enter *line commands* that affect specific lines. The rest of the panel is the *screen window*. Here, you can enter the data for a new member or change the data for an existing member.

In this figure, a new member is displayed, so the screen window is blank. To enter data into it, you just key in the characters you want in the positions you want. To move the cursor around the screen, you can use the terminal's arrow keys. If you want to change existing text, you type the new data over the old. When you're finished, you press the Enter key. Then, ISPF removes the lines you didn't key data into and assigns line numbers to the remaining lines (the line numbers replace the apostrophes in the line command area).

You can write your JCL from scratch using a blank screen like the one shown here. However, most new jobs are similar to existing jobs, so you'll usually want to start with existing JCL instead. To do that, you can use the COPY command to copy the existing JCL into the screen window. You'll learn more about the COPY command and other commands you can use with the editor in the next topic.

If the member contains more data than can be displayed on a single screen, you'll need to use the PF7/19 and PF8/20 keys to scroll backwards and forwards through it. When you use these keys, the number of lines that are scrolled is determined by the scroll setting. You can see this setting at the righthand side of the second line of the heading area. In this case, the setting is CSR, which means that the member will scroll so the line that contains the cursor is displayed at the top of the window. Three common scroll settings are listed in this figure.

The primary edit panel for a new data set

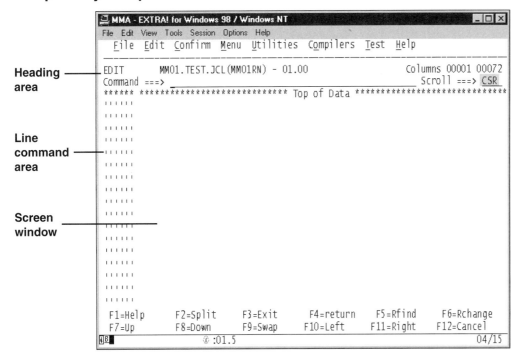

Heading area / **Line command area** / **Screen window**

Common scroll settings

Setting	Function
PAGE	Scrolls a whole page of data.
HALF	Scrolls half a page of data.
CSR	Scrolls to the line or column where the cursor is positioned.

Description

- The first line of the *heading area* in the *primary edit panel* identifies the file being edited and the leftmost and rightmost columns where editing is allowed.

- The second line of the heading area contains a command area where you can enter *primary commands* to invoke various editing functions. It also contains a scroll field where you can indicate the amount of data you want to scroll for each scroll operation.

- The six leftmost columns of lines 3 through 24 form the *line command area*. In this area, you can enter *line commands* that affect specific lines.

- The rest of the panel is the *screen window*. This is where the data for the member you're editing is displayed.

How to start a new member from an existing member

- Enter the COPY command in the command area and press the Enter key. Then, identify the existing member you want to copy in the panel that's displayed.

Figure 3-6   How to work in the primary edit panel

How to use line commands and primary commands

Figure 3-7 lists some of the most useful line and primary commands for the ISPF editor. As you can see, you can use line commands to delete lines, insert new lines, repeat lines, and move or copy lines. For example, when the Enter key is pressed, the line commands shown in the panel in this figure will move (M) the line that contains the CUSTMAST DD statement to the line just before (B) the line that contains SALESRPT DD statement.

Although the Move command shown in this figure operates on a single line, you can also enter line commands that operate on a block of lines. To delete a block of lines, for example, you can enter DD in the first and last lines to be deleted. You can also specify the exact number of lines you want a line command to affect by entering that number after the command. To insert 10 lines, for example, you can enter I10. Then, 10 empty lines will be displayed after the line where you entered the command.

The primary commands let you perform functions like locating specific lines or text, changing all occurrences of a character string to another string, retrieving data from other members, and terminating the editor. One command you'll use frequently is CHANGE. For example, you can change the output class assigned to all SYSOUT data sets in a job simply by coding this command:

```
CHANGE SYSOUT=A SYSOUT=* ALL
```

Another command you'll use regularly is COPY, to copy data in from another member. As I mentioned in the last topic, you'll often do that when you start a new JCL job stream so you don't have to code the job from scratch. The easiest way to use the COPY command is to simply enter COPY in the command area and press Enter. When you do, ISPF displays a panel that prompts you for the name of the member you want to copy. This panel also lets you specify the lines you want to copy if you don't want to copy the whole member.

As you experiment with the primary commands that are shown in this figure, you'll find that they're easy to use. Be aware, though, that most of the commands have more complicated formats than are shown here. So you may want to find out more about these and other commands by using PF1/13 to access ISPF's online help.

How to terminate an edit session

In most cases, you'll end an edit session by pressing the End key (PF3/15). When you do that, ISPF saves the changes you made and returns you to the Edit Entry panel where you can specify another member to edit. Occasionally, though, you may want to enter the CANCEL primary command to end the edit session without saving your changes.

The primary edit panel with M and B line commands

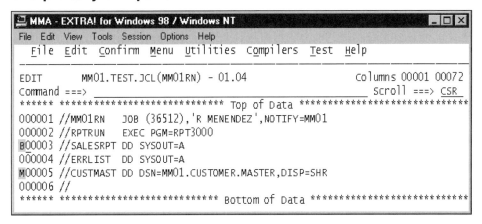

Basic line commands

I/I*n*	Insert one or *n* lines following this line.
D/D*n*/DD	Delete this line, *n* lines beginning with this line, or the block of lines beginning and ending with DD.
R/R*n*/RR/RR*n*	Repeat this line or the block of lines beginning and ending with RR one or *n* times.
C/C*n*/CC	Copy this line one or *n* times, or copy the block of lines beginning and ending with CC.
M/M*n*/MM	Move this line one or *n* times, or move the block of lines beginning and ending with MM.
A/A*n*	Copy or move lines one or *n* times after this line.
B/B*n*	Copy or move lines one or *n* times before this line.

Useful primary commands

LOCATE *line-number*	Moves to the indicated line.
FIND *string*	Finds the first occurrence of *string*, starting from the current line. To find the next occurrence, press PF5.
CHANGE *string-1 string-2* [ALL]	Finds the first occurrence of *string-1*, starting from the current line, and changes it to *string-2*. To find the next occurrence, press PF5. To change the next occurrence, press PF6. To change all occurrences, include the ALL option.
COPY *member-name*	Retrieves data from the specified member; use an A or B line command to specify where the data should be placed. If you omit *member-name*, ISPF displays a panel that lets you enter a library and member name.
PROFILE	Displays the profile settings for the edit session.
RECOVERY [ON	OFF]	Determines whether edit recovery mode is on. Edit recovery mode lets you recover data after a system failure or power outage. It also lets you reverse editing changes using the UNDO command.
UNDO	Reverses the last editing change.
SAVE	Saves changes and continues the edit session.
END (PF3/15)	Saves changes and returns to the Edit Entry panel.
RETURN (PF4/16)	Saves changes and returns to the Primary Option Menu.
CANCEL	Returns to the Edit Entry panel without saving changes.

Figure 3-7   How to use line commands and primary commands

How to manage job execution and output

Once you've used the editor to enter the JCL statements for a job, you can use ISPF job processing facilities to submit the job for processing in a batch address space. Then, when the job completes, you'll probably manage the job output with an optional facility called SDSF. However, if SDSF isn't installed on your system, you can use the standard ISPF Outlist utility to monitor the job's progress, display its output, and print or delete the output as needed.

How to submit a job for execution

Although there are several ways to submit a job for batch processing in ISPF, the easiest way is to enter a SUBMIT (or SUB) command while you're editing the member that contains the job stream, as shown in figure 3-8. The SUBMIT command places the job in the JES spool so it will be scheduled and executed.

ISPF acknowledges that you submitted the job by displaying a message like the one shown near the bottom of the second panel in this figure. Here, MM01RN is the name of the job and JOB09169 is the unique *job identifier* (or *job-id* or *job number*) since more than one job can have the same name. It's a good idea to record the job identifier because you may need it later.

The three asterisks after the message simply mean that you must press the Enter key to continue. They're displayed whenever ISPF invokes a function that displays data on the screen in a line-by-line format rather than using ISPF's full-screen display facilities.

Submitting a job for batch processing from the ISPF editor

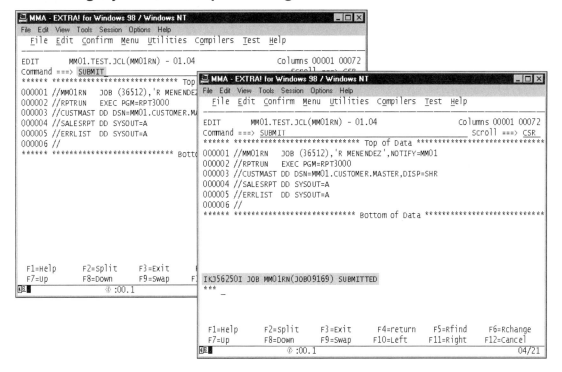

Description

- The easiest way to submit a job for batch processing is from the ISPF editor. Just enter the SUBMIT (or SUB) primary command to place the job in the JES spool for scheduling and execution.

- When you submit the job, ISPF responds with a message verifying the operation. This message includes the unique *job identifier* (or *job-id* or *job number*) that distinguishes this job from other jobs that have the same name.

- The job identifier can help you identify output that pertains to your job later on, so you may want to record it.

- When a message ends with three asterisks, it means that the function that's been invoked is displaying data on a line-by-line basis instead of in the full-screen format that's standard for ISPF. To continue after a message is displayed, you press the Enter key.

Figure 3-8   How to submit a job for execution

The basics of using SDSF to work with jobs and job output

The *System Display and Search Facility*, or *SDSF*, is a separately licensed program that makes it easy for you to monitor the progress of your jobs and handle their output. However, it isn't really a part of ISPF. So if it's not available at your installation, you can skip over the next few topics and learn how to use the Outlist utility instead.

The SDSF functions are listed on the SDSF Primary Option Menu shown in figure 3-9. The I option displays the *input queue*, which contains information about all of the jobs that are executing or waiting to be executed. The O option displays the *output queue*, which contains job output that's waiting to be printed. In contrast, the *held output queue* (option H) contains job output that's being held or that has a held output class that's not assigned to a printer. Finally, the ST option displays a status panel that contains information from all three queues.

Since the status panel is the most flexible panel, you'll learn how to use it first. Then, you'll learn how to use the held output panel to work with job output. Finally, you'll learn how to display output data sets. Although I won't present the input and output queues here, you shouldn't have any trouble using them if you understand how to use the other panels.

The SDSF Primary Option Menu

Access from the ISPF Primary Option Menu: S (SDSF)

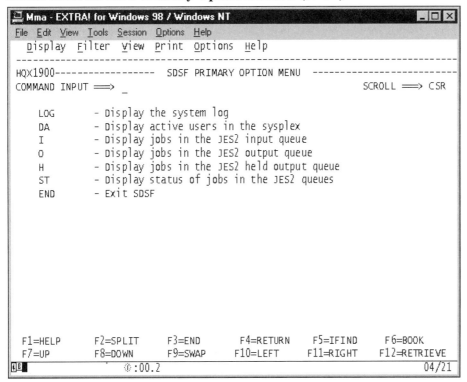

Description

- You can use *SDSF* (*System Display and Search Facility*) to monitor a job's progress and output. SDSF is a separately licensed product, so check whether it's available on your system. If not, you can use the Outlist utility to do similar functions (see figure 3-13).

- To display any of the panels listed on the SDSF Primary Option Menu, enter the appropriate option in the command area and press Enter.

- The *input queue* contains jobs that are waiting for execution and jobs that are currently executing.

- The *output queue* contains jobs that have completed execution and are waiting to be printed.

- The *held output queue* contains jobs that have completed execution and are being held or are assigned to a held output class.

- The status panel displays information from all of the queues.

Figure 3-9   The basics of using SDSF to work with jobs and job output

How to use SDSF to monitor job execution

The easiest way to monitor a job with SDSF is to use the status panel shown in figure 3-10. This panel lists all of the jobs on the system, whether they are waiting to be executed, are currently executing, or have completed execution. The current disposition of a job is indicated by the value in the Queue column. In this figure, for example, you can see that the first job is executing and that all the other jobs have completed execution and their output is waiting to be printed.

To pinpoint which job you're interested in, you use the job-id rather than the job name. In this figure, for example, two jobs are listed with the name MM01RN. The job-id for each is unique, though, so you can tell them apart.

Because TSO/E itself runs as a batch job even though it's controlling time-sharing functions on the system, the first job listed on this panel is for the current TSO/E session. That's why its job-id starts with TSU instead of JOB, and that's why this panel shows that it's executing.

In the NP column of the status panel, you can enter an *action character* to perform specific functions on the jobs. If you enter a question mark (?) as shown here, for example, SDSF will display a panel that lists the output data sets for JOB09169. Then, you can use that panel to display the contents of each data set individually.

In addition to using action characters, you can change the values of certain fields in the status panel by typing over them. The two fields you're most likely to change are the job class (C) and priority (PRTY) as they affect the scheduling of your jobs.

The SDSF status panel

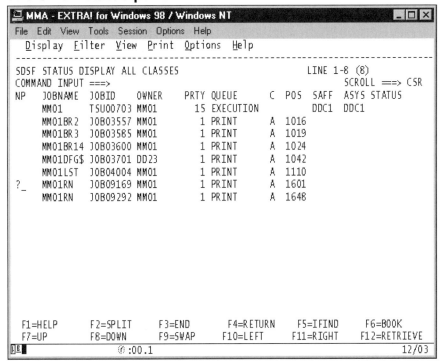

Common action characters

Character	Function
?	Displays a list of the output data sets for a job.
S	Displays one or more output data sets.
H	Holds a job.
A	Releases a held job.
O	Releases held output and makes it available for printing.
C	Cancels a job.
P	Purges a job and its output.

Description

- The status panel lists all of the jobs that are currently executing, that are waiting to be executed, and that have completed execution.

- The JOBID column lists the unique job identifier for each job. The QUEUE column indicates a job's current status.

- You can enter an *action character* in the NP column to perform one of the functions shown above.

- You can change some of a job's characteristics, such as its job class and priority, by typing over the appropriate fields.

Figure 3-10   How to use SDSF to monitor job execution

How to use SDSF to handle job output

Figure 3-11 shows the SDSF panel that displays the held output queue. It also lists the action characters you're most likely to use on this panel. To display all of the output for a job, for example, you can enter S in the NP column as shown.

If a job is listed in the held output queue, it means that (1) the output is on hold so that it isn't printed or (2) the output is assigned to a held class that isn't associated with a printer. If the output is on hold, you can use the O action character to release it so it can be printed. If the job is assigned to a held class, you also have to change the job's class in the queue to route the output to an appropriate printer.

However, aside from the reports that a job might generate, you usually won't print the output from a job. Instead, you'll display it at your terminal to check that the job executed without any problems. Then, once you've looked at it and are satisfied you don't need a copy of any of it, you can use the P action character to delete (purge) it from the system.

An SDSF panel that displays the held output queue

```
MMA - EXTRA! for Windows 98 / Windows NT              _ □ ×
File  Edit  View  Tools  Session  Options  Help
 Display  Filter  View  Print  Options  Help
-------------------------------------------------------------
SDSF HELD OUTPUT DISPLAY ALL CLASSES  LINES 414       LINE 1-7 (7)
COMMAND INPUT ===>                                    SCROLL ==> CSR
NP   JOBNAME  JOBID    OWNER    PRTY C ODISP DEST          TOT-REC  TOT-
     MMO1BR2  JOB03557 MM01      144 X HOLD  LOCAL              43
     MMO1BR3  JOB03585 MM01      144 X HOLD  LOCAL              62
     MMO1BR14 JOB03600 MM01      144 X HOLD  LOCAL              34
     MMO1DFG$ JOB03701 DD23      144 X HOLD  LOCAL              53
     MMO1LST  JOB04004 MM01      144 X HOLD  LOCAL              74
S_   MMO1RN   JOB09169 MM01      144 X HOLD  LOCAL              73
     MMO1RN   JOB09292 MM01      144 X HOLD  LOCAL              75




 F1=HELP     F2=SPLIT    F3=END      F4=RETURN   F5=IFIND   F6=BOOK
 F7=UP       F8=DOWN     F9=SWAP     F10=LEFT    F11=RIGHT  F12=RETRIEVE
                   :00.2                                       11/03
```

Common action characters

Character	Function
?	Displays a list of the output data sets for a job.
S	Displays one or more output data sets.
O	Releases output and makes it available for printing.
P	Purges output data sets.

Description

- You can enter an action character in the NP column to perform one of the functions shown above. You can also change some of a job's characteristics, such as its job class and priority, by typing over the appropriate fields.

- To print output in the held output queue, use the O action character to release the output and make it available for printing. If the output is assigned to a held output class, you must also change the class to one that's associated with a printer.

Figure 3-11   How to use SDSF to handle job output

How to use SDSF to display job output

As you've seen, you can use the S action character from any of the SDSF queue panels or the status panel to display all of the output from a job. In that case, the beginning of the display will look something like the one in figure 3-12. Here, you can see the beginning of the JES message log that gives you information on the job execution. The first thing you'll check here is the *return code* in the RC column that indicates whether your job executed successfully. A return code of 00 means that the job ran to completion with no errors. You'll learn more about the return codes you may encounter as you go through this book.

As you scroll down through the SDSF display, you'll find at least two other data sets are included in the output for any job: the JCL listing and the system message log. Beyond that, the job output may include one or more other data sets, depending on the options you specify for the job and the functions that the job performs.

For example, if the job compiles a program, the output will usually include a compilation listing and a summary of any errors that occurred during compilation. If the job runs a program that produces a report, the output will include the report plus any messages produced by the report program. Although the output can vary from job to job, it should always represent a complete record of the processing performed.

What if you want to look at a particular data set in the output instead of displaying all of it? In that case, you can enter the ? action character for a job from any of the queue panels or the status panel to list the individual data sets in the job output. Then, you can use the S action character to display a specific data set. Once you've reviewed the output on screen, you can print the data set if you want to look at the results more closely or if you need a printout for documentation.

To scroll through the output and locate particular entries, you can use the ISPF commands and function keys you've already learned about. When you display all of the output for a job, you can also move from one data set to another using two other primary commands, the NEXT and PREV commands (these don't work when you're displaying a single data set, however). As you become more familiar with ISPF, you won't have any trouble navigating through job output.

An SDSF browse panel that displays job output

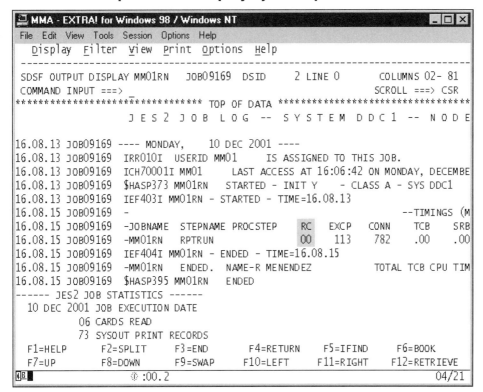

Description

- By looking through the output for a job, you can review the JES message log, JCL listing, and system message log to see whether the job executed as expected. Depending on the processing that's done, the job output may also include other information, such as a compilation listing or output data sets that were created by the job.

- The RC column in the JES message log gives the *return code* that indicates the level of errors that were encountered during the job execution. A return code of 00 means that there weren't any errors (you'll learn more about return codes in chapter 10).

- To display all of the output for a job, you can enter an S in the NP column for the job in any of the SDSF queue displays.

- To display an individual data set, you can enter a question mark (?) in the NP column for the job. This displays a list of all of the output data sets for the job, so you can then enter S for the one you want to look at.

- You can use the standard ISPF scrolling commands to browse job output. You can also use the FIND and LOCATE commands presented in figure 3-7 to find a particular line of data in the output.

- When you're displaying all of the output for a job, you can use two other primary commands, NEXT and PREV, to move to the next or previous data set within the display.

Figure 3-12   How to use SDSF to display job output

How to use the Outlist utility to work with jobs and job output

If SDSF isn't available on your system, you can use the ISPF *Outlist utility* to monitor a job's progress and control its output. Figure 3-13 shows the five functions available on the Outlist entry panel. You invoke the first four by using the one-letter option codes displayed on the screen and supplying the information needed for the function (like job name, job-id, or a new output class). The first option lets you check on the status of one or more jobs (option L). The next three let you handle job output by printing it (option P), by routing it to a job class associated with a particular printer (option R), or by deleting it (option D).

The fifth option, which lets you display job output, is invoked by leaving the option field blank. In this case, you must enter the job's name and, if there's more than one job with the same name, the job identifier. Once you do that, ISPF displays the output in a browse facility similar in format to the primary edit panel. Although you can't change any of the information displayed, you can use the scrolling PF keys to move up and down and left and right. In addition, you can use commands like LOCATE and FIND to search for specific lines of text.

The OUTLIST Utility entry panel

Access from the ISPF Primary Option Menu: 3 (Utilities) → 8 (Outlist)

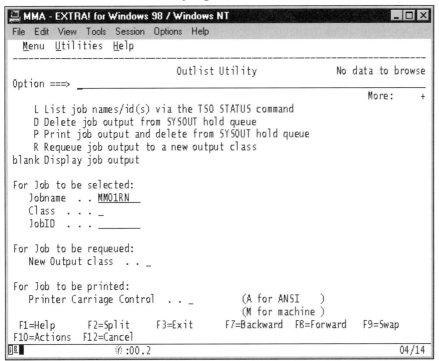

Description

*   The Outlist utility is a standard ISPF utility that you can use to monitor a job's progress and output if you don't have a more sophisticated tool, like SDSF, available to you.

*   To execute an Outlist function, you enter the appropriate option in the command line (or leave it blank if you want to display job output), supply the information necessary to identify the job, and press Enter.

*   Option L examines the JES spool for jobs you submitted and displays the name, identifier, and status for each job it finds. You don't have to include a job name with this option if your job names consist of your TSO/E user-id plus one letter (you'll learn about coding job names in chapter 4).

*   To display a job's output, enter the job name and, if there's more than one job with the same name, the job identifier.

*   To print held output, you can use the P option and direct the output to a particular printer, or you can use the R option to change the job's output class from a held class to a class associated with a printer.

*   To delete a job's output, you use the D option.

Figure 3-13   How to use the Outlist utility to work with jobs and job output

Perspective

ISPF is a feature-rich system that's designed to facilitate many different program-development tasks. Because of its complexity and keystroke-based interface, it may take some getting used to, but this chapter should be enough to get you started. As you become adept at creating, submitting, and managing your jobs, you'll want to experiment with other ISPF features that weren't covered in this chapter. Then, if you want to learn more about ISPF, you can use the online help facility (it's a better resource than the IBM manual) or get our book, *MVS TSO, Part 1: Concepts and ISPF*.

Terms

panel	screen window
graphical user interface	job identifier
GUI	job-id
action bar	job number
command nesting	System Display and Search Facility
ISPF editor	SDSF
edit profile	input queue
primary edit panel	output queue
heading area	held output queue
primary command	action character
line command area	return code
line command	Outlist utility

Section 2

JCL essentials

The best way to learn job control language is to start coding it, and that's the approach this section takes. So in chapter 4, you'll learn how to code basic JCL statements to perform the tasks that are required for just about every job you create. Then, in chapters 5-8, you'll build on the basics by learning how to use specific JCL facilities to manage job and program execution, DASD data set allocation, and tape and SYSOUT processing. Finally, in chapter 9, you'll learn how to use and create pre-coded segments of JCL called *procedures*. By the end of this section, then, you'll be coding the type of production jobs that are used every day in MVS, OS/390, and z/OS shops.

4

The basics of
Job Control Language

In this chapter, you'll learn how to code a basic subset of Job Control Language. This subset includes the JCL statements and parameters that you'll use the most. When you complete this chapter, you'll be able to code a wide variety of real-world jobs like the two that are presented at the end of this chapter.

How to code JCL statements

Before you can learn how to code individual JCL statements, you have to know some basic coding techniques that apply to all of the statements in a job. So to begin, you'll learn how to identify the elements that make up a JCL statement as well as how to follow the general rules that govern the punctuation and syntax of JCL code.

Job control language statements

Figure 4-1 presents the most commonly used JCL statements, all of which you'll learn about in this book. As you can see, there aren't that many. What makes JCL difficult to learn is not the number of statements, but the complexity of each one. In fact, most statements have a number of elements that can be coded in a variety of ways to achieve a desired effect. You'll get some sense of that as you learn to code the JOB, EXEC, and especially the DD statement in this chapter.

As you may remember from the simple job you saw in chapter 2, a job always starts with a JOB statement that identifies the job. After that, a job typically executes one or more programs. Each program is called a *job step* or *step*, and each job step begins with an EXEC statement that names the program to be executed. This is illustrated by the job example in this figure. This job consists of two job steps with the first one executing a program called PROGA and the second one executing a program called PROGB. In addition to the EXEC statement, both job steps contain several DD statements that provide the file information needed by the programs.

The last statement is a *null statement* that simply marks the end of the job. It consists of two slashes (//) at the beginning of the statement, with the rest of the statement remaining blank. Null statements aren't required because the operating system recognizes the end of the job stream or the beginning of a new job without them. Some programmers like to use null statements, though, when there's more than one job in a job stream just to clarify where one job ends and the next one begins.

Besides the JCL statements listed in this figure, you can include additional, non-JCL statements in a job if your installation has JES2 or JES3 installed. These JES2/JES3 control statements supply information that's processed directly by the Job Entry Subsystem. You'll learn how to code JES2 and JES3 control statements in chapter 5.

The basic job control language statements

Statement	Purpose
JOB	Identifies a job and supplies accounting information.
EXEC	Identifies a job step by indicating the name of the program to be executed.
DD	Identifies a data set to be allocated for the job step.
delimiter (/*)	Marks the end of an instream data set.
null (//)	Marks the end of a job.
comment (//*)	Provides comments.

The additional JCL statements that are covered in this book

Statement	Purpose
OUTPUT	Supplies options for SYSOUT processing (chapter 8).
PROC	Marks the beginning of a procedure (chapter 9).
PEND	Marks the end of a procedure (chapter 9).
JCLLIB	Identifies a private procedure library (chapter 9).
INCLUDE	Copies statements from another library member into the job (chapter 9).
SET	Sets default values for symbolic variables (chapter 9).
IF/THEN/ELSE/ENDIF	Provides conditional execution of a job step (chapter 10).
COMMAND	Identifies an MVS or JES command that is to be issued when the job runs (chapter 11).

A job begins with a JOB statement and consists of one or more job steps

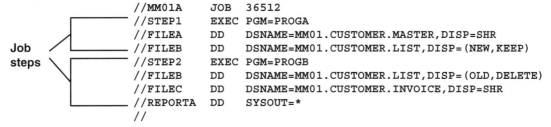

```
//MM01A     JOB  36512
//STEP1     EXEC PGM=PROGA
//FILEA     DD   DSNAME=MM01.CUSTOMER.MASTER,DISP=SHR
//FILEB     DD   DSNAME=MM01.CUSTOMER.LIST,DISP=(NEW,KEEP)
//STEP2     EXEC PGM=PROGB
//FILEB     DD   DSNAME=MM01.CUSTOMER.LIST,DISP=(OLD,DELETE)
//FILEC     DD   DSNAME=MM01.CUSTOMER.INVOICE,DISP=SHR
//REPORTA   DD   SYSOUT=*
//
```

Description

- OS/390 Job Control Language consists of a set of JCL statements that are used in jobs to control program execution, data allocation, and output processing.

- A job begins with a JOB statement. After that, most JCL statements are grouped into *job steps*. Each job step starts with an EXEC statement and contains the statements that are needed to execute one program.

- A *null statement* can be used to mark the end of a job. It consists of slashes in columns 1 and 2 and no other data on the rest of the line. It isn't required, though, so you probably won't use it.

- Depending on whether your installation uses the JES2 or JES3 Job Entry Subsystem, you can also include JES2 or JES3 control statements in your job to provide information that's processed directly by JES. You'll learn more about JES features in chapter 5.

Figure 4-1   Job control language statements

The fields in a JCL statement

JCL statements are coded as 80-byte records with 72 of those bytes available for JCL code and the last eight reserved for an optional sequence number. Within the 72 bytes, you can code JCL in a relatively freeform manner, following the basic format and rules shown in figure 4-2. As you can see, each JCL statement is logically divided into five fields: the identifier field, the name field, the operation field, the parameters field, and the comments field. The identifier, operation, and parameters fields are used by most JCL statements while the name and comments fields are optional.

The *identifier field* identifies a record as a JCL statement. For most JCL statements, the identifier field occupies the first two character positions and must contain two slashes (//). There are, however, two exceptions. First, the delimiter statement has a slash in column 1 and an asterisk in column 2 (/*). Second, the identifier field for a comment statement is three characters long with the first two columns containing slashes and the third containing an asterisk (//*). You'll learn about the comment and delimiter statements later in this chapter.

The *name field* associates a name with a JCL statement. It's always required on a JOB statement because it identifies your job to the system. It's optional on EXEC and DD statements, but you'll find that it's usually coded anyway. For the job in this figure, the name field for the JOB statement is MM01A; the name field for the EXEC statement is POST, and for the DD statements, the names are CUSTTRAN, CUSTMAST, TRANJRNL, and ERRLIST. The name field is not allowed on a delimiter or comment statement.

The *operation field* can be coded anywhere on the line as long as it's separated from the name field by at least one blank. If you start the operation field in column 12, though, that leaves enough space for the two-character identifier field, an eight-character name field, and one blank space. In addition, the listing is easier to read if all the operation fields are lined up. Delimiter and comment statements don't have an operation field because their unique identifier fields indicate their functions.

The *parameters field* begins at least one position after the end of the operation field and can extend all the way to column 71. In it, you code one or more *parameters* to supply information that influences how the statement is processed. It's easily the largest and most complicated of all the fields, so you'll learn about coding parameters in detail in the next topic.

After the parameters field, you can code a brief comment in the *comments field*. The comments field begins in the position after the space that marks the end of the parameters field and ends in column 71. The system ignores what you code here, so you can record any comments you wish. However, because space is limited in the comments field, you'll probably prefer to use the comment statement instead. You'll see examples of both the comments field and the comment statement later in this chapter.

Now that you've seen the basic format for JCL statements, you can understand how the null statement got its name. None of the fields can be coded in a null statement except the identifier field.

The basic format for JCL statements

```
identifier [name] [operation] [parameters] [comments]
```

Explanation

identifier	Starts in column 1 and generally consists of two slashes (//). There are two exceptions: (1) a delimiter statement (identifier is /*) and (2) a comment statement (identifier is //*).
name	One to eight alphanumeric or national ($,#,@) characters, starting with a letter or national character. Must begin in column 3 if coded.
operation	A valid operation code, such as JOB, EXEC, or DD. Must be preceded and followed by a space.
parameters	One or more parameters, depending on the operation. Individual parameters are separated from one another by commas, with no intervening spaces.
comments	Comments may follow the parameters, preceded by one space and not extending beyond column 71.

Typical fields in a JCL job

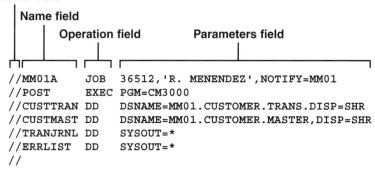

```
//MM01A     JOB  36512,'R. MENENDEZ',NOTIFY=MM01
//POST      EXEC PGM=CM3000
//CUSTTRAN  DD   DSNAME=MM01.CUSTOMER.TRANS.DISP=SHR
//CUSTMAST  DD   DSNAME=MM01.CUSTOMER.MASTER,DISP=SHR
//TRANJRNL  DD   SYSOUT=*
//ERRLIST   DD   SYSOUT=*
//
```

Description

- JCL statements are coded in 80-byte records although only 72 bytes are available for JCL code. The last eight columns of each record are reserved for an optional sequence number.

- Each statement can be logically divided into five fields. But all five fields don't necessarily appear on every statement.

- The *identifier field* starts in column 1 and for all standard JCL statements is two slashes (//).

- Immediately following the identifier field is the *name field*. Although required on JOB statements, the name is optional on EXEC and DD statements.

- The *operation*, *parameters*, and *comment fields* can be coded in a freeform style as long as there's at least one blank space between these fields. They can also begin in any column.

Figure 4-2   The fields in a JCL statement

The JCL parameters field

Learning how to code JCL is largely a matter of learning how to code the parameters correctly in the parameters field of each JCL statement. That's because most JCL statements can have dozens of parameters that can be coded in many different ways. Figure 4-3 shows the general guidelines you follow when coding parameters, no matter which statement you're dealing with.

To begin, you need to realize that JCL statement parameters are either positional or keyword, as shown in the examples in this figure. *Positional parameters* are coded first in the parameters field, and the operating system interprets their meaning based on the order in which they're presented. If you omit a positional parameter, you usually code an extra comma as a placeholder for it, as shown in the second example. You'll see many more examples of this later, so don't let it confuse you now.

Most JCL parameters are *keyword parameters*. A keyword parameter isn't interpreted based on its position in the parameters field. Instead, you identify the parameter by coding a keyword followed by an equals sign (=) and a value. When you code a JCL statement that has more than one keyword parameter, you can code the parameters in any order you wish. However, keyword parameters must always come after any required positional parameters.

If a parameters field consists of more than one parameter, you separate each with a comma. The system will assume that a parameters field is complete when a space is encountered. As a result, if a parameter value requires a space as part of its value, you have to enclose the value in apostrophes. You also have to use apostrophes for a value that contains any special characters other than a period (.) or a hyphen (-).

Some JCL parameters require *subparameters*, which are individual specifications within a single parameter. Subparameters are coded the same way as parameters. As a result, positional subparameters are coded first, followed by keyword subparameters in any order. Like positional parameters, omitted positional subparameters use commas as placeholders. And if a parameter specifies more than one subparameter, the entire list is enclosed in parentheses.

The DD statement examples in this figure should make some sense to you now. The first three contain two parameters each. The last two contain six parameters each, and four of those parameters have subparameters (DISP, VOL, SPACE, and DCB). Once you've finished this chapter, you'll understand all the coding in these examples, and you'll be able to code similar statements yourself.

Examples of positional and keyword parameters and subparameters

Two positional parameters

```
//MM01A     JOB   36512,'R MENENDEZ'
```

Two positional parameters when the first one isn't coded

```
//MM01A     JOB   ,'R MENENDEZ'
```

Two keyword parameters

```
//CUSTMAST DD    DSNAME=MM01.CUSTOMER.MASTER,DISP=SHR
```

Two keyword parameters with positional subparameters

```
//CUSTMAST DD    DSNAME=MM01.CUSTOMER.MASTER,DISP=(,CATLG,DELETE),
//               UNIT=SYSDA,VOL=SER=MPS800,
//               SPACE=(CYL,(10,5,2)),
//               DCB=DSORG=PO
```

Two keyword parameters with keyword subparameters

```
//DUNNING   DD    DSNAME=MM01.DUNNING.FILE,DISP=(NEW,KEEP),
//               UNIT=SYSDA,VOL=SER=MPS800,
//               SPACE=(CYL,(1,1)),
//               DCB=(DSORG=PS,RECFM=FB,LRECL=400)
```

How to code parameters

* The parameters field begins at least one position after the end of the operation field and can extend into column 71.

* There are two types of *parameters*: positional and keyword.

* The system interprets the meaning of a *positional parameter* based on its position in the parameters field. As a result, an omitted positional parameter that is followed by additional positional parameters must have a comma to mark its place.

* *Keyword parameters* are interpreted based on a keyword followed by an equals sign and a value. They can be coded in any order.

* Code positional parameters first in the parameters field, before any keyword parameters.

* All parameters must be separated by commas, not blanks. When the system encounters a blank in the parameters field, it assumes that it has reached the end of the field and treats any code that follows as comments.

* If a parameter contains any blanks or special characters other than a period (.) or hyphen (-), it must be enclosed in apostrophes.

How to code subparameters

* Some parameters require *subparameters*. Subparameters are coded the same way as parameters and can also be positional or keyword.

* If you code more than one subparameter for a parameter, enclose the list in parentheses.

Figure 4-3   How to code the parameters field

How to continue a JCL statement

Often, you'll find that you can't fit all of the parameters for a JCL statement on a single line. In that case, you can continue a statement onto a new line as shown in the top part of figure 4-4.

As you can see, the rules for coding continuation lines are straightforward. First, break the parameter field after the comma that follows a parameter or subparameter (don't forget to code the final comma at the end of the continued line). Second, code slashes in columns 1 and 2 of the following line. And third, code the next parameter or subparameter beginning anywhere in columns 4 through 16 (be careful not to start beyond column 16). You must always leave column 3 blank on a continuation line or the system will interpret it as a new statement and issue an error when you submit the job for processing.

If you look at the two examples of coding continuation lines, you'll see that both use the same DD statement. But the first one is coded with as many parameters as possible on the first line, while in the second example, there are only one or two parameters per line. If you compare the statements, you'll see that the second example presents a more organized and readable approach to coding JCL. It also makes the JCL easier to edit if you have to change or add parameters later on.

How to code comments in a job

The bottom part of figure 4-4 shows two ways to code comments in a job. The first example uses the comments field at the end of the statement, as described earlier. In this example, the comment starts with an asterisk, but that's not necessary. When the system reads the first blank after the parameters field, it treats any remaining text in the line as comments.

Since the size of the comments field is limited by the size of the parameters field, there's usually not enough room for meaningful comments. So more often, you'll use *comment statements* when you want to describe or clarify your JCL code, as shown in the second example. Although one comment statement would have been enough to describe this job step, the beginning of the step is more clearly defined by placing the comment in a "flower box."

Comment statements can be coded anywhere after the JOB statement, and they begin with two slashes and an asterisk (//*) in column 1. You can then follow the //* with any comment you want. Although the comment statement is ignored by the system, it's still printed along with the rest of the JCL listing.

Two ways to continue a JCL statement on more than one line

Code as many parameters on one line as possible

```
//DUNNING   DD    DSNAME=MM01.DUNNING.FILE,DISP=(NEW,KEEP),UNIT=SYSDA,
// VOL=SER=MPS800,SPACE=(CYL,(1,1)),DCB=(DSORG=PS,RECFM=FB,LRECL=400)
```

Code only one or two parameters per line

```
//DUNNING   DD    DSNAME=MM01.DUNNING.FILE,DISP=(NEW,KEEP),
//                UNIT=SYSDA,VOL=SER=MPS800,
//                SPACE=(CYL,(1,1)),
//                DCB=(DSORG=PS,RECFM=FB,LRECL=400)
```

Description

- The parameters field can be coded on more than one line. However, the field can only be divided after the comma at the end of a complete parameter or subparameter.

- The continued line must start with // in columns 1 and 2. Parameters on a continued line can start anywhere between columns 4 and 16.

- Column 3 of a continued line must be blank. If it isn't, the system will interpret the continued line as a new statement, and the job will abend.

Two ways to code comments in a job

How to code a comment in the comments field of a JCL statement

```
//MM01A     JOB   36512,MENENDEZ,NOTIFY=MM01
//POST      EXEC  PGM=CM3000    **Post cust transactions**
//CUSTTRAN  DD    DSNAME=MM01.CUSTOMER.TRANS.DISP=SHR
//CUSTMAST  DD    DSNAME=MM01.CUSTOMER.MASTER,DISP=SHR
//TRANJRNL  DD    SYSOUT=*
```

How to use JCL comment statements

```
//MM01RP    JOB   36512,'A PRINCE',MSGCLASS=X,MSGLEVEL=(1,1)
//************************************************************
//*   Prepare past-due reports from DUNNING file            *
//************************************************************
//AR7200    EXEC  PGM=AR7200
//DUNNING   DD    DSNAME=MM01.DUNNING.FILE,DISP=OLD,
//                UNIT=SYSDA,VOL=SER=MPS800
//ATB       DD    SYSOUT=*
//OVERDUE   DD    SYSOUT=*
```

Description

- Comments are typically used to help identify or clarify the purpose and operation of a job or job step.

- To code a comment within another JCL statement, simply leave one blank space between the end of the parameters field and the beginning of the comment.

- A JCL *comment statement* must begin in column 1 with two slashes and an asterisk (//*). In terms of processing, the entire comment statement is ignored, but it's printed along with the JCL listing.

Figure 4-4   How to code continuation lines and comments

How to code the JOB statement

The JOB statement has three basic functions. First, it identifies a job to OS/390 and supplies a job name that OS/390 uses to refer to the job. Second, it supplies accounting information so that OS/390 can determine who is responsible for the job and, if necessary, who should be billed for the computer resources the job uses. Third, it supplies various options that influence or limit how the job is processed.

The syntax of the JOB statement

Figure 4-5 shows a simplified format for the JOB statement. As you can see, there are two positional parameters (accounting information and programmer name) and three keyword parameters (MSGCLASS, MSGLEVEL, and NO-TIFY). The brackets in the syntax show that none of these parameters is required by the operating system. However, if you omit the accounting information but code the programmer name, you have to precede the programmer name with a comma to indicate the position of the missing parameter, as shown in the third example. In contrast, if you omit both positional parameters, you don't have to code any commas before the first keyword parameter, as shown in the fourth example.

Of all the JCL statements, the JOB statement is the one whose required format varies the most from one installation to the next. That's because OS/390 provides several ways for an installation to tailor the JOB statement so it provides appropriate accounting information. Many shops require that you code an account number in the accounting information parameter, followed by one or more options that determine who's responsible for the job and how its billing should be handled. In fact, JES2 provides a default for accounting information that includes subparameters like these (although JES3 doesn't). In contrast, some shops require only an account number, and a few don't require the accounting information parameter at all.

The examples in this figure show the types of variations you might run into. As you can see, the first two examples include the accounting information parameter, although each uses a different format, while the last two examples don't contain any accounting information at all. In any event, you'll have to find out exactly what the requirements are at your installation.

Once you know what parameters you need to include in your JOB statement, you may find it convenient to create a special JOBCARD member in the PDS library where you store your JCL. Then, you can copy it into each new job stream you create. Since the information on a JOB statement seldom changes from job to job, this saves you some work.

The syntax of the JOB statement

```
//jobname   JOB [ accounting-information ] [,programmer-name ]
                [ ,MSGCLASS=class ]
                [ ,MSGLEVEL=(stmt,msg) ]
                [ ,NOTIFY=user-id ]
```

Explanation

accounting-information	Specifies an account number or other accounting information. Typically used to charge the job's processing time back to a department or group. The requirements of this parameter vary from installation to installation, but it often has a format similar to this:

```
([account-number] [,accounting-options])
```

programmer-name	Identifies the owner of the job. The name can be from one to 20 characters long, but it may not be required depending on the installation.
MSGCLASS	Specifies a single-character output class to be used for the job's message output.
MSGLEVEL	Controls which JCL statements and system messages are produced by the job.
NOTIFY	Specifies the user-id of the TSO/E user to be notified when the job completes.

JOB statement examples

```
//PAY40B1   JOB    MMA2AB14
//PAY40B2   JOB    (MMA-001,'06/11/02',206),MENENDEZ,MSGCLASS=A
//PAY40B3   JOB    ,MENENDEZ,MSGCLASS=A
//PAY40B4   JOB    MSGCLASS=A,MSGLEVEL=(0,0),NOTIFY=MM01
```

A member named JOBCARD that contains a generic JOB statement

```
//MM01XXXX JOB   36512,'R MENENDEZ',
//               MSGCLASS=X,MSGLEVEL=(1,1),NOTIFY=MM01
```

Description

- The JOB statement must always be the first statement in a job.

- The most commonly used JOB statement parameters are listed above. Later in chapter 5, you'll learn about additional parameters that you may need to code in your shop.

- In contrast to the other JOB statement parameters, the format of the first positional parameter, accounting information, is installation-dependent. It often consists of several positional subparameters, the first of which is normally the *account number*. Check with your supervisor for details on how to code this parameter.

- Since the JOB statement seldom changes from job to job, you can create a PDS member that consists of a standard JOB statement and then copy it into each new job you code.

Figure 4-5   The syntax of the JOB statement

The job name

Every JOB statement you code must include a name in the name field. The name you supply becomes the *job name* OS/390 uses to identify your job, but it doesn't have to be unique. As you learned in chapter 3, if two or more active jobs have the same name, they're distinguished by the *job identifier* (or *job-id* or *job number*), which is assigned by the system and is unique for all active jobs.

Figure 4-6 shows the rules for coding the name field in any JCL statement and gives examples of valid and invalid job names. As you can see, there's quite a bit of flexibility when it comes to naming your job. Be aware, though, that your installation may have additional rules that govern how you can form job names. Often, the first two to four characters of a job name have to match an account number assigned to you by your installation. For example, suppose your account number and TSO user-id is MM01 and your installation requires that the first two characters of the job name match the first two characters of the account number. Under that scheme, job names like MMCOPY1 and MMXB14A would be acceptable.

If you're submitting a job from TSO/E or ISPF, it's a good idea to create job names that consist of your TSO user-id followed by one or two alphanumeric characters. For example, the TSO user-id used to test the examples in this book is MM01, so you'll see job names like MM01P and MM01RN throughout. If you don't follow this suggestion, it will be difficult to find your job output when you want to view it with SDSF or Outlist.

Rules for coding the name field of a JCL statement

- A name must start in column 3 of a JCL statement and must be followed by at least one blank.
- It can be from one to eight characters long, consisting of alphanumeric (A-Z and 0-9) and national (@,$,#) characters.
- The first character must be alphabetic or national.

Valid job names

```
//MM01A
//CS0166PR
//$PSP06B
```

Invalid job names

`// MM01C`	Doesn't start in column 3
`//(ABCDE)`	Starts with an invalid character
`//PR_001`	Contains an invalid character
`//PAYMENT805`	Contains more than 8 characters

Description

- A *job name* is required on every JOB statement you code.
- Although the job name is used to identify the job to the system, it does not have to be unique. If two or more jobs have the same name, they can still be distinguished by their *job identifier* (or *job-id* or *job number*), which is unique to all active jobs.
- Two jobs with the same name can't run at the same time. In such situations, one job is held until the other job with the same job name completes execution.
- Some installations have additional requirements for creating job names, such as that they be based on an account number or your TSO user-id. So check with your supervisor for any standards you need to follow.

Figure 4-6   How to create a job name

The programmer name parameter

The programmer name parameter may or may not be required at your installation. And even if it's required, the value you specify may or may not be important. At some installations, you have to code the programmer name parameter in a particular way to identify yourself. At others, the value you code is used for documentation. As you can see in the last example in figure 4-7, the parameter may not even represent a programmer's name. Here, DEPT-10 is listed as the originator of job MM01E.

Like any parameter value, the programmer name value must be enclosed in apostrophes if it contains special characters or spaces. So in this figure, 'R MENENDEZ' is enclosed in apostrophes because of the space between the R and the M, but R.MENENDEZ doesn't need apostrophes because periods aren't considered to be special characters. Beyond this, if the programmer name includes an apostrophe (as in O'Brien), you have to code two consecutive apostrophes and enclose the entire name in apostrophes.

The NOTIFY parameter

If you submit a job from a TSO/E terminal, you can code the NOTIFY parameter on the JOB statement so that you'll automatically be notified when the job completes. You can supply the NOTIFY parameter with either your TSO/E user-id or the &SYSUID system symbol. If you code your user-id, you'll be notified when the job ends whether or not you're the one submitting the job. In contrast, the &SYSUID system symbol is automatically replaced by the user-id of the person submitting the job. In a production environment, it's common to code &SYSUID. Then, if someone else submits a job stream you created, or copies your JOB statement to start a new job of their own, the user-id on the NOTIFY parameter doesn't have to be changed.

When the job completes, a message like the one in figure 4-7 will be sent to the TSO/E terminal identified by the user-id. If you're working under ISPF, you'll have to press the Enter key to receive the message, then press the Enter key again to return to the ISPF panel you were working in. If you aren't logged on to TSO/E when the message arrives, you'll receive the message when you log in.

Five JOB statements that use the programmer name parameter

```
//MM01A  JOB  36512,RMENENDEZ
//MM01B  JOB  ,R.MENENDEZ
//MM01C  JOB  ,'R MENENDEZ'
//MM01D  JOB  36512,'O''Brien'
//MM01E  JOB  ,DEPT-10
```

Two ways to code the NOTIFY parameter

```
//MM01A  JOB 36512,LOWE,NOTIFY=MM01
//MM01B  JOB 36512,LOWE,NOTIFY=&SYSUID
```

The message returned to your TSO/E terminal when the job completes

```
17.35.12 JOB02169 $HASP165 MM01B    ENDED AT DDC1NJE   MAXCC=0 CN(INTERNAL)
***
```

Description

- The programmer name parameter is a positional parameter that immediately follows the accounting information parameter. It may or may not be a required field in your installation.

- The name can be from one to 20 characters long and follows the rules for coding parameters. To include an apostrophe within a name, you code two consecutive apostrophes and enclose the entire name in apostrophes.

- If you code the NOTIFY parameter on the JOB statement, a message is sent to your TSO/E terminal when the job completes execution.

- The NOTIFY parameter requires either a valid TSO/E user-id or the &SYSUID system symbol. When &SYSUID is used, the system automatically inserts the user-id of whoever submits the job for processing.

Figure 4-7   How to code the programmer name and NOTIFY parameters

The MSGCLASS and MSGLEVEL parameters

As your job executes, the operating system lists JCL statements and produces various system messages. The MSGCLASS and MSGLEVEL parameters, when used together, let you manage that output. Figure 4-8 shows the syntax for both parameters as well as an example of how they're used in a typical JOB statement.

The MSGCLASS parameter lets you specify an output class that's associated with your job's message output. For example, if you specify MSGCLASS=A, your job's message output is assigned to output class A. At most shops, that means the output will be printed on one of the installation's high-speed printers. If you omit the MSGCLASS parameter, the system assigns a default. Usually, the default message class is A, but for jobs submitted from a TSO/E terminal, the default message class might be a held output class. For example, at my installation the default for jobs submitted from TSO/E is class X, a held class.

The MSGLEVEL parameter lets you specify the types of messages you want included in your output and consists of two positional subparameters. The first, *stmt*, controls which JCL statements appear in the JCL statement listing. The second, *msg*, controls which messages appear in the message log. This figure also lists the values you can code for each subparameter.

If you omit MSGLEVEL, a default value is used. At most installations, the default is MSGLEVEL=(1,1), which causes all of the JCL and system messages to be printed. Normally, that's what you want, so you can omit the MSGLEVEL parameter altogether.

For a production job that produces pages of JCL and message output, however, you may want to specify MSGLEVEL=(0,0). Then, only the JOB statement and the step completion messages will be printed if the job runs to completion. But if the job fails, the allocation and deallocation messages will be printed as well.

The syntax of the MSGCLASS parameter

```
MSGCLASS=class
```

Explanation

class   Identifies the output class for the job log. The class can only be one character long (A-Z or 0-9) and must be a valid output class specified at JES initialization.

The syntax of the MSGLEVEL parameter

```
MSGLEVEL=(stmt,msg)
```

Explanation

stmt   A single digit that specifies which JCL statements should be printed, as follows:

    0   Print only the JOB statement.

    1   Print only JCL statements, including those that come from procedures (the default).

    2   Print only JCL statements submitted through the input stream; don't print statements from procedures.

msg   A single digit that specifies which system messages should be printed, as follows:

    0   Print step completion messages only; don't print allocation and deallocation messages unless the job fails.

    1   Print all messages (the default).

A JOB statement with both the MSGCLASS and MSGLEVEL parameters

```
//MM01A  JOB 36512,'R MENENDEZ',MSGCLASS=X,MSGLEVEL=(0,0)
```

Description

- The MSGCLASS parameter allows you to assign an output class to your job log. The job log is a record of job-related information that you may find useful. The output classes you can use are defined by your installation.

- The MSGLEVEL parameter consists of two positional subparameters that let you control the printing of system statements and messages that are produced by the job.

- Normally, the default is MSGLEVEL=(1,1), but you may want to specify MSGLEVEL=(0,0) for large production jobs that would otherwise produce dozens of pages of JCL and message output.

- MSGCLASS and MSGLEVEL are typically coded together on a JOB statement.

Figure 4-8   How to code the MSGCLASS and MSGLEVEL parameters

How to code the EXEC statement

An EXEC statement is required to identify the program executed by each step in a job. Figure 4-9 shows the basic format of the EXEC statement as well as three examples of how it's typically coded.

Although the stepname field of an EXEC statement is optional, it's a good practice to code a step name for each step. Since system messages refer to job and step names, coding a step name will help you identify the source of errors indicated by such messages. In addition, coding a meaningful step name helps document the function of the job.

The PGM parameter

In the PGM parameter of the EXEC statement, you specify the name of the program you want to execute in the job step. Actually, the name you specify is the name of a member of a partitioned data set. The member must be a load module (a compiled program that's been link edited and is ready to execute). In the first example in this figure, the program name is PAY5B10, in the second example it's IEBDG, and in third example it's HEWL.

Normally, the program you specify must be a member of a system load library, such as SYS1.LINKLIB. In chapter 5, however, you'll learn how to execute a program that resides in a private library instead.

You should also know that even though the PGM parameter looks like a keyword parameter, it is in fact a positional parameter. So make sure that it's the first parameter coded on the EXEC statement. Note, too, that it's required (it isn't enclosed in brackets in the syntax).

The PARM parameter

The PARM parameter is used to pass information that can be accessed by the program you specify in the PGM parameter. The information is usually used to influence the way the program works. For example, many IBM-supplied programs, like utilities, compilers, and the linkage editor, use PARM information to set various processing options. User programs can take advantage of this parameter too.

In the PARM parameter, you have to code the information in a form that's expected by the program. As a result, there aren't any JCL rules that govern the format of this information other than the rules of punctuation you must follow for any parameter value. So if the PARM field contains special characters like commas, spaces, parentheses, and so on, you should enclose the entire field in apostrophes. As a result, the PARM values in the second and third examples of this figure are both enclosed in apostrophes.

The syntax of the EXEC statement

```
//stepname   EXEC PGM=program-name [ ,PARM=information ]
```

Explanation

PGM   Specifies the name of the program to be executed for this job step.

PARM   Optional; specifies information that's passed to the program.

Examples of the EXEC statement

An EXEC statement that executes program PAY5B10 in step PAYLIST

```
//PAYLIST   EXEC PGM=PAY5B10
```

An EXEC statement that passes a parameter value of LINECT=0050 to program IEBDG

```
//DATAGEN   EXEC PGM=IEBDG,PARM='LINECT=0050'
```

An EXEC statement that passes three parameters to program HEWL

```
//LINKED    EXEC PGM=HEWL,PARM='LET,MAP,XREF'
```

Description

- The EXEC statement is the first statement in each job step. It executes a program or invokes a procedure for each step (you'll learn about procedures in chapter 9).

- Although a *step name* is optional, it is recommended that you code one for each EXEC statement, following the same rules as for a job name (see figure 4-6). Since system messages refer to job and step names, coding a step name will help you identify the source of errors indicated by such messages. Also, coding a meaningful step name helps document the function of the job step.

- Although the PGM parameter looks like a keyword parameter, it's a positional parameter that must be coded first on the EXEC statement.

- The program specified in the PGM parameter must be a link-edited load module member of a partitioned data set. Normally, the member you specify belongs to a system load library like SYS1.LINKLIB. However, you can also execute a program residing in a private library. You'll learn how to do this in chapter 5.

- The PARM parameter lets you pass information to the program specified in the PGM parameter. This parameter information is typically used to influence the way the program works. For example, IBM programs like utilities, compilers, and the linkage editor use PARM information to set various processing options.

- Any information coded into the PARM field is program-dependent. As a result, there are no special JCL rules to adhere to other than the rules of punctuation you must follow for any parameter value.

Figure 4-9   The syntax of the EXEC statement

How to code the DD statement for DASD data sets

Before the program in a job step is executed, the operating system has to allocate any data sets that the program will process. To describe these data sets to the system, you code *Data Definition (DD) statements* after the EXEC statement that identifies the program. Normally, you code one DD statement for each data set your program will process.

The DD statement is the most complicated of all the JCL statements. This is because of the many parameters and subparameters it has, as well as the many ways you can code those parameters to allocate different types of data sets.

To start, you'll learn how to code DD statements for DASD data sets. Later in this chapter, you'll learn how to code DD statements that let you allocate instream data sets and SYSOUT data sets. Then, throughout the rest of this book, you'll build on this base of knowledge to learn how to code DD statements for other types of data sets, including temporary data sets, data sets that reside on tape, VSAM data sets, and data sets that are managed by SMS.

The syntax of the DD statement for DASD data sets

In general, DD statements provide the system with information about a data set's characteristics, such as its organization, storage requirements, and record length. As a result, the syntax of the DD statement for DASD data sets is fairly complex, as you can see in figure 4-10. The ellipsis (...) in JCL syntax means that the last element can be repeated, so you can code a series of options in the DCB parameter.

Actually, the syntax is even more complex than it might at first appear. That's because the parameters can be coded in various combinations, depending on whether the data set is new or old, temporary or permanent, and cataloged or uncataloged. There are also many other DD statement parameters that you'll learn about later in this book.

The two examples in this figure give you an overview of the type of information you code in the DD statement and the variations you get into. In the first example, the DD statement allocates an existing cataloged data set called MM01.INVNTORY.MASTER for shared access. VSAM files are typically described with a DD statement like this.

In the second example, the DD statement allocates a new data set named MM01.ACCOUNT.MASTER and catalogs it on the SYSDA-class volume called MPS8BV. This file receives 10 cylinders of primary space and 2 cylinders of secondary space. It has physical sequential organization and fixed-length, blocked records that are 100 bytes long. In contrast to the first example, you wouldn't use this type of DD statement for VSAM data sets. That's because new VSAM data sets are normally allocated using Access Method Services rather than JCL, as you'll see in chapter 16.

The syntax of the DD statement for DASD data sets

```
//ddname    DD DSNAME=data-set-name
               ,DISP=(status,normal-disp,abnormal-disp)
            [ ,UNIT=unit ]
            [ ,VOL=SER=serial-number ]
            [ ,SPACE=unit,(primary-qty,secondary-qty,dir) ]
            [ ,DCB=(option,option...) ]
```

Explanation

DSNAME   Specifies the file's data set name.

DISP   Specifies the file's status and normal and abnormal disposition.

UNIT   Specifies a group name, device type, or device number that identifies the device where the file resides. Not required for cataloged data sets.

VOL=SER   Specifies the six-character volume serial number of the volume that contains the file. Not required for cataloged data sets.

SPACE   Specifies the DASD space to be allocated for the file. Unit indicates the unit of measure; primary-qty and secondary-qty indicate the amount of space for the initial and secondary allocations; and dir indicates the number of directory blocks to allocate for a partitioned data set.

DCB   Specifies options to be used for the file's data control block.

Examples of the DD statement

A DD statement that allocates an existing data set

```
//INVMAST   DD    DSNAME=MM01.INVNTORY.MASTER,DISP=SHR
```

A DD statement that allocates a new data set and catalogs it

```
//INVMAST   DD    DSNAME=MM01.ACCOUNT.MASTER,DISP=(NEW,CATLG),
//                UNIT=SYSDA,VOL=SER=MPS8BV,
//                SPACE=(CYL,(10,2)),
//                DCB=(DSORG=PS,RECFM=FB,LRECL=100)
```

Description

- To describe the data sets that must be allocated for a job step, you code a DD statement for each data set after the EXEC statement that identifies the step.
- The DD statement provides the system with information about a data set, such as its organization, storage requirements, and record length.
- DD statement parameters can be coded in various combinations, depending on whether the data set is new or old, temporary or permanent, and cataloged or uncataloged. Although there are many more DD parameters available, the ones listed above are used most often.

Figure 4-10   The syntax of the DD statement for DASD data sets

The ddname and the DSNAME parameter

The *ddname* that's coded in the name field of a DD statement is a symbolic name that the processing program uses to refer to the data set. In a COBOL program, the ddname is the name specified in the ASSIGN clause of the file's SELECT statement. In an assembler language program, it's the name specified in the DDNAME parameter on the file's DCB or ACB macro. Other programming languages have similar facilities to specify a file's ddname.

It's important to realize that the ddname is not necessarily the actual name of the data set as indicated in the data set's label. Instead, the ddname is an intermediate name that lets a program refer to the file without using its actual data set name. That way, the program can be used to process different files, as long as the files have the same format.

The DSNAME parameter is always required for a permanent data set. It supplies the data set name as it's stored in the data set's label or in the file's catalog entry. In figure 4-11, the first example specifies the data set name MM01.INVMAST.DATA.

To refer to a member of a partitioned data set, you code a standard data set name followed by the member's one- to eight-character name in parentheses. In the second example in this figure, the member named TRANS in a partitioned data set named MM01.INV.DATA is allocated. When you refer to a PDS member in this way, only the member you specify is processed by the job step's program even though the entire library is allocated to your job step. In fact, the program doesn't even have to know it's processing a PDS. Instead, it can process the member as if it were a sequential data set.

Incidentally, you can abbreviate the DSNAME parameter as DSN, as shown in the syntax. Whenever you see braces, that means you can choose any one of the items listed. Sometimes, all the alternatives are listed on a single line between braces and a vertical line (|) is used to separate the choices (you'll see this convention used in the next chapter).

The syntax of the DSNAME parameter

```
{DSNAME}  = {data-set-name}
{DSN}        {data-set-name(member)}
```

Different ways to code the DSNAME parameter

A DD statement that accesses a sequential data set

```
//INVMAST   DD   DSNAME=MM01.INVMAST.DATA,DISP=SHR
```

A DD statement that accesses a PDS member

```
//INVTRAN   DD   DSN=MM01.INV.DATA(TRANS),DISP=SHR
```

Reserved ddnames used by the operating system

JCBIN	JCBLOCK	JCBTAB	JESInnnn	JESJCL	JESJCLIN
JESMSGLG	JESYSMSG	JOBCAT	JOBLIB	JOURNAL	JST
JS3CATLG	J3JBINFO	J3SCINFO	J3STINFO	STCINRDR	STEPCAT
STEPLIB	SYSABEND	SYSCHK	SYSCKEOV	SYSIN	SYSMDUMP
SYSUDUMP	TSOINRDR				

Description

* The *ddname* is a symbolic name that the program specified in the EXEC statement uses to refer to a data set. It follows the rules for job names (see figure 4-6).

* Each ddname should be unique within the job step. If not, the system will still perform device and space allocation for both DD statements but will direct all references to the first DD statement in the job step.

* Some ddnames have special meaning to the system and therefore cannot be used to identify data sets in a processing program. These reserved ddnames are listed above.

* The DSNAME parameter is required on a DD statement for a permanent data set. It supplies the data set name as it's stored in the data set's label or in the file's catalog entry. For a new data set, the name is assigned to the data set; for an existing data set, the name is used to locate the data set.

* The DSNAME parameter is optional for temporary data sets. You'll learn how to handle temporary data sets in chapter 6.

Figure 4-11   How to code the ddname and the DSNAME parameter

The DISP parameter

The DISP parameter has three positional subparameters: status, normal disposition, and abnormal disposition. Figure 4-12 shows the values you can code for each subparameter, describes each value, and explains how OS/390 selects default values for the subparameters you omit. This figure also shows two examples of the DISP parameter.

Status specifies whether the file is new (NEW), an existing file to which you want exclusive access (OLD), an existing file you want to access and allow others to access too (SHR), or an existing file to which you want to add records (MOD). *Normal disposition* specifies what the system should do with the data set if the job step ends normally. You can keep the file (KEEP), delete it (DE-LETE), catalog it (CATLG), uncatalog it (UNCATLG), or retain it for use by a subsequent job step (PASS). *Abnormal disposition* specifies what to do if your program fails. The same values used by normal disposition work here except for PASS.

As for the default values, you'll be able to remember how they're assigned if you keep in mind three simple rules. First, if you omit the status subparameter, OS/390 assumes NEW. Second, if you omit the normal disposition subparameter, the default depends on the status subparameter: if it's NEW, the default is DELETE; otherwise, it's KEEP. In other words, the default is to delete new files and keep existing files. Third, if you omit the abnormal disposition subparameter, it takes on whatever value you specify or let default for normal disposition.

To allocate an existing data set, you normally code just the status subparameter, letting the normal and abnormal disposition subparameters assume default values. The first example in this figure shows how to do this. Here, an existing file is allocated for shared access, so other jobs can access the file too. Because the disposition subparameters are omitted, both assume KEEP as their default value.

To create a new data set (non-VSAM), you specify NEW as the status and you code a normal disposition subparameter to indicate how you want the data set retained. In the second example, the file is retained and cataloged if the program ends normally and it is deleted if it fails. In this case, you can omit NEW because it's the default, but remember to code the comma to mark its position as shown. If you specify KEEP instead of CATLG for the normal disposition, the file is retained but no catalog entry is made.

For VSAM files, you specify just the status subparameter without a normal or abnormal disposition subparameter. That's because VSAM files are always cataloged, and they're created and deleted by the VSAM utility program called Access Method Services, which you'll learn more about in chapter 16. In most cases, you'll code the DISP parameter for a VSAM file as DISP=SHR.

The syntax of the DISP parameter

```
DISP=(status,normal-disp,abnormal-disp)
```

Status

NEW	The data set does not exist and should be created.
OLD	The data set exists and should be allocated for exclusive use.
SHR	The data set exists and should be allocated for shared use.
MOD	The data set is allocated for exclusive use and is positioned at the end of the data, so additional records may be added after the last record. If you also code VOL=SER, the data set must exist.

Normal and abnormal disposition

DELETE	The data set is deleted. If it was retrieved from the catalog, it is also uncataloged.
KEEP	The data set is retained.
CATLG	The data set is retained and a catalog entry is made.
UNCATLG	The data set is retained, but its catalog entry is removed.
PASS	Normal disposition only. The data set is retained for use by a later job step.

Default values

status	If omitted, NEW is assumed.
normal disposition	Depends on the value specified or assumed for status: if NEW, normal disposition is DELETE; if OLD, SHR, or MOD, normal disposition is KEEP.
abnormal disposition	Takes on the value specified or assumed for normal disposition.

Examples of the DISP parameter

The data set is allocated for shared access, and the normal and abnormal dispositions default to KEEP

```
DISP=SHR
```

The new data set is cataloged if the job step ends normally; otherwise, it's deleted

```
DISP=(,CATLG,DELETE)
```

Description

* The DISP parameter describes the status of a data set to the system and tells the system what to do with the data set after the step or job finishes. DISP has three positional parameters: *status*, *normal disposition*, and *abnormal disposition*.

* Although the DISP parameter is not necessary, it's a good idea to include it in your DD statement. If you don't, default disposition values will be used, and that may not be what you want.

Figure 4-12   How to code the DISP parameter

The UNIT and VOLUME parameters

Figure 4-13 shows the syntax for both the UNIT and VOLUME parameters. These parameters work together to specify the location of a data set. UNIT indicates the device where the data set resides, and VOLUME indicates the *volser*, or *volume serial number* of the data set's volume. You specify UNIT and VOLUME when you're creating a new data set or when you're retrieving an existing uncataloged data set. For a cataloged data set, the unit and volume information is stored in the catalog, so you don't need to code it in the JCL.

You can code the UNIT parameter in one of three ways. First, you can specify a group name that identifies devices that belong to categories set up by the installation. For example, SYSDA is a commonly used group name that typically refers to any DASD unit that's available for public use. This is the most common way to code the UNIT parameter, so be sure to find out what group names are used for DASD devices in your shop. Second, you can use a generic name that identifies a particular type of device. For example, if you specify UNIT=3390, a 3390 device will be used. Third, you can specify a device number, such as UNIT=301. Here, the unit at address 301 will be allocated. As a general rule, though, it's not a good idea to specify an actual device number in a UNIT parameter.

The VOLUME parameter lets you specify which volume you want to allocate for your data set. That's called a *specific volume request*. For a new data set, however, the VOLUME parameter is optional. If you omit it, OS/390 scans the eligible volumes based on how you code the UNIT parameter to determine which volume is best to contain your file. That's called a *non-specific volume request*. In general, if you code the VOLUME parameter in a DD statement, you should include a UNIT parameter too, as shown in the example in this figure.

The syntax of the UNIT parameter

```
         {group-name}
UNIT=    {device-type}
         {device-number}
```

Explanation

group-name   Specifies a group name that identifies devices that belong to categories set up by the installation. SYSDA and TAPE are commonly used group names. SYSDA typically refers to any DASD unit that's available for public use, and TAPE refers to any available tape drive (you'll learn about tape data sets in chapter 7).

device-type   Specifies a device by its machine type or model. For example, if you specify UNIT=3390, a 3390 device is used.

device-number   Specifies a device by a three- or four-digit hexadecimal address. A four-digit number must be preceded by a slash (/), as in UNIT=/2301.

The syntax of the VOLUME parameter

```
{VOLUME=}SER=serial-number
{VOL=}
```

Explanation

serial-number   Specifies which volume you want to allocate for your data set. If omitted, OS/390 scans for eligible volumes based on the UNIT parameter.

A DD statement that uses the UNIT and VOLUME parameters

```
//INVMAST  DD   DSNAME=MM01.INVNTORY.MASTER,DISP=(NEW,CATLG),
//               UNIT=SYSDA,VOL=SER=MPS8BV,...
```

Description

- The UNIT and the VOLUME parameters are used to specify the location of a data set.

- UNIT indicates the device that the data is written to. In a *specific volume request,* VOLUME (VOL) indicates the *volume serial number* (*vol-ser*) of the data set's volume. In a *non-specific volume request* for a new data set, no VOL=SER parameter is coded, so the system chooses an appropriate volume based on the UNIT parameter.

- The UNIT and VOLUME parameters are used to create new data sets or to retrieve existing uncataloged data sets. For cataloged data sets, the unit and volume information is stored in the catalog, so you don't need to code either of these parameters.

- If the VOLUME parameter is coded, the UNIT parameter should be coded too.

Figure 4-13   How to code the UNIT and VOLUME parameters

The SPACE parameter

For new, non-VSAM data sets, you code the SPACE parameter to tell the system how much primary and secondary space to allocate. Figure 4-14 shows the syntax for the SPACE parameter. As you can see, it consists of two positional subparameters with the second subparameter further divided into three additional subparameters (that's why there are two sets of parentheses).

The first subparameter indicates the unit of measure used for the space allocation. Most often, you'll allocate space in terms of cylinders (CYL) or tracks (TRK). But you can also allocate space in terms of block length or, if SMS is active, average record length.

The second SPACE subparameter indicates how much space to allocate to the data set. Its three positional subparameters specify primary, secondary, and directory allocations. The primary allocation indicates how many units of space to allocate for the data set's primary *extent*. If the file requires more space than that, secondary extents can be allocated, each as large as the secondary amount you specify. For standard sequential and partitioned data sets, up to 15 secondary extents can be allocated, although for other types of files (like those managed by SMS), the limit is 122.

The directory allocation is only used for partitioned data sets. It indicates how large the library should be. The directory allocation ignores the unit of measure you specify and allocates the directory instead in units called *directory blocks*, each of which is large enough to define 21 members. So if you expect the library to hold 40 members, allocate two directory blocks.

This figure also includes three examples of the SPACE parameter. The maximum amount of space allowed by the SPACE parameter in example 1 is 19 cylinders: one 4-cylinder primary extent and 15 one-cylinder secondary extents. It also allows for a directory that can accommodate up to 105 entries. In example 2, the maximum amount allocated is 35 tracks: one 5-track primary extent and 15 two-track secondary extents. And for example 3, the maximum space allocated is 2000 800-byte blocks: one 500-block primary extent and 15 100-block secondary extents.

The syntax of the SPACE parameter

```
SPACE= (unit,(primary-qty,secondary-qty[,dir]))
```

Explanation

unit	Specifies the unit used to allocate space to the data set, as follows:

	TRK	Allocates space in tracks.
	CYL	Allocates space in cylinders.
	blklgth	Allocates space in blocks, with the block size given in bytes.
	reclgth	Allocates space based on the average record length in bytes, but can only be used under SMS (see chapter 13).

primary-qty	Specifies the number of units to be initially allocated to the file.
secondary-qty	Specifies the number of units to be allocated to each secondary extent.
dir	Specifies the number of directory blocks to allocate for a partitioned data set.

Examples of the SPACE parameter

Example 1	Primary	Secondary	Directory
`SPACE=(CYL,(4,1,5))`	4 cylinders	1 cylinder	5 blocks

Example 2		
`SPACE=(TRK,(5,2))`	5 tracks	2 tracks

Example 3		
`SPACE=(800,(500,100))`	500 800-byte blocks	100 800-byte blocks

Description

- For new non-VSAM data sets, you code the SPACE parameter as part of the DD statement to tell OS/390 how much primary and secondary space to allocate to the data set.

- The first SPACE subparameter establishes the unit of measure for space allocation. In most cases, CYL (for cylinders) or TRK (for tracks) is used. But you can also allocate space based on block length or average record length.

- The first value in the second subparameter specifies the primary quantity, or *extent*, of disk space to allocate in terms of the unit specified. This is the amount of space that's allocated when the data set is created.

- The second value in the second subparameter specifies the quantity of additional space to be allocated if more is needed. Depending on the type of data set you're defining, up to 122 secondary extents can be allocated, each as large as the amount you specify. For standard sequential and partitioned data sets, the limit is 15 secondary extents.

- The third value in the second subparameter specifies the number of 256-byte records needed in the directory of a partitioned data set (PDS). Each *directory block* is large enough to define 21 members.

Figure 4-14   How to code the SPACE parameter

The DCB parameter

The last DD statement parameter covered in this chapter is the DCB parameter. It lets you specify file characteristics that are stored in the file's *Data Control Block*. You code the DCB parameter only for new files. For existing files, the information is retrieved from the data set label. In addition, you don't have to code the DCB parameter for a new file if your application program supplies the required information or if SMS is used.

Figure 4-15 shows four commonly used DCB subparameters. They're keyword subparameters, so you can code them in any order you want.

The DSORG subparameter specifies the organization of the data set. Usually, you'll code PS (for sequential files) or PO (for partitioned data sets). The RECFM subparameter specifies how the file's records are formatted. Most often, you'll code FB or VB, meaning that the file has fixed- or variable-length blocked records. The LRECL subparameter specifies the record length for the file, while the BLKSIZE subparameter specifies the block size. However, if BLKSIZE is omitted, the system automatically calculates the optimum block size for the data. For that reason, I recommend that you omit the BLKSIZE parameter from all your DD statements.

This figure also shows two examples of the DCB parameter. In the first example, a sequential file with fixed-length, 133-byte records is defined. The second example shows how to specify variable-length records. Here, LRECL specifies the maximum record length. You may notice that the subparameters in the second example aren't preceded by the DCB keyword and that they're not within parentheses. That's because most DCB subparameters can also be coded as separate DD statement parameters. However, DSORG must be coded as part of a DCB parameter.

The syntax of the DCB parameter

```
DCB=(option,option...)
```

Commonly used DCB options

`DSORG=x`	Specifies the data set's organization, as follows:

	PS	Physical sequential
	PO	Partitioned
	DA	Direct
	IS	Indexed sequential

`RECFM=x`	Specifies the format of the file's records, as follows:

	F	Fixed length, unblocked
	FB	Fixed length, blocked
	V	Variable length, unblocked
	VB	Variable length, blocked
	VBS	Variable length, blocked, spanned
	U	Undefined

`LRECL=n`	Specifies the length of the file's records.
`BLKSIZE=n`	Specifies the length of the file's blocks; for FB, BLKSIZE is normally a multiple of LRECL.

Examples of the DCB parameter

A DCB parameter for a sequential file with fixed-length records of 133 bytes

```
DCB=(DSORG=PS,RECFM=F,LRECL=133)
```

DD parameters for a file with variable-length records up to 500 bytes long

```
RECFM=VB,LRECL=500
```

Description

- The DCB parameter lets you specify data set attributes that are stored in the data set's *Data Control Block*. Because existing data sets retrieve their attribute information from the data set label, this parameter is used only for new data sets and then only if the application program that creates the data set doesn't supply the required information.

- The RECFM subparameter specifies how the data set's records are formatted. Most often, FB (fixed, blocked) or VB (variable, blocked) is used.

- If the BLKSIZE subparameter is omitted, the system will calculate the optimum block size for the data. As a result, you may never code the BLKSIZE subparameter.

- The RECFM, LRECL, and BLKSIZE subparameters can also be coded as separate DD statement parameters instead of as subparameters.

Figure 4-15   How to code the DCB parameter

How to code the DD statement for instream and SYSOUT data sets

In addition to DASD data sets, you'll probably want to allocate instream and SYSOUT data sets right from the start, depending on the types of programs you're executing. Both instream and SYSOUT data sets are allocated to the JES spool rather than to an actual file, so their DD statements are much simpler to code than those for DASD data sets.

The DD statement for instream data sets

Instream data sets are blocks of data that you include along with JCL statements in a job stream. JES copies the instream data to a spool volume from which your processing program can retrieve the data as it executes. The instream data is in the form of 80-byte records, and your program treats the data as if it were a standard sequential file.

Figure 4-16 shows portions of three job streams that use instream data sets (the shading identifies the instream data). Example 1 shows the most common way of coding instream data. First, a DD * statement indicates that the records that follow are data for the instream data set. The ddname on the DD * statement associates the instream data set with the file referred to by the program. A data set name isn't required because the file will reside in JES spool space. Following the data, a *delimiter statement* (/*) marks the end of the data. The delimiter statement is optional in this case. If you omit it, the next JCL statement (// in columns 1 and 2) indicates the end of the instream data set.

Since a subsequent JCL statement marks the end of an instream data set, what do you do if you want to include JCL statements as part of the instream data? You use the DD DATA statement. When you specify the DATA parameter instead of an asterisk, you *must* code a delimiter statement to mark the end of your data. That way, JCL statements can be read as data. Example 2 shows how the DD DATA statement works.

The DLM parameter lets you change the two-character code used to represent the delimiter statement. You might need to do that if your instream data set has records with /* in columns 1 and 2. Although that's an unlikely situation, it is possible. Example 3 shows you how to use the DLM parameter.

Although I don't recommend it, you can omit the DD statement for instream data altogether if the program expects the ddname to be SYSIN. That's because when OS/390 encounters data that it doesn't recognize as JCL or JES2/JES3 statements, it automatically generates a SYSIN DD statement to treat the data as an instream data set. Even if the expected ddname is SYSIN, however, it's a good idea to code the DD statement.

The syntax of the DD statement for instream data sets

```
//ddname  DD    {*}        [ ,DLM=xx ]
                {DATA}
```

Explanation

* or DATA	Indicates that instream data follows. If you code an asterisk, the next JCL statement ends the data. If you code DATA, you must include a delimiter statement to end the data.
DLM	Specifies the characters that identify a delimiter statement. If omitted, slash-asterisk (/*) is the default.

Three examples of coding instream data

Example 1

```
//INVTRAN  DD    *
A00101005995CH445
A00103010030CH445
A00272001950CJ550
/*
```

Example 2

```
//SYSUT1   DD    DATA
//STEP1       EXEC PGM=INV1040
//INVLSTA  DD    SYSOUT=A
//INVLSTB  DD    SYSOUT=A
/*
```

Example 3

```
//SYSIN    DD    DATA,DLM=##
//INVTRAN  DD    *
A00101005995CH445
A00103010030CH445
A00272001950CJ550
/*
##
```

Note: The shading indicates the records that are processed as data for the instream data set.

Description

- You can include *instream data sets* along with JCL statements in a job stream. JES will copy the instream data to a spool volume from which your processing program can retrieve the data as it executes.

- A program will treat the instream data as if it comes from a standard sequential file with 80-character records.

- The end of instream data is marked by either a *delimiter statement* (/*), the next JCL statement (// in columns 1 and 2), or a specially defined delimiter statement specified by the DLM parameter.

- If the instream data contains JCL statements (// in columns 1 and 2), the DATA parameter must be used.

Figure 4-16   How to code the DD statement for instream data sets

The DD statement for SYSOUT data sets

In a JES2 or JES3 environment, a program can produce *SYSOUT data sets* that are collected in JES spool space before they are actually printed. To identify these data sets to the system, you code the SYSOUT parameter of the DD statement. As you can see in the syntax in figure 4-17, the value you specify in the SYSOUT parameter represents the output class to be assigned to the data set.

In the first example in this figure, a SYSOUT data set identified by the ddname of SYSPRINT is assigned an output class of A. In most installations, class A is associated with a standard printer. As a result, once the job ends, this data set will be sent immediately to the printer.

You can also code an asterisk (*) instead of an output class in the SYSOUT parameter, as shown in the second example. Here, the output class defaults to the class you specified in the MSGCLASS parameter of the JOB statement. If you code SYSOUT=* for all print data sets and then want to change the output class later on, you can just change the output class in the MSGCLASS parameter and it applies to the entire job. That saves you having to change each SYSOUT parameter individually. Because this gives you the most flexibility in handling SYSOUT data, most of the SYSOUT data sets in this book specify SYSOUT=*.

The syntax of the DD statement for SYSOUT data sets

```
//ddname  DD  SYSOUT=x
```

Explanation

SYSOUT   Specifies a one-character output class to be associated with the SYSOUT data set. If you code an asterisk, the output class specified in the MSGCLASS parameter of the JOB statement is used.

Two ways to code the SYSOUT parameter

The data set identified by the ddname of SYSPRINT is a JES SYSOUT file with an output class of A

```
//SYSPRINT  DD  SYSOUT=A
```

The INVRPT data set is a JES SYSOUT file with an output class that defaults to the output class specified by MSGCLASS in the JOB statement

```
//INVRPT    DD  SYSOUT=*
```

Description

- Programs that produce reports typically use the SYSOUT parameter in their DD statements. JES2 and JES3 allow a program to produce SYSOUT data sets that are collected in JES spool space before they are actually printed. Therefore, by using the SYSOUT parameter in your DD statement, you are indicating that the data set should be processed by JES2/JES3.

- The SYSOUT parameter specifies an output class associated with the data set. Typically, class A is the class associated with an installation's standard printer devices.

- If you code an asterisk (*) instead of an output class in the SYSOUT parameter, the output class specified in the MSGCLASS parameter of the JOB statement is used.

Figure 4-17   How to code the DD statement for SYSOUT data sets

Two complete job streams

In the topics that follow, you'll see two complete jobs that use the JCL you learned in this chapter. The first is a relatively simple job that invokes a program to post a file of transaction records against a master file. The second job is a little more complex. It invokes several application programs to produce reports extracted from two master files: an accounts receivable file and a customer file.

The transaction-posting application

Figure 4-18 presents a system flowchart for a job that uses a file of customer transaction records to update a file of customer master records. Both files are VSAM files. A third VSAM file is used to accumulate any transaction records that contain incorrect data. The post-customer-transactions program (CM3000) produces three print files: a transaction journal that lists the transactions individually, a transaction summary report that highlights important summary data, and an error listing. This figure also includes the ddnames and data set names for the data sets that are processed by the CM3000 program.

The bottom part of this figure shows the JCL for the transaction-posting job. To start, the JOB statement assigns a job name of MM01PT to the job. Since this job will be submitted from a TSO/E terminal, the job name conforms to TSO/E naming conventions. The next statement is the EXEC statement. It assigns a step name of POST to this job step and invokes the CM3000 program.

The remaining statements are DD statements that allocate the files used by CM3000. In the first three, the ddnames CUSTTRAN, CUSTMAST, and ERRTRAN all refer to existing VSAM files, so the coding in the DD statements is fairly simple. In each case, the DSNAME parameter identifies the actual data set name for the file and the DISP parameter specifies that the file be available for shared access (DISP=SHR). The last three DD statements are for the three reports that the program produces, all allocated as SYSOUT data sets. In each case, the output class defaults to the job's message class, so all the job's output is printed together.

System flowchart for the transaction-posting application

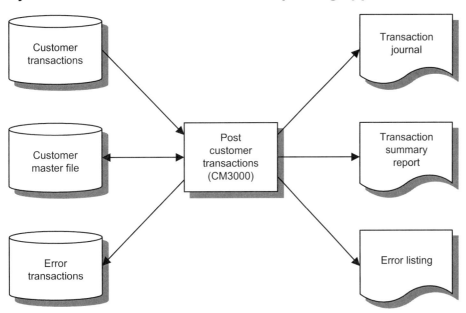

Data set requirements for the transaction-posting application

ddname	Data set name
CUSTTRAN	MM01.CUSTOMER.TRANS
CUSTMAST	MM01.CUSTOMER.MASTER
ERRTRAN	MM01.CUSTOMER.TRANS.ERRS
TRANJRNL	(SYSOUT data set)
TRANSUM	(SYSOUT data set)
ERRLIST	(SYSOUT data set)

The JCL for the transaction-posting application

```
//MM01PT    JOB  36512,'M MURACH',MSGCLASS=A,MSGLEVEL=(1,1),
//               NOTIFY=MM02
//POST      EXEC PGM=CM3000
//CUSTTRAN DD   DSNAME=MM01.CUSTOMER.TRANS,DISP=SHR
//CUSTMAST DD   DSNAME=MM01.CUSTOMER.MASTER,DISP=SHR
//ERRTRAN  DD   DSNAME=MM01.CUSTOMER.TRANS.ERRS,DISP=SHR
//TRANJRNL DD   SYSOUT=*
//TRANSUM  DD   SYSOUT=*
//ERRLIST  DD   SYSOUT=*
```

Figure 4-18   The job control requirements for a transaction-posting application

The job control requirements for a report-preparation application

Figure 4-19 shows the system flowchart for a report-preparation application. Here, the first application program (AR7100) creates a file with data from two master files (a customer file and an accounts receivable file). Before this program can be run, the receivables file, stored in invoice-number sequence, must be sorted into invoice-number within customer-number sequence. Then, AR7100 can match records from the sorted receivables file with records from the customer file, which is already stored in customer-number sequence. An IBM-supplied utility program called DFSORT (or just SORT) will do the sorting.

The output of the AR7100 program is the dunning file (to *dun* means to require payment), which is used to produce customer statements and three reports. Two of the reports, an overdue-invoices report and an aged-trial-balance report, are prepared in the dunning file's original sequence: invoice within customer. Because both of these reports are prepared from the same file, a single program (AR7200) is used so the file is read just once.

The other two output files in this application require that the dunning file be sorted into a different sequence: invoice within customer number within state. As a result, after the SORT program is run, AR7300 uses the sorted dunning file to prepare a cross-reference listing and the customer statements. Again, a single program prepares both output files, so the dunning file is read just once.

This figure also lists the data sets required by each program in the report-preparation job. For each ddname, you can see there's a data set name or an indication that the file is an instream data set, a temporary work file, or a SYSOUT data set. Only the names of the data sets that exist outside of the job are important. In this case, that's the customer master file and the accounts receivable master file. The names of the other files—for example, the sorted dunning file—aren't as important because they're created and deleted within a single job.

The job control requirements for a report-preparation application

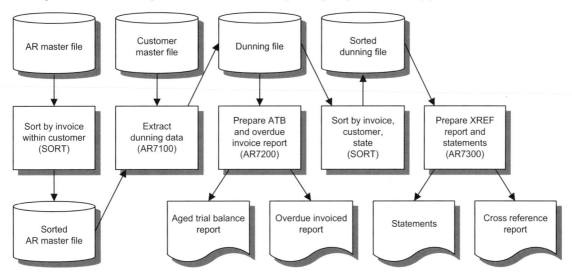

Data set requirements for the programs invoked by the report-preparation application

Step name	Program	ddname	Data set name
SORT1	SORT	SYSOUT	(SYSOUT data set)
		SORTIN	MM01.ACCOUNT.MASTER
		SORTOUT	MM01.ACCOUNT.MASTER.SORT
		SORTWK01	(temporary work file)
		SYSIN	(instream data set)
AR7100	AR7100	ARSORT	MM01.ACCOUNT.MASTER.SORT
		CUSTMAST	MM01.CUSTOMER.MASTER
		DUNNING	MM01.DUNNING.FILE
AR7200	AR7200	DUNNING	MM01.DUNNING.FILE
		ATB	(SYSOUT data set)
		OVERDUE	(SYSOUT data set)
SORT2	SORT	SYSOUT	(SYSOUT data set)
		SORTIN	MM01.DUNNING.FILE
		SORTOUT	MM01.DUNNING.FILE.SORT
		SORTWK01	(temporary work file)
		SYSIN	(instream data set)
AR7300	AR7300	DUNSORT	MM01.DUNNING.FILE.SORT
		XREF	(SYSOUT data set)
		STMTS	(SYSOUT data set)

Figure 4-19   The job control requirements for a report-preparation application

The JCL for the report-preparation application

Figure 4-20 shows the JCL for the report-preparation job. To help you understand this job stream, here is an explanation of each numbered statement.

1. The JOB statement assigns this job name to the job: MM01RP.

2. The first EXEC statement invokes SORT, which is the IBM system utility that sorts data sets. The step name is SORT1, and this step requires the five data sets that are defined by the DD statements that follow.

3. The SORT program writes output messages to a SYSOUT data set with a ddname of SYSOUT.

4. The file to be sorted is defined by the SORTIN DD statement. Here the A/R master file is MM01.ACCOUNT.MASTER. Because this is an existing cataloged file, only the data set name and disposition are specified.

5. The sorted output file, named MM01.ACCOUNT.MASTER.SORT, is identified by the SORTOUT DD statement. Here, the unit, volume, space, and DCB information is specified, and this file is kept but not cataloged.

6. The SORT program requires work space on a DASD device, so the SORTWK01 DD statement defines a temporary data set by specifying just unit, volume, and space information. No data set name is required since the file is deleted when the SORT program ends. Because there's no DISP parameter, the system assumes (NEW,DELETE).

7. The SYSIN DD statement defines an instream data set that contains a control statement that specifies which input positions to sort on. Don't worry about how this statement is coded because you'll learn more about it in chapter 19. A delimiter statement (/*) marks the end of this data set.

8. The EXEC statement for the AR7100 job step invokes the application program named AR7100. This program extracts data from the sorted A/R master file and the customer master file to create the dunning file, so it requires three data sets that are defined by the DD statements that follow.

9. The ARSORT DD statement defines the sorted A/R master file, so it has the data set name that's in the SORTOUT DD statement in the first job step. Since this file isn't needed after this step, it's deleted. And since the file is existing but uncataloged, the SPACE and DCB parameters aren't needed, but the UNIT and VOL=SER parameters are.

10. The CUSTMAST DD statement identifies the customer master file, which is an existing cataloged data set.

11. The DUNNING DD statement defines the output file that's created by the AR7100 program. Because this file is new, the DD statement includes unit, volume, space, and DCB information. The file is kept but not cataloged.

12. The EXEC statement for the AR7200 step invokes the application program named AR7200, which creates the aged-trial-balance and overdue invoices reports from the dunning file, so it requires three DD statements.

The JCL for the report-preparation application

```
1       //MM01RP    JOB   36512,'A PRINCE',MSGCLASS=X,MSGLEVEL=(1,1),
        //                NOTIFY=MM03
2       //SORT1      EXEC  PGM=SORT
3       //SYSOUT     DD    SYSOUT=*
4       //SORTIN     DD    DSNAME=MM01.ACCOUNT.MASTER,DISP=SHR
5       //SORTOUT    DD    DSNAME=MM01.ACCOUNT.MASTER.SORT,DISP=(NEW,KEEP),
        //                UNIT=SYSDA,VOL=SER=MPS800,
        //                SPACE=(CYL,(1,1)),
        //                DCB=(DSORG=PS,RECFM=FB,LRECL=400)
6       //SORTWK01 DD    UNIT=SYSDA,VOL=SER=MPS800,
        //                SPACE=(CYL,(1,1))
7       //SYSIN      DD    *
        SORT   FIELDS=(16,5,CH,A,1,5,CH,A)
        /*
8       //AR7100     EXEC  PGM=AR7100
9       //ARSORT     DD    DSNAME=MM01.ACCOUNT.MASTER.SORT,DISP=(OLD,DELETE),
        //                UNIT=SYSDA,VOL=SER=MPS800
10      //CUSTMAST DD    DSNAME=MM01.CUSTOMER.MASTER,DISP=SHR
11      //DUNNING  DD    DSNAME=MM01.DUNNING.FILE,DISP=(NEW,KEEP),
        //                UNIT=SYSDA,VOL=SER=MPS800,
        //                SPACE=(CYL,(1,1)),
        //                DCB=(DSORG=PS,RECFM=FB,LRECL=400)
12      //AR7200     EXEC  PGM=AR7200
13      //DUNNING  DD    DSNAME=MM01.DUNNING.FILE,DISP=OLD,
        //                UNIT=SYSDA,VOL=SER=MPS800
14      //ATB        DD    SYSOUT=*
        //OVERDUE  DD    SYSOUT=*
        //SORT2      EXEC  PGM=SORT
        //SYSOUT     DD    SYSOUT=*
        //SORTIN     DD    DSNAME=MM01.DUNNING.FILE,DISP=(OLD,DELETE),
        //                UNIT=SYSDA,VOL=SER=MPS800,
        //SORTOUT    DD    DSNAME=MM01.DUNNING.FILE.SORT,DISP=(NEW,KEEP),
        //                UNIT=SYSDA.VOL=SER=MPS800,
        //                SPACE=(CYL,(1,1))
        //                DCB=(DSORG=PS,RECFM=FB,LRECL=400)
        //SORTWK01 DD    UNIT=SYSDA,VOL=SER=MPS800,
        //                SPACE=(CYL,(1,1))
        //SYSIN      DD    *
        SORT   FIELDS=(43,2,CH,A,1,5,CH,A,50,5,CH,A)
        /*
        //AR7300     EXEC  PGM=AR7300
        //DUNSORT  DD    DSNAME=MM01.DUNNING.FILE.SORT,DISP=(OLD,DELETE),
        //                UNIT=SYSDA,VOL=SER=MPS800
        //XREF       DD    SYSOUT=*
        //STMTS      DD    SYSOUT=*
```

Figure 4-20   The JCL for the report-preparation application

13. The DUNNING DD statement identifies the dunning file that was created in the previous job step. Since the normal disposition defaults to KEEP, the file can be processed again in a subsequent job step.

14. The ATB and OVERDUE DD statements specify that the aged-trial-balance report and the overdue-invoices report are both SYSOUT data sets.

The statements in the rest of the job are similar to those you've already seen, so you should be able to follow them without too much trouble. In fact, the SORT2 step includes DD statements with the same ddnames as the SORT1 step. And the AR7300 uses a single input file to produce two SYSOUT files just like the AR7200 step.

Perspective

As you can tell from the job streams at the end of this chapter, the JCL statements you've learned so far form the basis for coding complex jobs. You can also tell that the bulk of your JCL coding will involve DD statements. In fact, much of what you learn in the chapters that follow will be additional DD parameters or alternate ways to allocate various types of data sets.

Now, if you understand the JCL coding in the examples, you're ready to go on to the next chapter. It teaches you additional JCL parameters and statements that give you more control over the way your job is executed in your operating environment. On the other hand, if you're having trouble with the code in these examples, it's worth taking the time to review the material that you don't understand because the rest of this book builds on this chapter.

Terms

job step	comment statement	vol-ser
step	account number	volume serial number
null statement	job name	specific volume request
identifier field	job identifier	non-specific volume
name field	job-id	request
operation field	job number	extent
parameters field	Data Definition statement	directory block
parameter	DD statement	Data Control Block
comments field	ddname	instream data set
positional parameter	status	delimiter statement
keyword parameter	normal disposition	SYSOUT data set
subparameter	abnormal disposition	

5

How to use JCL and JES facilities to manage program execution

In chapter 4, you learned how to code basic JOB and EXEC statements to identify jobs and job steps. In this chapter, you'll learn how to code additional parameters for both statements that allow you to exert greater control over how jobs and programs are scheduled and executed. You'll also learn about JES2 and JES3 statements and the controls they offer that are equivalent or related to those available in the JOB and EXEC statements.

The JOB and EXEC statements

Both the JOB and EXEC statements offer a variety of controls that influence job execution. In fact, as you'll see in a moment, several of the same parameters appear in both statements. Although this may seem redundant at first, it actually gives you added flexibility and control. If you want a parameter setting to apply to all of the steps in a job, you can include the parameter in the JOB statement. On the other hand, if the parameter setting applies to only one or two job steps, it makes more sense to code it in the EXEC statement. In most cases, parameter values specified on a JOB statement will override the same parameters specified in any subsequent EXEC statements.

More parameters of the JOB statement

Figure 5-1 presents the syntax for the new JOB statement parameters that are covered in this chapter, all listed after those that you learned about in chapter 4. As you can see, these parameters affect your job's overall performance by influencing the way it's scheduled or the system resources that are assigned to it.

Even though this syntax is more extensive than what you saw in chapter 4, there are still a number of JOB parameters that aren't included here. Some of them apply to specific types of job processing and will be covered in later chapters. Others are rarely used, so they aren't covered in this book at all.

By the way, the only new syntax element in this chapter is the underline, shown in the ADDRSPC parameter, which indicates the default value for a parameter or subparameter. Otherwise, remember that positional parameters come before keyword parameters, brackets ([]) indicate that a parameter or subparameter is optional, and braces ({}) indicate that you can only choose one of the elements listed.

The syntax of the JOB statement with the new parameters in this chapter

```
//jobname   JOB  [ accounting-information ] [ ,programmer-name ]
                 [ ,MSGCLASS=class ]
                 [ ,MSGLEVEL=(stmt,msg) ]
                 [ ,NOTIFY=user-id ]
                 [ ,ADDRSPC= {VIRT} ]
                             {REAL}
                 [ ,BYTES=(value[,action])]
                 [ ,CARDS=(value[,action])]
                 [ ,CLASS=jobclass ]
                 [ ,LINES=(value[,action])]
                 [ ,PAGES=(value[,action])]
                 [ ,PRTY=priority ]
                 [ ,REGION= {valueK} ]
                            {valueM}
                 [ ,TIME= {([minutes][,seconds])}  ]
                          {1440}
                          {NOLIMIT}
                          {MAXIMUM}
                 [ ,TYPRUN= {COPY}        ]
                            {HOLD}
                            {JCLHOLD}
                            {SCAN}
```

Explanation of the new parameters

ADDRSPC	Specifies whether the job requires virtual or real storage. The default is VIRT.
BYTES CARDS LINES PAGES	Specifies the maximum amount of SYSOUT data the job can produce and what action should be taken if that limit is reached.
CLASS	Specifies a single-character job class used to schedule the job.
PRTY	Specifies a number from 0 through 14 (JES3) or 15 (JES2) that indicates a job's scheduling priority within its job class.
REGION	Specifies the largest amount of virtual or real storage any of the job's steps may use.
TIME	Controls the amount of time the job can use the processor in minutes and seconds. You can also specify NOLIMIT or 1440 to allow the job to run indefinitely, or MAXIMUM to limit the job to 357,912 minutes.
TYPRUN	Indicates special JES processing, as follows:

COPY (JES2 only)	The job stream is printed as a SYSOUT data set but not processed.
HOLD	The job must be released by the operator before it will be processed.
JCLHOLD (JES2 only)	Similar to HOLD, but the job is held before its JCL is scanned rather than after.
SCAN	The job isn't executed but its JCL is scanned for syntax errors.

Figure 5-1   More parameters of the JOB statement

More parameters of the EXEC statement

Figure 5-2 shows the expanded syntax for the EXEC statement and describes the functions of the three parameters (REGION, ADDRSPC, and TIME) that are covered in this chapter. As you've seen, all three of them can be coded on the JOB statement as well. When they're coded on the EXEC statement, though, they affect only the job step and not the overall processing of the job. Here again, there are additional EXEC parameters that will be covered later in this book, as well as parameters that are rarely used so they aren't covered at all.

The syntax of the EXEC statement with the new parameters in this chapter

```
//stepname EXEC    PGM=program-name
                   [ ,PARM=information ]
                   [ ,ADDRSPC= {VIRT} ]
                               {REAL}
                   [ ,REGION= {valueK} ]
                              {valueM}
                   [ ,TIME= {([minutes][,seconds])} ]
                            {1440}
                            {NOLIMIT}
                            {MAXIMUM}
                            {0}
```

Explanation of the new parameters

ADDRSPC   Specifies whether the step requires virtual or real storage. The default is VIRT.

REGION   Specifies the largest amount of virtual or real storage the step may use.

TIME   Controls the amount of time the step can use the processor in minutes and seconds. You can also specify NOLIMIT or 1440 to allow the step to run indefinitely, MAXIMUM to limit the step to 357,912 minutes, or 0 to use any time left over from a previous step.

Figure 5-2   More parameters of the EXEC statement

How to code JES2/JES3 control statements

Under JES2 and JES3, a job stream can also include *JES2* or *JES3 control statements* that influence the way the Job Entry Subsystem processes your job. At one time, these statements provided for a number of parameters that weren't available on standard JCL statements. But as new versions of MVS and OS/390 have been released over the years, many of these parameters have been incorporated into existing JCL statements. As a result, JES control statements are seldom used today. Instead, programmers have found that using JCL statements results in code that's more portable from one system to another, and it saves you from having to be familiar with so many different statements. Still, you may come across JES control statements in older job streams, and occasionally, they provide for a function that isn't available in standard JCL.

The basic format for JES2/JES3 control statements

Figure 5-3 shows the basic format for JES2 and JES3 statements. Although it's similar to the format for a standard JCL statement, there are some key differences, as listed in this figure. Beyond that, there are differences depending on whether you're using JES2 or JES3.

As you can see, the identifier field for a JES2 control statement is the same as that of a JCL delimiter statement: a slash in column 1 followed by an asterisk in column 2 (/*). For JES3 control statements, the identifier field is the same as for a JCL comment statement: a slash in columns 1 and 2 and an asterisk in column 3 (//*). The only exceptions in JES3 are the /*SIGNON and /*SIGNOFF statements (which are also available in JES2), and the //**PAUSE statement.

Just like in a JCL statement, the operation field of a JES2/JES3 control statement indicates the statement's function. However, it immediately follows the identifier without a space. If you accidentally leave a space between the identifier and the operation field, OS/390 can't tell if the statement is a JES control statement or a JCL comment or delimiter statement.

JES control statement parameters are similar to JCL statement parameters. Many of them are positional parameters that are separated by commas. A few statements have positional parameters that are separated by spaces. And a couple of statements have keyword parameters that can be coded in any order you wish, as long as they're separated by commas.

With the exception of the /*OUTPUT command, JES2 statements can't be continued on more than one line. So if you need more than one line, simply code the same statement with the additional parameters on a second line. Keep in mind, though, that if the same parameter is encountered more than once on a JES2 statement, the system uses the last occurrence.

The syntax for JES2/JES3 control statements

```
identifier operation [parameters]
```

Explanation

identifier   For JES2 control statements, a slash in column 1 and an asterisk in column 2 (/*).

For JES3 control statements, slashes in columns 1 and 2 and an asterisk in column 3 (//*). There are two exceptions: (1) the JES3 SIGNON and SIGNOFF statements use the same identifier format as JES2 control statements (/*); and (2) the identifier for the PAUSE statement is two slashes followed by two asterisks (//**).

operation   The name of the JES2/JES3 control statement. It is coded immediately after the identifier with no intervening spaces and is followed by at least one space.

parameters One or more parameters, depending on the operation, coded similarly to JCL statement parameters.

Four differences between JES2/JES3 statements and JCL statements

1. JES2/JES3 statements use a different identifier field in the first columns of each statement.

2. JES2/JES3 statements don't have a name field.

3. JES2/JES3 statements follow different continuation rules.

4. The system ignores JES2/JES3 statements in cataloged or instream procedures (procedures are covered in chapter 9).

Description

*   *JES2/JES3 control statements* are normally coded between the job's JOB statement and the first EXEC statement. That way, JES2/JES3 can associate the statements with a particular job. Exceptions to this will be pointed out in the topics that follow.

*   The operation field in a JES2/JES3 statement identifies the statement's function. Unlike JCL statements, it immediately follows the identifier field without any spaces.

*   Except for the /*OUTPUT statement, JES2 statements can't be continued on another line. Instead, you code as many of the same statement as needed to provide for all the parameters. If you specify the same parameter more than once, the last occurrence is used.

*   To continue a JES3 statement on more than one line, you end the line with a comma and then code //* on the next line immediately followed by the next parameter.

Figure 5-3   The basic format for JES2/JES3 control statements

In contrast, it's easy to continue JES3 control statements. To do so, you end each line with a comma, code //* on the next line in columns 1 through 3, and continue the parameters in column 4. Be sure not to code a space in column 4, though, or the system will mistake the continued line for a JCL comment statement.

JES2 control statements

Figure 5-4 lists the control statements available in a JES2 environment and gives the syntax for the two that you're most likely to use to control job processing, the /*PRIORITY and /*JOBPARM statements. Actually, the /*JOBPARM statement includes a number of other parameters, but you probably won't ever need them. So in this chapter, you'll learn about the first four parameters shown, all of which deal with SYSOUT data. The RESTART parameter lets you handle recovery processing after a system failure, while the SYSAFF parameter lets you specify which processor should be used for a job. Both of these parameters are covered in chapter 11.

Like most JES2 statements, the /*JOBPARM statement must be coded after the JOB statement and is usually placed right before the first EXEC statement, as shown in the example in this figure. In contrast, the /*PRIORITY statement is one of the few JES2 statements that must be coded *before* the JOB statement.

The syntax for the JES2 /*PRIORITY statement

```
/*PRIORITY priority
```

The syntax for the JES2 /*JOBPARM statement

```
/*JOBPARM   [ ,BYTES=value ]
            [ ,CARDS=value ]
            [ ,LINES=value ]
            [ ,PAGES=value ]
            [ ,RESTART= {Y} {N} ]
            [ ,SYSAFF=(system[,IND]) ]
```

Other JES2 control statements

Statement	Function
/*$command-verb	Specifies JES2 operator commands. Must be placed *before* the JOB statement.
/*MESSAGE	Sends a message to the operator (see chapter 11).
/*NETACCT	Specifies the job account number.
/*NOTIFY	Notifies the specified user when the job is completed (same as the NOTIFY parameter on the JOB statement).
/*OUTPUT	Specifies SYSOUT processing options (see chapter 8).
/*ROUTE	Routes the job for execution or printing to a specific JES2 node.
/*SETUP	Instructs the operator to mount the specified tape volumes prior to job execution.
/*SIGNOFF	Ends a remote job session. May be placed anywhere in the job stream.
/*SIGNON	Begins a remote job entry session. Must be the first statement in the job stream.
/*XEQ	Routes the job to a specific JES2 node for execution.
/*XMIT	Transmits data to another JES2 node.

An example of a JES2 /*JOBPARM statement in a job stream

```
//MM01RN    JOB   (36512),'CS MOORE',MSGCLASS=X,MSGLEVEL=(1,1),
                  NOTIFY=&SYSUID
/*JOBPARM   SYSAFF=MVSA
//STEP1     EXEC  PGM=SORT
//SYSOUT    DD    SYSOUT=*
  .
  .
```

Description

- The /*PRIORITY statement specifies a job's priority within its job class. It's one of the few JES2 statements that must be coded before a JCL JOB statement.
- The /*JOBPARM statement specifies the job processing options for a job. It's placed after the JOB statement but before the first EXEC statement.
- The /*JOBPARM RESTART parameter is used for recovery processing if the system fails, while the SYSAFF parameter indicates which system may process the job. Both parameters are described in chapter 11.

Figure 5-4   JES2 control statements

JES3 control statements

Figure 5-5 shows the control statements available in a JES3 environment and gives the syntax for the //*MAIN statement parameters that are most useful in controlling job processing. Like most JES3 control statements, the //*MAIN statement must come after the JOB statement. Since it affects job-level facilities, you normally code it before the first EXEC statement so it will apply to all the steps in the job, as shown in this example.

As you can see, several of these parameters are similar to the ones on the JES2 /*JOBPARM statement. In this chapter, you'll learn how to code all of them except the FAILURE and SYSTEM parameters, which are covered in chapter 11. Four of the parameters (BTYES, CARDS, LINES, and PAGES) control SYSOUT processing. The CLASS parameter lets you override the default job class assigned to a job. The HOLD parameter lets you hold a job until the operator releases it for processing. And the LREGION parameter lets you give the system an estimate of the largest region size the job will require.

The syntax for the JES3 //*MAIN statement

```
//*MAIN     [ ,BYTES=(value[,action]) ]
           [ ,CARDS=(value[,action]) ]
           [ ,CLASS=job-class ]
           [ ,FAILURE=recovery-option ]
           [ ,HOLD= {YES} {NO} ]
           [ ,LINES=(value[,action]) ]
           [ ,LREGION=valueK ]
           [ ,PAGES=(value[,action]) ]
           [ ,SYSTEM=system ]
```

Other JES3 control statements

Statement	Function
//*DATASET	Supplies data for an instream data set. Must be placed immediately before the first record of the instream data. The data is terminated by an //*ENDDATASET statement.
//*ENDDATASET	Indicates the end of an instream data set. Must be placed immediately after the last record of the instream data.
//*ENDPROCESS	Indicates the end of a series of //*PROCESS statements.
//*FORMAT	Specifies options for SYSOUT data sets (see chapter 8).
//*NET	Specifies dependencies between jobs.
//*NETACCT	Specifies job accounting information that JES3 will transmit with a job to another node.
//*OPERATOR	Sends a message to the operator (see chapter 11).
//**PAUSE	Pauses the input reader until the operator issues a *START operator command. Must be placed *before* the JOB statement.
//*PROCESS	Controls JES3 job processing. An //*ENDPROCESS statement must follow any //*PROCESS statements.
//*ROUTE	Routes the job to another node in the network.
/*SIGNOFF	Ends a remote job session. May be placed anywhere in the job stream.
/*SIGNON	Begins a remote job entry session. Must be the first statement in the job stream.

An example of a JES3 //*MAIN statement in a job stream

```
//MM01RN    JOB   (36512),'CS MOORE',MSGCLASS=X,MSGLEVEL=(1,1),
//                NOTIFY=&SYSUID
//*MAIN     SYSTEM=MVSA
//STEP1     EXEC PGM=SORT
//SYSOUT    DD   SYSOUT=*
  .
  .
  .
```

Description

- The JES3 //*MAIN statement is used to control job processing options. It's coded after the JOB statement but before the first EXEC statement in a job stream.

- The //*MAIN FAILURE parameter is used for recovery processing if the system fails, while the SYSTEM parameter indicates which system or systems may process the job. Both parameters are described in chapter 11.

Figure 5-5   JES3 control statements

How to influence the way your job is scheduled

When you submit a job, JES2 or JES3 reads the job from a reader (usually the internal reader) and places it on a spool volume. Then, the job waits to be selected for execution by an active initiator. Coding certain JCL and JES2/JES3 parameters can help influence the way your job is scheduled for processing.

How to specify a job class

In order to achieve a balanced processing load on a system, installations need to control the types of jobs that are executing at any given time. That's why initiators select jobs for execution based on *job classes*. For example, an initiator that can process class A, B, and C jobs will only select jobs with a class of A, B, or C. By grouping jobs in this way, operators can start and stop whole classes to control the number of jobs processing on the system.

Installations usually establish job classes based on a number of factors, such as the size of the job, the resources it uses, the amount of I/O processing required, or the amount of CPU time required. As a rule, jobs that share the same characteristics or compete for the same resources belong in the same class.

Normally when you submit a job, JES2/JES3 assigns a default class that's determined by the reader that processes the job based on the job's characteristics. For instance, jobs submitted from within a TSO/E environment might have a different default job class than jobs submitted from an operator's console. It's easy to specify a job class that's different from the default, though. All you do is include a CLASS parameter in your JOB statement, as shown in the first example in figure 5-6. Here, job MM01A will be scheduled as a class F job.

You can also specify a job class on the JES3 //*MAIN statement, as shown in the second example in this figure. Coding a CLASS parameter on the //*MAIN statement overrides the CLASS parameter on a JOB statement. However, unless there's some compelling reason to specify the job class this way, I suggest you specify it on the JOB statement instead.

Unlike JES3, JES2 doesn't provide any control statement parameters for specifying a job class. As a result, if you're working in a JES2 environment, you have to use the CLASS parameter on the JOB statement.

Two ways to assign a job class

Assigning a job class with the CLASS parameter on a JOB statement

```
//MM01A     JOB  (36512),'B SYVERSON',MSGCLASS=X,MSGLEVEL=(1,1),
//          CLASS=F,NOTIFY=&SYSUID
```

Assigning a job class with the CLASS parameter on a JES3 //*MAIN statement

```
//MM01A     JOB  (36512),'B SYVERSON',NOTIFY=&SYSUID
//*MAIN CLASS=F
```

Types of jobs or job characteristics that classes might be set up for

- I/O bound jobs
- Processor-bound jobs
- Jobs using a particular resource
- Job size
- Held jobs

Description

- The *job class* is one character (A-Z or 0-9) and must be a valid class at JES initialization.
- Normally, JES2/JES3 assigns a default job class when a job is submitted. But you can override the default job class by specifying a CLASS parameter on your JOB statement.
- Installations establish job classes based on a number of factors such as how large or small jobs are, the types of I/O or CPU time requirements they may have, or the types of resources they may need.
- Job classes also help to determine the priority of the job. That means that jobs with the same job class are grouped together on the input queue to await execution. Also, the operator can start and stop whole job classes to control the number of jobs processing on a system at any given time.
- Under JES3, you can code the //*MAIN statement with the CLASS parameter. A CLASS parameter on the //*MAIN statement overrides the CLASS parameter on a JOB statement.

Figure 5-6   How to specify a job class

How to specify a job's scheduling priority

If there's more than one job with the same class in the JES spool, the initiator uses job *priorities* to determine which job to execute first. The system normally assigns the priority based on the job class for the job. That means that jobs with the same classes and priorities are processed in the order in which they were submitted. However, you can override the default priority in one of two ways, as shown in figure 5-7.

In the first example in this figure, the PRTY parameter is coded on the JOB statement to assign a priority of 12 to the job. This is the method you have to use in a JES3 environment. In the second example, a JES2 /*PRIORITY statement is used to assign the job priority. Notice that the /*PRIORITY statement is one of the few JES2 statements that's placed *before* the JOB statement for the job to which it applies.

There's a slight difference in the priority values you can specify on the PRTY parameter for JES2 and JES3 systems. Under JES2, you can specify a value from 0 to 15, and under JES3 you can specify a value from 0 to 14. In both cases, 0 has the lowest priority and the high value has the highest priority.

If the /*PRIORITY statement and the JOB PRTY parameter are both coded in the same job, the /*PRIORITY statement takes precedence. In general, though, I recommend you use the JOB PRTY parameter unless your installation standards say otherwise. Be aware, too, that occasionally a shop disables the JOB PRTY parameter, usually to prevent programmers from assigning their test jobs precedence over other test jobs when the system is bogged down.

Two ways to assign a scheduling priority

Assigning a priority with the PRTY parameter on a JOB statement

```
//MM01A     JOB  (36512),'A STEELMAN',MSGCLASS=X,MSGLEVEL=(1,1),
//               CLASS=F,PRTY=12,NOTIFY=&SYSUID
```

Assigning a priority with the JES2 /*PRIORITY statement

```
/*PRIORITY 12
//MM01A     JOB  (36512),'A STEELMAN',NOTIFY=&SYSUID
```

Description

- The PRTY parameter on the JOB statement lets you assign a processing *priority* within a job class for your job.

- The priority can be a number between 0 and 15 for JES2 systems and 0 and 14 for JES3 systems, with the highest number having the highest priority.

- If there's more than one job with the same class in the JES spool, jobs with a higher priority are executed first while jobs with the same priority are selected on a first come, first served basis.

- If the PRTY parameter is not coded in the JOB statement, an installation default is used.

- Under JES2, you can code the /*PRIORITY statement. This has the same effect as a PRTY parameter on the JOB statement. The /*PRIORITY statement is placed before the JOB statement to which it applies.

Figure 5-7   How to specify a job's scheduling priority

How to hold a job

Sometimes, you want a job to be placed in a hold status so it won't be scheduled for execution until an operator issues a command to release it. For example, you may want a tape processing job to remain in the job queue until the system operator is ready to mount the tape. Or you may want a job to wait until another job has completed.

Figure 5-8 shows four ways to specify that your job be held. In example 1, the TYPRUN=HOLD parameter on the JOB statement is specified, and in example 2, the TYPRUN=JCLHOLD parameter is specified. The difference between the two holds is that the HOLD option checks for JCL errors when the job is submitted, while the JCLHOLD option checks for JCL errors when the operator releases the job.

Another way to hold a job is to specify a *held job class* in the CLASS parameter of the JOB statement, as shown in example 3. All jobs submitted with a held job class are held whether or not the TYPRUN parameter is used. The use of held job classes is installation-dependent, however, so be sure to find out if there are any available to you.

Example 4 shows how to use the HOLD parameter of the JES3 //*MAIN statement. This has the same effect as coding TYPRUN=HOLD on the JOB statement. JES2 has no equivalent statement.

How to scan a job for syntax errors

In addition to placing jobs on hold, the TYPRUN parameter can be used to scan a job for syntax errors, as shown in the last example in figure 5-8. When a job is submitted with the TYPRUN=SCAN parameter, the system checks the job for errors and reports any found in the job message output without executing the job. Although the system can't detect any incorrect data set names or DCB data, it can catch misspelled parameters and incorrectly coded continuation lines.

The TYPRUN=SCAN option is useful if you want to check the syntax of a large job before submitting it for execution. Often, you'll need to prepare production JCL that's submitted by an operator during normal batch processing hours. Scanning the job for errors ahead of time can help avoid a call in the middle of the night by an operator informing you that your job failed because of a simple mistake.

The syntax for the TYPRUN parameter of the JOB statement

```
TYPRUN= {COPY}
        {HOLD}
        {JCLHOLD}
        {SCAN}
```

The syntax for the HOLD parameter of the JES3 //*MAIN statement

```
HOLD= {YES}
      {NO}
```

Four ways to hold a job

Example 1

```
///MM01A    JOB  (36512),'M MURACH',MSGCLASS=X,MSGLEVEL=(1,1),
//              CLASS=A,TYPRUN=HOLD,NOTIFY=&SYSUID
```

The TYPRUN parameter uses the HOLD option to hold a job in the queue until the operator issues a command to release it.

Example 2 (JES2 only)

```
///MM01A    JOB  (36512),'M MURACH',MSGCLASS=X,MSGLEVEL=(1,1),
//              CLASS=A,TYPRUN=JCLHOLD,NOTIFY=&SYSUID
```

The JCLHOLD option is similar to the HOLD option except that the JCL is not checked for errors until the operator releases the job.

Example 3

```
//MM01A     JOB  (36512),'M MURACH',NOTIFY=&SYSUID,CLASS=H
```

A held job class is specified in the CLASS parameter of the JOB statement. Once the operator changes the class, the job is released for processing.

Example 4 (JES3 only)

```
//MM01A     JOB  (36512),'M MURACH',NOTIFY=&SYSUID
//*MAIN     HOLD=YES
```

A JES3 //*MAIN statement HOLD parameter is used to hold the job in the queue. This has the same effect as coding TYPRUN=HOLD on the JOB statement.

How to scan a job for syntax errors

```
///MM01A    JOB  (36512),'M MURACH',MSGCLASS=X,MSGLEVEL=(1,1),
//              CLASS=A,TYPRUN=SCAN,NOTIFY=&SYSUID
```

Description

- A job can be placed in a hold status so it won't execute until an operator issues a command that releases it. This can be useful if the operator needs to mount a tape or if the job needs to wait until another job has completed.

- You can code the TYPRUN=SCAN parameter on a JOB statement to scan for any JCL errors without executing the job. Although it can't detect incorrect data set names or DCB data, it will catch misspelled parameters or incorrectly coded continuation lines.

Figure 5-8   How to hold a job and how to scan a job for syntax errors

How to specify a job's storage requirements

Each job on the system executes in its own private address space. Within that address space, a region is allocated to provide storage for the job steps. Depending on the size or purpose of a job, you may occasionally need to control the amount or type of storage allocated to it. Using standard JCL statements, there are two parameters you can code for this purpose, the REGION and ADDRSPC parameters. In addition, if you're working in a JES3 environment, the //*MAIN statement includes a parameter that lets you estimate the amount of storage space a job might use.

How to control a region size (the REGION parameter)

When a job step begins, the system allocates a region of storage space that's large enough to hold the program and any required control blocks. As the program executes, it can enlarge its region by acquiring additional storage. For example, programs that process VSAM files often need to acquire additional storage for buffer space as they execute. As a result, the amount of storage required and used by a program can vary as the program executes.

You can use the REGION parameter shown in figure 5-9 on a JOB or EXEC statement to control the maximum amount of storage that can be acquired for a job step's region. If you specify it on a JOB statement, the region size applies to all of the job steps within the job and overrides any REGION parameters coded on EXEC statements. Specifying the REGION parameter on an EXEC statement instead gives you more control over storage allocation for the job step.

You can specify the region size in terms of kilobytes or megabytes. For kilobytes, the system needs a value that's a multiple of 4, so if that's not what you code, it will round the value up to the nearest multiple of 4. Although the system also allows you to code REGION=0K or REGION=0M to allocate all available storage, you don't want to do that because it can cause storage problems, resulting in a region size that is unstable. Also, be sure to include an ample amount of storage space when you specify a REGION value, or the job will fail.

The examples in this figure show you how to code the REGION parameter. In the first example, a maximum of 4 megabytes of storage is allocated to each job step in the job, while in the second example, a maximum of 256 kilobytes of storage is allocated to program INV1000 in job step STEP3. If no REGION parameter is coded, the system uses the job step installation default specified at JES initialization. Since this default is adequate for most job steps, you only have to use the REGION parameter when you're executing a program with unusual storage requirements.

The syntax for the REGION parameter of the JOB and EXEC statements

```
REGION= {valueK} {valueM}
```

Explanation

valueK   Specifies the maximum amount of real or virtual storage for a job step in kilobyte units (1024 bytes). The value coded can be from 1 to 2096128. If the value coded is not a multiple of 4, the system will round it up to the next multiple of 4.

valueM   Specifies the maximum amount of real or virtual storage for a job step in megabyte units (1024 kilobytes). The value can be from 1 to 2047.

A JOB statement that specifies 4 megabytes of storage for each job step in the job

```
//MM03A JOB (36512),'A PRINCE',REGION=4M
```

An EXEC statement that specifies 256 kilobytes of storage for the job step

```
//STEP3    EXEC PGM=INV1000,REGION=256K
```

Description

- The REGION parameter is used on the JOB or EXEC statement to specify the maximum amount of storage a job step can use during execution.

- The amount of storage can be specified in terms of kilobytes or megabytes. If you use kilobytes, it's a good idea to choose a value that's a multiple of 4. Otherwise, the system has to round it up for you.

- A REGION parameter specified on a JOB statement applies to each job step within the job and overrides any REGION parameters specified on EXEC statements.

- If no REGION parameter is specified, the system uses a job step installation default specified at JES initialization.

- If a job step requires more space than what was specified by a REGION parameter, the job abends with an 804 or 80A completion code.

- Specifying a REGION size of 0K or 0M allocates all available storage, which can cause storage problems resulting in a region size that is unstable.

Figure 5-9   How to code the REGION parameter

How to specify a storage estimate (the JES3 LREGION parameter)

Under JES3, you can provide an estimate of the storage requirements of the largest step in a job by coding the LREGION parameter on the //*MAIN statement, as shown in the example in figure 5-10. Here, the estimate is 120 kilobytes. Unlike the REGION parameter, the LREGION parameter doesn't limit the amount of storage your job can acquire. Instead, JES3 uses it to improve job scheduling.

When you specify an accurate value for the LREGION parameter, JES3 utilizes the processors under its control as efficiently as possible. But it's not always easy to determine an accurate LREGION value. That's because LREGION doesn't indicate the total amount of virtual storage a job step needs to execute. Instead, it estimates the job step's *working set*, which indicates the amount of real storage required to support the job step's virtual storage requirements. For this reason, you should use the LREGION parameter sparingly because if the value you select is too small, your job may take longer to run.

How to request real storage (the ADDRSPC parameter)

You can code the ADDRSPC parameter shown in figure 5-10 to specify that a job step be assigned real *(non-pageable) storage* instead of the default virtual *(pageable) storage*. In other words, when you code ADDRSPC=REAL as shown in the examples, the system allocates to the job step an entire address space that is not subject to the normal paging process. That means that the storage pages within the address space are fixed in real storage and never paged out. You can code this parameter on either the JOB or EXEC statement depending on whether real storage is needed for each step in the job or only for a single step.

Although ADDRSPC=REAL can be appropriate for some time-dependent programs or specialized programs that perform system I/O operations, it's rarely used. In fact, some installations may not let you use this option at all because it can severely degrade the performance of other jobs running concurrently on the system.

The syntax for the LREGION parameter of the JES3 //*MAIN statement

```
LREGION=valueK
```

Explanation

valueK   Specifies an estimate of the storage requirements of the largest job step in kilobytes.

A JES3 //*MAIN statement that uses the LREGION parameter to estimate the largest storage requirement for any step in this job

```
//MM01A    JOB  (36512),'B MURACH',NOTIFY=MM01
//*MAIN    LREGION=120K
```

The syntax for the ADDRSPC parameter of the JOB and EXEC statements

```
ADDRSPC= {VIRT}
         {REAL}
```

Explanation

VIRT   Default; specifies that the region allocated for the job step can run in virtual storage. It gives the system permission to page the job step.

REAL   Specifies that the region allocated to the job step is not subject to paging processes. Instead, the allocated region is placed in real storage.

An ADDRSPC parameter that requests real storage for the entire job

```
//MM03A    JOB  (36512),'A PRINCE',REGION=4M,ADDRSPC=REAL
```

An ADDRSPC parameter that requests real storage for a job step

```
//STEP3    EXEC PGM=INV1000,ADDRSPC=REAL
```

Description

- The LREGION parameter provides JES3 with an estimate of the amount of real storage needed for the largest step in the job. Although an accurate value can improve job scheduling, this parameter should be used carefully because if the value selected is too small, the job may take longer to run.

- The ADDRSPC parameter is used on a JOB or EXEC statement to specify that a job step requires real rather than virtual storage.

- When coded on a JOB statement, the ADDRPC parameter applies to all the job steps within the job and overrides any ADDRSPC parameters specified on EXEC statements.

- When ADDRSPC=REAL is specified, the region allocated to the job step isn't subject to the paging process. That means that the storage pages are fixed in real storage and not paged out.

- The ADDRSPC=REAL parameter is sometimes used for time-dependent programs or specialized programs that modify channel programs during I/O operations. But most installations limit its use because it can severely degrade the performance of other jobs on the system.

Figure 5-10   How to code the LREGION (JES3) and ADDRSPC parameters

How to establish processing limits

OS/390 provides ways for an installation to control or limit how a job is processed. For example, by setting a default processing time limit, an installation can control how long a job is allowed to execute. And by specifying default SYSOUT limits, an installation can control the amount of SYSOUT data a job is allowed to produce. Although the defaults set by each installation are usually adequate, you may occasionally need to extend or reduce the amount of processing time or SYSOUT data a job is allowed. In such cases, you can use the parameters presented in the next two topics.

How to specify a job's execution time limit

Figure 5-11 shows the syntax for the TIME parameter that you can code on a JOB or EXEC statement to override the default execution time limit imposed at your installation. As you can see, the syntax is the same for both the JOB and EXEC statements with the exception of the 0 value, which can only be used in an EXEC statement.

You normally specify a value of minutes and seconds on the TIME parameter. For example, TIME=30 specifies a time limit of 30 minutes, and TIME=(2,30) specifies a time limit of 2 minutes and 30 seconds. If you choose to omit the minutes value, you must use parentheses and a comma to indicate the missing value. For example, TIME=(,30) specifies a limit of 30 seconds.

If you specify a time limit of 1440 minutes or code the keyword NOLIMIT, no time checking is done at all. You can use either value when you want a job to execute indefinitely. If you specify MAXIMUM, the maximum time limit of 357,912 minutes is used. This lets your job run uninterrupted for more than 248 days. And if you code TIME=0 on the EXEC statement, the job step can use the time remaining from the previous step. If it exceeds the remaining time available, the step will fail.

If you specify a TIME parameter on a JOB statement, the time applies to the entire job. As each step is executed, its execution time is added to the total execution time for the job. If the job's time limit is exceeded, the job is cancelled. On the other hand, when you specify a time limit on the EXEC statement, it applies only to that job step.

A potential conflict occurs when an EXEC statement specifies a time limit that's more than the limit remaining for the entire job. In that case, the job time limit takes precedence over the step time limit. The example in this figure illustrates this point. The overall time allocated to the job is 5 minutes, but the time allocated to STEP1 and STEP2 is 3 minutes each. If STEP1 runs for 2.75 minutes, STEP2 will only have 2.25 minutes left to run, not the 3 minutes specified in its EXEC statement.

The syntax for the TIME parameter of the JOB and EXEC statements

```
TIME= {([minutes][,seconds])}
      {1440}
      {NOLIMIT}
      {MAXIMUM}
      {0} (EXEC statement only)
```

Explanation

minutes	Specifies the maximum number of processor minutes a job or job step can use. The number of minutes can range from 0 to 357912 (248.55 days).
seconds	Specifies the maximum number of processor seconds a job or job step can use. The number of seconds can range from 0 to 59.
NOLIMIT	Specifies that a job or job step can use the processor for an unlimited amount of time.
1440	Specifies that a job or job step can use the processor for an unlimited amount of time. 1440 corresponds to the number of minutes in 24 hours.
MAXIMUM	Specifies that a job or job step can use the processor for the maximum amount of time (357,912 minutes).
0 (EXEC only)	Specifies that the job step can use the time remaining from the previous step. If the step exceeds the remaining time available, it will abend.

Reasons for coding the TIME parameter

* You want to decrease or increase the amount of processor time for a job or job step from the default installation value.

* The output messages the TIME parameter generates tell you how much processor time a job or job step used.

* If you're debugging a program, specifying the TIME parameter can limit the amount of time it runs if it gets caught in an endless loop.

* Your installation may require it.

A job that uses the TIME parameter on both JOB and EXEC statements

```
//MM03A     JOB (36512),'LE MENENDEZ',TIME=5
//STEP1     EXEC PGM=VIDUPD1,TIME=3
.
//STEP2     EXEC PGM=VIDRPT1,TIME=3
.
```

Description

* The TIME parameter on a JOB or EXEC statement allows you to override the default execution time limit. You can specify a value in minutes and seconds (or one or the other), or you can specify one of three alternate keywords that essentially give you an unlimited amount of processing time.

* Avoid coding TIME=0 on a JOB statement. The results are unpredictable.

Figure 5-11   How to specify a job's execution time limit

There are several reasons why you may want to use the TIME parameter in your job or job step. The most obvious is to increase or decrease the amount of processor time allocated by the installation default value. But the TIME parameter is also a handy tool for seeing how much processor time a job or a job step uses. That's because when the TIME parameter is present, it generates output messages specifying the amount of processor time each step used. Another way to use it is as a debugging aid. If you suspect that a program you are testing is looping endlessly, you can include a TIME parameter on the EXEC statement for that program to limit the amount of time it runs. Finally, and most importantly, you need to include the TIME parameter if your installation requires it.

How to specify SYSOUT limits

Figure 5-12 shows the syntax for various parameters you can use to control the amount of SYSOUT data a job produces. You can code these parameters on the JOB statement, the JES2 /*JOBPARM statement, or the JES3 //*MAIN statement, and they allow you to limit the output in terms of the total number of bytes, card, lines, or pages. (I haven't mentioned earlier that SYSOUT data can consist of cards to be punched, but that's an option even though it's not a commonly used form of output any more.) Notice that the value for BYTES and LINES has to be given in thousands, whereas the value for CARDS and PAGES represents the actual limit. You can also specify what action should be taken if the limit is exceeded if you're using the JOB or //*MAIN statement.

The example in this figure shows a JOB statement with a LINES parameter that includes both a value of 200 and an action of WARNING. That means that if the SYSOUT data sets produced by the job exceed 200,000 lines of output altogether, the system will issue a warning to the operator. If the action had been CANCEL or DUMP instead, the job would terminate or terminate and produce a storage dump if the output exceeded 200,000 lines.

In contrast to the JOB and //*MAIN statements, the parameters on the JES2 /*JOBPARM statement don't allow you to specify an action. So if the output limit is reached, the job will simply terminate. For that reason, I recommend that you use the parameters available on the JOB statement to specify SYSOUT limits.

The syntax for the SYSOUT parameters of the JOB and JES3 //*MAIN statements

```
BYTES=(value[,action])
CARDS=(value[,action])
LINES=(value[,action])
PAGES=(value[,action])
```

The syntax for the SYSOUT parameters of the JES2 /*JOBPARM statement

```
BYTES=value
CARDS=value
LINES=value
PAGES=value
```

Explanation

value   Specifies the maximum amount of SYSOUT output the job may produce. For the JOB and //*MAIN statements, the lowest value that can be coded is 1; for the /*JOBPARM statement, the lowest value can be 0. The highest value varies according to which parameter is used:

BYTES	Specifies the maximum number of bytes (in thousands) of SYSOUT data. The highest value allowed is 999999.
CARDS	Specifies the maximum number of SYSOUT card records. The highest value allowed is 99999999.
LINES	Specifies the maximum number of SYSOUT print records (in thousands). The highest value allowed is 999999.
PAGES	Specifies the maximum number of SYSOUT pages. The highest value allowed is 99999999.

action   Specifies the action to be taken if the maximum is exceeded:

WARNING or W	The system issues a warning message to the operator and continues processing.
CANCEL or C	The system cancels the job.
DUMP or D	The system cancels the job and produces a storage dump.

A JOB statement that sends a warning message to the operator if more than 200,000 SYSOUT lines are produced for this job

```
//MM01A    JOB  (36512),'R MENENDEZ',
//               LINES=(200,WARNING)
```

Description

- You can code the BYTES, CARDS, LINES, or PAGES parameter on a JOB statement to control the amount of SYSOUT data a job produces. If you don't specify any of the SYSOUT parameters in your job, the installation-defined limit is used.

- JES2 and JES3 also provide parameters in the /*JOBPARM and //*MAIN statements that control the amount of SYSOUT data a job produces.

- On the JOB or //*MAIN statement, you can also code an action subparameter that tells the system what to do if the specified limit is exceeded.

Figure 5-12   How to specify SYSOUT limits

How to specify execution-related data sets

So far, all of the features you've seen in this chapter have been either JOB or EXEC statement parameters or the JES2/JES3 statement parameters that provide similar functions. Now, you'll see how to code DD statements for two special types of data sets related to job processing. First, you'll learn how to specify a private program library from which programs can be retrieved for execution. Then, you'll learn how to specify the three SYSOUT data sets that the system uses to print storage dumps if a job step abends.

How to specify a private program library

When an EXEC statement with the PGM parameter is executed, the system searches a series of system libraries to find the program specified. Normally, the search is limited to libraries that contain programs of system-wide usage. These libraries are identified by system programmers and included as part of the initialization process for OS/390. The search always includes the system program library, SYS1.LINKLIB, and it usually includes other libraries, like installation-specific production libraries, as well.

There will be times, though, when you want to execute a program that doesn't reside in one of the default system libraries. In those situations, you code a DD statement in your job stream to identify a *private library* that's searched before the system libraries are searched. You can specify your private library as a *job library* or a *step library*. A job library applies throughout the job, while a step library only applies to the job step it's included in.

To specify a job library, you code a DD statement using JOBLIB as the ddname, as in the first example in figure 5-13. The JOBLIB DD statement must be the first JCL statement following the JOB statement for the job, although JES2/JES3 control statements can be placed between the two. When a job library is in effect, the system searches it first to locate any programs specified in EXEC statements. If a program isn't found in the job library, the standard system libraries are then searched.

To specify a step library for a job step, you code a DD statement named STEPLIB after the EXEC statement for that step, as shown in the second example in this figure. If you include both a JOBLIB and a STEPLIB DD statement, the step library is searched before the system libraries and the job library is ignored for the job step. To get a better idea of the search sequence for private libraries, take a look at the diagram at the top of this figure.

The search sequence for private libraries

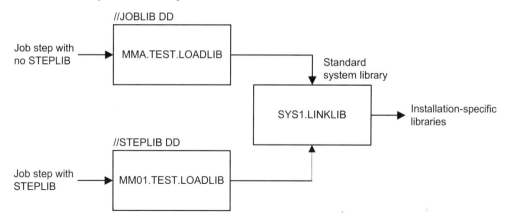

Establishing a job library

```
//MM01E     JOB   (36512),'LE MENENDEZ',NOTIFY=MM01
//JOBLIB    DD    DSNAME=MMA.TEST.LOADLIB,DISP=SHR
//STEP1     EXEC PGM=IEBGENER
  .
  .
  .
//STEP2     EXEC PGM=ORD2200A
  .
  .
  .
```

Establishing a step library

```
//MM01F     JOB   (36512),'LE MENENDEZ',NOTIFY=MM01
//STEP1     EXEC PGM=IEBGENER
  .
  .
//STEP2     EXEC PGM=ORD2200A
//STEPLIB   DD    DSNAME=MM01.TEST.LOADLIB,DISP=SHR
  .
  .
```

Description

- To execute programs that don't reside in the system libraries, you code a DD statement in your job stream that specifies a *private library* to be searched. You can specify your private library as a *job library* or a *step library*.

- To specify a job library that applies to an entire job, you code a DD statement using JOBLIB as the ddname. It must be the first JCL statement following a JOB statement, although JES2/JES3 statements can be placed between the two.

- To specify a step library that applies to only one step in a job, you code a DD statement named STEPLIB after the EXEC statement for that step.

- If you include both a JOBLIB and a STEPLIB DD statement, the step library is searched first, followed by the system libraries. The job library is ignored for the job step.

Figure 5-13   How to specify a private program library

How to specify a dump data set

When a job encounters an error it can't recover from, it ends in an *abnormal termination*, or *abend*. An abend can be caused by a JCL error, a system failure, or the failure of one of the programs that's executed in one of the job steps.

If a job step abends, OS/390 tries to print the contents of the virtual storage areas used by the program before it terminates the job step. This listing is called a *storage dump*, and it is often the only way to determine what caused the program to fail. To obtain a storage dump for a job step, you must provide a DD statement named SYSUDUMP, SYSABEND, or SYSMDUMP, as described in figure 5-14. Which ddname you specify depends on the type of information you want in the dump.

If you specify SYSUDUMP, you'll receive a listing of all of the virtual storage allocated to your program. In other words, SYSUDUMP provides a dump of the user region of your job's private address space. If you specify SYSABEND instead, the dump will include the user region along with system areas outside the user region that are associated with your job step. These system areas include the *local system queue area* (*LSQA*) and the *input/output system* (*IOS*) control blocks for the failing task.

As for SYSMDUMP, it provides a dump of the system areas and the entire private address space. It isn't as commonly used as SYSUDUMP or SYSABEND, however, because it's unformatted. To read it, you first write the dump to a disk or tape and later, a systems programmer prints it with the *interactive problem control system* (*IPCS*).

Unlike SYSMDUMP, both SYSUDUMP and SYSABEND produce formatted dumps that can be printed directly, so you'll usually specify these data sets as standard SYSOUT data sets. For example, the job stream in this figure shows how you can specify a SYSUDUMP data set with SYSOUT=*. Here, the SYSUDUMP data set will be printed using the same output class as the job's message output.

This example shows a single job step, but if you want a storage dump for each job step that abends, be sure to specify a dump DD statement for each step in the job. If a job step ends normally, this statement is ignored.

The three kinds of system dumps

ddname	Description
SYSUDUMP	Produces a formatted dump of the user region of the job's private address space.
SYSABEND	Produces a formatted dump of the user region and system areas.
SYSMDUMP	Produces an unformatted dump of the entire private address space and system areas.

A job that produces a formatted dump if STEP1 abends

```
//MM01RN    JOB  (36512),'J TAYLOR',MSGCLASS=X,MSGLEVEL=(1,1),
//               CLASS=A,NOTIFY=&SYSUID
//STEP1     EXEC PGM=INV2300
//STEPLIB   DD   DSN=MM01.TEST.LOADLIB,DISP=SHR
//INVMSTS   DD   DSN=MM01.INVMSTS.DATA,DISP=SHR
//RCTTRAN   DD   DSN=MM01.RCTTRAN.DATA,DISP=SHR
//RCTERR    DD   DSN=MM01.DCMERR.DATA,DISP=(NEW,CATLG,DELETE),
//               UNIT=SYSDA,VOL=SER=LIB788,
//               SPACE=(TRK,(1,1)),
//               DCB=(DSORG=PS,RECFM=FB,LRECL=23)
//SYSOUT    DD   SYSOUT=*
//SYSUDUMP  DD   SYSOUT=*
```

Description

- An *abnormal termination*, or *abend*, occurs when a job encounters an error that prevents it from running to completion.

- To obtain a *storage dump* for an abended step, you must provide the step with a DD statement named SYSUDUMP, SYSABEND, or SYSMDUMP. Which ddname you specify depends on the type of information you want in the dump.

- The system areas that are part of the dump when you specify SYSABEND or SYSMDUMP include the *local system queue area* (*LSQA*) and the *input/output system* (*IOS*) control blocks for the failing task.

- You can specify a data set name on the DD statement for SYSUDUMP or SYSABEND, but in most cases SYSOUT=* or SYSOUT=A will suffice since you'll probably want to print the dump report anyway.

- Since SYSMDUMP produces an unformatted, machine-readable dump, you'll want to write it to a disk or tape, so you will specify a data set name for it. That way, a system programmer can later print it with the *Interactive Problem Control System* (*IPCS*).

- If a job step ends normally, the dump DD statement is ignored.

Figure 5-14   How to specify a dump data set

Perspective

This chapter presented a number of JCL and JES2/JES3 parameters that are loosely related at best. Obviously, you won't use all of these parameters in every job you code. However, you should be familiar with all of them so that when the need for one arises, you'll know which parameter to use.

Terms

JES2/JES3 control statements	job library
job class	step library
priority	abnormal termination
held job class	abend
working set	storage dump
non-pageable storage	local system queue area (LSQA)
pageable storage	input/output system (IOS)
private library	interactive problem control system (IPCS)

6

How to use JCL facilities to allocate other types of DASD data sets

In chapter 4, you learned how to code DD statements to allocate the DASD data sets that are processed by a job step. This chapter builds on the basic DD statement format you learned there by presenting additional DD parameters that give you more control over how your data sets are allocated. In addition, it shows you how to allocate special types of DASD data sets that you'll only need in certain jobs.

How to allocate temporary data sets

Many jobs require *temporary data sets* that exist only for the duration of a job or a job step. For example, a job step that sorts a file may require temporary data sets that help with the sorting within that single job step. Those types of data sets are often referred to as *work files*. In other cases, temporary data sets are passed from one job step to another. For example, a sorted file can be passed from a sort program to a report program for printing. No matter how many job steps they're used for, temporary data sets are always deleted at the end of a job, unless you explicitly delete them sooner by specifying DELETE in the DISP parameter.

A temporary data set can also take advantage of another OS/390 facility called Virtual Input/Output, or just VIO. A VIO data set looks like a standard DASD data set to a program, but it doesn't reside on DASD. Instead, it resides in virtual storage, so it can be processed more efficiently than a standard DASD data set. VIO is used only for temporary data sets.

How to allocate a single-step temporary data set

To allocate a work file—a temporary data set that's created and deleted in a single step—you can code a bare minimum of information on the DD statement. In fact, only two DD statement parameters are required: UNIT, which should specify a DASD device type like SYSDA, and SPACE. You can code DISP=(NEW,DELETE) to indicate that the data set is created and deleted in the same job step, but that's the default anyway. And the DSNAME parameter isn't required since no other DD statement will have to refer to the data set. Besides these parameters, you may also need to include a DCB parameter to supply file characteristics such as record length if those characteristics aren't supplied by the program that's being run.

Figure 6-1 shows two examples of DD statements for work files. The first includes just the two required parameters: UNIT and SPACE. The second also specifies the DISP parameter, which duplicates the default value, and a DCB parameter that supplies the logical record length of the file.

Allocating a single-step temporary data set (a work file)

Example 1

```
//WORK1    DD    UNIT=SYSDA,SPACE=(CYL,(10,5))
```

Allocates a temporary data set on a SYSDA volume using 10 cylinders of primary and 5 cylinders of secondary space. DISP=(NEW,DELETE) is assumed.

Example 2

```
//WORK2    DD    UNIT=SYSDA,DISP=(NEW,DELETE),
//               SPACE=(3200,(500,500)),
//               DCB=LRECL=120
```

Allocates a temporary data set on a SYSDA volume using 500 blocks of primary and secondary space. DISP=(NEW,DELETE) is specified, but could be omitted since it's the default. The record length is 120 bytes.

Description

- To allocate a *temporary data set* that's created and deleted in a single step (also called a *work file*), the only two parameters you need to code on the DD statement are UNIT and SPACE. The DSNAME parameter isn't required since no other DD statement will refer to the data set.

- You may also need to include the DCB parameter to supply file characteristics such as record length if the program you're executing doesn't supply that information.

Figure 6-1   How to allocate a single-step temporary data set

How to allocate a multi-step temporary data set

There are two OS/390 terms, *pass* and *receive*, that describe how temporary data sets are typically processed when they're used by more than one job step. To *pass* a data set means to retain it so that a subsequent job step can process it. That means that when a temporary data set is deallocated, it's not deleted. To *receive* a temporary data set means to allocate a temporary data set that was previously passed.

OS/390 retains the unit and volume information for passed data sets in virtual storage, so subsequent DD statements that receive the passed data sets don't have to repeat that information. In fact, whenever you allocate a data set without specifying unit and volume information, OS/390 first checks to see if the data set has been passed. It only checks the catalog after determining that the data set wasn't passed.

To pass or receive a temporary data set, you must first assign it a data set name that follows a specific format, as shown in figure 6-2. A common mistake is coding only one ampersand at the beginning of a temporary data set name rather than two (&&). JCL procedures, which you'll learn about in chapter 9, use one ampersand to mark symbolic parameters that can be assigned variable values. If you code a data set name that starts with one ampersand, the system assumes you're specifying a symbolic parameter unless there's no value assigned to it. In that case, it does treat the name as a temporary data set name. However, this can lead to confusion and unintended results, so to avoid any trouble, be sure to use two ampersands.

The system creates the actual data set name for a temporary data set using the name you supply, the job name, and a date and time value. The same date and time value will be used for each temporary data set you create in a job. So don't create two temporary data sets using the same name in the same job because they won't be unique.

The DISP parameter controls whether a temporary data set is passed so that it can be received by a subsequent job step or deleted when the current step completes. In the job step that creates the temporary data set, the DD statement should specify DISP=(NEW,PASS). Then, subsequent job steps should specify DISP=(OLD,PASS) so the temporary data set will be received and passed on to additional job steps that need it.

In the last job step that processes the temporary data set, you should explicitly delete the file by specifying DISP=(OLD,DELETE) so the DASD space it uses is released as soon as possible. If you specify DISP=(OLD,PASS) again, the temporary data set isn't deleted until the job ends.

To see a typical use of temporary data sets, look at the two-step sort and report job in this figure. The first job step sorts an input file, producing a temporary data set that's passed to the next job step. In addition, the SORT step allocates sort work files, which are temporary data sets required by the sort program to do a large sort. Because the work files are only needed during the sort step, no data set names are coded for them.

Rules for coding temporary data set names

- Must be 1 to 8 alphanumeric or national characters, starting with an alphabetic or national character.
- Must be preceded by two ampersands (&&).
- Compound names joined by periods are not allowed.

Valid temporary data set names

```
&&CUSTOMER        &&TEMPRM        &&A             &&DD$1
```

Invalid temporary data set names

```
&&CUSTOMERS       &TRANSSRT       &&MM01.ARS      &&1ABC
```

A two-step job that uses temporary data sets

```
//MM01RN    JOB   (36512),'R MENENDEZ',MSGCLASS=X,MSGLEVEL=(1,1),
//                CLASS=A,NOTIFY=&SYSUID
//SORT      EXEC PGM=SORT
//SYSOUT    DD    SYSOUT=*
//SORTIN    DD    DSNAME=MMA2.AR.CUSTOMER.MASTER,DISP=SHR
//SORTWK01  DD    UNIT=SYSDA,SPACE=(TRK,(1,1))
//SORTWK02  DD    UNIT=SYSDA,SPACE=(TRK,(1,1))
//SORTWK03  DD    UNIT=SYSDA,SPACE=(TRK,(1,1))
//SORTOUT   DD    DSNAME=&&SORTCUST,DISP=(NEW,PASS),
//                UNIT=SYSDA,SPACE=(TRK,(1,1))
//SYSIN     DD    *
 SORT FIELDS=(2,13,A,20,1,A),FORMAT=CH
/*
//REPORT    EXEC PGM=CUSTLST
//SYSOUT    DD    SYSOUT=*
//CUSTMAST  DD    DSNAME=&&SORTCUST,DISP=(OLD,DELETE)
//ATB       DD    SYSOUT=*
//SYSUDUMP  DD    SYSOUT=*
```

Description

- Temporary data sets can be passed from one job step to another within the same job. OS/390 retains their unit and volume information in virtual storage.
- To identify a temporary data set that's going to be passed from one job step to another, you need to assign a name following the rules given above. Make sure that you don't accidentally code just one ampersand (&) or the name may be interpreted as a symbolic parameter (see chapter 9).
- To pass a temporary data set from one job step to another, the DD statement that creates the data set should specify DISP=(NEW, PASS). Then any subsequent job steps that process the temporary data set should specify DISP=(OLD,PASS). The last job step that processes the data set should explicitly delete it by specifying DISP=(OLD,DELETE).

Figure 6-2   How to allocate a multi-step temporary data set

How to allocate a VIO temporary data set

The *Virtual Input/Output facility* (*VIO*) lets you process temporary data sets that reside entirely in virtual storage rather than on DASD. To your program, a VIO data set looks like a standard DASD data set. But because the system can access data in virtual storage faster than it can access data in a standard DASD file, a VIO temporary data set can be processed more efficiently than an equivalent DASD temporary data set. You can use VIO temporary data sets that are created and deleted in a single job step, or you can use them for temporary data sets that are passed from step to step. However, you can't use VIO to create permanent data sets (that is, data sets that are retained at the end of the job).

To use VIO, you must specify a device type in the UNIT parameter that's eligible for VIO. Some installations define a group name of VIO to be used just for that purpose, so if you specify UNIT=VIO, the data set will use the VIO facility. In addition, an installation can specify that other groups are eligible for VIO, provided that certain conditions are met. SYSDA is usually defined in this way so that if you specify UNIT=SYSDA, the file will automatically use VIO if possible. There are three examples of DD statements that allocate VIO data sets in figure 6-3. As you can see, example 1 specifies UNIT=VIO, and examples 2 and 3 specify UNIT=SYSDA.

Besides specifying a VIO-eligible unit, there are two other requirements a file must meet before it can use VIO. First, as already mentioned, the file must be a temporary data set. That means the DISP parameter must specify PASS or DELETE (not KEEP or CATLG), and the DSNAME parameter must either be omitted or must specify a valid temporary data set name. Second, the file's allocation must be a non-specific volume request; in other words, the VOLUME parameter can't be coded.

Interestingly, the SPACE parameter is optional for a VIO data set. If you omit it, a default value of SPACE=(1000,(10,50)) is assumed. Keep in mind, however, that the default SPACE value works only for VIO data sets. For temporary data sets on DASD, you must specify a SPACE value. So if it's possible that the data set might be written to DASD rather than VIO space, be sure to include the SPACE parameter. In addition, remember to specify the DCB parameter for a VIO data set if your program doesn't provide complete DCB information.

Two advantages of using VIO data sets

- VIO data sets reside in virtual storage, so reading from and writing to them is performed at the speed of virtual storage access rather than at the speed of an I/O device.

- The VIO data set doesn't occupy space in the program's address space.

Examples of VIO temporary data sets

Example 1

```
//TEMP1    DD    UNIT=VIO
```

The data set is defined as a VIO temporary work file that's deleted at the end of the job step.

Example 2

```
//DD1      DD    UNIT=SYSDA,SPACE=(1000,(10,50)),
//               DCB=(RECFM=FB,LRECL=40)
```

If enough VIO space is available during the execution of the job step, the system will define the file as a VIO temporary data set. Otherwise, it'll be defined as a DASD temporary data set. In either case, it's deleted at the end of the job step.

Example 3

```
//SORTOUT  DD    DSNAME=&&PRODCD,DISP=(NEW,PASS),
//               UNIT=SYSDA,SPACE=(1000,(20,70))
```

&&PRODCD will be defined as a VIO or DASD temporary data set, depending on the available VIO space. In either case, DISP=(NEW,PASS) will allow the data set to be available to subsequent job steps.

Description

- The *Virtual Input/Output facility* (*VIO*) lets you process temporary data sets that reside entirely in virtual storage rather than on DASD. To programs, VIO data sets look and act like standard DASD data sets.

- You must always specify the UNIT parameter for VIO data sets. Sometimes, an installation defines a group name of VIO that is used just for VIO data sets. Other groups like SYSDA can also be defined as eligible for VIO data sets, provided that certain conditions are met.

- A non-specific volume request must be used for the file allocation for a VIO data set, so you don't code the VOL=SER parameter.

- The SPACE parameter is optional for VIO data sets. If omitted, the default is SPACE=(1000,(10,50)). However, DASD temporary data sets must specify a value for the SPACE parameter.

- You can specify the DCB parameter for a VIO temporary data set if your program doesn't provide complete DCB information.

Figure 6-3   How to allocate a VIO temporary data set

How to allocate other special-purpose data sets

Besides temporary data sets, the DD statement allows you to define other types of DASD data sets that you'll use only in certain situations. In the topics that follow, you'll learn how to allocate dummy data sets, how to treat two or more separate data sets as though they were a single file, and how to define a data set that requires more than one volume of DASD space.

How to allocate a dummy data set

Dummy data sets allow you to execute programs that process files without actually having the files present. When you use a dummy file, the system simulates all of the housekeeping tasks associated with file processing, including I/O operations. When a program tries to read a record from a dummy file, OS/390 indicates an end-of-file condition, and when a program writes a record to a dummy file, the data is discarded.

To understand why you would use a dummy data set, consider a report preparation program that reads the records of a master file and produces five reports, each written to a different SYSOUT data set. If you're testing just one of the reports, you may not want the others filling up your output queue. In this case, you could define the four SYSOUT data sets you don't need as dummy data sets.

The syntax at the top of figure 6-4 illustrates the two ways you can specify a dummy file on a DD statement. One way is to code the DUMMY parameter and the other is to specify NULLFILE as the DSNAME. DUMMY is a positional parameter, so if you code it, it must be the first parameter on the DD statement. The ellipsis (...) in JCL syntax simply means that the last element listed can be repeated, so you can code multiple parameters after DUMMY or NULLFILE.

In general, though, you don't need to code any additional parameters for a dummy data set. In fact, if you do, the system usually checks them for syntax errors but otherwise ignores them. There are a couple of exceptions, however. If a program doesn't internally specify a block size for a file it uses, you need to include a BLKSIZE parameter. Normally, the system computes an optimal BLKSIZE based on the I/O device specified in the UNIT parameter for the file. But because a dummy data set has no I/O device, the system can't determine a BLKSIZE on its own. Also, if the program expects a VSAM file, you need to specify AMP=AMORG on the DD statement (you'll learn more about the AMP parameter in chapter 15).

The examples in this figure show some of these coding variations. Example 1 shows the simplest way to allocate a dummy data set and illustrates a common use for one. The standard ddname, SYSIN, is often used to provide control statement input to system utility programs. Since some system utilities let you specify a dummy data set for SYSIN if there aren't any unusual processing requirements, you might see statements like this one in your shop.

The syntax for dummy data sets

```
//ddname    DD    DUMMY [,parameter]...

            or

//ddname    DD    DSNAME=NULLFILE [,parameter]...
```

Allocating a dummy data set

Example 1

```
//SYSIN    DD    DUMMY
```

Allocates a dummy data set. OS/390 simulates input and output processing, but no I/O operations are actually performed.

Example 2

```
//CUSTMAST DD    DUMMY,AMP=AMORG
```

Allocates a dummy VSAM data set.

Example 3

```
//TRANFILE DD    DUMMY,DSNAME=AR.TRANS.FILE,DISP=(NEW,KEEP),
//               UNIT=SYSDA,VOL=SER=MPS800,
//               SPACE=(CYL,(5,1)),
//               DCB=(DSORG=PS,RECFM=FB,LRECL=80)
```

Allocates a dummy data set using the specified file characteristics. When the DUMMY parameter is removed, this DD statement will allocate an actual data set.

Example 4

```
//TRANFILE DD    DSNAME=NULLFILE,DISP=(NEW,KEEP),
//               UNIT=SYSDA,VOL=SER=MPS800,
//               SPACE=(CYL,(5,1)),
//               DCB=(DSORG=PS,RECFM=FB,LRECL=80)
```

Allocates a dummy data set using the specified file characteristics. When NULLFILE is changed to a data set name, this DD statement will allocate an actual data set.

Description

- A dummy data set is a data set that doesn't exist. Instead, the system simulates the data set, allowing a program to process the file without actually having the file present.
- There are two ways to specify a dummy data set on a DD statement. You can code the DUMMY parameter, or you can specify DSNAME=NULLFILE. DUMMY is a positional parameter and, if coded, must be the first parameter on the DD statement.
- Although you can include parameters such as DISP, UNIT, and SPACE for a dummy data set, the system only checks their syntax and then ignores them.
- Since dummy data sets don't use actual I/O devices, the system can't automatically determine an optimal block size for them. So you'll need to include a BLKSIZE parameter if the program expects blocked records and doesn't provide a block size itself.
- If the program you're executing expects a VSAM file, specify AMP=AMORG (you'll learn about this parameter in chapter 15).

Figure 6-4   How to allocate a dummy data set

Example 2 shows you how to allocate a dummy data set when the program anticipates a VSAM file. And examples 3 and 4 show the full range of DD statement parameters that can be coded for a dummy file. Most of the parameters coded are checked for syntax but ignored. To actually process either file, you can remove the DUMMY parameter in example 3, or replace NULLFILE with the real data set name in example 4.

How to concatenate data sets

On occasion, you may need to treat two or more input data sets as if they were a single data set. To do this, you *concatenate* them, or link them together. Then, if the concatenated data sets are sequential files, the system processes them in the order in which you concatenate them. On the other hand, if you concatenate partitioned (PDS and PDSE) data sets, the system searches them in the order in which you concatenate them for a member you specify.

To concatenate files, you code the DD statement for the first file just as you normally would. Then, you code the next DD statement directly after it, but without a ddname, as shown in example 1 of figure 6-5. Here, three sequential data sets are concatenated. The program will first read all of the records from MMA1.TRANS.WEEK1. When an end-of-file condition is detected, OS/390 will switch to the next file in the concatenation so the records from MMA1.TRANS.WEEK2 are read. Similarly, after the records from the second file are all read, the records from MMA1.TRANS.WEEK3 are read. You can concatenate an unlimited number of sequential files in this way.

When you concatenate partitioned data sets, as in example 2, the effect is a little different. When a member is requested from a series of concatenated partitioned data sets, all of the concatenated libraries are searched (in other words, their directories are concatenated). Since the libraries are searched in the order in which you concatenate them, if more than one concatenated library has a member with the same name, the member from the library that's earlier in the concatenation will be used. You can concatenate up to 114 partitioned data sets in this way.

As a general rule, the characteristics of the data sets you concatenate should be similar. For example, you can't concatenate sequential and partitioned data sets together. As long as data sets are of the same type, though, certain data set attributes can vary. For example, you can concatenate sequential data sets on tape and DASD, partitioned data set members (which are treated as sequential files), and SYSIN data sets, in any combination you wish, as shown in example 3. However, you should avoid including dummy data sets as part of a concatenation because when the system encounters a dummy data set, the end-of-data set exit is taken immediately and any subsequent data sets are ignored.

You can also concatenate data sets with different block sizes (BLKSIZE) and logical record lengths (LRECL). Be aware, though, that in some older versions of MVS, the first data set in the concatenation must specify the largest block size and/or record length, regardless of the actual block size or record length for that particular data set.

Concatenating data sets

Example 1

```
//TRANS     DD    DSNAME=MMA1.TRANS.WEEK1,DISP=SHR
//          DD    DSNAME=MMA1.TRANS.WEEK2,DISP=SHR
//          DD    DSNAME=MMA1.TRANS.WEEK3,DISP=SHR
```

Allocates three sequential transaction files, processing them one after the other in the sequence in which they're listed.

Example 2

```
//SYSLIB    DD    DSNAME=MMA1.COBOL.OBJLIB,DISP=SHR
//          DD    DSNAME=SYS1.COBLIB,DISP=SHR
```

Allocates two partitioned data sets, searching their directories in the order in which they're listed.

Example 3

```
//SYSUT1    DD    DSNAME=MM01.TEXT,DISP=OLD,
//                UNIT=TAPE,VOL=SER=M00023
//          DD    DSNAME=MM01.ACCTG.DATA(ARMAST),DISP=SHR
//          DD    *
  (input data records)
/*
```

Allocates three files, processing them in the sequence in which they're listed: first the tape file, then the partitioned data set member, and finally, the instream data set.

Rules for concatenation

- You can only concatenate non-VSAM files that are used for input. Concatenating VSAM files or output files is not allowed.
- You can't mix sequential data sets and partitioned data sets together in a concatenation. You can concatenate PDS/PDSE members with sequential data sets, however, since the system treats members as if they were sequential files.
- Don't concatenate data sets to a dummy data set. When the system encounters a dummy data set, the end-of-data set exit is taken immediately and any subsequent data sets are ignored.
- The total number of partitioned data sets you can concatenate is 114. There's no limit to the number of sequential files you can concatenate.

Description

- To treat two or more data sets as a single data set, you *concatenate* them. Then, if the data sets are sequential input files, OS/390 will read the records in the concatenated data sets in the order in which they're concatenated.
- If you concatenate partitioned data sets, OS/390 searches them for a specified member in the order in which they're concatenated.
- To concatenate files, you code the DD statement for the first file as usual. Then, you code the DD statements for the additional files in the desired order, but *without* ddnames. The program will read the records from the first file and when an end-of-file condition is detected, OS/390 will automatically switch to the next file in the concatenation.

Figure 6-5   How to concatenate data sets

How to allocate multi-volume DASD data sets

In chapter 4, you learned how to code simple forms of the UNIT and VOLUME parameters to allocate data sets that reside on a single DASD or tape volume. Although most data sets fall into that category, some data sets are so large that more than one DASD or tape volume is required to store them. Data sets like that are called *multi-volume data sets* because they require multiple volumes.

Figure 6-6 shows you the syntax for the UNIT and VOLUME parameters and explains how you can use them to allocate multi-volume, non-VSAM data sets on permanently resident DASD. Later, in chapter 7, I'll introduce additional UNIT and VOLUME subparameters that apply specifically to multi-volume tape data sets.

To allocate a new or existing, but uncataloged, multi-volume DASD data set, you list all of the DASD volumes in the VOLUME parameter, as in the first example in this figure. Here, three DASD volumes are allocated: MVS300, MVS301, and MVS302. You can list up to 255 volume serial numbers in the VOLUME parameter, and the list must be enclosed in parentheses. For an existing data set, be sure you list the volume serial numbers in the same order as you listed them when you created the data set.

To allocate a cataloged multi-volume data set, you don't have to specify the VOLUME parameter. Instead, you include a unit count in the UNIT parameter that specifies how many non-specific volumes to allocate, as shown in the second example. As you can see, up to three volumes will be used for this multi-volume data set. Always remember to include CATLG as the data set's disposition if your program is adding records to the file. That way, if the data set is extended onto a new volume, the update volume information will be stored in the catalog.

When you create a multi-volume data set, the primary space you specify in the SPACE parameter is allocated on the first volume that's listed in the VOLUME parameter or chosen by the system. Then, for a standard sequential or partitioned data set, up to 15 secondary extents are allocated on the first volume. When a total of 16 extents have been allocated on the first volume, or when the first volume is full, a secondary extent is allocated on the next volume. When 16 secondary extents have been allocated on that volume, or the volume is full, a secondary extent is allocated on the next volume. This process can continue until all of the volumes you specify are used. On the other hand, if the file doesn't need as many volumes as you specified, the unused volumes aren't ever allocated to the file.

DD statement parameters used in multi-volume data set allocation

```
,UNIT=(device,unit-count)
,VOL=SER=(serial-number,serial-number...)
```

Explanation

device   Specifies a group name, device type, or device number that identifies the device where the file resides.

unit-count   Specifies the number of non-specific volumes to allocate.

serial-number   Species the six-character serial number of the volume that contains the file. Not required for cataloged data sets.

Allocating a multi-volume data set

Example 1

```
//CUSTMAST DD   DSNAME=MMA1.CUSTOMER.MASTER,DISP=(NEW,KEEP),
//             UNIT=SYSDA,VOL=SER=(MVS300,MVS301,MVS302),
//             SPACE=(CYL,(400,200))
```

Allocates a multi-volume uncataloged data set that uses DASD volumes MVS300, MVS301, and MVS302.

Example 2

```
//CUSTMAST DD   DSNAME=MMA1.CUSTOMER.MASTER,DISP=(NEW,CATLG),
//             UNIT=(SYSDA,3),SPACE=(CYL,(400,200))
```

Allocates a multi-volume cataloged data set that uses three DASD volumes chosen by the system.

Description

- Data sets that require more than one DASD volume to store their data are called *multi-volume data sets*. To allocate them, you can use the UNIT and VOLUME parameters on the DD statement.

- To allocate a new or existing uncataloged multi-volume data set, you list all of the DASD volume serial numbers to be used for this data set in the VOLUME parameter. You can list up to 255 volume serial numbers.

- To allocate a new or existing cataloged multi-volume data set, you specify a unit count in the UNIT parameter. The system then assigns non-specific DASD volumes to the data set. Since the data set is cataloged, the volume information is stored in the catalog.

- If the data set doesn't require all of the volumes assigned in the VOLUME or UNIT parameter, only the volumes required are allocated.

Figure 6-6   How to allocate multi-volume DASD data sets

How to use advanced space allocation subparameters

In chapter 4, you learned how to allocate DASD space for a data set by using the SPACE parameter on a DD statement. In the following topics, you'll learn how to use some advanced features of that parameter that allow you more control over the way that space is allocated. Although you may not often use these features, it's still a good idea to know what they are and what they do.

The complete syntax for the SPACE parameter

Figure 6-7 shows the complete syntax for the DD statement's SPACE parameter. It includes several positional subparameters that let you control the way OS/390 allocates DASD space to your data set. The RLSE subparameter lets you specify that unused space should be released so it can be allocated to other data sets. The CONTIG, MXIG, and ALX subparameters indicate that space should be allocated in groups of adjacent cylinders. And the ROUND subparameter indicates that space should be allocated in terms of whole cylinders even though you specify the amount of space in terms of blocks.

This figure also includes an alternate format for the SPACE parameter that allows you to allocate specific tracks to your data set. In this case, you specify ABSTR instead of CYL, TRK, or block size. Then, you specify the primary quantity of tracks to allocate to the data set followed by the track number of the first track in the allocation. The numbering offset used is 0, so track 1 has an address of 0, track 2 has an address of 1, and so on. Although you won't use this method often, it's included here for completeness.

The SPACE parameter for system assignment of space

```
SPACE=(unit,(primary[,secondary][,dir])[,RLSE][,{CONTIG}][,ROUND])
                                                 {MXIG}
                                                 {ALX}
```

Explanation

unit	Specifies the unit of measure for the primary and secondary allocations. Specify CYL for cylinders, TRK for tracks, or a decimal value representing a block size.
primary	Specifies the number of units to allocate for the file's primary space allocation.
secondary	Specifies the number of units to allocate for the file's secondary space allocations.
dir	Specifies the number of directory blocks to allocate for a partitioned data set.
RLSE	Specifies that space that's allocated but not used should be freed when the data set is closed.
CONTIG	Specifies that the primary allocation must be contiguous and satisfied in a single extent.
MXIG	Specifies that the primary allocation should be the largest available extent on the volume; the minimum size of the allocation is specified in the *primary* subparameter.
ALX	Specifies that up to five extents should be allocated; the minimum size of each extent is specified in the *primary* subparameter.
ROUND	Specifies that the primary allocation should be made in terms of cylinders, even though the *unit* subparameter specifies a block size.

The SPACE parameter for specific track requests

```
SPACE=(ABSTR,(primary,address [{,dir} ])
                              [{,index}]
```

Explanation

ABSTR	Requests that the data set be allocated at a specified location on the volume.
primary	Specifies the number of tracks to allocate to the file's primary space allocation.
address	Specifies the track number of the first track to be allocated. The first track on the first cylinder on the volume is 0, the second track is 1, and so forth. The data set starts on the track number you specify.
dir	Specifies the number of 256-byte records needed in the directory for a partitioned data set.
index	Specifies the number of tracks needed for the index of an indexed sequential data set.

Description

- As shown in chapter 4, you use the SPACE parameter to allocate space for a new data set on a DASD volume. The new syntax elements shown here give you more control over the way the system allocates the amount of space needed.

Figure 6-7   The complete syntax for the SPACE parameter

How to code the RLSE subparameter

Since you don't always know how much space a DASD file will require, it's often a good idea to specify a primary allocation on a data set's SPACE parameter that's relatively large. That way you avoid program abends due to an insufficient amount of file space. But on the other hand, you don't want to be wasteful of disk space. The solution is to include a RLSE subparameter so that DASD space that's not actually used by the file is released when the program finishes writing to it.

The first two examples in figure 6-8 show how to code the RLSE subparameter. In example 1, a primary allocation of 400 tracks and a secondary allocation of 100 tracks are specified. If the file uses less than that amount, the excess space is released. Example 2 shows how RLSE works with multi-volume data sets. In this case, the system will release any unused cylinders on the current volume.

The effect of the RLSE subparameter occurs when your program closes the file. During the CLOSE processing, OS/390 compares the space allocated to the file with the actual space occupied by the file's records. If the file's last extent, whether it's a primary or secondary extent, includes space that's not used by the file, that extent is trimmed back and the unused space is returned to the system as a free extent. Because RLSE happens during CLOSE processing, the unused space won't be released if the data set isn't properly closed or if the job step abends.

The advantage of using the RLSE subparameter is that your files use only the amount of DASD space they need. That's especially important if your installation charges for DASD use based on the exact amount of DASD space occupied by your files. There are, however, two disadvantages to using RLSE. First, if you expect your file to grow, RLSE releases space that would have otherwise been available for expansion without the need for allocating a secondary extent. As the file approaches its extent limit, that becomes important. Second, using RLSE may contribute to *volume fragmentation*, a situation where the available free space on a volume is spread out over a large number of small extents. If that happens, the amount of space released when your file is closed might be too small to be used by other files. Despite these disadvantages, I recommend you use the RLSE subparameter whenever possible.

How to code the ROUND subparameter

When you specify the SPACE allocation in terms of blocks instead of tracks or cylinders, the system converts the block allocation into tracks and allocates the required number of tracks. If you code the ROUND subparameter, however, the system converts the block allocation into cylinders instead. The advantage is that the data set will begin and end at a cylinder boundary. In some cases, that might give you a slight performance benefit.

DD statements that use the RLSE subparameter

Example 1

```
//EMPMAST  DD    DSNAME=MMA1.EMPLOYEE.MASTER,DISP=(,CATLG,DELETE),
//               UNIT=SYSDA,SPACE=(TRK,(400,100),RLSE)
```

The initial space allocation is 400 tracks of primary space and 100 tracks of secondary space. Any unused tracks are released if the job step ends normally.

Example 2

```
//INVMAST  DD    DSNAME=MMA1.INVENTORY.MASTER,DISP=(,CATLG,DELETE),
//               UNIT=SYSDA,VOL=SER=(MVS300,MVS301,MVS302),
//               SPACE=(CYL,(100,20),RLSE)
```

The initial space allocation for this multi-volume data set is 100 cylinders of primary space and 20 cylinders of secondary space. Any unused cylinders on the last volume used are released if the job step ends normally.

A DD statement that uses the ROUND subparameter

```
//INSMAST  DD    DSNAME=MMA1.INSURANCE.MASTER,DISP=(,CATLG,DELETE),
//               UNIT=SYSDA,SPACE=(3200,(5000,1000),,,ROUND)
```

Allocates the space, which is specified in terms of 3200-byte blocks, in units of whole cylinders.

Description

- To release any unused space when you close a data set that was opened for output, you code the RLSE subparameter within the SPACE parameter of a DD statement. That way, valuable DASD space isn't wasted.

- The effect of the RLSE subparameter occurs when a program closes the file. As the file is closed, the system compares the space allocated to the file with the actual space occupied by the file's records. If the file's last extent includes unused space, it's trimmed back and returned to the system as a free extent. RLSE won't happen if the program abends.

- For multi-volume data sets, the RLSE subparameter releases any unused space on the current volume. (If any of the assigned volumes are completely unused, they're released regardless of whether or not the RLSE subparameter is coded.)

- The RLSE subparameter is not recommended for files that grow over time because of the possibility of *volume fragmentation* (free space on a volume is spread out over a large number of small extents).

- If you allocate a data set's space in terms of blocks, specifying the ROUND subparameter will convert the block allocation into cylinders. Doing so will cause the data set to begin and end at a cylinder boundary, which may increase performance.

- Specifying CYL or TRK as the space allocation unit on the SPACE parameter will cause the ROUND subparameter to be ignored.

Figure 6-8   How to code the RLSE and ROUND subparameters

The third example in figure 6-8 shows you how to code the ROUND subparameter. Notice that three commas are required to mark the omission of two positional subparameters (RLSE and CONTIG/MXIG/ALX). Also notice that the primary and secondary space is specified in terms of 3200-byte blocks. ROUND is ignored if you allocate space in terms of tracks or cylinders.

How to code the CONTIG, MXIG, and ALX subparameters

If OS/390 can't locate an extent large enough to accommodate a file's primary space allocation, up to five extents will be combined. The resulting allocation will be the proper size, but two problems result. First, the space consists of two or more areas of DASD space that aren't adjacent; that is, they aren't *contiguous*. This can lead to slower processing and job performance. Second, each extent counts toward the extent limit. So, your primary allocation might use 5 of the file's 16 available extents. That could prove to be a problem if you expect the file to grow.

The CONTIG, MXIG, and ALX subparameters shown in figure 6-9 each address those problems by specifying that the primary space should be allocated using contiguous cylinders. You'll probably use CONTIG the most frequently, if at all. When you specify CONTIG, as shown in the first example, you tell the system that the primary allocation must be met with a single extent of contiguous cylinders. If the volume doesn't contain a free extent large enough to hold the primary allocation, the system terminates the job step. CONTIG applies only to the primary allocation amount; secondary allocations can still use up to five extents each. Notice in the example that an extra comma is coded to indicate that the positional RLSE subparameter is omitted.

MXIG is similar to CONTIG, except that it tells OS/390 to allocate the largest available free extent on the volume to your file. When you use MXIG, the primary allocation amount you specify indicates the minimum size of the file. As a result, OS/390 won't allocate an extent that's smaller than the primary allocation amount. The most common use of MXIG is to allocate an empty volume to a single file, so you won't code it very often.

ALX takes the function of MXIG one step further. With it, you can allocate up to five extents, each of which is at least as large as the primary allocation amount. ALX is designed to allocate all of the remaining space on a DASD volume to your file, but it accomplishes that only if there are five or fewer free extents on the volume. Like MXIG, I don't expect you to use ALX often.

Although you can use the MXIG or ALX subparameter to allocate an empty volume to a single file, IBM recommends that you use extreme caution when coding either subparameter. Depending on how much free space is available at the time the job step is executed, large amounts of space can be allocated. So if you have to use either subparameter, be sure to include the RLSE subparameter whenever possible to release unused space after the job step ends.

How to code the CONTIG, MXIG, and ALX subparameters

Example 1

```
//EMPMAST  DD   DSNAME=MMA1.EMPLOYEE.MASTER,DISP=(,CATLG,DELETE),
//              UNIT=SYSDA,SPACE=(CYL,(100,20),,CONTIG)
```

The primary allocation (100 cylinders) must be obtained from contiguous cylinders.

Example 2

```
//EMPMAST  DD   DSNAME=MMA1.EMPLOYEE.MASTER,DISP=(,CATLG,DELETE),
//              UNIT=SYSDA,VOL=SER=MVS300,
//              SPACE=(CYL,(100,20),RLSE,MXIG)
```

Obtains the largest extent available on the volume for the file's primary allocation. It must be at least 100 cylinders.

Example 3

```
//EMPMAST  DD   DSNAME=MMA1.EMPLOYEE.MASTER,DISP=(,CATLG,DELETE),
//              UNIT=SYSDA,VOL=SER=MVS300,
//              SPACE=(CYL,(100,20),RLSE,ALX)
```

Obtains up to five extents, each of which must be at least 100 cylinders, as the file's primary allocation.

Description

- To ensure that the primary space allocated to a data set uses contiguous (adjacent) cylinders, you can code the CONTIG, MXIG, or ALX subparameter as part of the SPACE parameter.

- Specifying the CONTIG subparameter tells the system that the primary space allocation for the data set must be made up of a single extent of contiguous cylinders. If the system can't find a free extent that's large enough, the job step will abend.

- Specifying the MXIG subparameter tells the system to allocate the largest available free extent on the volume to your file. It must be at least as large as the primary allocation amount.

- Specifying the ALX subparameter tells the system to allocate up to five extents, each at least as large as the primary allocation amount.

- IBM recommends that you use extreme caution when coding either MXIG or ALX because both subparameters have the ability to allocate large amounts of free space. Whenever possible, include the RLSE subparameter to free any unused space.

Figure 6-9   How to code the CONTIG, MXIG, and ALX subparameters

Other ways to allocate data sets

Usually, you'll code the DD statement as you've seen so far in this book when you want to allocate a data set. On occasion, though, you may want to use referbacks or the IEFBR14 program for data set allocation, or you may see these techniques used in other job streams at your installation.

How to obtain information from a previous DD statement

You can use a JCL facility called *backwards reference* or *referback* to obtain information from a previous DD statement within the same job, rather than code the information again. For example, if you want to allocate several data sets with the same DCB information, you can specify the DCB information on just the first DD statement. Then, you can code a referback in the DCB parameter on subsequent DD statements to copy the DCB information from the first statement.

Figure 6-10 shows the general format for a referback and gives you a list of the parameters that can use this facility. If the DD statement you want to reference is in a previous job step, the referback reference must include the step name as well as the ddname for the statement. However, if the DD statement is in the same job step, only the ddname is needed. If you use the referback facility on the VOLUME parameter, you must code VOL=REF instead of VOL=SER.

To get a better idea of how referbacks work, take a look at the job in this figure. The first DD statement in STEP1 is fairly straightforward. It allocates a data set with a ddname of TRANFILE. The next DD statement allocates another file that uses a referback for its DCB information. In this case, it will use the same DCB values that TRANFILE does.

The program in STEP2 reads in the TRANFILE data set produced in STEP1. Here, though, instead of giving the data set name, the DSNAME parameter simply refers back to it. The output file, TRANOUT, then uses the referback facility to reference the volume serial number and DCB values used by TRANFILE.

You can also use a referback in the PGM parameter of an EXEC statement, as shown in STEP5. This might seem odd, but remember that the PGM parameter names a member of a partitioned data set. Here, then, STEP5 will execute the PDS member defined by the LOADMOD DD statement in STEP3.

You probably won't use the referback facility often. In general, coding a referback is more error-prone than just duplicating the parameter you're referring to, and the ISPF editor makes it easy to copy code from a previous statement. Referbacks are best used in situations where you want to be sure several DD statements use the same parameter values and you expect those values to change frequently. In that case, you can set up your job so you have to change the parameter values in only one DD statement, then have all the other statements obtain the values through referbacks. However, JCL procedures, which you'll learn about in chapter 9, have better facilities for dealing with situations like this.

The general syntax for a referback

```
parameter=*.[stepname.]ddname
```

Parameters that can use the referback facility

```
DD CNTL
DD DCB
DD DSNAME
DD REFDD  (SMS only)
DD VOL=REF
EXEC PGM
```

A job that uses referbacks

```
//MM01AR    JOB   (36512),LYNCH,MSGCLASS=X,MSGLEVEL=(1,1),
//                CLASS=A,NOTIFY=&SYSUID
//STEP1     EXEC PGM=TRANS
//TRANFILE  DD    DSNAME=AR.TRANS.FILE,DISP=(NEW,KEEP),
//                UNIT=SYSDA,VOL=SER=MPS800,
//                SPACE=(CYL,(5,1)),
//                DCB=(DSORG=PS,RECFM=FB,LRECL=80)
//TRANERR   DD    DSNAME=AR.TRANS.ERR,DISP=(NEW,KEEP),
//                UNIT=SYSDA,VOL=SER=MPS801,
//                SPACE=(CYL,(2,1)),
//                DCB=*.TRANFILE
//STEP2     EXEC PGM=TRANSEP
//TRANIN    DD    DSNAME=*.STEP1.TRANFILE,DISP=SHR
//TRANOUT   DD    DSNAME=AR.TRANS.A.FILE,DISP=(NEW,KEEP),
//                UNIT=SYSDA,VOL=REF=*.STEP1.TRANFILE,
//                SPACE=(CYL,(5,1)),
//                DCB=*.STEP1.TRANFILE
   .
   .
   .
//STEP5     EXEC PGM=*.STEP3.LOADMOD
   .
   .
   .
```

Description

- Using the JCL facility called *backwards reference* or *referback* lets you obtain information from previous DD statements within the job. In other words, instead of coding all the parameters needed to allocate the data set, you can copy certain ones from a previous DD statement.

- Referbacks are best used in situations where several DD statements use the same parameters, and you expect those parameter values to change frequently.

- A referback can also be used in the PGM parameter of an EXEC statement when the DD statement it refers to allocates a member of a partitioned data set that's an executable program.

- If the DD statement you're referring to is in a previous job step, the referback must include the stepname for that step.

Figure 6-10   How to obtain information from a previous DD statement

How to use the IEFBR14 program to allocate data sets

The final data set allocation facility that you'll learn about in this chapter is not another DD statement parameter, subparameter, or coding feature. Instead, it's a special IBM-supplied program called IEFBR14 that you invoke with an EXEC statement.

IEFBR14 is unusual in that it doesn't do anything. In fact, its name is derived from an assembler language instruction that causes a return to the program that called it: a branch (BR) to register 14, which contains the address to return to after a call. In the case of IEFBR14, the BR14 instruction returns control directly to OS/390. That's all IEFBR14 does; it doesn't open or close data sets or do any other processing. When it's invoked, it returns immediately to OS/390.

IEFBR14 is useful, however, because it forces the system to perform step allocation and deallocation. In other words, even though the program itself doesn't do anything, it forces OS/390 to process any DD statements you include in the job step that executes it. As a result, any data sets you create by specifying DISP=(NEW,KEEP) or DISP=(NEW,CATLG) are allocated and kept or cataloged. Likewise, you can delete or uncatalog a data set by specifying DISP=(OLD,DELETE) or DISP=(OLD,UNCATLG). Figure 6-11 shows a simple IEFBR14 job step that creates one data set and deletes another.

In the past, IEFBR14 was the standard way of creating empty data sets or deleting data sets that were no longer needed. With TSO/E and ISPF, however, those functions can be done interactively. So if you have access to TSO/E or ISPF, you probably won't use IEFBR14 much.

An IEFBR14 job step

```
//STEP1     EXEC PGM=IEFBR14
//DD1       DD   DSNAME=MM01.COPYLIB.COBOL,DISP=(NEW,CATLG),
//               UNIT=SYSDA,VOL=SER=MPS8BV,
//               SPACE=(3200,(1000,250,5),,,ROUND),
//               DCB=(DSORG=PO,RECFM=FB,LRECL=80)
//DD2       DD   DSNAME=MM01.TEST.DATA,DISP=(OLD,DELETE)
```

Causes OS/390 to allocate and catalog the data set named MM01.COPYLIB.COBOL and delete the data set named MM01.TEST.DATA.

Description

- IEFBR14 is an IBM-supplied program that doesn't do anything. Instead, it performs an assembler language command that causes it to return control to OS/390 and terminate. This, however, also forces OS/390 to allocate and deallocate any data sets defined in the job step's DD statements.

- Although IEFBR14 was once the standard way of creating empty data sets or deleting data sets that were no longer needed, today you are more likely to use TSO/E or ISPF to perform these functions interactively.

Figure 6-11   How to use the IEFBR14 program to allocate data sets

Perspective

The DD statement parameters and coding techniques presented in this chapter give you more flexibility and more control when it comes to allocating DASD data sets. Although you'll use temporary data sets the most, the other features will come in handy in certain jobs. Now, you're ready to learn more about allocating two other types of data sets you'll use regularly: tape data sets (covered in the next chapter) and SYSOUT data sets (covered in chapter 8).

Terms

temporary data set
work file
pass a data set
receive a data set
Virtual Input/Output facility
VIO
dummy data set
concatenate
multi-volume data set
volume fragmentation
contiguous extents
backwards reference
referback

7

How to manage tape data sets

Although DASD data sets are used for the processing done by most business applications, tape data sets are still used on a daily basis in most IBM shops. That's because tape is still a cost-effective way to store data offline, and it's still a convenient way to transfer data to or from a mainframe system. As a result, you need to know how to manage data sets on tape, and that's what you'll learn in this chapter.

Introduction to tape data sets

To a large extent, processing a tape data set is like processing a sequential DASD data set. In fact, when you develop an application program, it doesn't matter much whether the sequential file is on DASD or tape. When you code JCL, though, it does matter. So you have to understand some basic tape concepts, how the labels on tapes are arranged, and how to use the DD statement parameters that are specific to tape data sets.

Tape concepts

In chapter 1, you learned how a tape drive reads and writes sequential data sets on magnetic tape. Originally, most tape drives used *tape reels* to store data sets. Depending on the *density* of the tape and how many tracks were written to it, you were able to store anywhere from 26 to 170 megabytes of information on each tape reel.

Although tape reels are still used today in some shops, most use 3590 *tape cartridges* instead. These tape cartridges have much higher densities than tape reels so each cartridge can store 10 to 20 gigabytes of information and three times that amount if the data is compressed. Tape cartridges are also smaller than tape reels, more durable, and easier to store.

Tape was once a popular way to store active sequential files that were used for daily processing. However, with the abundance of inexpensive DASD today, you use tape most often to back up data sets stored on disk, as shown in the diagram in figure 7-1. Here, a backup utility program copies a master file to a tape data set on one or more *tape volumes*…either tape reels or cartridges.

Although backup is the main use for tape data sets today, you may also use them for other purposes in your shop. For example, most companies are required to keep records of their transactions for at least seven to ten years. Keeping all of this data on DASD doesn't always make sense. Instead, data like this is often archived to tape, usually with an expiration date set for it. Once that date is reached, the system is free to delete or write over the data sets stored on the tape. In the meantime, the data can still be accessed and used by any program just like any other sequential file.

Another use for tape data sets is to transfer files from one system to another, which is often needed when two companies merge. If both companies use mainframes, of course, transferring the tape data sets is usually trouble-free. That's also true when tape data sets from smaller systems are transferred to mainframes, provided that the tapes use standard labels. Occasionally, though, the tapes to be transferred have non-standard labels or no labels, which makes reading the files more difficult, but you'll still be able to do it by using the skills that you'll learn later in this chapter.

A typical file backup process

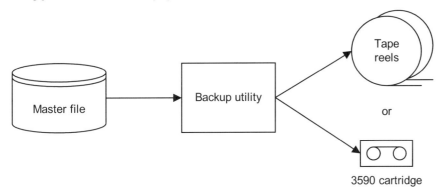

Reasons to store data on tape volumes

- To back up copies of data sets currently residing on DASD
- To archive older data sets no longer needed for day-to-day processing
- To transfer or distribute large quantities of information to other computer systems

Tape volumes and their capacities

Reel-to-reel system	Capacity
1600 bpi 9-track tape	26MB
6250 bpi 9-track tape	170MB

3590 cartridge subsystems	Capacity
High Performance tape/compressed	10GB/30GB
Extended High Performance tape/compressed	20GB/60GB

Description

- The two main types of tape storage are the *tape reel* and the 3590 *tape cartridge*. The 3590 tape cartridge has essentially replaced the older-style reel because of its superior storage capacity and greater durability.
- Each tape reel or tape cartridge is referred to as a *tape volume*.
- The *density* of a tape determines how much data can be stored on it. Density is measured in *bytes per inch* (*bpi*), which is the number of bytes of data that are stored per inch of tape. Some reel-to-reel tape drives can be set to store data at more than one density.
- A cartridge tape allows for *data compaction*, meaning that the data on the tape can be compressed to make more efficient use of storage.

Figure 7-1   Tape concepts

The labels on tape data sets

As you learned in chapter 2, the data sets on a tape volume are stored with labels. Figure 7-2 shows three arrangements of tape labels and data records. The first one, which is the most common case, shows how one data set is stored on one tape volume. The second one shows a *multi-volume file*, which means that one file requires more than one volume. And the third one shows a *multi-file volume*, which means that more than one file is stored on a single volume.

In all three cases, each volume starts with a *volume label* that includes identifying information like the volume serial number. This label is followed by at least one *file header label* that includes identifying information like the data set name. These labels are often referred to as the *VOL1 label* and *HDR1 label*.

The data records for a file come right after the header labels for the file, and each file ends with at least one *end-of-file label*, which is also known as a *file trailer label* or *EOF1 label*. For a multi-volume file, each volume except the last one ends with at least one *end-of-volume label*, or *EOV1 label*.

The labels are used by the operating system to make sure that the right volume is mounted and the right file is ready for processing. This is referred to as *label processing*. Although this processing can be complicated by the use of two file header labels, two file trailer labels, and optional user labels, the essential purpose of label processing is to make sure the right volumes and files are processed.

For data sets that are created and processed on an IBM mainframe, *IBM standard labels* are normally used. This processing assumes that the labels and data are stored in *EBCDIC format*, which is the standard format that is used by all IBM mainframes.

For data sets that are created and processed on other platforms, though, *ISO/ANSI/FIPS standard labels* are commonly used, and the labels and data are stored in *ASCII format*. This means that if a tape from some other platform is processed by an IBM mainframe, the mainframe has to convert the data from ASCII to EBCDIC and process the ISO/ANSI/FIPS standard labels. This, however, is done automatically when the label type is specified correctly in the DD statement for the data set. You'll see how this works later on.

Be aware, too, that tapes created on any platform can have non-standard labels or no labels at all instead of standard labels. Again, you can code a label type in the DD statement that helps you with processing a data set on a tape like this. However, it often takes some trial-and-error to access the records correctly when a tape is unlabelled or has non-standard labels.

The labels on a tape volume that contains just one file

Volume labels	File header labels	Data records	End-of-file labels	Unused

The labels for a file that requires four volumes (a multi-volume file)

Volume labels	File header labels	Data records	End-of-volume labels

Volume labels	File header labels	Data records	End-of-volume labels

Volume labels	File header labels	Data records	End-of-volume labels

Volume labels	File header labels	Data records	End-of-file labels	Unused

The labels for a volume that contains two files (a multi-file volume)

Volume labels	File header labels	Data records	End-of-file labels	File header labels	Data records	End-of-file labels

Description

- A tape volume begins with a *volume label* that provides the volume's serial number. This label is often referred to as the *VOL1 label* because VOL1 is stored in the first four characters of a standard volume label.

- After the volume label is a *file header label* that identifies the first file on the tape by providing its file name. This is often referred to as the *HDR1 label* because HDR1 is stored in the first four characters of a standard file header label.

- The data records for the file come after the file header label, and an *end-of-file label* (also called a *file trailer label* or *EOF1 label*) comes after the data records.

- If a file requires more than one volume, an *end-of-volume label* (or *EOV1 label*) is stored at the end of each volume, except the last volume for the file.

- There may be a second standard header label called the HDR2 label after the HDR1 label for each file, and there may be a second standard end-of-file label called the EOF2 label after the EOF1 label for each file.

- On IBM mainframes, *IBM standard labels* are typically used for tape data sets and the data is stored in *EBCDIC format*. On other types of systems, *ISO/ANSI/FIPS standard labels* and *ASCII format* are used.

- Although standard labels are the norm, tapes can also have non-standard labels or be unlabelled.

Figure 7-2   The labels on tape data sets

The DD statement for tape data sets

Figure 7-3 presents the DD statement parameters that you can use for tape data sets. Here, the only parameters that are new are the RETPD, EXPDT, and LABEL parameters. RETPD and EXPDT let you set a time limit for how long a data set should be kept, and LABEL is the parameter that you use to specify the label type. In addition, you're going to learn to use some subparameters for the UNIT, VOLUME (VOL), and DCB parameters that apply specifically to tape data sets. Otherwise, you code the DD statement for a tape data set much as you do for a sequential DASD data set.

For instance, for an existing tape data set that's cataloged, you only need to code the DSNAME and DISP parameters. This is illustrated by the first example in this figure. Then, the operating system gets the name and volume serial number from the catalog, and the label processing routines check to make sure that the right volume has been mounted and the right data set is available for processing.

Similarly, to allocate an uncataloged data set, you can code the UNIT and VOLUME parameters. In the second example, you can see that one tape volume has been specified for the file. In the third example, you can see that four volumes have been specified for a multi-volume file. And in the fourth example, you can see that no volume has been specified so the operating system will select one for you.

The syntax of a DD statement for a tape data set

```
//ddname    DD  DSNAME=data-set-name,DISP=(status,normal-disp,abnormal-disp)
            [ ,UNIT=(subparameters) ]
            [ ,VOL=(subparameters) ]
            [ ,RETPD=nnnn | EXPDT=date ]
            [ ,LABEL=(subparameters) ]
            [ ,DCB=(options) ]
```

Explanation

DSNAME	Specifies the data set's name.
DISP	Specifies the data set's status and normal and abnormal disposition.
UNIT	Can be used to specify a unit address, generic name, or group name that identifies the device where the file resides, but it also has some special subparameters for tape data sets. Not required for cataloged data sets.
VOL	Can be used to specify the volume serial number of the volume that contains the file, but it also has some special subparameters for tape data sets. Not required for cataloged data sets.
RETPD I EXPDT	Can be used to specify how long the data set should be considered current.
LABEL	Can be used to (1) specify which data set of a multi-file volume you want to process, and (2) indicate what format is used for the labels on the volume.
DCB	Can be used to specify tape options for the file's data control block.

Examples of simple DD statements for tape data sets

The allocation of an existing cataloged data set

```
//JOURNAL   DD    DSNAME=MMA2.AR.JOURNAL,DISP=OLD
```

The allocation of an existing uncataloged data set

```
//JOURNAL   DD    DSNAME=MMA2.AR.JOURNAL,DISP=OLD,
                  UNIT=TAPE,VOL=SER=300123
```

The allocation of an existing, uncataloged multi-volume data set

```
//JOURNAL   DD    DSNAME=MMA2.AR.JOURNAL,DISP=OLD,
                  UNIT=TAPE,
                  VOL=SER=(300123,300124,300125,300126)
```

The allocation of a new data set on an unspecified tape volume

```
//JOURNAL   DD    DSNAME=MMA2.AR.JOURNAL,DISP=(NEW,CATLG,DELETE),
                  UNIT=TAPE
```

Description

- The DSNAME and DISP parameters for tape data sets are coded just as they are for DASD data sets. For existing cataloged data sets, these are the only parameters you need to code.

- For some uncataloged tape data sets, you can code the UNIT and VOLUME (VOL) parameters much as you do for DASD data sets. In the UNIT parameter, you can use a generic name like 3590 or a group name like TAPE.

- For special types of tape processing, you need to code the UNIT, VOL, RETPD, EXPDT, LABEL, and DCB parameters as shown in the figures that follow.

Figure 7-3   The DD statement for tape data sets

How to code the DD statement parameters for tape data sets

The next five topics show you how to use the UNIT, VOLUME, RETPD, EXPDT, LABEL, and DCB parameters for tape data sets. Although you may never need to use some of the parameters and subparameters that are presented, you should at least know what they can do.

How to code the UNIT parameter

Figure 7-4 shows how to code the subparameters of the UNIT parameter. Of these, the most important one is the count subparameter, which lets you specify the number of tape units that you want used for a multi-volume file. Normally, this is coded as 2 or more so the operator can mount a tape volume on one unit while a tape volume on another unit is being processed. If only one unit is assigned to a multi-volume data set (the default), the job that's running has to wait while one tape volume is rewound and dismounted and the next tape volume is mounted.

The other two subparameters are used infrequently. The DEFER subparameter means that the volume shouldn't be mounted until the program that's running opens the file. But that means that the program has to wait once the file is opened while the operator mounts the tape volume. As a result, this only makes sense for a tape data set that *could* be processed by the program but normally isn't.

In contrast, the AFF (affinity) parameter means that a data set should be processed on the same unit that was used by an earlier data set in the same job step. This can be referred to as *unit affinity*. Because both data sets are processed by the same program, this only makes sense when the program completely processes one data set before it processes the next one. Nevertheless, this can be useful when you're creating and reading multi-file volumes.

The syntax for the UNIT parameter

```
{UNIT=(unit[,count][,DEFER])}
{UNIT=AFF=ddname}
```

Explanation

unit	Specifies the unit as a group name (like TAPE), device type (like 3590), or device number (a hexadecimal value).
count	Specifies how many of the requested unit type should be allocated.
DEFER	Specifies that the unit should be allocated when the step is initialized, but the requested volume should not be mounted on the unit until the data set is opened.
AFF	Specifies unit affinity, so the unit information is obtained from the DD statement for the specified ddname. This ddname must be allocated in the same job step.

Examples of UNIT parameters

A request for two tape drives
```
UNIT=(TAPE,2)
```

A request that defers the mounting of the tape until the data set is opened
```
UNIT=(TAPE,,DEFER)
```

A request for the same tape drive that was used for the data set described by the DD statement for TAPEDD1
```
UNIT=AFF=TAPEDD1
```

Description

- To allocate an existing cataloged data set, you don't have to code the UNIT parameter. However, you may need to code this parameter to provide for the three conditions that follow.
- To allocate more than one tape unit to a multi-volume data set, you can code the count subparameter. Then, the operator can mount the volumes of the file on the units that are specified. The value 2 is commonly coded for this subparameter so the operator can mount the next volume on one unit while the previous volume is being processed on the other unit.
- To defer the mounting of a tape volume until the related data set is opened, you can code the DEFER subparameter. This makes sense when there's a good chance that the data set won't be needed. DEFER is ignored on a DASD data set.
- To request *unit affinity*, you code the AFF subparameter. Then, that data set is processed on the same unit that was used for an earlier data set in the same job step. This only makes sense when the program completely processes one data set before it opens the next data set.

Figure 7-4 How to code the UNIT parameter for tape data sets

How to code the VOLUME parameter

Figure 7-5 shows how you can code the VOLUME parameter for a tape data set. As you can see, the first two subparameters apply to private volumes and the retention of a volume on a tape unit; the next two apply to multi-volume files; and the last one (SER) identifies the volumes for single- or multi-volume files, much as it does for DASD files.

In fact, one way to provide the volumes of a multi-volume file is to use the SER subparameter to specify the volume serial numbers as shown in the first example. Then, the operating system issues operator messages that specify which volumes to mount and in what sequence as the job is run. In this case, if the file doesn't require all of the volumes, the unused volumes are ignored.

Note, however, that you don't have to request specific volumes when you create a tape data set. If you omit the SER subparameter, the operating system tells the operator to mount a *scratch volume* (one with no data or expired data) on each of the units you allocate. This technique will work as long as you catalog the data set and make sure that it doesn't require more than five volumes.

If a file does require more than five volumes, you can code the volume-count subparameter to indicate how many volumes are likely to be needed. This is illustrated by the second example. As you can see in the explanation for this subparameter, if the count that you supply is over 20, it's increased by the operating system so it becomes a multiple of 15 plus 5.

If you need to start the processing of a job step with a volume other than the first one for a file, you can code the volume-sequence subparameter as shown in the third example in this figure. In this case, processing starts with the third volume instead of the first one. This can be useful if the processing for the first two volumes worked correctly, but an error occurred in the processing for the third volume. By using this subparameter, you can restart the job at the third volume and continue with all of the remaining volumes for the file.

If you want to identify a tape volume that you can use for your own private files, you can code the PRIVATE subparameter in the VOL parameter. Then, when the job step ends, the operating system rewinds and unloads the tape. Later, when you want to access the files on that volume, you must specifically request the volume by coding the SER subparameter as shown by the fourth example in this figure.

If you want to specify that a volume remain mounted on the tape unit after the job step is completed, you code the RETAIN parameter. This is useful when the volume is going to be needed by a later job step, and it can be used for a private volume as illustrated by the last example in this figure.

Please note that the first four VOLUME subparameters are positional, so if you omit one, you need to code a comma to mark its place as shown in the examples. The SER subparameter, however, is a keyword parameter, so it can be coded at any point.

The syntax for the VOLUME parameter

```
VOL=([PRIVATE][,RETAIN][,volume-sequence][,volume-count]
    [,SER=(serial,serial,...)])
```

Explanation

PRIVATE	Specifies that a private volume should be used. This volume should be dismounted when the step completes (unless RETAIN or DISP=(,PASS) is also coded), and this volume won't be used again unless specifically requested.
RETAIN	Specifies that the volume should remain mounted when the job step completes.
volume-sequence	For an existing multi-volume data set, this subparameter indicates that processing should begin at a volume that isn't the first volume. The volume sequence number can be from 1 to 255. This is ignored for a new data set.
volume-count	Specifies the maximum number of volumes that a multi-volume output data set will require. If you omit this count or specify 5 or less, 5 is used. If you specify a value between 6 and 20, 20 is used. And if you specify a value greater than 20, a multiple of 15 plus 5 is used (35, 50, 65, and so on, up to 255).
SER	Specifies one or more volume serial numbers for a specific volume request. You can specify up to 255 volume serial numbers.

Examples of VOLUME parameters

A specific request for four named volumes
```
VOL=SER=(163013,163014,163015,163016)
```

A non-specific request for up to 20 volumes
```
VOL=(,,,20)
```

A request for the third volume of a multi-volume data set
```
VOL=(,,3)
```

A specific request for two private volumes
```
VOL=(PRIVATE,SER=(MMA301,MMA302))
```

A specific request for a private volume that shouldn't be dismounted
```
VOL=(PRIVATE,RETAIN,SER=MMA400)
```

Description

- You don't have to code the VOLUME parameter when you create a new data set as long as you catalog it and it doesn't require more than five volumes.

- To request more than five volumes, you can use the volume-count subparameter.

- To request a private volume, you can code the PRIVATE subparameter. Once it's established as private, the volume must be specifically requested by volume serial number.

- To request that a volume not be rewound and unloaded at the end of a job step, you can code the RETAIN subparameter. Then, a subsequent job step can access the volume.

- To start the processing of a multi-volume file with a volume other than the first one, you can code the volume-sequence subparameter.

Figure 7-5   How to code the VOLUME parameter for tape data sets

How to code the RETPD and EXPDT parameters

Although you may need some of your data sets to stay on a tape volume for a specified or legal amount of time, you probably won't want to keep them on a shelf in your operations center forever. Instead, you'll eventually want to reuse the volume to store other data sets. That's why the DD statement provides the RETPD parameter and the EXPDT parameter that allow you to set the *retention period* or the *expiration date* for a file. Figure 7-6 includes the syntax for both parameters.

To set a retention period for a data set, you code the RETPD parameter with a value in days. This figure illustrates how to do this for a data set named MMA2.LN.MASTER. Here, the retention period is 30 days from the current date. So for a data set that's created on January 1, the operating system sets the expiration date to January 31. Once the calculated date is reached, the data set can be deleted or written over by another data set.

To set an expiration date for a data set, you code the EXPDT parameter with a *Julian date* value. In this figure, data set MMA2.AR.JOURNAL has an expiration date of 2002/365. That means that on December 31, 2002, the data set can be deleted or written over by another data set. Incidentally, specifying an EXPDT date of 1999/365 or 1999/366 indicates that the data set is never to be deleted or written over.

If a job is going to be used repeatedly, or if you place it in production, you should use the RETPD parameter to set any expiration dates within it. That's because RETPD will calculate the expiration date based on the current date. If you use the EXPDT parameter, you'll have to change the date each time the job is run.

The syntax for the RETPD parameter

```
RETPD=nnnn
```

Explanation

nnnn   Specifies a retention period in days for a data set. The four-digit number can be from 0 to 9999.

The syntax for the EXPDT parameter

```
EXPDT= {yyyy/ddd}
```

Explanation

yyyy/ddd   Specifies the expiration date for a data set. The format consists of a four-digit year from 1900 to 2155 followed by a three-digit day from 000 to 365 or 366 for leap years.

A RETPD parameter that sets a retention period of 30 days

```
//LNMAST    DD    DSNAME=MMA2.LN.MASTER,DISP=(NEW,KEEP),
                  UNIT=TAPE,VOL=SER=300123,RETPD=30
```

An EXPDT parameter that sets the expiration date to the last day of 2002

```
//JOURNAL   DD    DSNAME=MMA2.AR.JOURNAL,DISP=(NEW,CATLG,DELETE)
                  UNIT=TAPE,EXPDT=2002/365
```

Description

- To set a *retention period* for a tape data set, you code the number of days that the data set should be retained in the RETPD parameter on its DD statement. The system will add the number of days specified to the current date to produce an expiration date. Then, once the calculated date is reached, the data set can be deleted or written over by another data set.

- To set an *expiration date* for a tape data set, you code the EXPDT parameter with a *Julian date* value on the DD statement that defines the data set. Once the expiration date is reached, the data set can be deleted or written over by another data set.

- EXPDT parameter dates of 1999/365 or 1999/366 are never deleted or written over.

- You can't code both the RETPD and EXPDT parameters for the same data set.

Figure 7-6   How to code the RETPD and EXPDT parameters for tape data sets

How to code the LABEL parameter

The LABEL parameter is one that applies specifically to tape data sets, and it is summarized in figure 7-7. Although the LABEL parameter includes additional subparameters that aren't listed here, they're rarely used.

The example in this figure shows you how you can access an uncataloged data set on a multi-file tape volume when it's not the next data set in sequence on the tape. The DD statement specifies that data set MMA2.AR.JOURNAL is the third file on tape volume 300127. Although you don't need to code this parameter if the file is cataloged or passed from a previous job step, you do need to code it if it isn't. Otherwise, the first data set is processed (provided that the label information like the data set name and the volume serial number is correct).

If you're using IBM standard labels for your data sets, you don't need to use the label-type subparameter of the LABEL parameter. But if you are working with a file that has special labels, be aware that the label information isn't stored in the system's catalog. That means that even if the data set you're accessing is cataloged, you'll still need to include its label type and perhaps its data set sequence in the LABEL parameter, as shown in the next figure. Otherwise, the IBM standard of SL will be assumed, which can give you unexpected results.

The syntax for the LABEL parameter

```
LABEL=([data-set-sequence][,label-type])
```

Explanation

data-set-sequence   A one- to four-digit number indicating the relative position of the file on the volume. If you omit this subparameter or code 0 or 1, the first data set is processed unless the data set is cataloged or is a passed temporary data set, in which case the data set sequence number is obtained from the catalog or the original DD statement.

label-type   Specifies the format of the tape's label as shown in the next figure. SL (for IBM standard labels) is the default.

A LABEL parameter that requests the third file on a multi-file tape volume

```
//JOURNAL  DD   DSNAME=MMA2.AR.JOURNAL,DISP=OLD
               UNIT=TAPE,VOL=SER=300127,LABEL=3
```

Two reasons why you may need to code the LABEL parameter for a tape data set

- To read an uncataloged data set that isn't the first one on a tape volume.
- To process a data set that doesn't have IBM standard labels.

Description

- The data-set-sequence subparameter allows you to access an uncataloged data set on a multi-file tape volume out of sequence.

- You can omit the data-set-sequence subparameter if the data set is cataloged or if it's passed from a previous job step. That's because the system gets the sequence number from the catalog or from the passing step.

- The label-type subparameter specifies the type of label processing to be done for a tape data set that doesn't use IBM standard labels. This is typically the case for tapes generated on other types of systems.

- The system doesn't retain label information for a data set even if it's cataloged. That means that you need to specify the LABEL parameter on all non-IBM standard tape data sets, or the default SL type will be assumed.

- Although several other subparameters can be coded on the LABEL parameter, they aren't included here because they're rarely used. Two of them that you may see in older job streams, however, are RETPD and EXPDT. Although they were originally part of the LABEL parameter, IBM now recommends that you code them as separate parameters as shown in figure 7-6.

Figure 7-7   How to code the LABEL parameter for tape data sets

How to use the LABEL parameter to specify label formats

Figure 7-8 summarizes the eight types of label processing that you can request by coding the label-type subparameter of the LABEL parameter. If you're using IBM standard labels without user labels and you want standard label processing, you don't have to code this parameter. But in any other case, you do need to code it.

To start, you need to realize that *user labels* can be used with both IBM standard labels and ISO/ANSI/FIPS standard labels. When used, these labels follow the standard file header labels, and user routines are called to process them. In this case, you need to code SUL or AUL to alert the operating system that user labels are present.

As you learned earlier in this chapter, when tape data sets are created on non-IBM platforms, they usually have ISO/ANSI/FIPS labels, and the data is stored in ASCII format instead of EBCDIC format. To process these files, though, all you need to do is specify AL (or AUL if user labels are present). Then, the operating system will process the labels and convert the ASCII data to EBCDIC. Similarly, if you need to create a tape data set that can be processed on another platform, you can specify AL or AUL so the operating system will create the file in ASCII format with ISO/ANSI/FIPS labels.

Sometimes, though, the files that are created on other platforms have non-standard labels. Then, if you specify NSL, the operating system will try to find user routines for processing the non-standard labels. The other alternative is to specify BLP or LTM to skip the label processing entirely. Which one of these you use depends on whether the volume starts with a *tapemark*. This is a special indicator that is used on all types of tapes to separate sets of labels and data records for a file. Most tapes don't have a leading tapemark, but you can use LTM to process one that does.

When you bypass label processing, however, you usually need to code the data-set-sequence subparameter to indicate the location of the data records that you want processed. That's because the system treats the labels or data before each tapemark as a separate data set. For example, on an SL tape, the first tapemark comes after the volume header label and the first set of header labels, so those labels are data set sequence 1. The actual data records for the first file are data set sequence 2. The trailer records for the first file are data set sequence 3. The header records for the next file are data set sequence 4. And so on. In the third example in this figure, you can see that label processing is bypassed and the data records for the first file on the volume are supposed to be processed. With a poorly documented tape, though, you may not know for sure how the tapemarks are used, so it may take a few tries to get the data records that you want.

The last type of tape that you may encounter is an unlabelled tape. In this case, you code the label-type subparameter as NL, and the system reads the data before the first tapemark as the first data set on the volume. If the data records that you want aren't in the first data set on the volume, though, you need to code the data-set-sequence subparameter. Here again, with a poorly documented tape, it may take you a few tries to read the records that you want.

Valid codes for the label-type subparameter of the LABEL parameter

Code	Meaning
SL	The tape has standard IBM labels (the default).
SUL	The tape has standard IBM labels as well as user labels.
AL	The tape has ISO/ANSI/FIPS version 3 labels.
AUL	The tape has ISO/ANSI/FIPS version 3 labels and user labels.
NSL	The tape has non-standard labels.
NL	The tape has no labels.
BLP	The tape may or may not have labels, but label processing is bypassed.
LTM	Same as BLP, except that the leading tapemark on the volume is skipped.

Examples of LABEL parameters

Specifies IBM standard labels with user labels
```
LABEL=(,SUL)
```

Specifies processing of the fourth data set and ISO/ANSI/FIPS standard labels
```
LABEL=(4,AL)
```

Specifies that label processing be bypassed and that the second data set be processed (which is the first set of data records on a tape with standard labels)
```
LABEL=(2,BLP)
```

Specifies that the tape volume is unlabelled
```
LABEL=(,NL)
```

Description

- When you use IBM standard labels, the data is written and read in EBCDIC format. When you use ISO/ANSI/FIPS labels, the data is written and read in ASCII format.

- When using standard labels, the header labels may be followed by one or more *user labels*. In those cases, you need to code SUL or AUL as the label type.

- If a volume has non-standard labels, you can code NSL as the label type. This assumes that the operating system calls installation-specific routines to process these labels.

- To process a tape volume that doesn't have labels, you can code NL as the label type. Then, the system's label processing routines aren't called at all except to make sure that the tape volume doesn't start with a standard VOL1 label.

- To bypass label processing altogether, you can code BLP or LTM. Although neither checks for the VOL1 label, LTM assumes the tape starts with a *tapemark*, while BLP doesn't (all tapes use tapemarks to separate sets of labels and data records, but most unlabelled tapes don't have a leading tapemark).

- If you use BLP for a labelled tape, you have to code the data-set-sequence subparameter.

- The data set sequence depends on the tapemark positions. For an SL tape, the first tapemark is after the volume labels and the first set of header labels, making them data set sequence 1. The first set of data records is data set sequence 2. For tapes with non-standard labels or no labels, it may take several tries to determine the tapemark positions.

Figure 7-8   How to use the LABEL parameter to specify label formats

How to code the DCB parameter

As you learned in chapter 4, the DCB parameter lets you specify the data set attributes that are stored in the data set's Data Control Block, and those attributes get stored in the data set's label. In general, then, you only need to code the DCB parameter for new data sets. And if the application program that creates the data set supplies all of the DCB attributes, you don't need to code the DCB parameter at all.

When you work with tape data sets, though, you need to code the DCB parameter when you use an unlabelled tape or you bypass label processing because the attributes can't be extracted from the label. You also can use three new subparameters for special types of tape processing.

Figure 7-9 summarizes the DCB subparameters that you can use for tape data sets. The first four are the same ones that you use for sequential DASD data sets, and they were presented in figure 4-16 of chapter 4. These are the ones you need to code for an unlabelled tape data set or when you bypass label processing.

In contrast, the last three subparameters in this figure apply specifically to tape data sets. If, for example, you set the OPTCD subparameter to Q, you specify that the data set should be read or written in ASCII format. Although you don't need to code this for ISO/ANSI/FIPS data sets, you do need to code it for ASCII files with non-standard labels or no labels at all.

The next subparameter applies to tape drives that can record data at two different densities. By default, a *dual-density tape drive* writes data at the highest density it's capable of using. In some cases, though, you may want to use the DEN subparameter to specify a lower density for an output file if you know the file's going to be read by a tape drive that only has a lower density. When a dual-density tape drive reads the tape, it automatically recognizes the density used and adjusts accordingly, so you don't need this parameter for input files.

For cartridge tape drives, you can use the last subparameter, TRTCH, to specify that the data should be compacted (compressed) when it is written on the cartridge. Later, when the tape is read, the drive automatically determines whether or not data compaction has been used and adjusts accordingly.

DCB subparameters for tape processing

```
DCB=([DSORG=PS] [,RECFM=x] [LRECL=n] [,BLKSIZE=n]
     [,OPTCD=Q]
     [,DEN=n]
     [,TRTCH={COMP}{NOCOMP}]
```

Explanation

OPTCD   Q means that the data set should be read and written in ASCII format.

DEN   Specifies the recording density for a dual-density tape drive as a single digit where 1=556 bpi, 2=800 bpi, 3=1600 bpi, and 4=6250 bpi.

TRTCH   Specifies whether or not data compaction is used for cartridge tape drives. The default is NOCOMP for no compaction.

Examples of DCB parameters

The data set should be written in ASCII format

```
DCB=(DSORG=PS,RECFM=FB,LRECL=80,BLKSIZE=4000,OPTCD=Q)
```

The data set should be written with 1600 bpi on a dual-density tape drive

```
DCB=(DSORG=PS,RECFM=FB,LRECL=80,BLKSIZE=4000,DEN=3)
```

The data set should be written with data compaction on a cartridge tape drive

```
DCB=(DSORG=PS,RECFM=FB,LRECL=80,BLKSIZE=4000,TRTCH=COMP)
```

Description

* The DSORG, RECFM, LRECL, and BLKSIZE subparameters are used just as they are for sequential DASD files.

* When you process an unlabelled tape or bypass label processing for a labelled tape, OS/390 doesn't check the DD DSNAME against the tape label. Also, because the DCB can't be extracted from the label, you must code complete DCB information in the DCB parameter.

* If you need to process an unlabelled tape or a tape with non-standard labels in ASCII format, you can code Q as the OPTCD subparameter.

* If you need to specify the density to be used for a file on a *dual-density tape drive*, you can code the DEN subparameter.

* If you need to specify that data compaction be used for a file on a cartridge tape drive, you can code the TRTCH subparameter.

Figure 7-9   How to code the DCB parameter for tape data sets

Perspective

Remember that tape data sets are commonly used for offline storage and for transferring data between two different platforms. That's why you're likely to work with them at some point in your career, although it probably won't be on a daily basis. Most of the time, the data sets will have standard labels so you'll be able to code simple DD statements for them. But if your installation uses tapes that were created outside your company, perhaps as the result of a merger or some other business arrangement, you may also need to handle tapes with non-standard labels or no labels at all. No matter what you encounter, though, you should be able to refer back to this chapter for the specific skills that you need.

Terms

tape reel	file header label	ASCII format
tape cartridge	HDR1 label	unit affinity
tape volume	end-of-file label	scratch volume
density	EOF1 label	retention period
bytes per inch	file trailer label	expiration date
bpi	end-of-volume label	Julian date
data compaction	EOV1 label	user labels
multi-volume file	label processing	tapemark
multi-file volume	IBM standard labels	dual-density tape drive
volume label	EBCDIC format	
VOL1 label	ISO/ANSI/FIPS labels	

8

How to manage SYSOUT data sets

In chapter 4, you learned how to code a simple form of the DD statement for working with SYSOUT data sets. As you'll recall, SYSOUT data sets are output files that are designed to be printed rather than stored on DASD or tape. Now, in this chapter, you'll learn new techniques for handling SYSOUT data sets. For example, you'll learn how to print multiple copies of a data set without rerunning the entire job and how to send a data set to a printer in the department that needs the output.

As you read this chapter, please keep in mind that you only need these techniques for special SYSOUT processing. Also, since this chapter presents far more information than you can remember, you should read it first to get the general idea of what SYSOUT functions are available. Then, you can refer back to this chapter when you need to use one of these functions later on.

The basics of the OUTPUT JCL statement

As you might guess, a DD statement can include many more parameters to handle SYSOUT data than what you've seen so far, and you'll learn how to code them later in this chapter. First, though, you'll be introduced to another statement that you can use for SYSOUT processing, the OUTPUT JCL statement (or just OUTPUT statement).

The OUTPUT statement lets you specify many of the options for SYSOUT processing that you would otherwise code on a DD statement. The advantage of the OUTPUT statement is that the SYSOUT options can apply to multiple data sets in a job, so you don't have to code the same parameters on each DD statement. After you see how and when to use the OUTPUT statement, you'll learn how to code both the OUTPUT and SYSOUT DD parameters in detail.

The syntax for the OUTPUT statement

Figure 8-1 shows the syntax for the OUTPUT statement and lists the parameters that are presented in this chapter. Be aware, though, that this statement contains many more parameters. This figure simply summarizes the ones that you're most likely to use. For a complete list and description of all of the parameters available, please consult the IBM manual, *OS/390 MVS JCL Reference*.

In the next two figures, you'll see that the OUTPUT statement can be used in two ways. First, you can code a default OUTPUT statement that applics to all of the SYSOUT data sets produced by a job or job step. Second, you can code an OUTPUT statement that must be referred to directly by a DD statement before it takes effect.

The syntax for the OUTPUT statement

```
//name     OUTPUT [ ,CLASS=class ]
                  [ ,CONTROL= {PROGRAM} ]
                             {SINGLE }
                             {DOUBLE }
                             {TRIPLE }
                  [ ,COPIES= {nnn                                 } ]
                             {(,(group-value[,group-value...]))}
                  [ ,DEFAULT= {YES} ]
                             {NO }
                  [ ,DEST=destination ]
                  [ ,FCB=fcb-name ]
                  [ ,FLASH=overlay-name ]
                  [ ,FORMS=form-name ]
                  [ ,JESDS= {ALL} ]
                           {JCL}
                           {LOG}
                           {MSG}
                  [ ,LINECT=nnn ]
                  [ ,OUTDISP=(normal-disp[,abnormal-disp]) ]
                  [ ,PRTY=nnn ]
```

Explanation

CLASS	Assigns an output class for SYSOUT data sets.
CONTROL	Specifies the line spacing for each record that's printed.
COPIES	Specifies how many copies of the data set should be printed.
DEFAULT	Specifies whether or not this OUTPUT statement supplies default SYSOUT processing.
DEST	Specifies a destination for the SYSOUT data set.
FCB	Specifies the forms control buffer image to be downloaded to the printer when printing a special form.
FLASH	Specifies the name of the overlay to be used in printing a special form on a 3800 printing subsystem.
FORMS	Specifies the name of the form on which the SYSOUT data set is to be printed.
JESDS	Specifies the JES system data sets to which this OUTPUT statement applies.
LINECT	JES2 only; specifies the maximum number of lines to be printed on each page.
OUTDISP	JES2 only; specifies the disposition for a SYSOUT data set.
PRTY	Specifies a priority for the output data set.

Description

- The OUTPUT statement is used to set options that can apply to multiple SYSOUT data sets within a job.

- An OUTPUT statement can be used to provide default options for all the SYSOUT data sets produced by a job or a job step. Or it can be used only for those data sets that explicitly reference it in their DD statements.

Figure 8-1   The syntax for the OUTPUT statement

How to use default OUTPUT statements

Figure 8-2 shows the syntax for the DEFAULT parameter of the OUTPUT statement. To create a default statement, you code DEFAULT=YES or DEFAULT=Y along with any output processing options. Then, any subsequent SYSOUT data sets that don't refer to a specific OUTPUT statement in a job or job step will use the default statement for its output options.

If you code a default OUTPUT statement after the JOB statement but before the first EXEC statement, it is a *job-level default statement*. That means that the options in the OUTPUT statement apply to all SYSOUT data sets in the job that don't refer to other OUTPUT statements.

If you code a default OUTPUT statement within a job step, it is a *step-level default statement*. Then, the options apply to all SYSOUT data sets within the job step that don't explicitly refer to other OUTPUT statements. In other words, step-level OUTPUT statements override job-level OUTPUT statements.

When you're using default OUTPUT statements, the DD statements for the SYSOUT data sets in the job don't have to include any options. The SYSOUT parameter is still required, though, so you can code it as SYSOUT=(,) as shown in this figure. This specifies that no output class (also called a *null class*) is assigned to the data set. If you code a class or any other options on the DD SYSOUT statement, they will override the equivalent defaults in the OUTPUT statement.

To give you a better idea of how default OUTPUT statements work, look at the example in this figure. As you can see, there are two default OUTPUT statements coded for this job. OUT1 is a job-level default while OUT2 is a step-level default. When STEP1 executes, the TRANRPT data set prints to class H since that's what's specified in the OUT1 statement. In contrast, when STEP2 executes, the CUSTRPT data set prints to class A since OUT2 is a step-level statement that overrides the OUT1 statement. In addition, three copies of CUSTRPT are printed at remote printer R125.

If necessary, you can code more than one job-level or step-level default statement for a job or job step. Then, the SYSOUT data sets in the job are processed once for each OUTPUT statement that applies to them. Suppose, for example, that you code two job-level default OUTPUT statements: one that specifies normal class A printing, and another that specifies that the SYSOUT data should be routed to a remote destination. In this case, each SYSOUT data set produced by the job is printed twice: once using normal class A output processing, and again after being routed to the remote destination.

The syntax for the DEFAULT parameter of the OUTPUT statement

```
DEFAULT= {YES}
         {Y  }
         {NO }
         {N  }
```

Explanation

YES, Y   Indicates that the options in the OUTPUT statement apply to all SYSOUT data sets in the job or job step (in other words, the OUTPUT statement is implicitly referenced by the SYSOUT DD statements within the job).

NO, N   Indicates that the OUTPUT statement isn't implicitly referenced by the SYSOUT DD statements within the job. As a result, it must be explicitly referenced.

How to code a DD SYSOUT statement that doesn't specify any options

```
SYSOUT=(,)
```

A job that uses job-level and step-level OUTPUT statements

```
//MM01RN    JOB (36512),'R MENENDEZ',NOTIFY=MM01,MSGCLASS=X
//OUT1      OUTPUT DEFAULT=YES,CLASS=H
//STEP1     EXEC PGM=ARRPT1
//TRANIN    DD DSNAME=MMA2.AR.TRANS,DISP=SHR
//TRANRPT   DD SYSOUT=(,)
//STEP2     EXEC PGM=ARRPT2
//OUT2      OUTPUT DEFAULT=YES,CLASS=A,COPIES=3,DEST=R125
//MASTIN    DD DSNAME=MMA2.CUSTOMER.MASTER,DISP=SHR
//CUSTRPT   DD SYSOUT=(,)
```

Description

- The parameters in a default OUTPUT statement apply to all of the SYSOUT data sets in a job or job step that don't explicitly refer to another OUTPUT statement.
- To code a default OUTPUT statement, you must include the DEFAULT=YES or DEFAULT=Y parameter.
- A *job-level* OUTPUT statement appears after the JOB statement but before the first EXEC statement. Unless otherwise specified, its parameters apply to all of the SYSOUT data sets in the job.
- A *step-level* OUTPUT statement is coded within a job step after the EXEC statement. Unless otherwise specified, its parameters apply to all of the SYSOUT data sets that follow it within the job step.
- Step-level OUTPUT statements override job-level statements.
- If you code SYSOUT=* on a DD statement, the output class in the MSGCLASS parameter on the JOB statement is used for the data set. To use the output class given in a default OUTPUT statement, you have to specify a *null class* by coding SYSOUT=(,). (See figure 8-5 for more details.)
- If you code more than one job-level or step-level default statement, the SYSOUT data sets in the job or step are processed once for each default statement.

Figure 8-2   How to use default OUTPUT statements

How to use explicitly referenced OUTPUT statements

Sometimes, you want to use an OUTPUT statement for multiple SYSOUT data sets, but you don't want to use it as the default for the entire job or job step. In that case, you omit the DEFAULT parameter or code DEFAULT=NO or N. Then, whenever you want to use the OUTPUT statement for a data set, you have to code an OUTPUT parameter that points to it on the DD SYSOUT statement. This is summarized in figure 8-3.

If you look at the syntax for the OUTPUT parameter on the DD statement, you can see that the reference formats are similar to referbacks. If you specify just a name in the reference, you're referring to a job-level OUTPUT statement. If you specify a stepname and a name, you're referring to a step-level OUTPUT statement. And if you specify a stepname, procstepname, and name, you're referring to an OUTPUT statement in a cataloged or in-stream procedure, which you'll learn about in the next chapter.

To illustrate, the example in this figure includes several OUTPUT statements that are referred to explicitly by SYSOUT data sets. To start, INVLIST in STEP1 refers to OUT1, which is a job-level OUTPUT statement. It will be assigned to class C, and four copies of the data set will be printed at remote printer R125. Next, INVRPT explicitly refers both to OUT1 and to OUT2, which is a step-level OUTPUT statement. Here again, the data set will be assigned to class C. This time, however, four copies will be printed at printer R125 and two copies will be printed at printer R150. Last, LOGRPT doesn't explicitly refer to any OUTPUT statement, so its output will be handled according to the default OUTPUT statement. That means it will be assigned to class A and will be printed at the LOCAL (main) printer.

Although you can code explicitly referenced OUTPUT statements at either the job or step level, their placement doesn't affect processing the way it does with default OUTPUT statements. An OUTPUT statement that isn't a default just has to come before any DD statement that refers to it. As a result, some programmers group all of them at the beginning of a job, while others like to split them up, coding those that will be used throughout the job at the job level and those that will be used in a single step at the step level.

The syntax for the OUTPUT parameter of the DD statement

```
OUTPUT= {reference                      }
        {(,reference[,reference]...)}
```

Reference formats

*.name	Refers to a job-level OUTPUT statement.
*.stepname.name	Refers to a step-level OUTPUT statement.
*.stepname.procstepname.name	Refers to an OUTPUT statement in a procedure (see chapter 9).

A job that uses both default and explicitly referenced OUTPUT statements

```
//MM01RN   JOB (36512),'R MENENDEZ',NOTIFY=MM01
//DEFAULT OUTPUT DEFAULT=YES,CLASS=A,DEST=LOCAL
//OUT1     OUTPUT COPIES=4,CLASS=C,DEST=R125
//STEP1    EXEC PGM=AR4320
//OUT2     OUTPUT COPIES=2,CLASS=C,DEST=R150
//INVLIST DD    SYSOUT=(,),OUTPUT=*.OUT1
//INVRPT   DD    SYSOUT=(,),OUTPUT=(*.OUT1,*.STEP1.OUT2)
//LOGRPT   DD    SYSOUT=(,)
//
```

Description

- To code an OUTPUT statement that is explicitly referenced by a DD statement, omit the DEFAULT parameter or code DEFAULT=NO or N on the OUTPUT statement.

- To refer to an explicitly coded OUTPUT statement, include an OUTPUT parameter on the DD statement for the SYSOUT data set.

- The OUTPUT parameter can refer to a job-level or step-level OUTPUT statement. For a step-level statement, you must include the stepname.

- To refer to more than one OUTPUT statement in an OUTPUT parameter, list the references in parentheses and separate them with commas. Then, the data set is processed once for each statement that's referenced.

Figure 8-3   How to use explicitly referenced OUTPUT statements

How to use DD and OUTPUT statement parameters for SYSOUT processing

Many of the parameters of the OUTPUT statement have parallels on the DD statement. As a result, you can often invoke a specific SYSOUT function by coding an OUTPUT statement parameter, a DD statement parameter, or both. This topic begins by giving you an overview of the DD parameters that are related to SYSOUT processing. Then, you'll learn how to use these parameters along with those on the OUTPUT statement for specific processing functions.

DD statement parameters for SYSOUT processing

Figure 8-4 shows the format for the DD statement as it's used for SYSOUT data sets. If you compare it with the format for the OUTPUT statement in figure 8-1, you'll see that parameters such as COPIES, DEST, and FCB are available on both statements. You'll also see that the DD statement has some additional parameters that aren't available on the OUTPUT statement.

Whether you use DD or OUTPUT statement parameters to control SYSOUT processing is up to you. In general, though, you should use the DD statement parameters to control the processing for individual SYSOUT data sets. But when you want to control multiple SYSOUT data sets in the same way, you should use an OUTPUT statement.

Be aware, too, that the parameters you code on a DD statement will override equivalent parameters on any OUTPUT statements that are in effect. So if you're using OUTPUT statements in a job, be sure to code the DD statements carefully so you get the results you want.

Commonly used DD parameters for SYSOUT processing

```
//ddname    DD [ SYSOUT=(class[,writer][, {form-name} ]) ]
                                          {code-name}
               [ ,COPIES=nnn(,(group-value[,group-value])) ]
               [ ,DEST=destination ]
               [ ,FCB=fcb-name ]
               [ ,FLASH=overlay-name ]
               [ ,FREE= {END  } ]
                        {CLOSE}
               [ ,HOLD= {YES} ]
                        {NO }
               [ ,OUTLIM=number ]
               [ ,OUTPUT= {reference                   } ]
                          {(,reference[,reference]...)}
               [ ,SEGMENT=page-count ]
               [ ,SPIN= {UNALLOC} ]
                        {NO     }
```

Explanation

SYSOUT	Specifies the output class, the name of an output writer used to process the file, and the name of any special form needed to print the file.
COPIES	Specifies how many copies of the data set should be printed.
DEST	Specifies a destination for the SYSOUT data set.
FCB	Specifies the name of the forms control buffer to be downloaded to the printer when printing a special form.
FLASH	Specifies the name of the overlay to be used in printing a special form on a 3800 printing subsystem.
FREE	Specifies that the data set should be unallocated at the end of the last job step that uses it or when a program closes it.
HOLD	Specifies whether or not the data set should be held.
OUTLIM	Specifies a limit for the number of records that can be written to the data set.
OUTPUT	Associates the SYSOUT data set with the named OUTPUT statement.
SEGMENT	JES2 only; allows a job's output to start printing while the job step is still executing.
SPIN	Specifies when the data set should be released for printing.

Description

* The DD statement provides specific parameters that control output processing for SYSOUT data sets. Many of these are equivalent to parameters on the OUTPUT statement.

* To control the characteristics of a specific SYSOUT data set, code the parameters on the DD statement. To control multiple SYSOUT data sets in the same way, code an OUTPUT statement.

* When both an OUTPUT statement and a DD statement apply to a data set, the DD statement parameters override equivalent parameters on the OUTPUT statement.

Figure 8-4   DD statement parameters for SYSOUT processing

How to specify an output class

A SYSOUT data set's output class can affect the way the data set is printed by indicating which printer or printers may print the data set, whether the data set should be held, and the data set's importance relative to data sets with other output classes. To assign a class to a SYSOUT data set, you normally use the SYSOUT parameter of the DD statement, as shown in the syntax at the top of figure 8-5. As you can see, you can specify the class directly in this parameter, using an appropriate value as defined by your installation. It's more common, though, to code SYSOUT=*, and that's what you'll see in most of the examples in this book. Then, the job's message class, specified in the MSGCLASS parameter on the JOB statement, is used (if the MSGCLASS is omitted, the installation's default message class is used).

Either of these values will override the class setting in any OUTPUT statements that are in effect, though. So if you want to use an OUTPUT statement to set the class, you specify SYSOUT=(,). Then, the class that's coded in the CLASS parameter of the OUTPUT statement is used. The syntax for this parameter is also shown in this figure.

The job in this figure assigns output classes to the SYSOUT data sets in a variety of ways. Here, the first four data sets are all created according to the default OUTPUT statement, but only ARPLIST and ARRP15 use the default output class of A. The DD statement for ARPLOG overrides the default and uses the MSGCLASS parameter on the JOB statement to obtain an output class of X, and the DD statement for ARRP10 overrides the default by directly assigning an output class of D. Finally, ARSTMT refers to OUTPUT statement OUT1, so it's created with an output class of C.

Incidentally, if you code SYSOUT=(,) and then don't provide a CLASS parameter on an OUTPUT statement, the job's message class is used. And if you don't code a MSGCLASS parameter on the JOB statement, an installation-dependent default message class is used.

How to specify an output priority

Normally, SYSOUT data sets are printed on a first-come, first-served basis, as soon as a printer that's eligible for the output class becomes available. However, in some cases, a SYSOUT data set contains important information and must be printed sooner than other SYSOUT data sets waiting in the output spool. To alter the printing sequence, you can code the PRTY parameter on the OUTPUT statement to specify an output priority.

The job in figure 8-5 includes two OUTPUT statements that use the PRTY parameter. The default OUTPUT statement has a priority of 50 and the OUT1 OUTPUT statement has a priority of 200. When the SYSOUT data sets are sent to the printer, the ones assigned to the OUT1 OUTPUT statement (in this case, ARSTMT) will print before those created according to the default OUTPUT statement (ARPLOG, ARPLIST, ARRP10, and ARRP15).

The syntax for the SYSOUT class of the DD statement

```
SYSOUT= {class}
        {*}
        {(,)}
```

The syntax for the CLASS parameter of the OUTPUT statement

```
CLASS= {class}
       {*    }
```

Explanation

class   Specifies the output class for the SYSOUT data set. The class is a one-character identifier that can be A through Z or 0 through 9.

*   Specifies that the output class in the JOB statement's MSGCLASS parameter be used.

(,)   Specifies a null class (in other words, no output class is specified for the data set). If an OUTPUT statement is in effect, the output class in the CLASS parameter is used for the data set. If not, the output class in the JOB statement's MSGCLASS parameter is used.

The syntax for the PRTY parameter of the OUTPUT statement

```
PRTY=nnn
```

Explanation

nnn   Specifies the priority of the SYSOUT data set as it enters the output queue. The number specified can be from 0 to 255 where 0 is the lowest priority.

A job that uses output classes and sets printing priorities

```
//MM01RN   JOB (36512),'R MENENDEZ',NOTIFY=MM01,MSGCLASS=X
//DEFAULT  OUTPUT DEFAULT=YES,CLASS=A,PRTY=50
//OUT1     OUTPUT CLASS=C,PRTY=200
//STEP1    EXEC PGM=AR5000
//ARPLOG   DD   SYSOUT=*
//ARPLIST  DD   SYSOUT=(,)
//ARRP10   DD   SYSOUT=D
//ARRP15   DD   SYSOUT=(,)
//ARSTMT   DD   SYSOUT=(,),OUTPUT=*.OUT1
//
```

Description

- To assign an output class to SYSOUT data sets using an OUTPUT statement, code the class in the CLASS parameter.
- To assign an output class to a single SYSOUT data set, code the class in the DD SYSOUT parameter.
- If a SYSOUT data set isn't assigned an output class in a DD or OUTPUT statement, the job's MSGCLASS is used. If no MSGCLASS is coded, the installation's default output class is used.
- To specify an output priority for a data set in the print queue, code the PRTY parameter on the OUTPUT statement.
- Omitting the PRTY parameter causes the installation-specific priority to be used.

Figure 8-5   How to specify an output class and priority

How to release a SYSOUT data set for immediate processing

In most cases, a job's SYSOUT data sets are held in the JES output queue until the job completes. Then, they're all printed together. There will be times though, when you won't want to wait until a job finishes to begin printing a SYSOUT data set. For example, suppose a job has two steps: the first produces a long report, and the second sorts a huge file. If the sort step takes several hours to complete, the user must wait unnecessarily for the report to begin printing. In a case like this, you can use the three DD parameters shown in figure 8-6 to begin printing the SYSOUT data set before the job finishes.

The SPIN parameter allows you to specify when a SYSOUT data set is to be released. Specifying SPIN=UNALLOC makes the data set available before the job ends and specifying SPIN=NO makes it available after the job ends. The outcome of SPIN=UNALLOC depends on how your system is set up, however. It may mean that the data set is available as soon as the application closes it, or it may mean that the data set isn't available until the job step ends.

The FREE parameter allows you to specify whether a data set should be made available after the last step that uses it unallocates it or when the current program closes it. You'll typically code FREE=CLOSE with SPIN=UNALLOC to ensure that a SYSOUT data set is available for immediate printing.

Under JES2, the SEGMENT parameter causes a SYSOUT data set to be spun-off for output processing while the job is still executing. The number you specify in the parameter represents the number of pages to produce for each segment. When that page count is reached, that segment of the data set is sent to the printer for processing.

The syntax for the SPIN parameter of the DD statement

```
SPIN= {UNALLOC}
      {NO     }
```

Explanation

UNALLOC　　Specifies that the data set is to be available for processing immediately after it is unallocated. Depending on system configurations, this can be as soon as the file is closed or at the end of the job step.

NO　　　　Specifies that the system make the data set available only when the job completes, regardless of when it's unallocated.

The syntax for the FREE parameter of the DD statement

```
FREE= {END  }
      {CLOSE}
```

Explanation

END　　Specifies that the system unallocate the data set at the end of the last step that uses it.

CLOSE　　Specifies that the system unallocate the data set when the program closes it.

The syntax for the SEGMENT parameter of the DD statement (JES2 only)

```
SEGMENT=page-count
```

Explanation

page-count　　Specifies the number of pages to produce for each segment of a SYSOUT data set. When the page count is reached, the segment is released for output processing.

Three ways to start printing a SYSOUT data set before a job finishes

A report that starts printing after the job step ends but before the job finishes

```
//REPORT    DD   SYSOUT=A,SPIN=UNALLOC
```

A report that starts printing as soon as the SYSOUT data set is closed

```
//REPORT    DD   SYSOUT=A,SPIN=UNALLOC,FREE=CLOSE
```

A report that starts printing after the first 100 pages are produced

```
//REPORT    DD   SYSOUT=A,SEGMENT=100
```

Description

- The SPIN parameter lets you specify whether a SYSOUT data set is to be made available for printing before the job ends. Depending on how your system is set up, coding SPIN=UNALLOC will make the data set available (1) as soon as the application closes the file or (2) when the job step ends.

- The FREE parameter lets you specify whether a data set should be made available after the last step that uses it unallocates it or when a program closes it.

- In JES2, the SEGMENT parameter causes a SYSOUT data set to be spun-off for output processing after a given number of pages are produced, even though the job is still running.

Figure 8-6　　How to release a SYSOUT data set for immediate processing

How to route a SYSOUT data set to a specific destination

Normally, the system determines which printer to use based on the output class for the data set, the source of the job, and which printers are currently available. But what if you want to send your output to the remote printer near your desk rather than the default LOCAL printer it would normally print to? In such situations, you can specify the DEST parameter on either the OUTPUT statement or the DD statement for the SYSOUT data set in question.

The rules for specifying a destination vary from installation to installation. So you'll need to get a list of destinations that are valid at your installation. In general, though, you can use the DEST parameter to route output data to a remote or local printer, a node, a node and printer or terminal, or a user-id. The chart at the top of figure 8-7 lists some of the types of destinations you can specify as well as the JCL statements you can code them on. It also shows what values can be used in a JES2 or JES3 environment.

When using the DEST parameter, be mindful of the size of the output data set going to a remote printer. If you send a huge report to a slow-speed departmental printer, you'll hold up everyone else's output while yours is printing.

The syntax for the DEST parameter of the OUTPUT and DD statements

```
DEST=destination
```

Destination	OUTPUT	DD	JES2	JES3	Description
ANYLOCAL	X	X	X		Routes output to a local device.
LOCAL	X	X	X	X	Routes output to a local device.
Name	X	X	X		Routes output to a destination identified by a symbolic name up to 8 characters long.
Nnnnn	X	X			Routes output to a node. The number can be from 1 to 1000.
Rnnnn, RMnnnn, RMTnnnn	X	X	X		Routes output to a remote terminal. The number can be from 1 to 9999.
Userid	X	X	X		Routes output to a user-id at the local node.
nodename.userid	X		X		Routes output to a node and a user-id within the node.
(node,userid)		X	X	X	Routes output to a node and a user-id within the node.
'IP:ipaddr', 'nodename.IP:ipaddr'	X		X	X	Routes output to a TCP/IP routing designation.

A SYSOUT data set that's routed to remote printer R100

```
//REPORT  DD  SYSOUT=A,DEST=R100
```

An OUTPUT statement that routes output to a node named FRESNO and a printer with an IP address of main-2

```
//DEFAULT  OUTPUT DEFAULT=YES,DEST='FRESNO.IP:main-2'
```

Description

- The DEST parameter lets you route a SYSOUT data set to a specific destination. The destination can be a remote or local printer or terminal, a node, a node and printer or terminal, or a user-id.

- Installations determine the rules and the format for specifying a destination. So you'll have to find out what destinations are valid at your installation.

Figure 8-7   How to route a SYSOUT data set to a specific destination

How to specify the disposition for a SYSOUT data set

In chapter 4, you saw how to code a DISP parameter on a DD statement for a data set that's stored on disk, but those DD values don't apply to SYSOUT data sets. In a JES2 system, though, you can use the OUTDISP parameter on an OUTPUT statement to specify the disposition of a SYSOUT data set, as shown in figure 8-8.

As you can see, the OUTDISP parameter allows you to specify two dispositions. The first one tells JES2 what to do if the job terminates normally, and the second one tells it what to do if the job terminates abnormally. If you don't specify an abnormal disposition, JES2 uses the normal disposition if the job terminates abnormally. If you specify an abnormal disposition without a normal disposition, the normal disposition defaults to WRITE. And if you omit the OUTDISP parameter, JES2 uses the normal and abnormal dispositions specified in the SYSOUT class for the data set.

To illustrate how the OUTDISP parameter might be used, suppose you have a report that should print on a printer in the corporate office as long as there's no problem with the output. However, if the job terminates abnormally, the report data set should be held on the local printer so a programmer can look at it to determine the problem. Then, the data set can either be purged or printed if further examination is required.

The OUTPUT statements in the first example in this figure set up this processing. In the GOOD statement, the OUTDISP parameter specifies KEEP to print the report at the remote printer if the job ends normally and PURGE so the corporate office won't see the report if the job ends abnormally. In the BAD statement, the OUTDISP parameter says to purge the report at the local destination if the job completes normally and hold it for review if the job terminates abnormally. Then, the DD SYSOUT statement says to process the data set once for each OUTPUT statement. As a result, if the job completes successfully, the output for data set REPORT is printed at remote printer R100. On the other hand, if the job doesn't end successfully, the output is held until a programmer can examine it.

If you want to hold the output from a SYSOUT data set no matter what its disposition is, you can code the HOLD parameter on the DD statement as shown in this figure. An alternate way to hold a SYSOUT data set using the DD statement is to specify a held output class in the SYSOUT parameter.

The syntax for the OUTDISP parameter of the OUTPUT statement (JES2 only)

```
OUTDISP=(normal-disp[,abnormal-disp])
```

The dispositions that can be coded on the OUTPUT statement

WRITE   Specifies that the SYSOUT data set is to be printed and then deleted.

HOLD   Specifies that the system is to hold the SYSOUT data set until the user or operator releases it. Once printed, the SYSOUT data set is deleted.

KEEP   Specifies that the SYSOUT data set is to be printed. After printing, its disposition is changed to LEAVE.

LEAVE   Specifies that the SYSOUT data set is to be kept in the output queue.

PURGE   Specifies that the SYSOUT data set is to be deleted without being printed.

How the OUTDISP parameter can be used to manage output processing

```
//GOOD     OUTPUT  OUTDISP=(KEEP,PURGE),DEST=R100
//BAD      OUTPUT  OUTDISP=(PURGE,HOLD)
//REPORT   DD      SYSOUT=A,OUTPUT=(*.GOOD,*.BAD)
```

The syntax for the HOLD parameter of the DD statement

```
HOLD= {YES}
      {Y  }
      {NO }
      {N  }
```

Explanation

YES, Y   Requests that the system hold the SYSOUT data set until it is released by a user or operator.

NO, N   Requests that the system perform installation-defined processing for the SYSOUT data set based on its output class.

How the HOLD parameter can be used keep a report from printing immediately

```
//REPORT  DD  SYSOUT=A,HOLD=YES
```

Description

- In a JES2 system, you can use the OUTPUT statement's OUTDISP parameter to indicate the disposition of a SYSOUT data set. Like the DD DISP parameter, you code two dispositions. This first one applies if the job step completes normally, and the second one applies if it doesn't.

- If you omit the abnormal disposition, the system uses the normal disposition you specify. If you omit the normal disposition, the system defaults to WRITE.

- You can use the DD statement's HOLD parameter to hold a SYSOUT data set until it's released for printing by a user or system operator. The HOLD parameter overrides the OUTDISP parameter.

Figure 8-8   How to specify the disposition for a SYSOUT data set

How to produce multiple copies of a SYSOUT data set

From time to time, it may be necessary to print more than one copy of a report. Generally, if several departments or individuals need to view a report, this will be the case. To print multiple copies, you can use the COPIES parameter on either the OUTPUT or DD statement, as shown in figure 8-9.

If you look at the examples in this figure, you'll see that the first DD statement and the first OUTPUT statement show how to code the COPIES parameter in its simplest form. In both cases, two copies of the data set are produced. When you print multiple copies of a data set this way, the data set is sent to the printer twice. When the first copy has finished printing, JES2/JES3 sends the second copy. If the two copies are to be sent to different users, this is efficient for the operator, who can just separate the copies and deliver them. However, it's inefficient for the system because the data set must be processed twice.

For efficiency, there is an alternative method for printing multiple copies of a data set if you're using a laser printer such as the 3800 printing subsystem. The alternative is to code a group value in the COPIES parameter, which tells the system to print multiple copies of each page as the data set is processed. For example, if you request two copies of a data set, the copies are printed in this order: two copies of page 1, two copies of page 2, and so on. This way, JES processes the data set just once (of course, this makes it more difficult for the operator to separate the copies).

The second DD and OUTPUT statement examples in this figure show how to use group values. In the DD example, the first subparameter is omitted and a comma marks its position. Then, the next three subparameters, all group values, are enclosed in parentheses. The result is that two copies of each page will be printed before moving on, then three copies for each page, and then finally one copy for each page. Why not simply specify a single group value of 6 since the copies will need to be collated anyway? A parameter like this might be used if different departments needed different numbers of copies. Then, the copies would be delivered to the departments uncollated, as printed.

In the second OUTPUT example, the group values specify that five copies of the data set are to be printed in two groups if they're printed on a laser printer. Here, though, the first subparameter is also coded, specifying five copies. As a result, if the output device is not a laser printer, five collated copies are produced.

The syntax for the COPIES parameter of the OUTPUT and DD statements

```
COPIES= {nnn                                       }
        {(nnn,(group-value[,group-value...]))}
        {(,(group-value[,group-value...]))    }
```

Explanation

nnn	Specifies how many copies of the SYSOUT data set to print. You can specify up to 255 copies in JES2 and 254 copies in JES3. On a laser printer system, this value is ignored if a group value is coded.
group-value	Specifies the number of copies to be printed of each page before the next page is printed. You can code up to 8 group values but the sum of the pages printed must not exceed 255 pages for JES2 and 254 pages for JES3. Valid only for laser printer systems.

Specifying the COPIES parameter on the DD statement

2 collated copies of the data set are printed on any type of printer

```
//REPORT1   DD   SYSOUT=A,COPIES=2
```

On a laser printer, 6 uncollated copies are printed in 3 sets

```
//REPORT2   DD   SYSOUT=A,COPIES=(,(2,3,1))
```

Specifying the COPIES parameter on an OUTPUT statement

2 collated copies of the data set are printed on any type of printer

```
//OUT1    OUTPUT  CLASS=A,COPIES=2
```

On an impact printer, 5 collated copies are printed; on a laser printer, 5 uncollated copies are printed in 2 sets

```
//OUT2    OUTPUT  CLASS=A,COPIES=(5,(2,3))
```

Description

- The COPIES parameter lets you specify how many copies of a SYSOUT data set are to be printed. The printed output is in page sequence for each copy.

- If you're printing on a 3800 printing subsystem or other laser printer system, you can print multiple copies of each page together by coding group values on the COPIES parameter. A group value specifies the number of copies to be printed for each page before moving on to the next.

- The number value and the group values are mutually exclusive. If both are coded and the data set is sent to an impact printer, the number value is used. If the data set is sent to a laser printer, the group values are used.

Figure 8-9   How to produce multiple copies of a SYSOUT data set

How to set an output limit

If you need to limit the number of records written to a SYSOUT data set, you can code an OUTLIM parameter on the DD statement, as shown in figure 8-10. As you can see, the OUTLIM parameter allows you to specify the number of logical records, or lines, that can be written to a SYSOUT data set. If the limit is reached, the system will either exit to an installation-written routine or terminate the job. In the example in this figure, the SYSOUT data set named REPORT is to be no longer than 2000 lines.

There may be many reasons for coding such a parameter. For example, you may suspect that one of the reports in a job is looping, generating the same lines of output over and over again. Then, you can save your installation a lot of paper by using the OUTLIM parameter.

Of course, you already learned in chapter 5 that you can also code the LINES, BYTES, PAGES, or CARDS parameters on the JOB, EXEC, /*JOBPARM, or //*MAIN statements to achieve a similar effect. The difference is that the limits specified in these parameters apply to the entire job or job step rather than to an individual SYSOUT data set.

The syntax for the OUTLIM parameter of the DD statement

```
OUTLIM=number
```

Explanation

number   Specifies the number of logical records that can be written to the SYSOUT data set. The value can be from 1 to 16777215.

A SYSOUT data set with an output limit

```
//REPORT    DD    SYSOUT=A,OUTLIM=2000
```

Description

- You can use the OUTLIM parameter on a DD statement to limit the number of records written to a SYSOUT data set.
- If the output limit is reached, the system will either exit to an installation-written routine or terminate the job.
- If no OUTLIM parameter is specified or OUTLIM=0 is coded, the system will use a default limit established by your installation.
- An alternate way of limiting the number of records produced is by specifying the LINES, BYTES, PAGES, or CARDS parameters on the JOB, EXEC, /*JOBPARM, or //*MAIN statements, but these options apply to the entire job or job step, not to a specific SYSOUT data set.

Figure 8-10   How to set an output limit

How to control line spacing and the number of lines on each page

Two OUTPUT statement parameters, CONTROL and LINECT, let you control the line spacing and the number of lines on each page of SYSOUT output. Figure 8-11 shows the syntax for both parameters.

The CONTROL parameter lets you vary the line spacing of a SYSOUT data set. If you omit CONTROL or specify CONTROL=PROGRAM, JES assumes that the first position of each line in the SYSOUT data set contains a carriage-control character that affects line spacing. That's normally the case. However, you can override the carriage-control settings by specifying single, double, or triple spacing instead.

This figure includes a job that uses the CONTROL parameter in two OUTPUT statements. The NORM OUTPUT statement defers line spacing to the program. The LSTING OUTPUT statement requires that the data set be double-spaced when printed.

The LINECT parameter, available only under JES2, changes the JES default for the maximum number of lines printed on each page of a SYSOUT data set. Usually, the default LINECT value is 66 lines per page. That's the physical maximum that can be printed with normal line spacing using standard 11 x 14 paper on an impact printer or 8-1/2 x 11 paper on a laser printer in landscape mode. If you want fewer lines per page or if you're using smaller-sized paper, you should reduce the line count accordingly.

The syntax for the CONTROL parameter of the OUTPUT statement

```
CONTROL= {PROGRAM}
         {SINGLE }
         {DOUBLE }
         {TRIPLE }
```

Explanation

PROGRAM   Specifies that each record in the SYSOUT data set begins with a carriage-control character that determines the line spacing.

SINGLE   Specifies forced single spacing.

DOUBLE   Specifies forced double spacing.

TRIPLE   Specifies forced triple spacing.

A job that uses the CONTROL parameter to control line spacing

```
//MM01RN  JOB (36512),'R MENENDEZ',NOTIFY=MM01
//NORM    OUTPUT CLASS=A,CONTROL=PROGRAM
//LSTING  OUTPUT CLASS=A,CONTROL=DOUBLE
//STEP1   EXEC PGM=AR7000
//ARLIST  DD   SYSOUT=(,),OUTPUT=*.LSTING
//ARRPT   DD   SYSOUT=(,),OUTPUT=*.NORM
//
```

The syntax for the LINECT parameter of the OUTPUT statement (JES2 only)

```
LINECT=nnn
```

Explanation

nnn   Specifies the maximum number of lines allowed per page. The number can be from 0 to 255.

An OUTPUT statement that uses the LINECT parameter to control the number of lines on each page

```
//LSTING  OUTPUT CLASS=A,LINECT=66
```

Description

- The CONTROL parameter on the OUTPUT statement lets you specify whether each record in a SYSOUT data set starts with a carriage-control character or whether the records should be printed with single, double, or triple spacing.
- Specifying SINGLE, DOUBLE, or TRIPLE overrides the line spacing specified by any carriage-control characters in the data set.
- In JES2, the LINECT parameter on the OUTPUT statement lets you specify the maximum number of lines the system can print on each page. If you omit it, a JES2 initialization default value is used.

Figure 8-11   How to control line spacing and the number of lines on each page

How to use special forms

Although most SYSOUT data sets are printed on standard computer paper, some have to be printed on special forms. For example, payroll checks are usually printed on blank check forms, and invoices are printed on blank invoice forms. As a result, the DD and OUTPUT statements provide several parameters for printing SYSOUT data sets on special forms. The parameters you code in a given job depend on whether you're using an impact printer or a laser printer such as a 3800 printing subsystem.

On an impact printer, pre-printed forms are typically used. These forms usually vary in size and color; they may also contain your company's logo and contact information. Another common feature of pre-printed forms is that they include a number of boxes that your SYSOUT data set will fill with data.

To print on these types of forms, you need to provide two elements: the form name and the FCB name. The form name identifies the form you want to use. Then, when the data set is released for printing, this name is used in a message to the operator that indicates which form to mount on the printer. You can specify the form name in the SYSOUT parameter of a DD statement or in the FORMS parameter of an OUTPUT statement. The results are the same either way.

As for the FCB name, it identifies a *forms control buffer* that corresponds to the form. A forms control buffer is a series of coded instructions that's loaded into the printer's memory. It provides information that the printer needs to print on the form, such as the length of the form. Usually, the FCB name is the same as the form name. You specify it in an FCB parameter on either a DD or OUT-PUT statement.

On a laser printer, pre-printed forms aren't generally used. Instead, you use the *forms-flash technique* to print the form itself along with the data on a blank piece of paper. This technique requires that the operator load a photographic negative image of the form into the printer. As a result, you specify an overlay name in the FLASH parameter on a DD or OUTPUT statement to identify which negative the operator needs to mount into the printer before the data set is printed.

The examples in this figure show three different ways to code for special forms. The first two are for forms printed on an impact printer. In either case, the same output is produced. Then, the third example shows how to print the same form on a laser printer.

The syntax for the forms-handling parameters of the DD statement

```
SYSOUT=(class,,form-name)
FCB=fcb-name
FLASH= {overlay-name}
       {STD         }
```

The syntax for the forms-handling parameters of the OUTPUT statement

```
FORMS= {form-name}
       {STD       }
FCB=fcb-name
FLASH= {overlay-name}
       {STD         }
```

Explanation

form-name	Specifies the form to be used for the output. In the SYSOUT parameter, the name can be 1 to 4 alphanumeric or national characters. In the FORMS parameter, the name can be 1 to 8 alphanumeric or national characters.
fcb-name	Specifies the FCB image. The name can be 1 to 4 alphanumeric or national characters.
overlay-name	Specifies the name of a form's photographic negative image. Valid only for laser printers.
STD	A form or overlay specified on system initialization.

Three ways to print invoices

Specifying the name of a pre-printed invoice form on the DD statement

```
//INVOICE  DD   SYSOUT=(C,,INV1),FCB=INV1
```

Specifying the name of a pre-printed invoice form on the OUTPUT statement

```
//OUT1     OUTPUT CLASS=C,FORMS=INV1,FCB=INV1
```

Printing the invoice on a laser printer with a blank sheet of paper

```
//OUT1     OUTPUT FLASH=INV1
```

Description

- To print on special forms on an impact printer, you specify a form name and an FCB name on either the SYSOUT DD statement or an OUTPUT statement.

- The form name is used in a message to the operator that tells which form to mount on the printer.

- The FCB name identifies a *forms control buffer* that corresponds to the form. It provides information the printer needs to print on the form, such as the length of the form.

- To print forms on a laser printer, you include a FLASH parameter on either the SYSOUT DD statement or OUTPUT statement. The overlay specified by the parameter represents a form image that's printed along with the data. The operator is instructed to load the image into the printer before the data is printed.

Figure 8-12   How to use special forms

How to code the OUTPUT statement for JES system data sets

When a job executes, JES produces system-managed SYSOUT data sets that contain information relating to the job's execution. The JES message log lists messages produced by JES2/JES3 as it processes the job. The JCL listing simply lists the JCL statements for the job. And the system message log contains allocation and other messages produced as the job executes. Together, they can be used to verify that the job executed successfully or to help you debug any errors produced during execution.

In chapter 4, you learned that you can use the MSGCLASS and the MSGLEVEL parameters on the JOB statement to control the output processing for these system-managed data sets. The MSGLEVEL parameter lets you suppress some or all of the output, while the MSGCLASS parameter lets you associate an output class with the JES data sets. To be honest, though, MSGCLASS and MSGLEVEL are limited in their capabilities. For example, you can't control how many copies of the data sets to print or what remote printer they should be sent to.

For greater control over the JES data sets produced by your job, you can code the JESDS parameter on the OUTPUT statement, as shown in figure 8-13. With this parameter, you can associate an OUTPUT statement with one or more JES data sets. In most cases, you'll want to specify JESDS=ALL.

The OUTPUT statement in this figure shows how the JESDS parameter allows for more flexibility than the MSGCLASS and MSGLEVEL parameters. Here, the JESDS parameter says that this OUTPUT statement applies to all three JES system data sets. In addition, the OUTPUT statement specifics that three copies should be produced of all the JES output and those three copies should be sent to remote printer R100.

The syntax for the JESDS parameter of the OUTPUT statement

```
JESDS= {ALL}
       {LOG}
       {JCL}
       {MSG}
```

Explanation

ALL   Specifies that the OUTPUT statement applies to all of the system-managed data sets for the job.

LOG   Specifies that the OUTPUT statement applies only to the JESMSGLG data set (the message log).

JCL   Specifies that the OUTPUT statement applies only to the JESJCL data set (the JCL listing).

MSG   Specifies that the OUTPUT statement applies only to the JESYSMSG data set (the system message log).

An OUTPUT statement that controls JES data sets

```
//OUT1   OUTPUT   CLASS=A,JESDS=ALL,COPIES=3,DEST=R100
```

A JOB statement that controls JES data sets

```
//MM01RN JOB (36512),'R MENENDEZ',MSGCLASS=A,MSGLEVEL=(1,1)
```

Description

- You can code the JESDS parameter on the OUTPUT statement to control how the system-managed data sets for the job are printed.

- The system-managed data sets consist of a JES message log, a JCL listing, and a system message log.

- An alternate way to control the printing of these data sets is to include the MSGCLASS and MSGLEVEL parameters in your JOB statement. Refer to chapter 4 for more information about these two parameters.

Figure 8-13   How to code the OUTPUT statement for JES system data sets

JES2/JES3 control statements for SYSOUT data

Both JES2 and JES3 provide control statements that let you manage how SYSOUT data is handled. Since most of their functions duplicate those provided by the standard DD and OUTPUT JCL statements, you probably won't ever code them. However, because you may come across them in a production environment, it's a good idea to be familiar with two of these statements: the JES2 /*OUTPUT statement and the JES3 //*FORMAT PR statement.

The basic syntax for both statements is shown in figure 8-14. Like the OUTPUT JCL statement, they specify SYSOUT parameters but then have to be related to specific SYSOUT data sets for the parameters to take effect. This figure focuses on how those relationships are coded rather than on the parameters that can be used. However, if you ever have to code one of these statements yourself, you can find the information you need in IBM's *OS/390 MVS JCL Reference* manual.

The JES2 /*OUTPUT statement

The JES2 /*OUTPUT statement lets you specify output processing parameters for SYSOUT data sets under JES2. As you can see in the syntax in this figure, a code is used to identify the statement, followed by one or more parameters. For example, in the /*OUTPUT statement that's shown, the code is OUT1 and a COPIES parameter just like the one on the OUTPUT JCL and DD statements is used to produce four copies of a SYSOUT data set.

In a job, the /*OUTPUT statement is placed after the JOB statement and before the first EXEC statement. Then, to relate a SYSOUT data set to the /*OUTPUT statement, you specify the /*OUTPUT statement's code in the form-name position of the DD SYSOUT parameter, as shown in this figure. Unlike the OUTPUT JCL statement, there's no way to specify a default /*OUTPUT statement, so you have to specify the code in the DD statement for *each* data set that should use the /*OUTPUT options.

The JES3 //*FORMAT PR statement

The JES3 //*FORMAT PR statement lets you specify output processing parameters for SYSOUT data sets under JES3. As you can see in its syntax, it includes a DDNAME parameter that specifies the SYSOUT data set or data sets to which the statement applies. In the example in this figure, the REPORT DD statement in job step GO is referenced. If the ddname is omitted in the DDNAME parameter, the statement will apply to each SYSOUT data set the job produces other than the SYSOUT data sets referred to explicitly by other //*FORMAT PR statements.

The basic syntax for the JES2 /*OUTPUT statement

```
/*OUTPUT  code [,parameter][,parameter]...
```

Explanation

code   A one- to four-character value that's coded in a DD statement SYSOUT parameter
            to refer to the /*OUTPUT statement.

parameter   A variety of parameters similar to those on the DD SYSOUT and OUTPUT JCL
            statements can be coded, including COPIES, DEST, and FORMS.

How to use the /*OUTPUT statement

An /*OUTPUT statement that specifies four copies

```
/*OUTPUT  OUT1  COPIES=4
```

A SYSOUT data set that refers to the /*OUTPUT statement

```
//REPORT  DD  SYSOUT=(A,,OUT1)
```

The basic syntax for the JES3 //*FORMAT PR statement

```
//*FORMAT  PR,DDNAME=[ddname-specification] [,parameter][,parameter]...
```

Explanation

DDNAME   Specifies the SYSOUT data set to which the //*FORMAT PR statement applies.
            You can specify stepname.ddname or SYSMSG, JESJCL, or JESMSG.

parameter   A variety of parameters similar to those on the DD SYSOUT and OUTPUT JCL
            statements can be coded, including COPIES, DEST, and FORMS.

A //*FORMAT PR statement that applies to the REPORT DD statement in the GO step

```
//*FORMAT PR DDNAME=GO.REPORT,COPIES=4
```

Description

- Although rarely used, the JES2 /*OUTPUT statement and the JES3 //*FORMAT PR statement are two alternate ways of managing SYSOUT data. Whenever possible, though, use the DD SYSOUT and OUTPUT JCL parameters instead.

- The purpose of this figure is to show you how to relate a JES2 /*OUTPUT statement or a JES3 //*FORMAT PR statement to a specific SYSOUT data set. For detailed information on the parameters that can be coded in these statements, please see IBM's *OS/390 MVS JCL Reference* manual.

Figure 8-14   The JES2 /*OUTPUT statement and the JES3 //*FORMAT PR statement

Perspective

Managing SYSOUT data can be confusing. That's because SYSOUT data sets can be processed in many different ways depending on an installation's environment, and because there are often three or four ways to request the same function. The good news is that you won't need to do any special SYSOUT processing in the majority of jobs. Instead, coding SYSOUT=* on the DD statement will be sufficient. So keep the information presented in this chapter in that perspective. It's here to refer to when you need it.

Terms

job-level default statement
step-level default statement
null class
forms control buffer
forms-flash technique

9

How to use JCL procedures

As you code JCL, you'll discover that there are many job steps…and series of job steps…that are used over and over in an installation, often by different programmers. That's why OS/390 provides for procedures that can be stored in libraries and made available to any programmer on the system. With this facility, you can usually code just a few JCL statements to execute procedures that contain dozens or even hundreds of JCL statements. In fact, IBM supplies complex procedures that let you interface easily with software products like compilers, CICS, and DB2, and you'll use them all the time. In addition, in most shops, you'll create and use procedures that are specific to your installation.

The basics of using JCL procedures

A *JCL procedure* (or just *procedure*) is a pre-written segment of code consisting of one or more job steps that you can include in a job stream. By using procedures, the amount of JCL coding you have to do is reduced, resulting in fewer coding errors and greater productivity. Although you can code a procedure directly in a single job stream, you're more likely to invoke cataloged procedures that are available throughout an installation.

How to create and use cataloged procedures

A *cataloged procedure* is a series of JCL statements that are stored in a partitioned data set and may be invoked by any job on the system. For example, in the middle of figure 9-1, you can see the JCL statements that make up a cataloged procedure named INV3000. This procedure consists of two job steps that execute the programs INV3010 and INV3020 and allocate seven different data sets.

To invoke a cataloged procedure in a job stream, you specify its name in an EXEC statement. As you can see in the syntax for the EXEC statement in this figure, the PROC parameter is optional and is usually omitted. But it's positional, so if you do code it, it must be the first parameter on the EXEC statement. Note that because a procedure is always invoked by an EXEC statement in a job, the procedure itself doesn't contain a JOB statement.

Invoking a procedure is much like invoking a program. Rather than invoke a program directly, however, a procedure-invoking EXEC statement searches for the cataloged procedure in the system's procedure libraries and causes its JCL statements to be read into your job stream. Then, the procedure statements invoke programs and allocate files. In the example in this figure, then, when STEP1 invokes procedure 3000, it causes the programs named INV3010 and INV3020 to be executed and their files to be allocated.

An important point to realize here is that the JCL statements in a procedure are processed by the reader/interpreter component of JES. In other words, the procedure statements are actually processed *before* the job begins to execute. Then, if the procedure can't be located or errors are found, the job won't execute. In most cases, though, the procedure statements will be executed just as if they had been coded directly in the job stream.

As I mentioned earlier, the main reason for using procedures is to avoid coding the same JCL over and over again. In fact, IBM puts their JCL code for common system functions in cataloged procedures because the jobs are often lengthy and complicated and because they need to be used in conjunction with many jobs in a system. So you'll frequently use IBM-supplied procedures for functions like compiling or running programs. Beyond IBM-supplied procedures, however, your shop may create cataloged procedures for jobs that are run regularly (like backups), job steps that are used by many jobs, and jobs that have been thoroughly tested and put into production.

The syntax for invoking a JCL procedure

```
EXEC [PROC=]procedure-name
```

Explanation

procedure-name   Identifies the procedure to be called and executed. For cataloged procedures, it's the member name of the procedure. For instream procedures (see figure 9-2), it's the name on the PROC statement that begins the procedure.

A job that invokes a cataloged procedure

```
//MM01RN   JOB (36512),'R MENENDEZ',NOTIFY=MM01
//STEP1    EXEC INV3000
//
```

The cataloged JCL procedure named INV3000 that is invoked

```
//INV3000  PROC
//INV3010  EXEC PGM=INV3010
//SYSOUT   DD   SYSOUT=*
//INVMAST  DD   DSNAME=MMA2.INVENTRY.MASTER,DISP=SHR
//INVSEL   DD   DSNAME=&&INVSEL,DISP=(NEW,PASS),
//              UNIT=SYSDA,SPACE=(CYL,(20,10))
//SELCTL   DD   DUMMY
//INV3020  EXEC PGM=INV3020
//SYSOUT   DD   SYSOUT=*
//INVMAST  DD   DSNAME=&&INVSEL,DISP=(OLD,DELETE)
//INVSLST  DD   SYSOUT=*
```

Typical types of cataloged procedures

- IBM-supplied procedures that compile, link, and run programs
- JCL steps that back up, delete, and define VSAM files
- Programs that are required by many jobs
- Large jobs where it makes sense to separate the steps into manageable procedures (most production jobs fall into this category)

Description

- *JCL procedures* are pre-written segments of code that you can include in a job stream just by coding the procedure name in an EXEC statement.
- A procedure consists of job steps and is always invoked from a job. As a result, the procedure itself doesn't include a JOB statement. In addition, the EXEC statements within a procedure must all invoke programs, rather than other procedures.
- *Cataloged procedures* are stored in partitioned data sets and can be invoked by any job on the system.
- When you invoke a cataloged procedure, the system looks for it in the system procedure library, SYS1.PROCLIB, unless you specify otherwise (see figure 9-3 for more details).
- Although the PROC statement can be coded as the first statement in a cataloged procedure, it's not required.

Figure 9-1   How to create and use cataloged procedures

How to create and use instream procedures

Before cataloging a procedure in a procedure library, it's usually a good idea to test the JCL code it contains, and the easiest way to do that is with an instream procedure. An *instream procedure* consists of a PROC statement, any number of procedure steps, and a PEND statement. Then, you place the instream procedure near the beginning of your job stream, before any EXEC statement that refers to it. In contrast to a cataloged procedure, an instream procedure is available only to the job that contains it.

To give you a better understanding of how this works, figure 9-2 presents a job stream that contains an instream procedure. The first statement after the JOB statement is a PROC statement that marks the beginning of procedure INV3000. The lines that follow are the JCL statements that make up the procedure. Then, to mark the end of the procedure, a PEND statement is coded. After the PEND statement are two EXEC statements, each of which invokes the instream procedure by specifying the name that's coded on the PROC statement, INV3000.

The EXEC statements between the PROC and PEND statements are not executed when they're first encountered in the job stream. Instead, they're saved as a procedure so they can be processed later. Then, when the EXEC statement in STEPB1 is processed, the two job steps in the INV3000 instream procedure are executed. Next, the STEPB2 EXEC statement is processed and it too invokes the instream procedure.

An instream JCL procedure

```
//MM01RN    JOB (36512),'R MENENDEZ',NOTIFY=MM01
//             MSGCLASS=X,MSGLEVEL=(1,1)
//INV3000   PROC
//INV3010   EXEC PGM=INV3010
//SYSOUT    DD   SYSOUT=*
//INVMAST   DD   DSNAME=MMA2.INVENTRY.MASTER,DISP=SHR
//INVSEL    DD   DSNAME=&&INVSEL,DISP=(NEW,PASS),
//               UNIT=SYSDA,SPACE=(CYL,(20,10))             Instream
//SELCTL    DD   DUMMY                                      procedure
//INV3020   EXEC PGM=INV3020
//SYSOUT    DD   SYSOUT=*
//INVMAST   DD   DSNAME=&&INVSEL,DISP=(OLD,DELETE)
//INVSLST   DD   SYSOUT=*
//          PEND
//STEPA     EXEC PGM=INV1000
//INVMAST   DD   DSNAME=MMA2.INVENTORY.MASTER,DISP=SHR      Executing
//INVLIST   DD   SYSYOUT=*                                  code
//STEPB1    EXEC INV3000
//STEPB2    EXEC INV3000
//
```

The order in which the programs in the job are executed

```
INV1000
INV3010
INV3020
INV3010
INV3020
```

Description

- Before cataloging a procedure in a procedure library, it's a good idea to test it. You can do that by inserting the procedure into a job as an *instream procedure*.

- An instream procedure consists of a PROC statement, followed by the JCL for the procedure, followed by a PEND statement.

- A name is always required on the PROC statement for an instream procedure. You can also specify a name on the PEND statement, but it's optional.

- JCL statements falling between the PROC and PEND statements are not executed when first encountered. Instead, they're scanned for errors and retained as a temporary procedure. Any JCL statements after the PEND statement are recognized as normal statements and are executed.

- An instream procedure should be placed near the beginning of a job stream, before any EXEC statement that refers to it.

- The maximum number of instream procedures you can code in any job is 15.

Figure 9-2   How to create and use instream procedures

How to use the JCLLIB statement to identify private procedure libraries

As I said earlier, the cataloged data sets at an installation are stored as members in the installation's procedure libraries. When JES2 or JES3 is initialized, the system procedure library, typically named SYS1.PROCLIB, is allocated to the JES address space. SYS1.PROCLIB contains mostly system-oriented and IBM-supplied procedures. Each installation also concatenates various libraries to SYS1.PROCLIB, so if a procedure isn't found in one library, another is searched.

When a procedure is stored in a partitioned data set other than SYS1.PROCLIB, you use the JCLLIB statement shown in figure 9-3 to identify the PDS as a *private procedure library*. The JCLLIB statement is placed after the JOB statement and before the first EXEC statement in a job. Then, the private procedure libraries that you list on the JCLLIB statement are searched, in the order given, for any cataloged procedures that are invoked in the job. If a procedure is still not found once all of those libraries have been searched, the system searches SYS1.PROCLIB. As a result, using the JCLLIB statement doesn't affect your ability to invoke standard procedures like those supplied by IBM.

The example in this figure shows how the JCLLIB statement is commonly used. Here, when the EXEC statement is executed, the system searches for a procedure named INV3000 in a private procedure library called MMA2.TEST.PROCLIB. If the procedure isn't a member of that library, the private procedure library called MMA2.PROD.PROCLIB is searched. Last, if INV3000 is not located in either library, SYS1.PROCLIB is searched.

Specifying the JCLLIB statement in this way is a common technique to use when testing a procedure in a job that has several procedures. The test procedure library will only contain those procedures that are being tested and the rest will default to the production procedure library.

The syntax for the JCLLIB statement

```
//[name] JCLLIB ORDER=(library[,library]...)
```

Explanation

ORDER   Specifies the names of the libraries to be searched for cataloged procedures. You can
specify private libraries, system libraries, and installation-defined libraries. The
system will search the libraries in the order specified.

A job that invokes a cataloged procedure in a test library

```
//MM01RN    JOB  (36512),'R MENENDEZ',NOTIFY=MM01
//          JCLLIB ORDER=(MMA2.TEST.PROCLIB,MMA2.PROD.PROCLIB)
//STEP1     EXEC INV3000
//
```

The search sequence used to find procedure INV3000

```
MMA2.TEST.PROCLIB  →  MMA2.PROD.PROCLIB  →  SYS1.PROCLIB
```

Description

* SYS1.PROCLIB is normally used to store system-oriented cataloged procedures, like
those supplied by IBM. It can also be used to store other types of cataloged procedures
(like those for production jobs, job steps, or jobs that are in development), but other
private procedure libraries are often created for these.

* The JCLLIB statement lets you identify libraries as private procedure libraries that the
system should search to find a specified cataloged procedure.

* The job will search the JCLLIB libraries in the order in which they're coded. If the
procedure is not found in any of the named libraries, SYS1.PROCLIB is searched.

* The JCLLIB statement must appear after the JOB statement but before any EXEC
statements in the job.

* The system and private libraries you specify in the JCLLIB statement can contain both
procedures and INCLUDE groups. You'll learn about the INCLUDE statement in
figure 9-5.

Figure 9-3   How to use the JCLLIB statement to identify private procedure libraries

How to identify procedure statements in job listings

A job's output JCL listing will incorporate any procedures you specified in the job as part of the job stream. As a result, a job that consists of only a couple of lines, like the example in figure 9-4, can end up being much longer in the output listing. If you examine the JCL listing, you'll notice that the original JCL appears at the top and that procedure INV3000 is inserted immediately after the EXEC statement that invoked it.

You'll also notice that the statements in the JCL listing are marked to distinguish procedure JCL statements from job JCL statements. The chart in this figure shows what these identifiers are. In this case, the // in columns 1 and 2 of the procedure statements have been replaced by XX to show that they came from a cataloged procedure. Had an instream procedure been used instead, ++ would have appeared in columns 1 and 2.

You can see from the chart that procedure statements can be marked in other ways as well. Later in this chapter, you'll see statements in job listings that begin with X/. This means that the cataloged procedure statement was changed by a JCL statement that you coded in your job stream.

A JCL job stream that invokes a cataloged procedure

```
//MM01RN    JOB  (36512),'R MENENDEZ',NOTIFY=MM01
//STEP1     EXEC INV3000
//
```

The JCL listing in the job output

```
//MM01RN    JOB  (36512),'R MENENDEZ',NOTIFY=MM01
//         JCLLIB ORDER=MMA2.PROCLIB
//STEP1     EXEC INV3000
XXINV3000  PROC
XXINV3010  EXEC PGM=INV3010
XXSYSOUT   DD   SYSOUT=*
XXINVMAST  DD   DSNAME=MMA2.INVENTRY.MASTER,DISP=SHR
XXINVSEL   DD   DSNAME=&&INVSEL,DISP=(NEW,PASS),
XX              UNIT=SYSDA,SPACE=(CYL,(20,10))
XXSELCTL   DD   DUMMY
XXINV3020  EXEC PGM=INV3020
XXSYSOUT   DD   SYSOUT=*
XXINVMAST  DD   DSNAME=&&INVSEL,DISP=(OLD,DELETE)
XXINVSLST  DD   SYSOUT=*
//
```

Identifiers for procedure statements in a job's JCL listing

Cataloged procedure	Instream procedure	Meaning
//	//	Statement from input JCL.
XX	++	Statement from procedure.
X/	+/	Procedure statement that you modified.
XX*	++*	Procedure statements, other than comment statements, that were converted to comments (probably because of an error).
***	***	Comments and JES2/JES3 control statements.

Description

- In a job listing, JCL statements that are retrieved from cataloged or instream procedures are identified by X's or plus signs instead of slashes in columns 1 and 2.

- If you modify a procedure statement to tailor it for the job you want to do, the statement is marked by X/ or +/ in columns 1 and 2. You'll see how to modify procedure statements later in this chapter.

Figure 9-4   How to identify procedure statements in job listings

How to use the INCLUDE statement to copy JCL into a job stream

In addition to or in conjunction with a JCL procedure, you can use an INCLUDE statement to copy text directly into your job stream, as shown in figure 9-5. Then, when the job is submitted, the *INCLUDE group* replaces the INCLUDE statement, and the system processes the embedded text as part of the job stream.

The INCLUDE statement works much like a cataloged procedure, except that the JCL copied into the job stream doesn't have to consist of entire job steps. As a result, you can use INCLUDE to copy just portions of a step, such as a single DD statement or a group of commonly used DD statements.

Like cataloged procedures, INCLUDE groups are stored in PDS libraries. In fact, you can store INCLUDE groups in the same libraries that you use to store your procedures. Typically, though, you're better off keeping INCLUDE groups in separate libraries, so they're easily distinguished. In any case, if an INCLUDE group is stored in a private procedure library instead of SYS1.PROCLIB, you use the JCLLIB statement to specify its location just as you do for cataloged procedures.

In the example in this figure, a private library member called INVMAST contains the DD statement used to allocate a data set with a ddname of INVMAST. Then, instead of coding a DD statement for INVMAST in the job stream, the INCLUDE statement copies the INVMAST member into the job. The effective JCL shows how the system retrieves the INVMAST member and inserts the INCLUDE group to be processed as if the INVMAST DD statement had been coded directly in the job stream.

You can also nest INCLUDE statements if you wish. In other words, an INCLUDE group can itself contain an INCLUDE statement. You can't, however, code any of the JCL statements listed in this figure in an INCLUDE group.

The syntax for the INCLUDE statement

```
//[name]    INCLUDE MEMBER=name
```

Explanation

MEMBER   Specifies the name of the member you want to include. The member must exist in a private library specified in a JCLLIB statement or in SYS1.PROCLIB.

A job that uses an INCLUDE statement

The JCL submitted for processing

```
//MM01RN    JOB    (36512),'R MENENDEZ',NOTIFY=MM01
//          JCLLIB ORDER=MMA2.PROCLIB
//INV3010   EXEC PGM=INV3010
//SYSOUT    DD    SYSOUT=*
//          INCLUDE INVMAST
//INVSEL    DD    DSNAME=&&INVSEL,DISP=(NEW,PASS),
//                UNIT=SYSDA,SPACE=(CYL,(20,10))
//SELCTL    DD    DUMMY
//INV3020   EXEC PGM=INV3020
//SYSOUT    DD    SYSOUT=*
//INVMAST   DD    DSNAME=&&INVSEL,DISP=(OLD,DELETE)
//INVSLST   DD    SYSOUT=*
```

The INVMAST library member

```
//INVMAST   DD    DSNAME=MMA2.INVENTRY.MASTER,DISP=SHR
```

The effective JCL

```
//INV3010   EXEC PGM=INV3010
//SYSOUT    DD    SYSOUT=*
//INVMAST   DD    DSNAME=MMA2.INVENTRY.MASTER,DISP=SHR
//INVSEL    DD    DSNAME=&&INVSEL,DISP=(NEW,PASS),
//                UNIT=SYSDA,SPACE=(CYL,(20,10))
//SELCTL    DD    DUMMY
//INV3020   EXEC PGM=INV3020
//SYSOUT    DD    SYSOUT=*
//INVMAST   DD    DSNAME=&&INVSEL,DISP=(OLD,DELETE)
//INVSLST   DD    SYSOUT=*
```

JCL statements not allowed in an INCLUDE group

- JOB, PROC, PEND, JCLLIB, DD*, DD DATA
- JES2 and JES3 statements and commands

Description

- The INCLUDE statement is similar to the EXEC statement for a procedure in that it lets you copy text directly into your job stream. When the job is submitted, the *INCLUDE group* (the JCL statements in the library member that's specified) replaces the INCLUDE statement, and the system processes the embedded text as part of the job stream.
- You can use the INCLUDE statement to copy portions of a step, such as a single DD statement or a group of commonly used DD statements.
- INCLUDE statements can be nested up to 15 levels deep.

Figure 9-5   How to use the INCLUDE statement to copy JCL into a job stream

How to modify the statements in a procedure

There will be times when you'll need to make minor adjustments to the JCL statements contained within procedures to meet varying processing needs. So in the topics that follow, you'll learn how to code job stream statements that let you change or supplement the statements in a procedure.

How to modify EXEC statements

To change a parameter that's coded on an EXEC statement within a procedure or to add a parameter to one of the procedure's EXEC statements, you code a *parameter override* on the EXEC statement that invokes the procedure. The syntax for a parameter override is included in figure 9-6. As you can see, you code the parameter name you want to override as well as the procedure step in which it occurs. If you want to override more than one parameter, you separate the parameter overrides with commas. Because it's necessary to associate parameters with procedure step names, it's important that each step in a procedure has a unique name.

It's also important to realize that overrides are done on a parameter-by-parameter basis. In other words, if you code an override for a parameter, it replaces the entire parameter in the procedure, including any subparameters that are set there. As a result, if the parameter in a procedure includes a subparameter that you want to keep unchanged, you have to repeat it in the parameter override or it will be lost. In contrast, if the procedure includes multiple parameters for an EXEC statement, you only need to code overrides for the ones you want to change; the others will not be affected.

To illustrate how to code parameter overrides, look at the examples in this figure. The first one is for an IBM-supplied COBOL compile-and-link procedure. Here, the DATEPROC and XREF parameters are added to the COBOL step, so the program will be compiled with these options. If the COBOL step in the procedure already has PARM parameters specified, they'll be overridden.

The second example overrides the TIME parameter in STEP3 of the procedure to allow the job step 3 minutes of processor time instead of 1 minute, 30 seconds. Notice that because the override completely replaces the TIME parameter in the procedure, the value for the seconds subparameter (30) is lost.

If you code a parameter without specifying a procedure step name, it usually overrides or is added to each EXEC statement in the procedure, as shown in the third example. The only exceptions are the PARM and TIME parameters. If you code a PARM parameter without a step name, it applies just to the first step of the invoked procedure. If you code a TIME parameter without a step name, the entire procedure is timed as if it were a single job step.

To nullify the effect of an EXEC parameter in a procedure, you code the parameter and procedure step name on the invoking EXEC statement, but omit the value after the equals sign. The last example in this figure nullifies the TIME parameter coded on the procedure step named PSTEP1.

The syntax for modifying EXEC statements in a procedure

```
//[name]   EXEC [PROC=]procedure-name,parameter.procstepname=value
```

The functions of parameter overrides in an invoking EXEC statement

* Modify the existing parameters on an EXEC statement within a procedure
* Add parameters to an EXEC statement within a procedure
* Add parameters to all EXEC statements within a procedure
* Nullify the effects of a parameter on an EXEC statement within a procedure

Invoking EXEC statements that modify EXEC statements in procedures

Adding compilation parameters to the COBOL step in the IGYWCL procedure

```
//COMP1     EXEC PROC=IGYWCL,PARM.COBOL='DATEPROC,XREF'
```

Overriding the TIME parameter in the STEP3 step of procedure INV3200

The procedure statement	`//STEP3`	`EXEC PGM=3230,REGION=256K,TIME=(1,30)`
The parameter override	`//INV3200`	`EXEC PROC=INV3200,TIME.STEP3=3`
The result	`//STEP3`	`EXEC PGM=3230,REGION=256K,TIME=3`

Applying a REGION parameter to all of the steps in procedure ACT1000

```
//ACT1000   EXEC PROC=ACT1000,REGION=4M
```

Nullifying the TIME parameter in the PSTEP1 step of procedure ARS2010

```
//ARS2010   EXEC ARS2010,TIME.PSTEP1=
```

Description

* To change or add a parameter that's coded on an EXEC statement within a procedure, you can code a *parameter override* on the EXEC statement that invokes the procedure.
* To identify the parameter you want to override, you have to provide the parameter name and the step name that are coded on the EXEC statement within the procedure. For parameter overrides to work right, each step in the procedure should have a unique name.
* If you code a parameter without specifying a procedure step name, it will override or add the parameter to each EXEC statement in the procedure.
* To nullify the effects of a parameter in a procedure step, you code the parameter and procedure step name on the invoking EXEC statement, but omit the value after the equals sign.
* If you override a parameter on an EXEC statement that has multiple parameters, you only need to code the parameter you want to change. All the other parameters remain the same.
* If you override an EXEC parameter that has multiple subparameters, you have to repeat all of the subparameters in the override, even if they're not changed. That's because a parameter override completely replaces the original parameter in the procedure EXEC statement.

Figure 9-6   How to modify EXEC statements

How to modify or add DD and OUTPUT statements

If you want to change the parameters in DD or OUTPUT statements in a procedure, or add new statements altogether, you use the syntax shown in figure 9-7. Then, the parameter overrides or new statements are applied to the procedure that's invoked.

To understand how this works, look at the example in this figure. To start, STEPB1 in this job invokes procedure INV3000. That statement is immediately followed by an OUTPUT override statement. Since OUT1 is a job-level OUTPUT statement within the procedure, the override doesn't have to include a procedure step name. It does, however, include an override parameter of COPIES=4 that will replace the value of 2 in the procedure statement. The OUTPUT statement in the procedure also includes a CLASS=A parameter that isn't affected by the override. (In the JCL output listing, the highlighted statements beginning with // are the parameter overrides, while the statements beginning with X/ are the original procedure statements that are affected.)

The next two override statements are for the SYSOUT and INVSEL DD statements in procedure step INV3010. Since SYSOUT is the first DD statement for that step, the procedure step name is included as part of its identification. In contrast, the INVSEL override statement doesn't have to include the procedure step name. That's because it's in the same procedure step as the SYSOUT DD statement and because it's coded in the same order as the DD statements in that step. If you don't want to worry about the coding order, however, always include the procedure step name in DD overrides. On the INVSEL override, only the SPACE parameter for the data set is changed. The other INVSEL parameters are not affected.

This figure doesn't include an example of adding a DD or OUTPUT statement to a procedure because the technique is the same. The only difference is that you need to include all of the parameters necessary for the DD or OUTPUT statement to properly function. Also, all added statements within a procedure step must follow all override statements for the same step.

The syntax for modifying or adding DD/OUTPUT statements in a procedure

```
//[name]                  EXEC   [PROC=]procedure-name
//[procstepname.]ddname   DD     parameter=value
//[procstepname.]ddname   OUTPUT parameter=value
```

The functions of parameter overrides in DD and OUTPUT statements

- Modify existing parameters on DD and OUTPUT statements within a procedure
- Add parameters to existing DD and OUTPUT statements within a procedure
- Add DD and OUTPUT statements to an existing job step within a procedure
- Nullify the effects of a parameter on DD and OUTPUT statements within a procedure

A job that modifies DD and OUTPUT statements in a procedure

The invoking JCL

```
//STEPB1    EXEC INV3000
//OUT1        OUTPUT COPIES=4
//INV3010.SYSOUT DD DUMMY
//INVSEL    DD    SPACE=(CYL,(5,5))
```

The JCL listing in the job output

```
//STEPB1    EXEC INV3000
XXINV3000  PROC
//OUT1        OUTPUT COPIES=4
X/OUT1        OUTPUT CLASS=A,COPIES=2
XXINV3010  EXEC PGM=INV3010
//INV3010.SYSOUT DD DUMMY
X/SYSOUT    DD    SYSOUT=*
XXINVMAST   DD    DSNAME=MMA2.INVENTRY.MASTER,DISP=SHR
//INVSEL    DD    SPACE=(CYL,(5,5))
X/INVSEL    DD    DSNAME=&&INVSEL,DISP=(NEW,PASS),
XX                UNIT=SYSDA,SPACE=(CYL,(20,10))
XXSELCTL    DD    DUMMY
XXINV3020  EXEC  PGM=INV3020
XXSYSOUT    DD    SYSOUT=*
XXINVMAST   DD    DSNAME=&&INVSEL,DISP=(OLD,DELETE)
XXINVSLST   DD    SYSOUT=*
```

Description

- To modify or add DD and OUTPUT statements in a procedure, you code the appropriate parameters on DD and OUTPUT statements that follow the invoking EXEC statement. To nullify a parameter, you code the parameter but omit the value after the equals sign.

- The procedure step name is only required on the first override DD statement for a step. However, if you omit it from subsequent DD overrides for the step, the overrides must be coded in the same sequence as the DD statements in the procedure step.

- The procedure step name is not required for override OUTPUT statements at the job level.

- All added DD and OUTPUT statements within a procedure step must follow all statement overrides for the same step.

- As with EXEC overrides, DD and OUTPUT overrides are done on a parameter-by-parameter basis, so be sure to include all subparameters that should remain unchanged.

Figure 9-7   How to modify or add DD and OUTPUT statements

How to use the DDNAME parameter for DD statements in procedures

A DDNAME parameter lets you relate a DD statement to another DD statement with a different ddname within a job or procedure step, as shown in figure 9-8. Although you usually don't need to use this parameter in a normal job stream, it can come in handy when you're coding a procedure.

What makes the DDNAME parameter particularly useful in procedures is that the DD statement referred to in the DDNAME parameter is optional. If the specified DD statement is present, it's used. But if it isn't, the data set is treated as if DUMMY were specified and all I/O operations for the data set are ignored. As a result, using the DDNAME parameter is a good way to provide for data sets that are optional.

You might be wondering at this point why you wouldn't just code DUMMY on the DD statement in the procedure and provide an override DD statement if the data set is needed. The reason is that the only way to override a DUMMY parameter is to code a DSNAME parameter on the overriding DD statement in the invoking JCL. However, when you do that, you can't provide instream data to the procedure, as I've done in the example in this figure. So if you want to allow an instream data set to override a DUMMY data set, you'll have to use DDNAME instead of DUMMY. Then, you code the instream data set in the invoking JCL using the ddname that the DDNAME parameter points to. This adds the instream data set to the specified procedure step, and when the DD statement with the DDNAME parameter is executed, the instream data set is used.

If you code a DDNAME parameter, you can only code a few other parameters with it, as listed in this figure. Any other DD statement parameters will result in a syntax error.

The syntax for the DDNAME parameter of the DD statement

```
DDNAME=ddname
```

Explanation

ddname   Refers to a later DD statement within the same job step or calling job step.

How to get around the restriction on instream data sets in procedures

The cataloged procedure with a DDNAME parameter

```
//INV3000  PROC
//INV3010  EXEC PGM=INV3010
//SYSOUT   DD   SYSOUT=*
//INVMAST  DD   DDNAME=INPUT
//INVSEL   DD   DSNAME=&&INVSEL,DISP=(NEW,PASS),
//              UNIT=SYSDA,SPACE=(CYL,(20,10))
//SELCTL   DD   DUMMY
//INV3020  EXEC PGM=INV3020
//SYSOUT   DD   SYSOUT=*
//INVMAST  DD   DSNAME=&&INVSEL,DISP=(OLD,DELETE)
//INVSLST  DD   SYSOUT=*
```

The JCL that invokes the procedure and provides it with instream data

```
//MM01RN JOB (36512),'R MENENDEZ',NOTIFY=MM01
//STEP1  EXEC INV3000
//INV3010.INPUT  DD *
   .
   instream data
   .
/*
//
```

Description

- The DDNAME parameter on a DD statement lets you relate a DD statement coded in a procedure to an overriding DD statement with a different ddname.

- If the DD statement specified in the DDNAME parameter is not present, the data set will be treated as if DUMMY were specified.

- One reason for using the DDNAME parameter in a procedure is to provide for instream data, something you can't do directly in a procedure. In this case, you use a parameter override to add the DD * statement and instream data to the procedure step when the procedure is executed, and use the DDNAME parameter to point to that new data set.

- The only other DD statement parameters you can code with DDNAME are BLKSIZE, BUFNO, DIAGNS, LIKE, and REFDD.

- The DDNAME parameter can be coded in regular job streams, as well as in procedures.

Figure 9-8   How to use the DDNAME parameter for DD statements in procedures

How to use symbolic parameters within a procedure

The techniques presented so far for modifying procedures are fairly flexible, but they can be awkward to use. A better way to create procedures for generalized use is with *symbolic parameters*. When you use symbolic parameters, you don't code the actual parameter values in the procedure's JCL statements. Instead, you code symbolic parameters that can take on specific values when you invoke the procedure. The topics that follow will show you how to code symbolic parameters and the different ways you can use them.

How to code and use symbolic parameters

You code symbolic parameters within a procedure when you want the values of certain parameters to remain variable. Then, when you invoke the procedure, you assign values to the symbolic parameters in the invoking EXEC statement, as shown in figure 9-9. As a result, the procedure is executed with those values.

To code a symbolic parameter in a procedure, you use a name that starts with an ampersand (&). The name can be any meaningful name you want as long as it isn't a keyword parameter on an EXEC statement. For example, &TIME or &REGION would not be valid names because both are keyword parameters on an EXEC statement. But &SPACE and &CLASS are acceptable names.

You can use the same symbolic parameter in a procedure as many times as you like. For example, you can use a symbolic parameter called &CLASS as the value for the SYSOUT parameter in all of the SYSOUT DD statements in a procedure. That way, you can be sure that all SYSOUT data sets are processed using the same output class. If you need to assign different classes to the SYSOUT data sets, however, you have to use more than one symbolic parameter.

To illustrate the use of symbolic parameters, this figure shows another version of the INV3000 procedure that you've seen throughout this chapter. Here, three symbolic parameters are used to make the procedure easier to customize. In the DD statements for the SYSOUT data sets, &CLASS is used so that the output class can be changed when the procedure is invoked. Similarly, &DEPT is specified as part of the data set name for the INVMAST data set. Notice that there are two periods coded following &DEPT. You'll learn why in the next topic. Finally, &SPACE is specified as a subparameter in the SPACE parameter of the INVSEL DD statement. That way, a different amount of space can be allocated to the data set each time the procedure is invoked.

To supply the values for symbolic parameters on the EXEC statement that invokes the procedure, you code the symbolic parameter name but without the ampersand. If the value you're assigning contains any special characters like commas or asterisks, you have to enclose the entire value in apostrophes. In this example, then, &CLASS is assigned a value of M, &DEPT is assigned a value of MMA2, and &SPACE is assigned a value of 5,1.

The syntax for assigning values to symbolic parameters in a procedure

```
//[name]  EXEC [PROC=]procedure-name,symbolic-parameter=value
```

Explanation

symbolic-parameter   A one- to seven-character name that is referenced by the procedure. The name can't be a keyword parameter used by the EXEC statement.

A procedure that uses symbolic parameters

The INV3000 procedure

```
//INV3000   PROC
//INV3010   EXEC  PGM=INV3010
//SYSOUT    DD    SYSOUT=&CLASS
//INVMAST   DD    DSNAME=&DEPT..INVENTRY.MASTER,DISP=SHR
//INVSEL    DD    DSNAME=&&INVSEL,DISP=(NEW,PASS)),
//                UNIT=SYSDA,SPACE=(CYL,(&SPACE))
//SELCTL    DD    DUMMY
//INV3020   EXEC  PGM=INV3020
//SYSOUT    DD    SYSOUT=&CLASS
//INVMAST   DD    DSNAME=&&INVSEL,DISP=(OLD,DELETE)
//INVSLST   DD    SYSOUT=&CLASS
```

The invoking EXEC statement

```
//STEPA1    EXEC  INV3000,CLASS=M,DEPT=MMA2,SPACE='5,1'
```

The effective JCL

```
//INV3010   EXEC PGM=INV3010
//SYSOUT    DD   SYSOUT=M
//INVMAST   DD   DSNAME=MMA2.INVENTRY.MASTER,DISP=SHR
//INVSEL    DD   DSNAME=&&INVSEL,DISP=(NEW,PASS),
//               UNIT=SYSDA,SPACE=(CYL,(5,1))
//SELCTL    DD   DUMMY
//INV3020   EXEC PGM=INV3020
//SYSOUT    DD   SYSOUT=M
//INVMAST   DD   DSNAME=&&INVSEL,DISP=(OLD,DELETE)
//INVSLST   DD   SYSOUT=M
```

Description

- *Symbolic parameters* can be used in procedures to represent a value later supplied by the invoking JCL. This allows you to create procedures that can be customized for many different jobs.

- In a procedure, the symbolic parameter consists of an ampersand (&) followed by a one- to seven-character name. The name can be anything you want as long as it's not a keyword parameter name on an EXEC statement.

- In a procedure, you can code a symbolic parameter anywhere you would normally code a JCL statement parameter or subparameter.

- To supply the value for a symbolic parameter, you code its name *without* the ampersand along with its value on the EXEC statement that invokes the procedure.

- If the value for a symbolic parameter contains special characters, like commas and asterisks, you enclose the entire value in apostrophes.

Figure 9-9   How to code and use symbolic parameters

This figure also shows the effective JCL for the procedure as it's interpreted using the symbolic parameter values supplied by the EXEC statement. As you can see, all of the SYSOUT data sets now have an output class of M, the INVMAST DD statement now has a proper data set name, and the INVSEL DD statement now has an appropriate number of cylinders assigned to it. Although this isn't the way the listing appears in your job output, it helps you see the effect of using symbolic parameters.

Coding rules for symbolic parameters

To illustrate the flexibility of symbolic parameters, as well as the coding rules that govern their use, figure 9-10 presents seven examples. For each example, assume that the value of &VAR1 is TEST and the value of &VAR2 is LIST, as shown in the procedure-invoking EXEC statement at the top of this figure.

The first example shows a simple case. Here, the &VAR1 symbolic parameter is used to assign a value to the DSNAME parameter. As a result, when the procedure is invoked, TEST will be used as the data set name.

The second example illustrates how a symbolic parameter can be used with other text to form the final parameter value. Here, the letter A is combined with &VAR1's value to form the data set name ATEST. In this example, no special coding is required to combine the text with the symbolic parameter value. That's because the ampersand acts as the delimiter to separate the text from the symbolic parameter name.

Adding text to the end of a symbolic parameter isn't a problem either as long as the text starts with a special character, as in the third example. Here, the DSNAME becomes TEST(LIST). Because the left parenthesis is a special character, no special coding is needed to distinguish it from the &VAR1 symbolic parameter name.

Adding text after a symbolic parameter when the text begins with a letter or digit, however, is another matter. That's because the system can't separate the start of the text from the end of the symbolic parameter name. To solve this problem, you must use a period as a delimiter between the symbolic parameter and the text, as in the fourth example. As a result, although you code &VAR1.A, the result is TESTA.

Unfortunately, the use of a period as a delimiter can be a problem if you want a period to appear in the final JCL statement. In such situations, you code two periods, as shown in the fifth example. Here, the first period is the delimiter that marks the end of the symbolic parameter name, and the second period becomes a part of the data set name. You may recall seeing this technique in figure 9-9 where the &DEPT symbolic parameter was used as the high-level qualifier for the inventory master data set.

Example 6 shows that you don't need to use a period to place two symbolic parameters back to back. That's because the ampersand itself separates them. Although you can use a period if you wish (&VAR1.&VAR2), it's not necessary. If you want the period to remain between the two symbolic parameters, however, you must again code two periods, as in example 7.

Examples of coding symbolic parameters

The symbolic parameter values used

```
//          EXEC proc-name,VAR1=TEST,VAR2=LIST
```

Example	As coded in procedure	As interpreted by JES
1	DSNAME=&VAR1	DSNAME=TEST
2	DSNAME=A&VAR1	DSNAME=ATEST
3	DSNAME=&VAR1(&VAR2)	DSNAME=TEST(LIST)
4	DSNAME=&VAR1.A	DSNAME=TESTA
5	DSNAME=&VAR1..A	DSNAME=TEST.A
6	DSNAME=&VAR1&VAR2	DSNAME=TESTLIST
7	DSNAME=&VAR1..&VAR2	DSNAME=TEST.LIST

Rules for coding symbolic parameters in JCL statements

* You can use the same symbolic parameter in a procedure as many times as you wish.

* Symbolic parameters can be mixed with text to form a final parameter value.

* If you want text to appear immediately after a symbolic parameter, you must code a period (.) as a delimiter between the symbolic parameter name and the text that follows it.

* If you want a period to appear immediately after a symbolic parameter, you have to code two periods in a row. The first one acts as a delimiter marking the end of the symbolic parameter and the second one becomes part of the JCL statement.

* To nullify the value of a symbolic parameter, you code the symbolic parameter's name followed by an equals sign without a value.

Figure 9-10   Coding rules for symbolic parameters

You can also nullify the value of a symbolic parameter by coding the symbolic parameter's name followed by an equals sign without a value. When you do this, however, you have to be sure that the JCL statement has a valid syntax after the symbolic parameter's value is applied. If a null value is encountered where one isn't valid, a JCL error will occur.

How to assign default values to symbolic parameters

So far, you've learned how to code symbolic parameters and how to assign values to them when you invoke a procedure. As you code your own procedures, though, you'll soon realize that many symbolic parameters will have certain values that are used most of the time. So rather than having to assign values to all of the symbolic parameters in a procedure each time it's invoked, you can assign default values on the procedure's PROC statement.

To illustrate, figure 9-11 shows yet another version of the INV3000 procedure that supplies default values for the &CLASS and &SPACE parameters. Here, the default output class for &CLASS is * so that the job's message output class is used. In addition, &SPACE has been assigned a reasonable amount of disk space. Note, however, that no default value has been assigned to &DEPT, so DEPT must always be coded on the EXEC statement that invokes the procedure. This figure also shows the effect of invoking the procedure with an EXEC statement that provides a value for &DEPT, overrides the default for &SPACE, and relies on the default value for &CLASS.

A procedure that uses default symbolic parameters

The INV3000 procedure

```
//INV3000  PROC CLASS='*',SPACE='1,1'
//INV3010  EXEC PGM=INV3010
//SYSOUT   DD   SYSOUT=&CLASS
//INVMAST  DD   DSNAME=&DEPT..INVENTRY.MASTER,DISP=SHR
//INVSEL   DD   DSNAME=&&INVSEL,DISP=(NEW,PASS),
//              UNIT=SYSDA,SPACE=(CYL,(&SPACE))
//SELCTL   DD   DUMMY
//INV3020  EXEC PGM=INV3020
//SYSOUT   DD   SYSOUT=&CLASS
//INVMAST  DD   DSNAME=&&INVSEL,DISP=(OLD,DELETE)
//INVSLST  DD   SYSOUT=&CLASS
```

The invoking EXEC statement

```
//STEPA1   EXEC INV3000,DEPT=MMA2,SPACE='10,5'
```

The effective JCL

```
//INV3010  EXEC PGM=INV3010
//SYSOUT   DD   SYSOUT=*
//INVMAST  DD   DSNAME=MMA2.INVENTRY.MASTER,DISP=SHR
//INVSEL   DD   DSNAME=&&INVSEL,DISP=(NEW,PASS),
//              UNIT=SYSDA,SPACE=(CYL,(10,5))
//SELCTL   DD   DUMMY
//INV3020  EXEC PGM=INV3020
//SYSOUT   DD   SYSOUT=*
//INVMAST  DD   DSNAME=&&INVSEL,DISP=(OLD,DELETE)
//INVSLST  DD   SYSOUT=*
```

Description

- To provide a default value for a symbolic parameter in a procedure, you code the value on the procedure's PROC statement. Then, if an EXEC statement that invokes the procedure doesn't provide a value for the symbolic parameter, the default value is used.

- If an EXEC statement that invokes the procedure does provide a symbolic parameter value, it will override the default value.

Figure 9-11   How to assign default values to symbolic parameters

How to use the SET statement to assign values to symbolic parameters

The SET statement, shown in figure 9-12, is another way to assign values to symbolic parameters. In contrast to a PROC statement that assigns default values or a procedure-invoking EXEC statement that provides runtime values, the SET statement lets you set the values of symbolic parameters at any point or time within your JCL. Be aware, however, that SET values are overridden by any values that are assigned in subsequent PROC or EXEC statements in the job.

This figure shows how you can use SET statements to set parameter values before invoking a cataloged procedure. Instead of specifying parameter values on the invoking EXEC statement, two SET statements are used to set the values of the symbolic parameters &SPACE and &DEPT. Although these values could be combined into a single SET statement, coding separate SET statements makes it easier to change the values for each parameter later on.

If you study the effective JCL, you'll see that the parameter value for &DEPT established in the SET statement is reflected in the procedure. But the value for &SPACE assigned by the SET statement is overridden by the default value assigned by the PROC statement in the procedure. This illustrates that you have to use the SET statement with care, or your jobs won't execute as you expect them to.

An advantage of the SET statement is that you don't have to use it in conjunction with procedures at all. In fact, it enables you to use symbolic parameters in any job stream. For example, suppose you have a job that you use frequently with only minor variations. If you use a SET statement at the beginning of the job to set a symbolic parameter that's used throughout the job, you can change the value in only one place rather than having to hunt through the entire job to make the equivalent changes. In some cases, this type of coding can eliminate the need for a cataloged procedure altogether.

The syntax for the SET statement

```
//[name]    SET symbolic-parameter=value[,symbolic-parameter=value]...
```

Explanation

symbolic-parameter   The name of a symbolic parameter you want to assign a value to.

A job that uses the SET statement to assign values to symbolic variables

The INV3000 procedure

```
//INV3000  PROC CLASS='*',SPACE='1,1'
//INV3010  EXEC PGM=INV3010
//SYSOUT   DD   SYSOUT=&CLASS
//INVMAST  DD   DSNAME=&DEPT..INVENTRY.MASTER,DISP=SHR
//INVSEL   DD   DSNAME=&&INVSEL,DISP=(NEW,PASS),
//              UNIT=SYSDA,SPACE=(CYL,(&SPACE))
//SELCTL   DD   DUMMY
//INV3020  EXEC PGM=INV3020
//SYSOUT   DD   SYSOUT=&CLASS
//INVMAST  DD   DSNAME=&&INVSEL,DISP=(OLD,DELETE)
//INVSLST  DD   SYSOUT=&CLASS
```

The invoking JCL

```
//MM01RN JOB (36512),'R MENENDEZ',NOTIFY=MM01
//         SET  SPACE='10,5'
//         SET  DEPT=MMA2
//STEPA1   EXEC INV3000
```

The effective JCL

```
//INV3010  EXEC PGM=INV3010
//SYSOUT   DD   SYSOUT=*
//INVMAST  DD   DSNAME=MMA2.INVENTRY.MASTER,DISP=SHR
//INVSEL   DD   DSNAME=&&INVSEL,DISP=(NEW,PASS),
//              UNIT=SYSDA,SPACE=(CYL,(1,1))
//SELCTL   DD   DUMMY
//INV3020  EXEC PGM=INV3020
//SYSOUT   DD   SYSOUT=*
//INVMAST  DD   DSNAME=&&INVSEL,DISP=(OLD,DELETE)
//INVSLST  DD   SYSOUT=*
```

Description

- The SET statement is an alternate way to assign values to symbolic parameters. In contrast to an EXEC statement or PROC statement, the SET statement allows you to assign values to symbolic parameters at any time or point in your JCL.

- A SET statement can appear anywhere within a job after the JOB statement.

- Symbolic parameter values assigned by the SET statement are overridden by any subsequent values that are coded in invoking EXEC statements or PROC statements.

- Although typically used to assign a value to a symbolic parameter within a procedure, the SET statement also allows you to code symbolic parameters in regular JCL streams.

Figure 9-12   How to use the SET statement to assign values to symbolic parameters

Perspective

You'll work with procedures regularly using the facilities covered in this chapter. So check with your supervisor to find out what procedure libraries are available to you as you develop new job streams and what the standards are for creating and storing procedures of your own. Then, in chapter 17, you'll use what you've learned in this chapter to work with IBM-supplied procedures for jobs like compiling your programs.

Terms

JCL procedure
procedure
cataloged procedure
instream procedure
private procedure library
INCLUDE group
parameter override
symbolic parameter

Section 3

Other JCL skills

The chapters in this section expand on the JCL basics to teach you about OS/390 features that you'll use regularly, although you won't need them in every job. Chapter 10 teaches you how to control job processing based on the outcome of previous job steps. Chapter 11 teaches you how to restart a job if it terminated abnormally due to a job or system failure. Chapter 12 teaches you how to manage generation data groups that make it easier for you to create and process multiple backup copies of the same file. And chapter 13 teaches you how to use the Storage Management Subsystem (SMS) if it's installed in your shop.

Because these chapters are independent of each other, you can read them in any sequence you like. What's more, you don't have to read them right after you read section 2. If you prefer, you can skip to section 4 to learn about VSAM file handling or to section 5 to learn about other OS/390 facilities that save you time and work as you develop application programs.

10

How to process jobs conditionally

In the course of coding JCL jobs, you'll often find that job steps are dependent on one another. If one step ends abnormally, for example, you may not want to continue processing any subsequent steps. That's why OS/390 provides facilities that allow you to execute programs conditionally. In other words, you can specify whether to execute a job step based on the results of previous steps in the job.

OS/390 return codes

When a program in a job step completes execution normally (that is, it doesn't abend), it passes a value called a *step return code* back to OS/390. This value indicates whether there were any problems with the execution and, if so, how severe they were. Then, at the end of a job, a *system completion code* indicates whether the job completed normally or not.

Since you will have to deal with job errors during the course of your career, understanding how to interpret both step return codes and system completion codes will allow you to resolve your JCL problems more quickly. It will also allow you to use these codes in your JCL to control job execution.

Step return codes

A step return code (or just a *return code* or *condition code*) indicates whether or not a job step ran successfully. If a step ends normally, the return code is usually 0. But if the step does not end normally, the return code can have a value from 1 to 4095.

The program that's executed during the step determines what the return code will be and what it represents. All IBM compilers, linkage editors, and utility programs follow the same general numbering conventions shown in figure 10-1. A return code of 0 indicates that the step ran successfully with no errors encountered. A 4 indicates that some minor errors were encountered but the program was able to recover from them. For instance, compilers will typically return a code of 4 if the program source code generated any warning messages during the compilation. A code of 8 indicates that the program encountered a problem that prevented it from performing a successful execution. A 12 is similar to an 8 but more serious. And a return code of 16 indicates that the program encountered a serious error and was not able to continue.

Application programming languages allow you to generate your own return codes for your programs. For example, this figure shows you the syntax needed to generate a return code in some of the programming languages that are used on an OS/390 system. In most cases, you simply pass a numeric value to a predefined field or subprogram. The value you choose is up to you (as long as it's between 0 and 4095) and can depend on the results the program produces. Before you assign your own return codes in an application program, however, be sure to check your installation standards for any additional guidelines on their use.

Typical step return codes issued by OS/390 programs

Return code	Meaning
0	Program ran to successful completion.
4	Program encountered a minor error but was able to recover.
8	The program encountered a problem that inhibited successful execution.
12	The program encountered a problem that inhibited successful execution; normally, this indicates a more serious error than return code 8.
16	The program encountered a serious error and was not able to continue.

A step return code message in a JCL output listing

```
IEF142I MM01A STEP1 - STEP WAS EXECUTED - COND CODE 0000
```

How different programming languages issue return codes

Language	Syntax
COBOL	MOVE *return-code* TO RETURN-CODE
Java	System.exit(*returnCode*);
PL/I	CALL PLIRETC(*return-code*);
FORTRAN	STOP *return-code*
C/C++	exit(*return-code*);
Assembler	Specify a return code in register 15

Description

- A *step return code* (or just *return code* or *condition code*) is issued for every job step executed in a job. If the step ends normally without encountering any unusual conditions, the return code is 0. If it runs into any problems while processing, though, a value from 1 to 4095 is assigned.

- All of the IBM compilers, linkage editors, and utility programs follow the same general numbering conventions shown in the return code chart above.

- Most of the application programming languages that run in an OS/390 environment provide language syntax or a special register for issuing a return code. As a result, a programmer can specify a return code value ranging from 0 to 4095, depending on the results a program produces.

Figure 10-1   Step return codes

System completion codes

Figure 10-2 includes some of the more common system completion codes (or just *completion codes*) you may encounter. As you can see, if a job ends normally, the system completion code is 000. Otherwise, the system completion code is generated in the JCL message output and consists of an *S* followed by a three-digit hexadecimal number that indicates the reason for the abnormal job termination. Many of these *abend codes* also include an additional *reason code* to help further explain the source of the problem. For example, if a job has a system completion code of S0C4, reason 4, it indicates that a program abended because of a protection exception. More than likely, the program tried to access an array table with an invalid index or subscript.

This figure also includes a sample of what a system completion code may look like in the JCL message output. Here, the output line includes information like the job identifier, the job name and step name, and the abend code and reason code, all of which help you track down the cause of the problem. If you have to deal with abend codes or reason codes that aren't listed in this figure, please refer to the IBM manual, *OS/390 MVS System Codes*, for more information.

System completion codes

Code	Reason	Explanation
000		Normal completion. The job ended successfully.
0C1	1	Operation exception. Can be caused by an invalid program branch or program data overwriting the instruction area of the program.
0C4	4	Protection exception. The program tried to access a storage area other than its own. Often happens when a storage array is accessed with an invalid index or subscript.
	10	Segment-translation exception. The program tried to access storage that has not been obtained.
	11	Page-translation exception. The program tried to access storage that was paged out.
0C5	5	Addressing exception. The program tried to access an invalid storage address.
0C7	Varies	Data exception. Caused by invalid data used in a calculation.
122		The operator cancelled the job and requested a dump.
222		The TSO/E user cancelled the job without requesting a dump.
322		The job exceeded the CPU time limit specified by the TIME parameter or the default time allowed for the job.
722		The job output limit specified by the OUTLIM, BYTES, CARDS, LINES, or PAGES parameter was exceeded.
804		The job's virtual storage requirements exceeded the amount specified in the job or job step REGION parameter.
806		Program not found. The system could not find the program module to execute.
822		The region size requested is not available. Typically occurs when the REGION parameter requests a region size larger than what is currently available on the system.
B37		Disk volume is full. The volume requested in the DD statement is out of space or ran out of space during execution.

The completion code message in a JCL output listing

```
19.08.15 JOB02444  IEF450I MM01B STEP1 - ABEND=S806 U0000 REASON=00000004
```

Description

- A *system completion code* (or just *completion code*) is generated when a job ends.

- If the job ends normally, the completion code is 000. If the job abends, the completion code consists of a three-digit code with a prefix of *S*, and it appears in the job output. In this case, it can also be called an *abend code*.

- Most completion codes include an additional *reason code* that helps further define what the problem is. For a complete listing of completion codes and their explanations, see the IBM manual, *OS/390 MVS System Codes*.

Figure 10-2   System completion codes

How to use the COND parameter

The COND parameter allows you to specify the conditions that will allow a job step to execute. Specifically, it allows you to check return codes from earlier steps so you can decide whether to execute the current step. You can code this parameter on either the JOB or EXEC statement depending on whether you want to specify a condition that applies to each step in the job or only to a single step.

How to code the COND parameter on a JOB statement

When you specify the COND parameter in a JOB statement as shown in figure 10-3, you specify the conditions that cause the job to stop processing. For example, suppose you have a job with several steps. If any of the steps issues a return code of 4 or more, the job should stop processing, bypassing the remaining steps. In such a case, the COND parameter would be coded like this: COND=(4,LE). This means that if 4 is less than or equal to the return code issued by any job step, the remaining job steps are to be bypassed. So if the return code is 8, the remaining steps are bypassed because the condition is true. In contrast, if the return code is 0, the condition is not true, so the job continues with the next step.

The table near the top of this figure shows the relational operators you can code in the COND parameter, and the table right below it illustrates how different types of conditions are handled. To be honest, many programmers find that this condition handling logic is confusing. So as you look at these examples, remember that the value you code in the COND parameter is compared with the actual return code using the relational operator you specify. If the relationship is true, all remaining job steps are bypassed. In other words, the COND parameter specifies not the conditions under which processing is to continue, but rather the conditions under which processing is to be terminated.

This figure also shows three examples of the COND parameter on the JOB statement. The first example consists of a single condition, like those you've already seen. The second and third examples show how you can combine up to eight conditions on the COND parameter. When you combine conditions, job processing stops if any of the conditions you specify are true. Note in these last two examples how each condition is enclosed in a set of parentheses, and the entire list of conditions is enclosed in parentheses too.

Chapter 10   How to process jobs conditionally   **279**

The syntax for the COND parameter in a JOB statement

```
COND=((value,operator)...)
```

Relational operators for the COND parameter

Operator	Meaning
GT	Greater than
GE	Greater than or equal to
LT	Less than
LE	Less than or equal to
EQ	Equal to
NE	Not equal to

How the COND parameter handles return codes (RC)

COND parameter	Continue job	Terminate job
COND=(4,GT)	RC >= 4	RC < 4
COND=(8,GE)	RC > 8	RC <= 8
COND=(0,LT)	RC <= 0	RC > 0
COND=(8,LE)	RC < 8	RC >= 8
COND=(12,EQ)	RC <> 12	RC = 12
COND=(0,NE)	RC = 0	RC <> 0

Examples of the COND parameter on a JOB statement

The job will terminate if any job step has a return code of 8

```
//MM01C    JOB (36512),'R MENENDEZ',COND=(8,EQ)
```

The job will terminate with a return code of 8 or a return code of 16 or greater

```
//MM01C    JOB (36512),'R MENENDEZ',COND=((8,EQ),(16,LE))
```

The job will terminate with a return code of 8, 12, or 16

```
//MM01C    JOB (36512),'R MENENDEZ',COND=((8,EQ),(12,EQ),(16,EQ))
```

Description

- You can code the COND parameter on a JOB statement to specify the conditions that cause a job to stop processing. If any of the steps within the job issues a return code that satisfies the condition, the system bypasses the remaining steps and terminates the job.

- You can combine up to eight conditions on a single COND parameter. Then, if any one of the conditions is true, the job terminates. This can be useful in situations where you are interested in stopping the job only if certain return codes are issued.

Figure 10-3   How to code the COND parameter on a JOB statement

How to code the COND parameter on an EXEC statement

The COND parameter of the EXEC statement is more flexible than the COND parameter of the JOB statement. It lets you specify a return code and a relational operator to determine whether to skip a particular job step instead of all subsequent steps. In addition, you can specify a step name in order to test the return code for a specific job step. It also provides two additional subparameters, EVEN and ONLY, that let you specify how an abend affects job step execution.

Figure 10-4 gives you the syntax for the COND parameter on an EXEC statement and shows you five ways to code it. In the first example, the COND parameter specifies that the job step should be bypassed if 7 is less than the return code issued by any previous step. In other words, a return code of 8 or more causes the step to be bypassed. In the second example, the return code from the step named SORT1 is tested; if it's equal to 8, the current job step is bypassed. The third example shows that you can specify multiple conditions just as on the JOB statement. Here, this job step will be bypassed if 8 is equal to the return code from step SORT1 or if 12 is less than or equal to the return code from step VIDUPD1.

The fourth example uses the EVEN subparameter. This tells OS/390 to execute the job step whether or not a previous step has abended. The ONLY subparameter, shown in the fifth example, tells OS/390 to execute the job step only if a previous step has abended. In other words, if an abend has not occurred, the step is not executed. ONLY is useful for steps that perform recovery processing in the event of an abend and is usually coded in the last step of a job. EVEN is useful for steps that don't depend on the successful completion of previous steps. If EVEN or ONLY aren't specified anywhere in a job, an abend in any job step causes the rest of the job steps to be bypassed.

Incidentally, if the condition of a COND parameter on a JOB statement is satisfied, the job terminates regardless of any COND parameters on EXEC statements. For example, suppose a JOB statement has a COND parameter coded COND=(7,LE) and STEP2 has a COND parameter coded COND=(12,EQ,STEP1). If STEP1 issues a return code of 8, the job will terminate without executing STEP2.

The syntax for the COND parameter in an EXEC statement

```
COND=([(value,operator[,stepname])...]
      [ ,{EVEN} {ONLY}])
```

Explanation

EVEN   Tells the system to execute the job step even if a previous job step abended.

ONLY   Tells the system to execute the job step only if a previous job step abended.

Examples of the COND statement on an EXEC statement

The job step is bypassed if any previous step has a return code of 8 or greater

```
//VIDUPD1    EXEC PGM=VIDUPD1,COND=(7,LT)
```

The job step is bypassed if the SORT1 job step's return code is 8

```
//VIDRPT3    EXEC PGM=VIDRPT3,COND=(8,EQ,SORT1)
```

The job step is bypassed if SORT1 has a return code of 8 or VIDUPD1 has a return code of 12 or greater

```
//VIDRPT4    EXEC PGM=VIDRPT4,COND=((8,EQ,SORT1),(12,LE,VIDUPD1))
```

The job step is executed even if a previous job step abended

```
//VIDLOG     EXEC PGM=VIDLOG,COND=EVEN
```

The job step is executed only if a previous job step abended

```
//VIDERR     EXEC PGM=VIDERR,COND=ONLY
```

Description

- You can use the COND parameter on an EXEC statement to test return codes from previous job steps to determine whether or not to bypass the current job step.

- You can code an expression with a relational operator in the COND parameter to test the return code from a particular job step or from every job step that has completed processing.

- You can code the EVEN or ONLY subparameter to specify how an abend affects job step execution.

- You can combine up to eight conditions on a single COND parameter. Then, if any one of the conditions is true, the job step is bypassed.

- If the condition of a COND parameter on a JOB statement is satisfied, the job terminates regardless of any COND parameters coded on EXEC statements.

Figure 10-4   How to code the COND parameter on an EXEC statement

How to use the IF construct

At one time, the COND parameter was the only option for handling conditional processing in JCL. But because it's awkward and confusing to use, later versions of the operating system added three JCL statements that work together for that purpose: IF/THEN, ELSE, and ENDIF. Like the COND parameter, the IF/THEN/ELSE/ENDIF statement construct (or just the IF construct, as we'll refer to it here) allows you to conditionally execute job steps based on the results of the conditions you set. In contrast to the COND parameter, however, you can code the conditions in much the same way as you would in COBOL, Java, C++, or any other high-level programming language.

The syntax of the IF/THEN, ELSE, and ENDIF statements

Figure 10-5 shows the syntax for the IF/THEN, ELSE, and ENDIF statements. To begin conditional execution, you code an IF statement that includes the condition you want to test. After the condition, you code a THEN clause followed by whatever JCL statements you want to execute if the condition is true (there must be at least one). Then, if necessary, you code an ELSE statement followed by whatever JCL statements you want to execute if the condition is false. Finally, you code an ENDIF statement to end the conditional structure.

You specify the condition you want to test in an IF statement by coding a relational expression that can contain the keywords and operators shown in this figure. If you look through the explanations of these elements, you'll see that you can code expressions to check for specific return codes or abend codes or to determine whether a job, job step, or procedure step completed normally. To make these options clearer, the next topic shows you a number of coding examples.

The syntax for the IF/THEN, ELSE, and ENDIF statements

```
//[name] IF (relational-expression) THEN
.
    statements-executed-if-true
.
//[name] ELSE
.
    statements-executed-if-not-true
.
//[name] ENDIF
```

The syntax for a relational expression

```
keyword [operator value]
```

Operator		Meaning	Operator		Meaning
NOT	or ¬	Logical not	EQ	or =	Equal to
GT	or >	Greater than	NE	or ¬=	Not equal to
LT	or <	Less than	GE	or >=	Greater than or equal to
NG	or ¬>	Not greater than	LE	or <=	Less than or equal to
NL	or ¬<	Not less than	AND	or &	And
			OR	or |	Or

Keyword	Meaning
RC	The highest return code issued by any job step previously executed.
stepname[procstep.]RC	The return code issued by the specified job step or procedure step.
ABEND	True if an abend has occurred.
stepname.[procstep.]ABEND	True if the specified job step or procedure step has abended.
¬ABEND	True if an abend has not occurred.
stepname.[procstep.]¬ABEND	True if the specified job step or procedure step has not abended.
ABENDCC=Sxxx	True if the most recent system abend code is the abend code specified.
ABENDCC=Uxxxx	True if the most recent user abend code is the abend code specified.
stepname.[procstep.]RUN	True if the specified job step or procedure step started execution.
stepname.[procstep.]¬RUN	True if the specified job step or procedure step did not start execution.

Description

- An IF/THEN/ELSE/ENDIF construct (or just IF construct) consists of the IF statement, followed by the condition you want to test and the word THEN. You can omit the ELSE statement if it isn't needed, but an ENDIF statement must always be coded.
- To specify the condition you want, you code a relational expression. A relational expression is made up of the operators and keywords listed above.
- To continue a relational expression on the next line, break the first line wherever a blank is valid and start the next line of the expression beginning in column 4 through 16.
- To test the results of a step within a cataloged procedure, you code the procedure step name after the step name in a keyword expression.

Figure 10-5   The syntax of the IF/THEN, ELSE, and ENDIF statements

How to code the IF/THEN, ELSE, and ENDIF statements

Figure 10-6 shows seven examples of conditions coded in the IF/THEN statement. In each case, a true condition would cause the job to execute any statements that are coded in the THEN clause.

The first example in this figure includes a simple condition that tests to see if the highest return code issued by any prior job step is greater than 0. The condition in the second example is true if the return code issued by job step STEP1 is equal to 6. The third example shows how you can use AND to test two conditions at once. This statement evaluates to true if STEP1 issues a return code of 6 and STEP2 issues a return code less than 16. The fourth and fifth examples show how you can test to see if a specific job step has abended. The sixth example shows how you can test to see if a specific job step abended with a specific system abend code. And the last example shows how you can test to see if a specific step in a cataloged procedure started execution.

Notice in the first three examples that a space is included both before and after each operator in the relational expressions. Although this isn't necessary, it can help make the statements more readable. On the other hand, if you're using the mnemonic equivalents of the operators (GT, LT, EQ, etc.), a space before and after the operator is always necessary.

The example at the bottom of this figure shows how you can use the IF/THEN, ELSE, and ENDIF statements together in a job stream. Here, the job step TRERR is executed if any previous job step has issued a return code greater than or equal to 8. Otherwise, the step named TRSUM is executed. Notice that the name field wasn't coded for any of the conditional statements. If you omit the name field, you must leave column 3 blank. Then, you can start the operation field (IF/THEN, ELSE, or ENDIF) anywhere after column 3.

IF constructs can appear anywhere in a job after the first EXEC statement, and they can be nested up to a maximum of 15 levels. I recommend you avoid coding them any more than two levels deep, however, to avoid confusion and possible coding errors. And by all means, make sure that each IF statement has a corresponding ENDIF statement. If you accidentally omit ENDIF, the system will treat additional statements as though they're still part of the IF construct and will execute them conditionally.

Examples of IF/THEN conditions

Example	IF/THEN condition	Evaluates to true if...
1	`IF RC > 0 THEN`	Any previous job step has issued a return code greater than 0.
2	`IF STEP1.RC = 6 THEN`	The return code for job step STEP1 is 6.
3	`IF STEP1.RC = 6 AND STEP2.RC < 16 THEN`	The return code for job step STEP1 is 6 and the return code for STEP2 is less than 16.
4	`IF STEP1.ABEND THEN`	STEP1 ended abnormally.
5	`IF STEP1.¬ABEND THEN`	STEP1 ended normally.
6	`IF STEP1.ABENDCC=S0C4 THEN`	STEP1 ended abnormally with a system abend code of S0C4.
7	`IF STEP1.ORD2000A.RUN THEN`	The step named ORD2000A in the procedure invoked by STEP1 started execution.

Part of a job stream that uses IF/THEN, ELSE, and ENDIF statements

```
// IF RC >= 8 THEN
//TRERR     EXEC PGM=AR5340
//SYSOUT    DD   SYSOUT=*
//ERRLOG    DD   DSNAME=MMA2.ERRLOG,DISP=MOD
// ELSE
//TRSUM     EXEC PGM=AR5350
//SYSOUT    DD   SYSOUT=*
//TRANFILE  DD   DSNAME=MMA2.TRANFILE,DISP=SHR
// ENDIF
```

Description

- An IF construct can appear anywhere in the job after the first EXEC statement. The THEN clause and, if used, the ELSE clause must each contain at least one EXEC statement.
- You can nest IF constructs up to a maximum of 15 levels.

Figure 10-6   How to code the IF/THEN, ELSE, and ENDIF statements

Perspective

Although conditional processing isn't an issue for most jobs, from time to time you may need to set conditions that determine whether or not a job step should be executed based on the result of a previous step. When you do, you can use either the COND parameter or an IF construct, depending on your personal preference and your shop standards. The COND parameter has been around longer and is still the preferred method of conditional handling in some shops, so you're likely to run into it at some time in your career. However, given a choice, I prefer to use IF constructs because their syntax makes conditions easier to code and understand and they more closely resemble the method of conditional coding that I'm used to using in application programs.

Terms

step return code
return code
condition code
system completion code
completion code
abend code
reason code

11

How to use RESTART and other program execution facilities

When a program abends or the system fails, you may need to restart a job from the point where the failure occurred. So in this chapter, you'll learn about the facilities that OS/390 provides for doing that. You'll also learn about a couple of additional facilities that let you control other aspects of program execution. Although you probably won't use these facilities often, it's good to know that they're available if you should ever need them.

How to restart a job

As you learned in chapter 10, jobs may terminate before they complete due to a program or system error. In either case, it's possible to restart a job at a point other than at the beginning. To be specific, you can restart a job from a designated step (a *step restart*), or you can restart a step from a checkpoint within a program (a *checkpoint restart*).

OS/390 provides two parameters for restarting a job. The RESTART parameter can be coded on the JOB statement to handle job failures, while the RD parameter can be coded on the JOB or EXEC statement to handle job or system failures. In addition, JES2 and JES3 both provide statements that restart jobs automatically in case of a system failure.   ·

How to code checkpoints in your jobs

When you set up *checkpoints* for individual job steps, the status of the executing program is recorded periodically in a data set assigned for that purpose. That way, if the job terminates without successfully completing the job step, it can be restarted from the last recorded checkpoint rather than having to start at the beginning of the step again.

Not all programming languages that run on OS/390 systems allow checkpoint recording, but the chart in figure 11-1 shows you the languages and utilities that do. As you can see, COBOL provides a clause called RERUN that allows you to assign the file where the checkpoints are to be stored and to specify the frequency of the checkpoints that are to be taken. In PL/I, you use a special module called PLICKPT. And in assembler language, you store your checkpoints by executing the CHKPT macro instruction.

In JCL, the CHKPT parameter on a DD statement allows you to record a checkpoint whenever a multi-volume sequential data set reaches the end of any volume except the last one. That way, if the job step abends, the program can restart at the beginning of the most recent data set volume. The example in this figure shows you how to code a job step with these *end-of-volume checkpoints*. Here, the data set named MM01.INV.OUT is a sequential file that is written to two tape volumes. By specifying CHKPT=EOV in its DD statement, a checkpoint will be written to the data set defined by SYSCKEOV after the end-of-volume is reached for the first volume (TAPE01). The checkpoint data set must have the ddname SYSCKEOV, it must be a sequential or partitioned data set, and it must be defined with DISP=MOD so that each new checkpoint is written beyond the previous one.

To be honest, you probably won't use checkpoints often, if at all. In fact, most installations discourage their use because they don't work well in most situations. With today's processor speeds, jobs tend to run much faster than they did just a few years ago, so the difference between restarting a job from the beginning of a step rather than at some point within it is inconsequential. Still, the JCL parameters for restart processing do allow for checkpoints, so I wanted you to be familiar with them before going on.

Programming languages and utilities that support checkpointing

COBOL
Use the RERUN clause in the I-O-CONTROL paragraph of the Input-Output Section to generate checkpoints within a COBOL program. The ddname for the data set that stores the checkpoints is specified in the RERUN clause.

PL/I
Use the CALL PLICKPT feature to generate checkpoints within a PL/I program. The ddname for the checkpoint data set is SYSCHK.

Assembler language
Use the CHKPT macro instruction to generate checkpoints. The DCB macro specifies the ddname for the checkpoint data set.

JCL
Use the CHKPT parameter on the DD statement to generate check points whenever the end of a volume is reached for a sequential data set. The ddname for the checkpoint data set is SYSCKEOV.

DFSORT
Use the CKPT parameter in sort control statements to generate checkpoints. The ddname for the checkpoint data set is SORTCKPT.

The syntax for the CHKPT parameter of the DD statement

```
CHKPT=EOV
```

Explanation

EOV   Requests a checkpoint at the end of the volume.

A job step with end-of-volume checkpoints

```
//STEP1     EXEC PGM=INVUPD
//INVOUT    DD   DSN=MM01.INV.OUT,DISP=(NEW,KEEP),
                 UNIT=TAPE,VOL=SER=(TAPE01,TAPE02),CHKPT=EOV
//SYSCKEOV DD    DSN=CHECK.SAVE,DISP=MOD
```

Description

- *Checkpoints* can be set up on individual job steps so that periodic snapshots are taken of the executing program's status and are stored in a designated data set. If the job terminates for whatever reason, it can be restarted from the last recorded checkpoint rather than from the beginning of the step.

- Not all programming languages allow checkpoint recording. For those that do, refer to their language reference manuals for specific instructions on how to set up a checkpoint.

- Use the CHKPT parameter on the DD statement to record a checkpoint whenever a multi-volume sequential data set reaches the end of a volume. Checkpoints are written for each volume except the last.

- If you use the CHKPT parameter on a DD statement, be sure to include a SYSCKEOV DD statement that defines the data set where the checkpoints are stored. The SYSCKEOV data set must be a sequential or partitioned data set defined with DISP=MOD so that each new checkpoint is written beyond the previous one.

Figure 11-1   How to code checkpoints in your jobs

How to code the RESTART parameter for deferred restarts

Figure 11-2 shows the syntax for the RESTART parameter of the JOB statement, which lets you restart a job when one of the job steps has failed. Normally, you specify the job step name where you want to restart the job, but you can also specify a procedure step name if the job calls a procedure. If you code an asterisk (*) in place of a step name, the job will simply start at the first job step—the same as not specifying RESTART at all.

The most common way to restart a job is shown in the first example in this figure. Here, the job is simply restarted at the beginning of the step named STEP3. The second example shows how you can include a procedure step name to restart the job from within a procedure. Here, the job is restarted at the beginning of the step named INV3020 in the procedure that's invoked by STEP3. Restarting a job at the beginning of a step as in these examples is called a *deferred step restart.*

Restarting a job from a checkpoint within a job step, as shown in the third example, is called a *deferred checkpoint restart.* Here, job MM01G will restart at the checkpoint named CKPT4 that was recorded in job step STEP2. The CKPT4 checkpoint reference can be found in the data set named by the SYSCHK DD statement. You must always include this DD statement when using a deferred checkpoint restart. In addition, you must make sure that all of the data sets used in the original run of the job step are present. In other words, the checkpoint process only records the position each data set was in when the checkpoint was generated; it doesn't save the data records themselves.

In coding the RESTART parameter, keep in mind that you may not always be able to restart a job at the job step that failed. That's because the step may depend on references or temporary data sets created by previous steps. For example, suppose you want to restart a job at a step that was executing a report program when it failed. However, the report program reads in a sorted temporary data set created in a previous step. Since the sorted file was temporary, it was automatically deleted when the job abended and now doesn't exist. In a case like this, you need to restart the job at the step where the temporary data set is created. Also be aware that you need to delete any data sets the job step created in a previous run before restarting.

In general, you add the RESTART parameter to a job once it's failed and then resubmit the job for processing. However, some programmers like to code RESTART=* in all their jobs. Then, when a job fails, they simply replace the * with the values needed for the step or checkpoint restart.

The syntax for the RESTART parameter of the JOB statement

```
RESTART= ({*                       } [,checkid] )
         {stepname                 }
         {stepname.procstepname}
```

Explanation

*	Specifies that the system is to restart the job at the first job step.
stepname	Specifies that the system is to restart the job at the beginning of the named job step or at a checkpoint within that job step.
stepname.procstepname	Specifies that the system is to restart the job at the beginning of the named job step of the cataloged procedure or at a checkpoint within that job step. *Stepname* identifies the EXEC statement that calls the procedure and *procstepname* identifies the job step within the procedure.
checkid	Specifies the name of the checkpoint at which the system is to restart execution.

The two ways to use the RESTART parameter

A deferred step restart

```
//MM01F    JOB (36512),'LE MENENDEZ',RESTART=STEP3
//MM01G    JOB (36512),'J TAYLOR',RESTART=STEP3.INV3020
```

A deferred checkpoint restart

```
//MM01H    JOB (36512),'M MURACH',RESTART=(STEP2,CKPT4)
//SYSCHK   DD  DSNAME=MM01.CHECK,DISP=OLD
```

Description

- The RESTART parameter on the JOB statement allows you to restart a job from a specified job step, procedure step, or checkpoint within a job step.

- If the job is restarted from a job or procedure step, it's called a *deferred step restart*. If the job is restarted from a checkpoint, it's called a *deferred checkpoint restart*.

- The *stepname* and *procstepname* specified in a RESTART parameter must be unique in order for the system to determine the correct restart step. If not, the results are unpredictable.

- When using a deferred checkpoint restart, you have to include a SYSCHK DD statement to identify the data set where the checkpoint reference can be found.

- Before resubmitting a job with the RESTART parameter, check to be sure that all backward references to EXEC statement PGM parameters and data sets are either accounted for or eliminated. If a temporary data set passed from a previous job step is used, it may be necessary to restart the job from the step that creates the data set. Also make sure that any data sets created by the job step in a previous run are deleted.

Figure 11-2   How to code the RESTART parameter for deferred restarts

How to code the RD parameter for automatic restarts

Figure 11-4 shows the syntax for the RD parameter for both the JOB and EXEC statements. This parameter is primarily used to specify whether a job, or the individual jobs steps within it, can be automatically restarted after a system failure. Chances are, though, that you'll seldom use it. For the most part, installations prefer that you use the RESTART parameter to restart any failed jobs. Still, it's included here so you'll know how to code it in case it's ever required.

The system will perform an *automatic restart* when three conditions are met. First, the JOB statement or at least one of the EXEC statements within the job must have the RD parameter coded with the R or RNC keyword. This tells the system that an automatic restart with or without checkpoints is allowed for the job or job step. Second, the job step to be restarted must have a restartable abend code. If the system failed, chances are that this condition will be true. And third, the operator must authorize the restart. That means that after the system is reinitialized or the job has been requeued, the operator has the option of releasing the job or canceling it.

Assuming these conditions are met, an automatic restart is still only possible if the job had a job journal at the time of the failure. A *job journal* is a sequential data set that contains job-related control blocks needed for the restart. Job journals are internal system files controlled by either JES2 or JES3, so you don't have to worry about keeping track of them. They're automatically created by the system whenever a job is executed provided that certain parameters are specified during JES2 or JES3 initialization.

Although the RD parameter is used most often to enable automatic restarts, it can also be used to control whether or not checkpoints are to be allowed for deferred restarts. Specifying RD=NR indicates that a job or job step can't be restarted automatically but checkpoints are allowed if a deferred restart is used. In contrast, specifying RD=NC indicates that the job or job step can't be restarted automatically and that deferred checkpoint restarts aren't allowed either.

The syntax for the RD parameter of the JOB and EXEC statements

```
RD= {R}
    {RNC}
    {NR}
    {NC}
```

Explanation

R   Restart, checkpoints allowed. This option allows the system to automatically restart execution of a job or job step from the beginning or from the last checkpoint.

RNC   Restart, no checkpoints. This option allows the system to perform an automatic step restart when the job or job step fails. Automatic and deferred checkpoint restarts aren't allowed.

NR   No automatic restart, checkpoints allowed. This option suppresses automatic restarts but permits deferred checkpoint restarts.

NC   No automatic restart, no checkpoints. This option indicates that the system can't perform an automatic step restart if the job or job step fails and that checkpoint restarts aren't allowed.

The system will perform an automatic restart on a job or job step when:

- RD=R or RD=RNC is present on a JOB or EXEC statement
- The step to be restarted has a restartable abend code
- The operator authorizes the restart

A JOB statement that uses the RD parameter

```
//MM01A JOB (36512),MENENDEZ,RD=R
```

An EXEC statement that uses the RD parameter

```
//STEP2   EXEC  PGM=APRUPD,RD=RNC
```

Description

- If a job abends due to a program or system failure, the entire job or the individual job steps within it can be automatically restarted if you code the RD parameter on the JOB or EXEC statement. The RD parameter can also be used to control checkpoint restarts.

- To have a job automatically restart after a system failure, code RD=R or RD=RNC on either the JOB or EXEC statement. If coded on the JOB statement, all of the job steps in the job are restarted. If coded on the EXEC statement, only the individual job step is restarted. An RD parameter in the JOB statement overrides any RD parameters specified in the EXEC statements.

- The system can perform an *automatic restart* on a job only if the job has a job journal. A *job journal* is a sequential data set that contains job-related control blocks needed for the restart. It's an internal system file that's not part of your JCL.

- Specifying RD=NR or RD=NC will prevent an automatic restart from occurring, so you'll probably never code it that way.

Figure 11-3   How to code the RD parameter for automatic restarts

How to code the JES2 /*JOBPARM RESTART parameter

In a JES2 environment, you can code the /*JOBPARM RESTART parameter to automatically restart a job from the beginning in the event that the system fails while the job is executing. As you can see in figure 11-4, coding RESTART=Y ensures that JES2 will queue the job for re-execution after the system is reinitialized. In contrast, coding RESTART=N specifies that JES2 is to take no special action, so the effect is the same as not coding the parameter at all.

How to code the JES3 //*MAIN FAILURE parameter

To control whether or not your job restarts automatically after a system failure in a JES3 environment, you code the FAILURE parameter on the //*MAIN statement, as shown in figure 11-4. Specifying RESTART on this parameter instructs JES3 to restart the job when the processor is restarted. CANCEL instructs JES3 to first print and then cancel the job. HOLD causes JES3 to hold the job for restart until the operator releases it. And PRINT tells JES3 to first print the job and then hold it for restart until the operator releases it. If you don't code the FAILURE parameter at all, a default keyword is assigned to the job based on job class.

The //*MAIN statement shown in this figure specifies FAILURE=HOLD. As a result, if the system fails while this job is executing, JES3 will automatically resubmit the job for restart once the system is reinitialized. But instead of starting immediately, the job won't be processed until the operator manually releases it.

The syntax for the RESTART parameter of the JES2 /*JOBPARM statement

```
RESTART= {Y}
         {N}
```

Explanation

Y   Specifies that JES2 queue the job for re-execution from the beginning of the job when the processor is restarted.

N   Specifies that JES2 take no special action (the default).

The syntax for the FAILURE parameter of the JES3 //*MAIN statement

```
FAILURE= {RESTART}
         {CANCEL}
         {HOLD}
         {PRINT}
```

Explanation

RESTART   Specifies that JES3 restart the job when the processor is restarted.

CANCEL   Specifies that JES3 first print and then cancel the job.

HOLD   Specifies that JES3 hold the job for restart until an operator releases it.

PRINT   Specifies that JES3 first print then hold the job for restart.

A job that uses the JES2 RESTART parameter

```
//MM01A     JOB (36512),MENENDEZ,NOTIFY=MM01
/*JOBPARM   RESTART=Y
```

A job that uses the JES3 FAILURE parameter

```
//MM01B     JOB (36512),MENENDEZ,NOTIFY=MM01
//*MAIN     FAILURE=HOLD
```

Description

* If the system fails, you can automatically restart a job using a JES control statement.

* In a JES2 environment, you use the RESTART parameter on a /*JOBPARM statement to queue the job for re-execution after a system IPL. If a RESTART parameter isn't coded, N is assumed unless the installation overrides the default during JES2 initialization.

* In a JES3 environment, you use the FAILURE parameter on a //*MAIN statement to indicate the recovery option to use if the system fails. If the FAILURE parameter isn't coded, a default failure option will be assigned based on job class.

Figure 11-4   How to code JES2 and JES3 parameters to restart a job when the system fails

Other facilities that influence the way a job is executed

In chapter 5, you learned about the facilities you use most often to control job execution. In the topics that follow, you'll learn about three additional JCL features that you may use in your jobs from time to time.

How to code the PERFORM parameter

In an OS/390 installation, systems programmers create several *performance groups*. Each performance group has performance characteristics associated with it so an installation can control the rate at which jobs or steps access the processor, storage, and channels. For example, a performance group for TSO/E users would emphasize fast response time for a relatively short duration. Performance groups can also control how frequently a job's address space is swapped in and out.

Each job class is associated with a default performance group. The default group can be defined by your installation, or it can be a built-in system default of 1 for non-TSO/E jobs or 2 for TSO/E sessions. If you want to override the performance group associated with the job class, however, you can specify the PERFORM parameter on a JOB or EXEC statement. For example, the JOB statement in figure 11-5 includes a PERFORM=10 parameter that specifies performance group 10 should be used for the job instead of the default group.

The second example in this figure shows how you can specify a PERFORM parameter on an EXEC statement so that a performance group is applied to a single job step. Here, performance group 3 will be used only for job step APRCALC. Keep in mind, though, that if you include a PERFORM parameter on a JOB statement, it overrides any PERFORM parameters specified on EXEC statements.

The PERFORM parameter will function differently depending on which mode the system's *Workload Manager* is set to. If the system is set to *WLM compatibility mode*, the performance group you specify in your JOB or EXEC statement will function in the way described above. But if the system is set to *WLM goal mode*, the PERFORM parameter is used in the JOB statement to classify jobs and procedures to a service or report class instead (these classes are set up to meet the installation's workload goals). In addition, the PERFORM parameter on an EXEC statement is ignored. More than likely, your system's running in WLM compatibility mode, but it's a good idea to check that with your systems programmer before using the PERFORM parameter.

The syntax for the PERFORM parameter of the JOB and EXEC statements

```
PERFORM=group
```

Explanation

group   An installation-defined performance group with a value from 1 to 999.

The effect of the PERFORM parameter depends on the workload management mode

WLM compatibility mode

The PERFORM parameter in the JOB or EXEC statement specifies a performance group for the job or step. If a PERFORM parameter isn't coded, the system uses an installation default if there is one. Otherwise, it uses a built-in system default of 1 for non-TSO/E job steps and 2 for TSO/E sessions.

WLM goal mode

The system uses the value in the PERFORM parameter in the JOB statement to classify jobs and procedures to a service or report class that is appropriate for the workload goals the installation has set. The PERFORM on an EXEC statement is ignored in this mode.

A JOB statement that uses the PERFORM parameter

```
//MM02D    JOB (36512),'G MURACH',PERFORM=10
```

An EXEC statement that uses the PERFORM parameter

```
//APRCALC   EXEC PGM=APRCALC,PERFORM=3
```

Description

- The PERFORM parameter assigns a job or step to a *performance group* defined by the installation.

- Each performance group has performance characteristics associated with it that determine the rate at which jobs or steps have access to the processor, storage, and channels. For example, a performance group can control how frequently a job or step's address space can be swapped in and out.

- Although the PERFORM parameter can be used in either *WLM compatibility mode* or *WLM goal mode*, more than likely, your installation will have it configured to run in WLM compatibility mode.

- If a PERFORM parameter isn't specified on a JOB or an EXEC statement, the default performance group assigned to the job class is used.

- A PERFORM parameter specified on a JOB statement applies to all the steps within the job and overrides any PERFORM parameters specified on EXEC statements.

Figure 11-5   How to code the PERFORM parameter

How to issue operator commands

From time to time, you'll find it necessary to include running instructions for a job you submit. These instructions can include telling the operator to have a specific tape ready to be mounted or to notify you if the job abends. Rather than contacting the operator by phone or email, you can include a JES2 /*MESSAGE statement or a JES3 //*OPERATOR statement in your job stream with a message that will appear on the operator's console as the job is read in.

The syntax for both statements is shown in figure 11-6, along with an example of each. As you can see, you code the statement name, followed by a blank space and then the message you want displayed on the operator's console. In displaying the message, the JES2 /*MESSAGE statement also appends the job number to the beginning of the display line.

You can also communicate with the operator using the JCL COMMAND statement shown in this figure. The effect of this statement is different than that of the JES2 /*MESSAGE and JES3 //*OPERATOR statements, however. The COMMAND statement allows you to code an MVS or JES command that is displayed on the operator's console. The operator then has to authorize the execution of the command. As you can see in the syntax, the parameter field in the COMMAND statement is enclosed in parentheses and consists of the command you want to use along with any of the command's operands. To find out what commands and operands you can code here, see the IBM manual, *OS/390 MVS System Commands.*

To illustrate how this statement works, look at the example in this figure. In this case, the COMMAND statement includes the MVS SEND command. The syntax of the SEND command allows for a message along with the user-id the message should be sent to. (Note that the message is enclosed in double apostrophes. Normally, it would be enclosed in single apostrophes, but since the entire SEND command has to be enclosed in apostrophes on the COMMAND statement, the double apostrophes are required.) When the MSG1 COMMAND statement is encountered, the system sends a message to the operator's console requesting authorization to execute the SEND command. The operator can reply with a Y or N depending on whether or not the SEND command should be executed.

The syntax for the JES2 /*MESSAGE statement

```
/*MESSAGE message
```

Explanation

message   Specifies a message to be sent to the operator. The message can be coded anywhere between columns 11 and 71.

The syntax for the JES3 /*OPERATOR statement

```
//*OPERATOR message
```

Explanation

message   Specifies a message for the operator. The message can be coded anywhere between columns 13 and 80.

The syntax for the JCL COMMAND statement

```
//[name]   COMMAND  'command command-operand'
```

Explanation

parameter field   Specifies the name of an MVS or JES command and any operands that the command uses, all enclosed in apostrophes. The maximum length of the command is 123 characters. If the command doesn't fit on one line, you can continue it on the next line starting in column 16.

A /*MESSAGE statement that sends a message to the operator

```
/*MESSAGE NOTIFY ON-CALL PROGRAMMER IF JOB ABENDS
```

A //*OPERATOR statement that sends a message to the operator

```
//*OPERATOR CALL R MENENDEZ - EXT 22 WITH RESULTS
```

A COMMAND statement that requests the execution of a SEND command

```
//MSG1     COMMAND 'SEND ''PRODUCTION JOB ACCTNG1B IS NOW COMP
            LETE.'',USER=(MM01)'   **SENDS MESSAGE TO MM01**
```

Description

- To notify an operator about special instructions for running a job, you can code a JES2 /*MESSAGE statement or a JES3 //*OPERATOR statement. These statements can be placed anywhere after the JOB statement, and the message you include will appear on the operator's console as the job is read in.

- To include an MVS or JES command in a job, you can code the command in the JCL COMMAND statement. In this case, the system sends a message to the operator requesting authorization to run the command specified. The operator can reply with a Y or N.

- Because MVS and JES commands can be confusing, it's common to include comments in a COMMAND statement to clarify the purpose of the command.

- The SEND command is an MVS command that allows you to send a message to a specified user.

Figure 11-6   How to issue operator commands

How to schedule a job for a specific system

As you know, JES2 and JES3 can be used to manage a *multiprocessor network* that consists of more than one system. In a multiprocessor network, each system operates under the control of its own copy of OS/390. However, the JES components of each processor's operating system are connected in various ways to the JES components of the other processors, and a common spool is used to service all the processors in the network. As a result, JES2 and JES3 can control how jobs are processed by the systems within the multiprocessor network.

When you log on under TSO/E, you're connected to one of the systems in the network. By default, that system is used to process any batch jobs you submit. Although standard JCL doesn't provide any way to change that default, both JES2 and JES3 do, as shown in figure 11-7. In both versions of JES, the term *system affinity* is used to describe the relationship between a job and the system on which it executes.

On a JES2 system, you code the SYSAFF parameter of the /*JOBPARM statement to specify which system should execute the job. Each system within a JES2 network is given a unique four-character name, so the easiest way to execute a job on a particular system is to specify that system's name, as shown in the first JES2 example. Then, the second example shows how to specify that any of several systems can execute the job. When this job is ready to be scheduled, JES2 will assign it to one of the two processors listed in parentheses (MVSA or MVSB).

There are two other ways you can code the SYSAFF parameter. First, you can specify that the job should run on the system from which it is submitted by coding SYSAFF=*. However, there's little reason to code this since it's the default. Second, you can tell JES2 to decide which system to use for the job by coding SYSAFF=ANY, as shown in the third example. Then, JES2 selects any available processor to execute the job.

Under JES3, you use the SYSTEM parameter of the //*MAIN statement to indicate which processor or processors are eligible to process the job. The first JES3 example in this figure shows that you can code this parameter much like you code the SYSAFF parameter under JES2. In addition, you can code ANY, JGLOBAL, or JLOCAL as in the second JES3 example. ANY means that any available processor can be used to process the job. JGLOBOL means that the JES3 *global processor*, the processor in charge of the network, must process the job. And JLOCAL means that any JES3 *local processor* can be used for the job.

If you code a slash after the equals sign in the SYSTEM parameter, JES3 will use a processor other than the one you list to process the job. This might be useful if, for example, any processor in the network except one can process a job. The last example illustrates how to do this. Here, any processor except the one named MVSB can process the job.

The syntax for the SYSAFF parameter of the JES2 /*JOBPARM statement

```
SYSAFF= {*} {(system-name,...)} {ANY}
```

Explanation

*	The job will run on the system that reads it (the default).
system-name	A one- to four-character system-id defined in the multiprocessor network that identifies which processor will run the job. If more than one system-name is specified, the job can run on any one of the processors listed.
ANY	The job can run on any available processor.

The syntax for the SYSTEM parameter of the JES3 //*MAIN statement

```
SYSTEM= {[/](main-name,...)} {JGLOBAL} {JLOCAL} {ANY}
```

Explanation

main-name	A system-id defined in the multiprocessor network that identifies which processor will be used to run the job. If more than one main-name is specified, the job can run on any one of the processors listed.
/	The job can run on any processor *except* the one(s) listed.
JGLOBAL	The job must run on the global processor.
JLOCAL	The job can run on any local processor.
ANY	The job can run on any available processor.

Specifying system affinity

Under JES2

```
/*JOBPARM   SYSAFF=MVSA
/*JOBPARM   SYSAFF=(MVSA,MVSB)
/*JOBPARM   SYSAFF=ANY
```

Under JES3

```
//*MAIN     SYSTEM=(MVSA,MVSC,MVSD)
//*MAIN     SYSTEM=JLOCAL
//*MAIN     SYSTEM=/MVSB
```

Description

- JES2 and JES3 can be used to manage a *multiprocessor network* that consists of more than one system. Each system operates under control of its own copy of OS/390, but the JES components for each system are connected. As a result, JES2 and JES3 can control how systems within the network process jobs.

- The term *system affinity* can be used to describe the relationship between a job and the system on which it executes.

- Under JES2, you use the SYSAFF parameter of the /*JOBPARM statement to specify system affinity. Under JES3, you use the SYSTEM parameter of the //*MAIN statement.

- The *global processor* is the processor that's in charge of the entire network. A *local processor* is one that's controlled by the global processor.

Figure 11-7   How to schedule a job for a specific system

Perspective

Sooner or later, you're probably going to want to restart a job that failed. So of the job execution facilities presented in this chapter, the one you're most likely to use is the RESTART parameter for a deferred step restart. The others are of more limited use and depend to a greater extent on your installation's practices. However, you can come back to this chapter if you ever need the details on how to use them.

Terms

step restart
checkpoint restart
checkpoint
end-of-volume checkpoint
deferred step restart
deferred checkpoint restart
automatic restart
job journal
performance group
Workload Manager
WLM compatibility mode
WLM goal mode
multiprocessor network
system affinity
global processor
local processor

12

How to manage generation data groups

Several generations of a data set are commonly maintained for those data sets that contain the critical data of an organization. Then, if something goes wrong, you can restore the data set to a known point and redo the processing from that point on. To facilitate the processing of these generations, OS/390 provides for generation data groups. In this chapter, you'll learn how to create and use those groups.

How to use a generation data group

The illustration in figure 12-1 gives the general idea of how a *generation data group* (*GDG*) works. Here, three generations of a master file are maintained: one for the current month and one for each of the two preceding months. Each month when this master file is updated and a new master file is created, the new master file becomes the *current generation* and the file that was the current generation becomes the *previous generation*. Each file in the GDG can be referred to as a *generation data set*.

Keeping more than one generation of a master file is a common practice for all of the critical data sets of an installation. Then, if something goes wrong with the current data set, it can be recreated from the previous generation. If, for example, a disk drive fails and the September master file can't be read, it can be recreated by processing the September transactions against the August master file. In practice, three or more generations of each master file are kept and generation processing is often done on a daily or even more frequent basis.

If you had to create your own procedures for doing generation processing, you would have to establish naming conventions that let you identify successive generations of a data set. However, the GDG facility that OS/390 uses makes this easier by keeping track of the generations for you. This feature works with non-VSAM sequential data sets on either DASD or tape, and it depends on the use of both relative generation numbers and absolute generation numbers.

The relative generation numbers of GDG members

In figure 12-1, you can see how *relative generation numbers* work. Quite simply, the current generation is referred to as generation 0, and the previous generations are referred to as generations -1, -2, -3, and so on. While the current generation is being updated, the next generation is referred to as +1. But as soon as the job is finished, the next generation becomes the current generation (0), and the other relative generation numbers are reduced by 1. As you will see in a moment, you can use these generation numbers in your JCL when you set up the jobs that process the GDG generations.

How the relative positions of the GDG members change

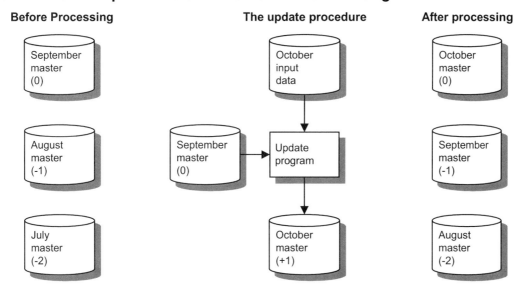

Description

- A *generation data group*, or *GDG*, is a collection of two or more chronologically related versions of the same data set. Each version is called a *generation data set*.

- Generation data sets are non-VSAM sequential data sets that reside on tape or DASD.

- Each time a generation data set is processed, a new *generation* of the data set is added to the GDG. This new version becomes the *current generation*, and the old current generation becomes the *previous generation*.

- If necessary, a previous generation can be processed. Normally, though, the current generation is processed the next time the job is run.

- To refer to the generations of a GDG, you can use *relative generation numbers*. When using these numbers, 0 refers to the current generation; -1, -2, and -3 refer to the three previous generations; and +1 refers to the next generation.

- The GDG and each generation data set in it must be cataloged. Then, OS/390 uses the GDG's catalog entry to keep track of the relative generation numbers.

- When you create the catalog entry for a GDG, you specify how many generations should be maintained. Then, after each processing cycle, the oldest generation is removed from the group.

Figure 12-1   How generation data group processing works

The absolute generation numbers of GDG members

Although OS/390 lets you use relative generation numbers in your JCL, it uses *absolute generation numbers* to identify each generation on the system itself. These numbers are added to the data set names as shown in figure 12-2. As you can see, each absolute generation number consists of a generation number like G0013 followed by a version number like V00.

Although the version number lets you create more than one version of a generation, you normally don't need to do that, so the version number is usually V00. If you do create more than one version of a generation, though, OS/390 uses only the latest version for GDG processing. That means you have to specify the absolute generation number in your JCL if you want to process a version other than the latest version.

In this figure, you can see how the relative and absolute generation numbers for a data set are related. Because the GDG and each generation data set in it are cataloged, OS/390 is able to maintain these relationships for you each time the current generation is updated.

An update procedure that uses a generation data group

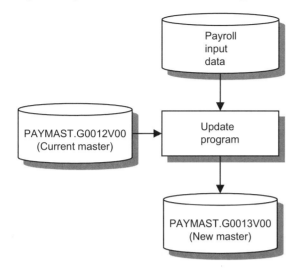

How the absolute generation numbers for the GDG members change

Relative name	Data set name before processing	Data set name after processing
PAYMAST(0)	PAYMAST.G0012V00	PAYMAST.G0013V00
PAYMAST(-1)	PAYMAST.G0011V00	PAYMAST.G0012V00
PAYMAST(-2)	PAYMAST.G0010V00	PAYMAST.G0011V00
PAYMAST(-3)	PAYMAST.G0009V00	PAYMAST.G0010V00

The format of the generation and version numbers in a data set name

```
datasetname.GnnnnVnn
```

Description

- Although OS/390 lets you use relative generation numbers in your JCL, OS/390 itself uses *absolute generation numbers* to uniquely identify each generation data set. This number is added to the end of the data set name.

- The absolute generation number consists of four digits for the generation number and two digits for the version number as shown above. Because these numbers require 9 characters (including the preceding period), the data set name of a generation data group is limited to 35 characters (not 44).

- The version number lets you create more than one copy of a single generation. For instance, G0013V01 is the second version of a generation data set. However, only the version with the highest number is considered to be part of the GDG (that is, it's the only one that's assigned a relative number).

Figure 12-2   The absolute generation numbers of GDG members

How to code jobs that process GDG members

Figure 12-3 shows how you use relative generation numbers when you code the JCL for a job that updates a generation data set. In the DD statement for a generation data set, you just code the data set name followed by the relative generation number in parentheses. For the update program, then, the current generation is referred to as MM01.PAYROLL.MASTER(0) and the next generation is referred to as MM01.PAYROLL.MASTER(+1). You can imagine how much easier this is than keeping track of the unique names for each generation of a data set.

When you code the JCL for generation data sets, you must remember that the relative generation numbers are updated after the completion of the job, not the completion of a job step. This is illustrated by the two examples in this figure. The first example, which consists of two job steps, creates a new generation of the master file in the first step and refers to it as relative number +1. Then, the second job step uses this +1 version of the master file as input and in turn creates a new master file, which it refers to as relative number +2. Here, the second job step has to refer to the two versions of the master file as +1 and +2 because the numbers haven't been updated yet.

In contrast, the second example consists of two separate jobs. In this case, though, the second job refers to the old and new master files as 0 and +1, because the generation numbers are updated at the end of the first job.

You may have noticed that in the first example, the DCB parameter isn't coded in the DD statement for the new generation of the master file in each step. That's because this information is obtained from the model data set control block for the GDG, which you'll learn about in a moment. However, you can override or add to this DCB information by coding the DCB parameter as illustrated by the first job in the second example.

The syntax for referring to a GDG member

```
dsname(relative-number)
```

A two-step job that updates a GDG master file twice

```
//MM01PY1  JOB   (36512),'R MENENDEZ',NOTIFY=&SYSUID
//UPDATE1  EXEC PGM=PAY3200
//OLDMAST  DD    DSNAME=MM01.PAYROLL.MASTER(0),DISP=OLD
//NEWMAST  DD    DSNAME=MM01.PAYROLL.MASTER(+1),DISP=(NEW,CATLG),
//               UNIT=SYSDA,VOL=SER=MPS8BV,
//               SPACE=(CYL,(10,1))
//PAYTRAN  DD    DSNAME=MM01.PAYROLL.TRANS.CORP,DISP=OLD
//PAYCORP  DD    SYSOUT=*
//UPDATE2  EXEC PGM=PAY3210
//OLDMAST  DD    DSNAME=MM01.PAYROLL.MASTER(+1),DISP=OLD
//NEWMAST  DD    DSNAME=MM01.PAYROLL.MASTER(+2),DISP=(NEW,CATLG),
//               UNIT=SYSDA,VOL=SER=MPS8BV,
//               SPACE=(CYL,(10,1))
//PAYTRAN  DD    DSNAME=MM01.PAYROLL.TRANS.BRANCH,DISP=OLD
//PAYLIST  DD    SYSOUT=*
```

Two one-step jobs that update the GDG master file

```
//MM01PY2  JOB   (36512),'R MENENDEZ',NOTIFY=&SYSUID
//UPDATE1  EXEC PGM=PAY3200
//OLDMAST  DD    DSNAME=MM01.PAYROLL.MASTER(0),DISP=OLD
//NEWMAST  DD    DSNAME=MM01.PAYROLL.MASTER(+1),DISP=(NEW,CATLG),
//               UNIT=SYSDA,VOL=SER=MPS8BV,
//               SPACE=(CYL,(10,1)),
//               DCB=(LRECL=80)
//PAYTRAN  DD    DSNAME=MM01.PAYROLL.TRANS.CORP,DISP=OLD
//PAYCORP  DD    SYSOUT=*

//MM01PY3  JOB   (36512),'R MENENDEZ',NOTIFY=&SYSUID
//UPDATE2  EXEC PGM=PAY3210
//OLDMAST  DD    DSNAME=MM01.PAYROLL.MASTER(0),DISP=OLD
//NEWMAST  DD    DSNAME=MM01.PAYROLL.MASTER(+1),DISP=(NEW,CATLG),
//               UNIT=SYSDA,VOL=SER=MPS8BV,
//               SPACE=(CYL,(10,1))
//PAYTRAN  DD    DSNAME=MM01.PAYROLL.TRANS.BRANCH,DISP=OLD
//PAYLIST  DD    SYSOUT=*
```

Description

- To retrieve an existing generation data set or to create a new one, you code the name of the GDG followed by a relative generation number.

- Relative generation numbers are updated after the completion of the job, not the completion of a job step. As a result, any step that refers to a generation created in a preceding step must refer to it in relation to the generation that was current when the job began.

- When creating new generation data sets, the DCB information is usually obtained from the generation data group and can therefore be omitted from the DD statement. However, you can override the DCB information by specifying DCB attributes of your own.

Figure 12-3   How to code jobs that process GDG members

How to manage a generation data group

Before you can process a generation data set, you need to create a generation data group. To do that, you need to create a catalog entry for the GDG. You also need to create a model data set control block that is used to get the DCB information for each new generation data set. Figure 12-4 shows how to do both.

How to create a GDG catalog entry

To create a GDG catalog entry, you execute the VSAM utility program known as IDCAMS (or AMS) and issue a DEFINE GDG command. (Yes, you use a VSAM program to define a GDG, even though GDG data sets are non-VSAM sequential files.) In the job stream in figure 12-4, you can see that the IDCAMS program requires a SYSIN data set that contains the DEFINE GDG command. This figure also gives you the syntax for coding the parameters of this command.

The NAME parameter of the DEFINE GDG command supplies the name of the generation data group, and the LIMIT parameter indicates how many generations you want to keep in the group. If, for example, you want the current generation plus four previous generations, you code 5 as the limit.

The other two parameters that you normally code are the NOEMPTY and SCRATCH parameters. NOEMPTY means that the oldest generation should be removed from the group when a new generation is added, while SCRATCH means that the removed data set is actually deleted from the volume. In contrast, EMPTY means that all of the previous generations are removed from the group when a new generation is added, while NOSCRATCH means that a removed data set is uncataloged but not deleted.

If you haven't worked with AMS before, you can simply copy this command and format it as shown, substituting your GDG name and the number of generations to be kept for the shaded values. Then, chapter 16 will teach you more about this and other AMS commands.

How to create a model DSCB

The second requirement for processing a generation data group is that there must be a *model data set control block* (or *model DSCB*) on the same volume as the catalog that contains the GDG entry. This model DSCB is used by OS/390 to get DCB information for new generations of the group. Usually, no space is allocated to the model DSCB, so it's a VTOC entry without any space allocation.

In the job in figure 12-4, the MODEL DD statement creates the model DSCB for the GDG defined by the DEFINE GDG command. Although the ddname for the model DSCB can be any name, the data set name should be the same as for the GDG (unless it's a general-purpose model DSCB as shown in the next figure). Because the data set name is the same as the GDG, though, the model DSCB can't be cataloged (otherwise, a duplicate entry would occur).

The syntax for the AMS DEFINE GDG command

```
DEFINE GDG|GENERATIONDATAGROUP
              ( NAME(entry-name)
                LIMIT(limit)
              [ EMPTY | NOEMPTY ]
              [ SCRATCH | NOSCRATCH ]
              [ OWNER(owner-id) ]
              [ TO(yyyyddd) | FOR(nnnn) ] )
```

Explanation

NAME	Specifies the name of the generation data group. This name follows normal data set naming conventions but is limited to 35 characters.
LIMIT	Specifies how many generation data sets are to be maintained in the group. The maximum limit is 255.
EMPTY | NOEMPTY	Specifies what action should be taken when the LIMIT value is reached. EMPTY means that all generations should be removed from the group. NOEMPTY means that just the oldest generation should be removed.
SCRATCH | NOSCRATCH	Specifies whether the data sets that are removed from the group should be scratched (deleted) or just uncataloged.
OWNER	Specifies a 1- to 8-character owner-id for the generation data group.
TO | FOR	Specifies an expiration date or a retention period for the GDG.

A job that defines a GDG and allocates a model DSCB

```
//MM01DFG  JOB   (36512),'R MENENDEZ',NOTIFY=&SYSUID
//         EXEC PGM=IDCAMS
//SYSPRINT DD    SYSOUT=*
//MODEL    DD    DSNAME=MM01.PAYROLL.MASTER,DISP=(,KEEP),
//               UNIT=SYSDA,VOL=SER=MPS800,SPACE=(TRK,(0)),
//               DCB=(DSORG=PS,RECFM=FB,LRECL=400)
//SYSIN    DD    *
 DEFINE GDG ( NAME(MM01.PAYROLL.MASTER)   -
              LIMIT(5)                     -
              NOEMPTY                       -
              SCRATCH )
 /*
```

Description

- To create a GDG, you must (1) create a catalog entry for the GDG, and (2) create a model data set control block on the same volume as the catalog entry for the GDG.

- To create a GDG catalog entry, you invoke the VSAM utility program, AMS, and issue a DEFINE GDG command. (For more information on AMS, please see chapter 16.)

- To create a *model data set control block*, you code a DD statement in the job that defines the GDG. This *model DSCB* is a data set that's used to obtain DCB information for new generations of the group. Normally, the SPACE parameter allocates no space, so the model DSCB is a VTOC entry with no space allocated to it.

- The data set name for the model DSCB should be the same as for the GDG, and the VOL parameter should specify the volume that contains the user catalog where the GDG is defined. Then, the DCB parameter defines the characteristics of each generation data set.

Figure 12-4   How to create a generation data group

When you code the DD statement for the model DSCB, the VOLUME parameter must specify the vol-ser for the volume that contains the user catalog where the GDG is defined. Then, the DCB parameter defines the characteristics that OS/390 will use for each generation data set in the group.

How to use a general-purpose model DSCB

You can also code a general-purpose model DSCB that can be used for more than one GDG instead of a specific model for each GDG. To do that, it's common to use the IEFBR14 utility, as shown in the first job in figure 12-5. As you may recall from chapter 6, IEFBR14 doesn't do anything but force OS/390 to process the DD statements in a job. So a job like this sets up the VTOC entry for the general-purpose model DSCB.

If you compare this DD statement to the one for the model DSCB in figure 12-4, you'll see that the DSNAME parameter specifies a unique name instead of the name of a GDG, so the data set can be cataloged. Also, no logical record length is given in the DCB parameter in this figure. Since a general-purpose model DSCB can be used for many different generation data sets, it makes sense to supply the record length in the JCL that does the generation processing instead.

To define a GDG that's going to use a general-purpose model DSCB, you don't have to include a DD statement for the model, as shown by the second job in this figure. Instead, when you code the JCL that creates the next generation of the GDG, you code the DSCB name in the DCB parameter of the DD statement for the generation data set. This is illustrated by the third job in this figure. Here, the first DCB subparameter, which is positional, identifies the general-purpose model DSCB that's created by the JCL in the first example. You also code whatever DCB subparameters are needed to override or add to the subparameters given in the general-purpose model.

One other thing to notice here is that the vol-ser for the GDG is different than the one for the model DSCB. They don't have to reside on the same volume when a general-purpose model DSCB is used.

Which type of DSCB works better? I prefer specific model DSCBs because that way you don't have to remember the data set name of the general-purpose model DSCB. Remember, though, that one of the requirements for using specific models is that the model must be on the same volume as the catalog entry for the GDG. If you have a problem meeting that requirement, you can use a general-purpose model to get around it.

A job that creates a general-purpose model DSCB

```
//MM01BR14 JOB   (36512),'R MENENDEZ',NOTIFY=&SYSUID
//         EXEC PGM=IEFBR14
//DD1      DD    DSNAME=MODLDSCB,DISP=(NEW,CATLG),
//               UNIT=SYSDA,VOL=SER=MPS800,
//               SPACE=(TRK,(0)),
//               DCB=(DSORG=PS,RECFM=FB)
```

A job that defines a GDG with a general-purpose model DSCB

```
//MM01DFG  JOB   (36512),'R MENENDEZ',NOTIFY=&SYSUID
//         EXEC PGM=IDCAMS
//SYSPRINT DD    SYSOUT=*
//SYSIN    DD    *
 DEFINE GDG ( NAME(MM01.PAYROLL.MASTER)   -
              LIMIT(5)                     -
              NOEMPTY                      -
              SCRATCH )
/*
```

The JCL for updating a GDG that uses a general-purpose model DSCB

```
//MM01PY4  JOB   (36512),'R MENENDEZ',NOTIFY=&SYSUID
//UPDATE   EXEC PGM=PAY3200
//OLDMAST  DD    DSNAME=MM01.PAYROLL.MASTER(0),DISP=OLD
//NEWMAST  DD    DSNAME=MM01.PAYROLL.MASTER(+1),DISP=(NEW,CATLG),
//               UNIT=SYSDA,VOL=SER=MPS8BV,
//               SPACE=(CYL,(10,1)),
//               DCB=(MODLDSCB,LRECL=400)
//PAYTRAN  DD    DSNAME=MM01.PAYROLL.TRANS,DISP=OLD
//PAYCORP  DD    SYSOUT=*
```

Description

- If you create a general-purpose model DSCB, it can be used as the model for more than one GDG.

- To create a general-purpose model DSCB, you use a data set name that isn't the same as the name of a GDG. The easiest way to create this data set is with the IEFBR14 utility, which produces an empty file.

- When you create a new generation of a GDG that uses a general-purpose model DSCB, you code the name of the model DSCB as the first positional subparameter in the DCB parameter. You also code whatever DCB subparameters you need to override or add to the subparameters in the model DSCB.

- A model DSCB doesn't have to reside on the same volume as the GDGs that use it.

Figure 12-5   How to create and use a general-purpose model DSCB

How to list GDG catalog information

Although you normally don't use the absolute generation numbers of a GDG in your JCL, you can if you need to. If, for example, the current version of a payroll master file is G0195V00, you can do a special update of that version by referring to the new version as MM01.PAYROLL.MASTER.G0195V01. This is useful when testing because it lets you continue to refer to one version of a data set, no matter how many times you update it.

Before you can use absolute generation numbers in your JCL, though, you have to know what they are for the GDG you're working with. There are two ways to find out. Usually, the fastest way is through the ISPF DSLIST screen shown in figure 12-6. To access the DSLIST utility from the ISPF Primary Option Menu, you select option 3 (Utilities) followed by option 4 (DSLIST). Then, you specify the GDG entry you want to view on the DSNAME LEVEL line and press Enter. If any generation data sets exist for the GDG entry, they'll be displayed on the screen.

If you want additional information about the generations (for example, when each was created), you can use the LISTCAT command that is part of the VSAM AMS utility instead of ISPF. This figure shows a LISTCAT command that lists all the generations of a GDG named MM01.PAYROLL.MASTER. Then, from that list, you can find out what the absolute generation numbers are. If you haven't worked with the LISTCAT command before, you can simply copy this command as shown, substituting the correct GDG name. Then, chapter 16 will teach you more about the syntax and output of this command.

The ISPF DSLIST screen for the MM01.PAYROLL.MASTER GDG

```
MMA - EXTRA! for Windows 98 / Windows NT                          _ □ X
File  Edit  View  Tools  Session  Options  Help
  Menu  Options  View  Utilities  Compilers  Help
 ────────────────────────────────────────────────────────────
 ISRUDSL0 Data Sets Matching MM01.PAYROLL.MASTER        Row 1 of 6
 Command ===> _____        Scroll ===> CSR

 Command - Enter "/" to select action          Message       Volume
 ────────────────────────────────────────────────────────────
          MM01.PAYROLL.MASTER                                  ??????
          MM01.PAYROLL.MASTER.G0006V00                         LIB79A
          MM01.PAYROLL.MASTER.G0007V00                         LIB79A
          MM01.PAYROLL.MASTER.G0008V00                         LIB79A
          MM01.PAYROLL.MASTER.G0009V00                         LIB79A
          MM01.PAYROLL.MASTER.G0010V00                         LIB79A
 *********************** End of Data Set list ***********************




  F1=Help   F2=Split   F3=Exit   F5=Rfind   F7=Up    F8=Down   F9=Swap
  F10=Left  F11=Right  F12=Cancel
 ◄█           ◌:00.3                                    04/15
```

An AMS LISTCAT command for the MM01.PAYROLL.MASTER GDG

```
//MM01LST   JOB  (36512),'R MENENDEZ',NOTIFY=&SYSUID
//          EXEC PGM=IDCAMS
//SYSPRINT DD   SYSOUT=*
//SYSIN    DD   *
 LISTCAT ENTRIES(MM01.PAYROLL.MASTER) -
            GDG                        -
            ALL
/*
```

A DD statement that refers to a data set by absolute generation number

```
//OLDMAST   DD   DSNAME=MM01.PAYROLL.MASTER.G0009V00,DISP=OLD
```

Description

- One way to find out what the absolute generation numbers are in a GDG is to view a listing of the GDG data sets in the ISPF DSLIST screen. To do this, choose option 3 (Utilities) from the ISPF Primary Option Menu, followed by option 4 (DSLIST). Then, enter the name of the GDG you want to view on the DSNAME LEVEL line and press Enter to display a screen like the one above.

- Another way to check on absolute generation numbers is to use the LISTCAT command for the AMS utility. You can code this command as shown above, substituting the correct GDG name in the ENTRIES parameter. (To learn more about this command, please see chapter 16.)

Figure 12-6   How to list GDG catalog information

How to delete a GDG catalog entry

As you know, individual generation data sets are deleted as new generations are added based on the limit specified in the GDG catalog entry. However, the only way to delete the GDG entry itself is with a job like the one in figure 12-7. Here, the AMS DELETE command is used to delete the catalog entry for the GDG named MM01.PAYROLL.MASTER.

This figure also shows the syntax for the parameters of the DELETE GDG command. When you code the FORCE parameter, the GDG catalog entry and all of its GDG members are deleted. When you code the PURGE parameter, the catalog entry...and its members, if FORCE is coded...are deleted whether or not they've reached their expiration dates. Both of these parameters are commonly coded when you delete a GDG catalog entry because, in most cases, you know you want to get rid of the entire GDG.

The syntax for the AMS DELETE GDG command

```
DELETE    entry-name
          GDG|GENERATIONDATAGROUP
     [ PURGE|NOPURGE ]
     [ FORCE|NOFORCE ]
```

Explanation

entry-name	Specifies the name of the GDG catalog entry that is to be deleted.
GDG	Specifies that the entry to be deleted is a generation data group.
PURGE	Deletes the catalog entry even if the expiration date hasn't been reached. When used with FORCE, it deletes the catalog entry and the GDG members even if any of their expiration dates haven't been reached.
FORCE	Forces the GDG catalog entry and all of its members to be deleted, assuming that the expiration dates have passed or that PURGE is coded.

A job that deletes a GDG

```
//MM01DELG JOB   (36512),'R MENENDEZ',NOTIFY=&SYSUID
//         EXEC PGM=IDCAMS
//SYSPRINT DD   SYSOUT=*
//SYSIN    DD   *
 DELETE MM01.PAYROLL.MASTER GDG    -
                            PURGE -
                            FORCE
/*
```

Description

- To delete a GDG catalog entry, you invoke the VSAM utility program, AMS, and issue a DELETE GDG command.
- If you don't code the PURGE parameter, the GDG entry is deleted only if its expiration date has passed.
- If you don't code the FORCE parameter, only the GDG catalog entry is deleted. Since that orphans the data sets that were part of the GDG, you usually include the FORCE parameter.

Figure 12-7   How to delete a GDG catalog entry

Perspective

Because GDG processing makes it easier to provide for several generations of a data set, it's a feature that's commonly used in OS/390 shops. Although you usually don't need to use this feature during program development, you often need it when a master data set is put into production. So when a situation like that occurs, you can come back to this chapter to refresh your memory on the details of creating, processing, and managing a generation data group.

Terms

generation data group
GDG
generation data set
generation
current generation
previous generation
relative generation number
absolute generation number
model data set control block
model DSCB

13

How to use
the SMS facilities
for data set allocation

SMS is an automated storage management system that reduces the need for many of the manual procedures that you normally use for managing data sets. Among other features, it lets you define new data sets with a minimum of DD statement parameters. Although this facility isn't installed on all systems, you need to know how to use it if it is installed on yours.

Introduction to SMS

SMS, which stands for *Storage Management Subsystem*, is an optional, automated storage management system that can be used for creating and managing data sets. This subsystem does tasks like determining which volume a data set should be stored on, calculating the amount of space to allocate to the data set, and determining when a data set is no longer needed so it can be deleted or moved to offline storage. As such, SMS eliminates the need for many of the procedures and much of the JCL that you normally use for managing data sets.

How SMS manages data sets

SMS manages data sets by establishing classes for each type of data set. This is illustrated by the diagram in figure 13-1. Three of these classes are the *storage class*, *data class*, and *management class*. The SMS administrator (or systems programmer) sets up these classes so they provide for the types of data sets that are commonly used in an installation. For example, one type of data class might be used for data sets that contain COBOL source statements, while another might be used for VSAM key-sequenced data sets.

The SMS administrator also sets up *Automatic Class Selection (ACS) routines* that pick the storage class, data class, and management class for each new data set that's created. These ACS routines analyze the information provided in JOB statements, EXEC statements, and DD statements to determine which classes should be used.

The diagram in this figure illustrates the use of ACS routines. Here, the routines have determined that the new data set is a transaction file because the low-level qualifier in the data set name is TRANS. Then, since all the transaction files in the system have the same format, the ACS routines choose the appropriate storage, data, and management class for a transaction file. As a result, those classes provide the attributes for the new data set.

As you go through this chapter, you will learn what type of information each class provides. In brief, though, the storage class determines what volume a data set will be stored on. The data class determines the characteristics of a data set, like its organization, record format, and default space allocation. And the management class determines how long the data set will be kept online and how often it will be backed up. (A fourth class, called the *security class*, can be used for security management, but it isn't presented in this book because you usually don't need to be concerned with it.)

SMS can be used to manage all the types of data sets listed in this figure. However, it's normally used for DASD-intensive files, rather than for temporary or VIO files that make little or no long-term use of disk storage. Many shops also use SMS to manage VSAM data sets because then you don't have to use the Access Methods Services utility presented in chapter 16 of this book. This makes it much easier to create a VSAM data set.

How SMS manages the creation of a new data set

The complete DD statement for the data set that is being created

```
//TRANS   DD   DSNAME=MM01.AR.TRANS,DISP=(NEW,CATLG)
```

Storage classes · Data classes · Management classes → ACS routines ← JCL DD statement → MM01.AR.TRANS

The types of data sets SMS can manage

Sequential data sets

Partitioned data sets (PDS and PDSE)

VSAM data sets

Generation data group (GDG) data sets

Temporary data sets

Virtual Input/Output (VIO) data sets

Description

- *SMS (Storage Management Subsystem)* is an automated storage management system that may or may not be present on your OS/390 or z/OS system.

- SMS manages files by establishing *storage classes*, *data classes,* and *management classes* for different types of data sets. These classes determine what volume a data set is written to, what the characteristics of the data set are, how long it will reside on the volume before it is archived offline, and how often it should be backed up.

- The *Automatic Class Selection (ACS) routines* that are set up for a system automatically pick the storage class, management class, and data class for each new data set based on information in the JOB, EXEC, and DD statements.

- The SMS administrator sets up the SMS classes as well as the ACS routines. In general, the administrator sets up classes for the common types of data sets that are used in a shop.

- Besides normal data set management, SMS consolidates fragmented disk space and tries to balance DASD volume usage.

Figure 13-1   How SMS manages data sets

Regardless of the data set type, though, SMS only works well for a few basic data set configurations. For example, transaction files often have the same characteristics, so ACS routines can easily be set up to define them. In contrast, master files tend to be very different from one another, so you'll usually need to define them using standard JCL. Also, even when a data set can be created through SMS, you need to code the JCL in such a way that the ACS routines will recognize the data set type and assign the right classes to it. So check with your SMS administrator on the guidelines for using SMS in your shop.

The two ways you can use SMS

The most obvious way to use SMS is to create SMS-managed data sets. This gives you all the benefits that SMS has to offer. In fact, to create an SMS-managed data set, you usually code a minimum of DD parameters and let the ACS routines assign the right storage, data, and management class to it, as shown in the first example in figure 13-2. Here, a new data set is created by a DD statement with just two parameters. In other words, all the other data set information is derived from the classes that are automatically assigned by the ACS routines.

There may be times, though, when you want to modify the automatic SMS assignments. Some data set attributes can be modified just by coding appropriate DD parameters, as you'll see later in this chapter. In addition, SMS provides its own parameters that can be coded on the DD statement to give you more control over SMS-managed files. To illustrate, in the second example in this figure, an SMS parameter is used to specify the data class for the data set instead of letting the ACS routines choose it. In this case, though, the ACS routines still determine the storage and management classes.

But you aren't limited to using SMS just for SMS-managed data sets. In fact, the second way to use SMS is to code SMS parameters for data sets that aren't managed by SMS. For example, the third DD statement in this figure shows how you can use the SMS AVGREC parameter in creating a new, non-SMS data set. This parameter lets you specify the space allocation in terms of records, which isn't possible with standard JCL.

After the examples, you can see a summary of the SMS parameters, divided into two parts. The first part shows the parameters you'll use most often when you create an SMS-managed data set. The second part shows the parameters that can be used for both SMS-managed and non-SMS data sets, although they're rarely coded for SMS-managed data sets. In the topics that follow, you'll see examples of all seven parameters, so you'll have a better idea of when you might want to use them.

How SMS can be used to create an SMS-managed data set

A DD statement that lets the ACS routines choose the classes

```
//TRANS    DD    DSNAME=MM01.AR.TRANS,DISP=(NEW,CATLG)
```

A DD statement that specifies the data class

```
//TRANS    DD    DSNAME=MM01.AR.TRANS,DISP=(NEW,CATLG),DATACLAS=TRAN2
```

How an SMS parameter can be used to create a data set that isn't managed by SMS

```
//TRANS    DD    DSNAME=MM01.AR.TRANS,DISP=(NEW,CATLG),
//               UNIT=SYSDA,VOL=SER=MPS8BV,
//               SPACE=(1000,(5,3),RLSE),AVGREC=U
//               DCB=(RECFM=FB,LRECL=120)
```

SMS parameters for the DD statement

Parameters for SMS-managed data sets	
STORCLAS	Specifies the storage class for a data set.
DATACLAS	Specifies the data class for a data set.
MGMTCLAS	Specifies the management class for a data set.
DSNTYPE	Allows you to specify the type of data set being created.

Parameters that can be used for non-SMS data sets as well as SMS-managed data sets	
AVGREC	Specifies (1) that the space allocation should be based on record size and (2) how many records should be used for each extent.
LIKE	Copies data set characteristics from a specified data set.
REFDD	Refers back to a DD statement to copy data set characteristics.

Description

- Normally, you use SMS to manage data sets. In that case, you can use SMS parameters on the DD statement to affect the automatic SMS settings. However, you can also use three SMS parameters with data sets that aren't managed by SMS.

- When you work with SMS-managed data sets, you can use any of the parameters shown above, but you'll probably use only the first set. The first three let you override the storage, data, or management class that is established by the ACS routines. The fourth one lets you override the data set type specified in a data class.

- When you work with data sets that aren't managed by SMS, you can use the last three parameters shown above. AVGREC lets you allocate space in terms of records. The other two let you model a new data set based on the characteristics of an existing data set.

- If SMS is not active when SMS parameters are coded, the system checks the syntax of the parameters but then ignores them.

Figure 13-2   The two ways you can use SMS

How to use SMS parameters in creating SMS-managed data sets

In most cases, the SMS processes and ACS routines set up by the SMS administrator work seamlessly with the JCL you code. In fact, as an application programmer, you're usually not aware of what functions SMS is carrying out, nor do you have to be. So you'll usually create new SMS-managed data sets using simple DD statements that specify only the data set name and disposition (like the first example you saw in figure 13-2), and you'll let SMS do the rest.

Occasionally, though, you may want to override some of the attributes assigned to a data set by SMS. Or the data set may have requirements that won't be recognized by the ACS routines, so you want to make sure that the right storage, data, or management class is assigned to it. In cases like these, you can use the STORCLAS, DATACLAS, MGMTCLAS, and DSNTYPE parameters to provide SMS with the information it needs to create the data set properly.

How to set the storage class (STORCLAS)

As figure 13-3 shows, SMS uses the storage class to select an appropriate volume on which to store a new data set. That's why you can omit the UNIT and VOLUME parameters when you create an SMS-managed data set. In fact, if you code the UNIT parameter, it's ignored. The VOLUME parameter is usually ignored as well, depending on how the storage class itself is defined. In most cases, then, you should let the storage class determine the volume as well as the unit information.

To specify a storage class directly instead of leaving the choice to an ACS routine, you code the STORCLAS parameter on the DD statement as shown in this figure. Here, the STORCLAS parameter tells SMS to assign a storage class named MVPS100 to the data set. Of course, you will have to check with your SMS administrator to find out what values can be coded here and what storage classes are appropriate for the type of data set you're creating. In fact, you'll have to check to see whether you can code the STORCLAS parameter at all, since the ACS routines are sometimes set up to ignore it. Note that only a storage class is specified in this example, so the ACS routines will still choose a data class and management class for the data set.

The syntax for the STORCLAS parameter

```
STORCLAS=storage-class-name
```

A DD statement that sets the storage class to MVPS100

```
//TRANX    DD    DSNAME=MM01.TRANS.NEW,DISP=(NEW,CATLG),
//                STORCLAS=MVPS100
```

What a storage class does

- The storage class provides the information normally supplied by the UNIT and VOL-UME parameters. As a result, any UNIT parameter coded for the data set is ignored.

- In most cases, any VOLUME parameter coded for the data set is ignored, too. But if the SMS administrator specifies GUARANTEED_SPACE=YES for a storage class, the volume serial numbers that you specify in the VOL=SER parameter will override the volume serial numbers provided by SMS.

- The SMS administrator defines the storage class names as well as the UNIT and VOL-UME attributes for each storage class.

How to use the STORCLAS parameter

- If you don't specify the STORCLAS parameter when SMS is active and an ACS routine is present, the ACS routine will select the storage class for the data set. When you code the STORCLAS parameter, you name the storage class that you want to use for the data set instead.

- Even when you use the STORCLAS parameter, the ACS routine can be set up to ignore it. So check your installation's standards before coding this parameter.

Figure 13-3   How to set the storage class (STORCLAS)

How to set the data class (DATACLAS)

The data class for an SMS-managed data set specifies many of the attributes you would normally have to code in the DD statement for a data set, as shown in the table in figure 13-4. In contrast to the storage class, you can override any or all of the attributes set in a data class by including the appropriate DD parameters in your JCL. For instance, suppose that the data class to be assigned to a new data set specifies a record length of 80 characters, but you know the data set you're creating contains 85-character records. In this case, you can simply include an LRECL=85 parameter in the DD statement to override the LRECL=80 attribute in the data class.

If you want to assign a data class to a data set directly instead of letting an ACS routine make the choice, you include a DATACLAS parameter that gives the data class name in the DD statement. As with STORCLAS, the name you code in this parameter must already be defined in SMS, so you'll have to check to see what values you can use. Also, be aware that the ACS routine assigned to the type of file you're defining may be set up to override the attributes for the data class specified in the DATACLAS parameter.

The two examples in this figure illustrate the use of the DATACLAS parameter. In the first example, a data class named MVPD050 is assigned to MM01.TRANS.NEW, while an ACS routine selects the storage and management classes. The same is true in the second example, but here the SPACE and LRECL parameters modify the space allocation and logical record length that are set in MVPD050.

The syntax for the DATACLAS parameter

```
DATACLAS=data-class-name
```

The attributes that are defined by a data class

DD parameter	Description
RECFM	Record format.
LRECL	Logical record length.
SPACE and AVGREC	Space allocation.
volume-count (VOLUME parameter)	Number of volumes in the data set (see chapter 7).
RETPD or EXPDT	Retention period or expiration date (see chapter 7).
RECORG, KEYLEN, KEYOFF, IMBED, REPLICATE, CISIZE, FREESPACE, and SHAREOPTIONS	VSAM options (see chapter 16).

A DD statement that sets the data class to MVPD050

```
//TRANX    DD    DSNAME=MM01.TRANS.NEW,DISP=(NEW,CATLG),
//                DATACLAS=MVPD050
```

A DD statement that overrides the SPACE and LRECL parameters of the data class

```
//TRANX    DD    DSNAME=MM01.TRANS.NEW,DISP=(NEW,CATLG),
//                DATACLAS=MVPD050,SPACE=(TRK(1,1)),
//                LRECL=1000
```

What a data class does

- The data class provides many of the attributes that you normally code on the DD statement for a data set.

- You can override any or all of the data set attributes in a data class by coding the equivalent parameters in the DD statement.

- The SMS administrator defines the data class names as well as the attributes for each data class.

How to use the DATACLAS parameter

- If you don't specify the DATACLAS parameter when SMS is active and an ACS routine is present, the ACS routine will select the data class for the data set. When you code the DATACLAS parameter, you specify the data class that you want to use for the data set instead.

- Even when you code the DATACLAS parameter, the ACS routine assigned to the type of file you're defining may override the attributes for the data class you specify.

Figure 13-4   How to set the data class (DATACLAS)

How to set the management class (MGMTCLAS)

As shown in figure 13-5, management classes typically govern activities such as how often a data set should be backed up and how many of the backup versions to keep. They also delete data sets with a retention or expiration date that has already passed. And they can archive data sets to tape or offline DASD storage if they haven't been used in a while.

Note that the management class can assign a maximum value for an expiration or retention date for a data set. This takes precedence over what's specified in any EXPDT or RETPD DD parameters or in the data class for the data set. For example, if the management class assigns a data set a maximum expiration date of 12/31/2002, you can't code an EXPDT parameter to change the date to 6/30/2003. Keep this in mind if you ever need to extend the retention or expiration date on a tape data set because the data set's management class may limit your options.

Apart from the expiration and retention dates, the data set attributes provided in the management class can't be coded with JCL statements. As a result, you can't override the options for a management class in a DD statement as you can the options for a storage or data class.

If you want to assign a specific management class to a data set, you code the MGMTCLAS parameter, as shown in this figure. In this example, the MGMTCLAS parameter assigns the MVPM010 management class to a data set named MM01.TRANS.NEW. Since neither a STORCLAS nor a DATACLAS parameter is included in this DD statement, an ACS routine will select the storage and data classes.

The syntax for the MGMTCLAS parameter

```
MGMTCLAS=management-class-name
```

Typical functions of a management class

- Determine how often to back up the data set.
- Determine how many backup versions of the data set to maintain.
- Determine when to migrate the data set to archival storage.
- Delete the data set when its expiration date or retention date expires.
- Assign a maximum expiration or retention date to a data set.
- If the data set is partitioned, routinely compress it.

A DD statement that sets the management class to MVPM010

```
//TRANX    DD   DSNAME=MM01.TRANS.NEW,DISP=(NEW,CATLG),
//              MGMTCLAS= MVPM010
```

What a management class does

- The management class determines how backup and disk storage space are managed for a data set.
- You can't override management class attributes with JCL statements.
- A management class can override the EXPDT or RETPD parameters in a data class or DD statement by setting a maximum value for an expiration or retention date.

How to use the MGMTCLAS parameter

- If you don't specify the MGMTCLAS parameter when SMS is active and an ACS routine is present, the ACS routine will select the management class for the data set. When you code the MGMTCLAS parameter, you specify the management class that you want to use for the data set instead.
- Even when you use the MGMTCLAS parameter, the ACS routine can be set up to ignore it. So check your installation's standards before coding this parameter.

Figure 13-5   How to set the management class (MGMTCLAS)

How to create a partitioned data set (DSNTYPE)

The DSNTYPE parameter is used to create SMS-managed data sets that aren't sequential or VSAM data sets. You can code the DSNTYPE parameter directly in your DD statement for a new data set, or an SMS administrator can include it in a data class definition.

The DSNTYPE parameter is most often used to define *PDSE (partitioned data set extended)* libraries, a type of data set that's available only under SMS. PDSE libraries are similar to PDS libraries in that you can create and store members in them. But PDSE libraries process and manage members more efficiently. I've listed some of the advantages of PDSE libraries in the chart in figure 13-6. Perhaps the two most important features are that they release unused storage space when it is no longer needed by the library and that you can access the data within the members much faster.

To create a PDSE library when it's not provided for by the data class, you include DSNTYPE=LIBRARY in the DD statement for the data set, as shown by the example in this figure. Here, a member called TRANERR is created in a new PDSE library called MM01.LIB.ERR. In this case, the programmer knows that the data class assigned by the ACS routine will be for a normal PDS library (DSNTYPE=PDS), so the DSNTYPE parameter is included to override that setting.

Please note that you can specify data set types other than LIBRARY and PDS in the DSNTYPE parameter. However, they aren't used as often, so they aren't included here. You can check with your supervisor to find out what other data set types can be used at your installation.

The syntax for the DSNTYPE parameter

```
DSNTYPE= {LIBRARY}
         {PDS}
```

Explanation

LIBRARY   Specifies an SMS-managed PDSE (partitioned data set extended).

PDS   Specifies a PDS (partitioned data set).

A DD statement that overrides the data class file type to create a PDSE

```
//TRANERR  DD   DSNAME=MM01.LIB.ERR(TRANERR),DISP=(NEW,CATLG),
//               DSNTYPE=LIBRARY
```

The advantages of a PDSE over a PDS

* A PDSE doesn't need to be periodically compressed. When a member is deleted, the space is made available for reuse.

* A PDSE provides faster access.

* Individual members in a PDSE can be concurrently updated.

* A PDSE can contain up to 524,286 members.

Description

* The DSNTYPE parameter can be used to specify the data set type for several different kinds of non-sequential, SMS-managed data sets.

* The DSNTYPE parameter can be coded in a data class or DD statement. When it's coded in a DD statement, it overrides the data set type specified in the data class.

* Although this parameter can be used to define several different types of data sets, only the two most common options are shown above. You'll use it most often to create a type of library called a *PDSE (partitioned data set extended)* that's available only under SMS.

Figure 13-6   How to create a partitioned data set (DSNTYPE)

How to use SMS parameters in creating non-SMS data sets

When you're defining non-SMS data sets, you can use the AVGREC parameter to help you with space allocation and you can use the REFDD and LIKE parameters to save JCL coding by creating new data sets that are modeled after existing data sets. Although you can use these parameters for SMS-managed files as well, you won't do that very often. It's usually easier to let the storage, data, and management classes take care of these functions.

How to allocate space in terms of records (AVGREC)

When you code the SPACE parameter, you normally specify the units in terms of blocks, tracks, or cylinders. However, if SMS is active on your system, you can also allocate space in terms of records, as shown in figure 13-7. To do that, you specify the record size for the unit subparameter of the SPACE parameter, and you code the AVGREC parameter. This parameter tells the system that you're coding a record size rather than a block size. In addition, it supplies a multiplier that affects how the primary and secondary allocation amounts are interpreted.

To get a better understanding of how to code the AVGREC parameter, look at the example in this figure. Here, the AVGREC parameter tells the system that 120 bytes is the average record length of a record and that the primary and secondary allocation amounts are to be multiplied by 1024 (1K). As a result, the primary allocation will be large enough to store 5120 (5K) 120-byte records, and the secondary allocation will be large enough to store 3072 (3K) 120-byte records.

The syntax for the AVGREC parameter

```
         {U}
AVGREC=  {K}
         {M}
```

Explanation

U	Specifies that the primary and secondary allocations in the SPACE parameter represent the number of records in units.
K	Specifies that the primary and secondary allocations in the SPACE parameter represent the number of records in thousands of units (a multiple of 1024).
M	Specifies that the primary and secondary allocations in the SPACE parameter represent the number of records in millions of units (a multiple of 1,048,576).

A DD statement that uses the AVGREC parameter

```
//TRANS    DD    DSNAME=MM01.AR.TRANS,DISP=(NEW,CATLG),
//                UNIT=SYSDA,VOL=SER=MPS8BV,
//                SPACE=(120,(5,3)),AVGREC=K
```

Description

- The AVGREC parameter allows you to allocate space in terms of records. It lets the system know that the first SPACE subparameter is a record size rather than a block size, and it supplies a multiplier that affects how the primary and secondary allocations are interpreted.

- Don't code the AVGREC parameter if CYL, TRK, or ABSTR is specified in the SPACE parameter.

Figure 13-7   How to allocate space in terms of records (AVGREC)

How to model a new data set after an old one (REFDD and LIKE)

You use the REFDD or LIKE parameter to create a new data set based on a *model data set* that already exists. To be specific, these parameters copy the data set attributes summarized in figure 13-8 from the model data set. For the REFDD parameter, the model data set must be defined by an earlier DD statement in the same job. For the LIKE parameter, the model data set must be cataloged. For either parameter to work, the model data set must reside on DASD, although it doesn't have to be managed by SMS.

The examples in this figure illustrate the use of both parameters. In the first example, the DD statement in STEP2 shows how you can use the REFDD parameter to copy the attributes from the model data set that's defined in STEP1. As you can see, you code this parameter with a backwards reference. In the second example, the DD statement uses the LIKE parameter to copy the attributes of the cataloged data set named MM01.AR.TRANS.

With either REFDD or LIKE, you can supply DD parameters for the attributes that won't be copied. For instance, the REFDD example includes a UNIT parameter since unit information isn't copied from a model data set. In addition, you can code parameters to override the values in the model data set, as shown in the LIKE example. It includes a SPACE parameter to override the space allocation in the model data set. This is a common practice, especially when you know that your new data set will require less DASD storage than is used for the model.

The syntax for the REFDD and LIKE parameters

```
REFDD=*.stepname.ddname

LIKE=model-dataset-name
```

DD parameters that are copied from the model data set by REFDD and LIKE

Parameter	Explanation
RECFM	Record format used by the model data set.
LRECL	Logical record length used by the model data set.
SPACE	Primary space allocation based on the first three extents of the model data set.
AVGREC	Unit of measure specified by AVGREC on the model data set.
DSNTYPE	File type of the model data set.
RECORG KEYLEN KEYOFF	VSAM only. Record organization, key length, and key offset of the model data set (see chapter 16).

How to use the REFDD parameter to model a new data set after one that's defined earlier in the job

```
//STEP1    EXEC PGM=TRNSPR1
//ARTRANS DD    DSNAME=MM01.AR.TRANX,DISP=(NEW,CATLG),
//               UNIT=SYSDA,VOL=SER=MPS8BV,
//               SPACE=(TRK,(5,3),RLSE)                  } Model data set
//               DCB=(RECFM=FB,LRECL=120)
//STEP2    EXEC PGM=TRNSPR2
//ROTRANS DD    DSNAME=MM01.RO.TRANX,DISP=(NEW,CATLG),
//               UNIT=SYSDA,REFDD=*.STEP1.ARTRANS
```

How to use the LIKE parameter to model a new data set after a cataloged data set

```
//STEP1    EXEC PGM=TRNSPR1
//TRANS   DD    DSNAME=MM01.AP.TRANS,DISP=(NEW,CATLG),
//               UNIT=SYSDA,LIKE=MM01.AR.TRANS,
//               SPACE=(TRK,(1,1))
```

Description

* The REFDD parameter lets you define a new data set based on a *model data set* defined earlier in the same job. It uses a backwards reference to identify the model data set.

* The LIKE parameter also lets you define a new data set based on a model data set. In this case, the model data set must be cataloged.

* A model data set must reside on DASD, and it cannot be a temporary data set, a member of a partitioned data set, or a generation data group in which a relative generation number is used.

* Any DD parameters that are coded for the new data set will override those in the model data set.

* If the new data set resides on tape, the model data set must have sequential organization, and only the RECFM and LRECL attributes will apply.

Figure 13-8   How to model a new data set after an old one (REFDD and LIKE)

Perspective

If SMS is installed and active on your system, using the various SMS features can make your life easier when it comes to coding DD statements for new data sets, especially those that are managed by SMS. Keep in mind, though, that SMS works well for only a few basic types of standard data set configurations. So be sure to check your installation standards for how and when to use SMS. In many cases, you'll find that you have to code the standard JCL DD parameters to create the exact data set you need.

Terms

SMS
Storage Management Subsystem
storage class
data class
management class
ACS routine
Automatic Class Selection routine
PDSE
partitioned data set extended
model data set

Section 4

VSAM data management

VSAM is the access method that is used for indexed files on an IBM mainframe. It can also be used as the access method for two other kinds of files. It provides a catalog facility that can be used for both VSAM and non-VSAM files. And it provides a multi-function utility program called Access Method Services (AMS) that lets you perform a variety of functions for VSAM as well as non-VSAM files.

In this section, you'll learn how to use VSAM. In chapter 14, you'll learn the concepts and terms that you need for working with VSAM. In chapter 15, you'll learn how to code JCL for VSAM data sets. And in chapter 16, you'll learn how to use AMS.

14

VSAM concepts and terms

This chapter presents the concepts and terms that you need to know when you're working with VSAM. First, it describes the three types of file organizations that are supported by VSAM. Then, it explains how VSAM manages data sets that have these organizations.

As you read through this chapter, you'll find many references to efficiency considerations. So it's important to remember how data access works on DASD (which is the only type of device that can be used for VSAM files). The most time-consuming part of any DASD I/O operation is moving the access mechanism on the device to the record that needs to be read or written. While the actual transfer of data takes place at electronic speeds, the access mechanism movement is a slower, mechanical process.

As a result, many techniques are used on a mainframe to minimize access mechanism movement. For example, records are blocked so that an entire set of records can be read with a single access mechanism movement, instead of having to move the read/write heads to each record individually. Keep this in mind as you learn about how VSAM handles data organization and access.

The three types of VSAM data sets

VSAM, which stands for *Virtual Storage Access Method*, provides for three types of data sets: entry-sequenced, key-sequenced, and relative-record. Since these correspond to the sequential, indexed, and relative file organizations that are supported on all platforms that allow for COBOL programming, they are not unique to VSAM. What is unique, though, is the way they're implemented by VSAM. So after you learn the basic concepts that apply to these file organizations, you'll learn how VSAM implements them.

As you read this chapter, you will come upon occasional references to *AMS* (*Access Method Services*). That is the multi-function utility program that you use to define VSAM data sets. In chapter 16, you'll learn how to use AMS, and there you will see that you need to know many of the VSAM terms that are presented in this chapter.

Entry-sequenced data sets (ESDS)

Figure 14-1 summarizes the concepts and terms that apply to an *entry-sequenced data set*, or *ESDS*. Here, you can see a file of employee records that's in sequence by employee number. When the records are read or written, they are always accessed in sequence by disk location, which can be referred to as *sequential access*. On other platforms, this type of data set is referred to as a *sequential file*.

When the records in an ESDS are processed, they usually need to be in sequence by one or more of the fields in the records. These fields are referred to as the *key fields*, and the values in the fields are referred to as *keys*. If the records aren't in the sequence that's needed by a processing program, an ESDS can be sorted into the proper sequence.

A record in an ESDS can also be processed directly via its *relative byte address* (*RBA*). The RBA gives the starting location of an ESDS record relative to the start of the file, which is byte 0. If, for example, a file contains fixed-length 200 byte records, the RBAs for the first three records are 0, 200, and 400. Although this method of access is rarely used, the notion of the RBA is useful because VSAM keeps track of the highest RBA that's used by a data set. You'll learn how that comes into play with reusable data sets later on in this chapter.

Curiously, entry-sequenced data sets aren't in common use today. That's because non-VSAM sequential data sets are just as efficient and they're easier to work with. The non-VSAM access method that's used instead is called QSAM, which stands for Queued Sequential Access Method.

An ESDS that's in sequence by employee number

Disk location	Employee number	Social security number	First name	Last name	Dept. number
1	00001	499-35-5079	Stanley	Abbott	101
2	00002	279-00-1210	William	Collins	140
3	00004	899-16-9235	Alice	Crawford	122
4	00005	703-47-5748	Paul	Collins	101
5	00008	558-12-6168	Marie	Littlejohn	130
6	00009	559-35-2479	E	Siebert	140
7	00010	334-96-8721	Constance	Harris	101
8	00012	213-64-9290	Thomas	Bluestone	122
9	00013	572-68-3100	Jean	Glenning	101
10	00015	498-27-6117	Ronald	Westbrook	140

Description

* In an *entry-sequenced data set* (*ESDS*), the records are stored one after the other in consecutive disk locations. On other platforms, this is called a *sequential file*.

* To retrieve records from a sequential file, you must read them sequentially by disk location. This type of record retrieval is referred to as *sequential access*.

* The records in an ESDS are often in ascending or descending sequence based on the values in one or more of the fields within the records. The field or fields that contain these values are called *key fields*, and the values in those fields are called *keys*.

* Before an application program can process the records in an ESDS, the records may have to be sorted into another key sequence.

* Although it's rarely done, you can also access an ESDS record directly by its *relative byte address* (or *RBA*). The RBA gives the starting location of a record measured from the first byte of the file, which is byte 0.

* Because VSAM entry-sequenced data sets didn't improve on the non-VSAM access method for sequential data sets (QSAM), non-VSAM sequential data sets are still used in most OS/390 shops.

Figure 14-1   Entry-sequenced data sets (ESDS)

Key-sequenced data sets (KSDS)

Figure 14-2 summarizes the concepts and terms that apply to a *key-sequenced data set*, or *KSDS*. In this type of data set, the records can be read sequentially, but they can also be read randomly. On other platforms, this type of file is referred to as an *indexed file*.

To make *random access* possible, a KSDS consists of a *data component* and an *index component*. The *index component* of a KSDS contains the *primary key* values for the records in the data set. For each key value, the index also contains the record's disk location in the data component of the file. That way, the index can be used to randomly access the record for any key value.

Because key-sequenced data sets provide for both sequential and random access, they are commonly used for master files, like inventory, customer, and employee master files. That way, the records in the file can be updated using random access, and reports can be prepared from the file using sequential access.

Historically, the problem with indexed files on all platforms has been that they're inefficient. For instance, reading a record on a random basis means that one or more index records have to be read before the master record can be read. And adding a record to an indexed file means that the index must be updated and the record must be inserted somewhere in the file. These are problems you don't have with sequential files.

When VSAM became available in the mid-1970s, though, it provided major performance improvements over the Indexed Sequential Access Method (ISAM) that had been in use. As a result, key-sequenced data sets quickly replaced ISAM files. In the second half of this chapter, you'll learn about some of the VSAM record management techniques that help make key-sequenced data sets more efficient than ISAM files.

A KSDS that's indexed by employee number

Index component

Employee number	Disk location
00001	1
00002	2
00004	3
00005	4
00008	5
00009	6
00010	7
00012	8
00013	9
00015	10

Data component

Disk location	Employee number	Social security number	First name	Last name	Dept. number
1	00001	499-35-5079	Stanley	Abbott	101
2	00002	279-00-1210	William	Collins	140
3	00004	899-16-9235	Alice	Crawford	122
4	00005	703-47-5748	Paul	Collins	101
5	00008	558-12-6168	Marie	Littlejohn	130
6	00009	559-35-2479	E	Siebert	140
7	00010	334-96-8721	Constance	Harris	101
8	00012	213-64-9290	Thomas	Bluestone	122
9	00013	572-68-3100	Jean	Glenning	101
10	00015	498-27-6117	Ronald	Westbrook	140

Description

- A *key-sequenced data set* (*KSDS*) consists of two parts: an *index component* and a *data component*. Within the index component, each entry contains a key field value that points either to a lower-level index or to a record in the data component of the file. On other platforms, this type of data set is called an *indexed file*.

- An indexed file must have at least one index, which is the *primary index*. The key for this index is called the *primary key*, and each key in the primary index must be *unique*, which means that *duplicate keys* aren't allowed.

- In the data component of a KSDS, the records are stored in primary key sequence. That way, the records can be accessed sequentially without using the index component. This is referred to as *sequential access*.

- The index component can be used to access a record directly by getting the disk location for any primary key value. This is referred to as *random access*.

- Because VSAM key-sequenced data sets offered significant improvements in performance, they soon replaced the non-VSAM access method for indexed files (ISAM).

Figure 14-2 Key-sequenced data sets (KSDS)

Alternate indexes for key-sequenced data sets

Besides its primary index, an indexed file can have one or more *alternate indexes*. These indexes make it possible to access records sequentially or randomly based on the values of *alternate keys*. This is illustrated by the examples in figure 14-3.

In the first example, an alternate index is used for social security numbers. In this case, the alternate keys are unique since there is only one social security number for each worker. This gives a program the ability to access the records in the data set by either employee number (the primary key) or social security number.

In the second example, an alternate index is used for department numbers. These keys, however, are *non-unique*, which means that the index provides for *duplicate keys*. This gives a program the ability to access all of the employee records for a specific department.

By using alternate keys, you can access the data in a file in whatever way is most logical. As you might guess, though, alternate keys add to the overhead that's associated with an indexed file. If, for example, a record is added to this employee file, three different indexes need to be updated: employee number, social security number, and department number.

But here again, the efficiency of alternate keys depends to a large extent on how they're implemented. With VSAM, an alternate index is actually a KSDS that has the alternate keys for a data set in its index component and the primary keys in its data component. Then, the primary keys in the alternate index are used to find the records in the *base cluster*, which contains the index and data components of the original data set. In this way, VSAM provides for any number of alternate indexes with a reasonable degree of efficiency for all of the indexes.

A KSDS with unique alternate keys

Alternate index

Social security number	Employee number
213-64-9290	00012
279-00-1210	00002
334-96-8721	00010
498-27-6117	00015
499-35-5079	00001
558-12-6168	00008
559-35-2479	00009
572-68-3100	00013
703-47-5748	00005
899-16-9235	00004

Base cluster

Employee number	Social security number	Last name	Dept. number
00001	499-35-5079	Abbott	101
00002	279-00-1210	Collins	140
00004	899-16-9235	Crawford	122
00005	703-47-5748	Collins	101
00008	558-12-6168	Littlejohn	130
00009	559-35-2479	Siebert	140
00010	334-96-8721	Harris	101
00012	213-64-9290	Bluestone	122
00013	572-68-3100	Glenning	101
00015	498-27-6117	Westbrook	140

A KSDS with non-unique alternate keys

Alternate index

Dept. number	Employee numbers
101	00001 00005 00010 00013
122	00004 00012
130	00008
140	00002 00009 00015

Base Cluster

Employee number	Social security number	Last name	Dept. number
00001	499-35-5079	Abbott	101
00002	279-00-1210	Collins	140
00004	899-16-9235	Crawford	122
00005	703-47-5748	Collins	101
00008	558-12-6168	Littlejohn	130
00009	559-35-2479	Siebert	140
00010	334-96-8721	Harris	101
00012	213-64-9290	Bluestone	122
00013	572-68-3100	Glenning	101
00015	498-27-6117	Westbrook	140

Description

- An indexed file can have one or more *alternate indexes*. The keys used in each alternate index are called *alternate keys*. An alternate index can contain unique or *non-unique* (duplicate) *keys*.

- The entries in an alternate index are maintained in alternate key sequence so the file can be read sequentially and randomly by the alternate key.

- In VSAM, an alternate index is actually a KSDS with the alternate keys in the index component and the primary keys in the data component. The index and data component in the original KSDS are called the *base cluster* for the alternate index.

Figure 14-3   Alternate indexes for key-sequenced data sets

Relative-record data sets (RRDS)

Figure 14-4 presents the concepts and terms that apply to a *relative-record data set*, or *RRDS*. Although the records in an RRDS can also be accessed both sequentially and randomly, not many files can be easily adapted to this type of organization. On other platforms, this type of file is called a *relative file*.

Each *record area* in an RRDS is addressed by a *relative record number* from one through the number of record areas in the file. Since a relative record number can easily be converted to a disk address without using an index, the data in a record area can be efficiently accessed on a random basis. Similarly, since the record areas are read in sequence without using an index, sequential access is more efficient than it is with indexed organization.

The trick to using an RRDS is converting a key field like employee number to a relative record number without creating duplicate record numbers and without wasting too many record areas. In the example in this figure, the employee numbers are unique keys that range from 1 through 15 so they can be used as the relative record numbers. Because five of the first 15 numbers aren't used, however, five of the first 15 record areas are wasted. This often happens as the records in a file are deleted.

But what if a master file of 10,000 inventory records has item numbers that range from 100,000 to 2,000,000? How then do you convert those item numbers to relative record numbers that range from 1 through 12,000 (assuming 2,000 record areas are left empty for later additions)? Although you can try to develop a *randomizing routine* that does the conversion, it is likely to be impractical. That's the primary reason why relative-record data sets are rarely used.

Reusable data sets

As you learned in chapter 6, some applications call for temporary data sets that are created, used, and deleted each time the application is run. To provide for this type of processing, VSAM lets you define an ESDS, a KSDS, or an RRDS as a *reusable data set*. When a reusable data set is opened for output, VSAM resets the data set so all of its records are ignored and the records of the new data set overwrite the old records.

With a reusable ESDS, for example, VSAM keeps track of the highest relative byte address (RBA) that is used by the data set. Then, when the data set is opened for input or for I/O, VSAM reads all the records sequentially until it reaches the highest RBA. But when the data set is opened for output, VSAM resets the RBA to zero so the old records can be overwritten by the new records. By using a reusable data set, you are able to define a VSAM data set just once and use it repeatedly.

An RRDS with empty record areas for deleted records

Relative record number	Employee number	Social security number	First name	Last name	Dept. number
1	00001	499-35-5079	Stanley	Abbott	101
2	00002	279-00-1210	William	Collins	140
3					
4	00004	899-16-9235	Alice	Crawford	122
5	00005	703-47-5748	Paul	Collins	101
6					
7					
8	00008	558-12-6168	Marie	Littlejohn	130
9	00009	559-35-2479	E	Siebert	140
10	00010	334-96-8721	Constance	Harris	101
11					
12	00012	213-64-9290	Thomas	Bluestone	122
13	00013	572-68-3100	Jean	Glenning	101
14					
15	00015	498-27-6117	Ronald	Westbrook	140

Description

- A *relative-record data set* (*RRDS*) consists of *record areas* that can contain one record. Each of these areas is identified by a *relative record number* that indicates its relative position in the file. On other platforms, this type of data set is called a *relative file*.

- When the records in an RRDS are accessed sequentially, the areas that don't contain records are skipped.

- To access a record randomly, a program must specify the relative record number of the area that contains the record. Then, the record is read or written directly without going through an index. As a result, this is more efficient than random access of an indexed file.

- The relative record number for a record is usually derived from a key field. In the simplest case, the key can be used as the relative record number as shown above. Usually, though, the key value has to be converted to a relative record number by using a *randomizing routine*.

- The purpose of a randomizing routine is to convert the values in key fields to relative record numbers that fall between one and the number of record areas allocated to the file. If two or more records randomize to the same relative record number, additional routines must be used to put the record with the duplicate record number in an available area.

- When the keys in a file can be converted to relative record numbers with a minimum of duplicates and unused record areas, an RRDS is an efficient file organization. These data sets are used infrequently, though, because the keys in most files don't meet those qualifications.

Figure 14-4   Relative-record data sets (RRDS)

How VSAM manages data sets

To keep track of the VSAM data sets used by a system, all VSAM data sets are cataloged in a VSAM catalog facility. To provide for efficient record processing, VSAM uses some improved techniques for *record management*. In the topics that follow, you'll learn about these features.

The Integrated Catalog Facility (ICF)

The catalog facility that's commonly used with OS/390 is the *Integrated Catalog Facility*, or *ICF*. Although you were introduced to it in chapter 2, it is summarized again in figure 14-5. As you can see, you can use ICF for cataloging both VSAM and non-VSAM files.

Unlike non-VSAM files, VSAM data sets *must* be cataloged. The catalog information for each VSAM data set not only includes location and extent information like what volumes a data set is stored on, but also data set characteristics like data set type, key location, and so on. By keeping this information in the catalog, the JCL for working with a data set is simplified.

As you have already learned, the high-level qualifier in the data set name for a user data set usually identifies the *user catalog* that the data set is cataloged in. However, a user catalog can also have one or more *aliases* that are defined through AMS. That way, you can use different high-level qualifiers to identify data sets that arc in thc samc uscr catalog.

The relationships among the master catalog, user catalogs, and data sets

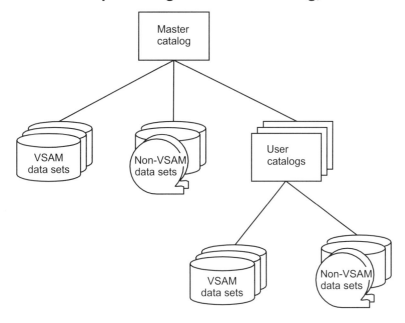

Description

- The catalog facility that's commonly used with OS/390 is the *Integrated Catalog Facility*, or *ICF*.

- ICF provides for two types of catalogs: *master catalogs* and *user catalogs*. Each system typically has just one master catalog and an unlimited number of user catalogs. The master catalog contains entries that identify system data sets and user catalogs, while the user catalogs contain entries that identify user data sets.

- ICF can be used to catalog both VSAM and non-VSAM data sets. Although non-VSAM data sets don't have to be cataloged, cataloging makes them easier to work with because you don't have to provide volume information for existing data sets.

- All VSAM data sets must be cataloged. Each catalog entry not only contains information about the location of the file, but also about the characteristics of the file. This simplifies the DD statements for existing files.

- By convention, the high-level qualifier in a data set name is the name of the user catalog in which it is entered. Because user catalogs typically have several *aliases*, data sets with different high-level qualifiers can be cataloged in the same user catalog.

Figure 14-5   The Integrated Catalog Facility (ICF)

Control intervals and control areas

In VSAM, a data set can also be referred to as a *cluster*. For an ESDS or RRDS, the cluster consists of just a data component. But for a KSDS, the cluster consists of both a data component and an index component.

When a VSAM data set is stored on a DASD, the records in the data component of the cluster are grouped into *control intervals*, which are grouped into *control areas*. This is illustrated in figure 14-6. This is one of the VSAM record management techniques that leads to more efficient processing, and it works the same way for all three types of data sets.

The control interval is the unit of data that VSAM transfers between disk storage and virtual storage, and a control interval usually contains more than one record. As a result, the size of the control interval can have a significant effect on processing efficiency. This is similar to blocking for non-VSAM files, which can also have a significant effect on processing efficiency.

As for the control area, its size is based on the amount of space allocated to the data set and the characteristics of the DASD that's used for the data set. When possible, though, control areas are normally full cylinders, and additional extents are allocated in units of adjacent control areas. In general, this leads to improved efficiency.

In the illustration in this figure, the assumption is that each control interval contains three records of the same length. In practice, though, the records in a control interval may not fill it completely, so there's usually some unused space in cach control intcrval. Also, records of varying lengths may be stored in a control interval.

Beyond that, VSAM lets you define clusters that allow *spanned records*. These are records that flow from one control interval to the next. If, for example, record 24 started in control interval 8 and finished in interval 9, it would be a spanned record. Normally, though, spanned records are avoided because they degrade processing efficiency. The only time they are required is when the maximum record size for a data set is larger than the control interval size, but that should be avoided whenever possible.

A cluster consists of control intervals within control areas

Control area 1

Control interval 1	Logical record 1	Logical record 2	Logical record 3
Control interval 2	Logical record 4	Logical record 5	Logical record 6
Control interval 3	Logical record 7	Logical record 8	Logical record 9
Control interval 4	Logical record 10	Logical record 11	Logical record 12
Control interval 5	Logical record 13	Logical record 14	Logical record 15
Control interval 6	Logical record 16	Logical record 17	Logical record 18

Control area 2

Control interval 7	Logical record 19	Logical record 20	Logical record 21
Control interval 8	Logical record 22	Logical record 23	Logical record 24
Control interval 9	Logical record 25	Logical record 26	Logical record 27
Control interval 10	Logical record 28	Logical record 29	Logical record 30
Control interval 11	Logical record 31	Logical record 32	Logical record 33
Control interval 12	Logical record 34	Logical record 35	Logical record 36

Description

- In VSAM, a data set can be referred to as a *cluster*. For a KSDS, the cluster consists of an index component and a data component. For an ESDS or RRDS, the cluster consists of just a data component.

- For all VSAM clusters, the data component consists of one or more *control areas*, and each control area consists of one or more *control intervals*.

- The control interval is the unit of data that VSAM transfers between virtual storage and disk storage as a data set is processed. As a result, the size of a control interval can have a significant effect on performance.

- VSAM determines the size of a control area based on the space allocated to the data set and the characteristics of the device on which the data set is stored. Whenever possible, each control area is a full cylinder, and additional extents are added to a data set in units of adjacent control areas.

- A *spanned record* is a record that flows from one control interval to the next. For most data sets, though, spanned records aren't allowed.

Figure 14-6   Control intervals and control areas

Free space and record additions for a KSDS

Another VSAM record management technique is its use of *free space* in both the control intervals and control areas of a KSDS. If, for example, you know that a data set is going to have frequent record additions, you can assign free space in each control interval as well as free control intervals in each control area. This can improve the performance of the KSDS.

This is illustrated in figure 14-7, which shows the primary keys of the records in the data component of a KSDS right after the data set has been created. Note that the records are in sequence by their primary keys. Note also that some free space has been provided in each control interval, and a free control interval has been provided in the control area. This free space is also provided in all of the other control intervals and areas of the data set.

Because the records are in key sequence, they can be read with minimal use of the index component of the data set. This leads to efficient sequential processing of a KSDS. But what happens when records are added to the data set? By using the free space, VSAM is able to keep the records in the control intervals in sequence by their primary keys, so the sequential processing efficiency is maintained.

This works particularly well when there is enough free space in the control intervals for all of the records that are added to a data set. When there isn't enough free space in a control interval for a new record, though, a *control interval split* occurs. And if there isn't a free control interval when a control split occurs, a *control area split* occurs. These splits, which are described in more detail in this figure, start to degrade the performance of record additions. Eventually, then, you need to recreate the KSDS so the free spaces are restored and the records are written in sequence in the control intervals.

One way to recreate a KSDS is to use the REPRO command of the AMS utility. Then, AMS reads the old KSDS and writes a new KSDS. In the new KSDS, the original free space allocations are restored, and all of the records are written in sequence in the data component of the cluster. Most installations routinely REPRO their KSDS files because it restores them to maximum efficiency.

You can assign free space to control intervals and control areas

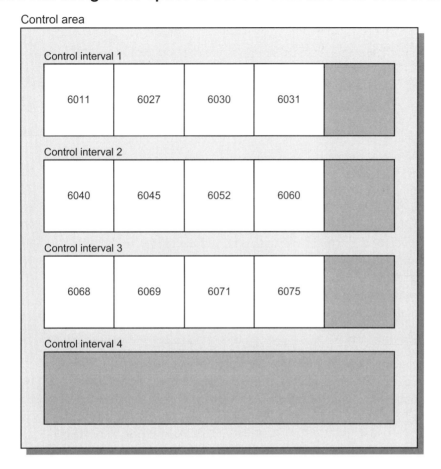

Figure 14-7   Free space and record additions for a KSDS

Description

- To facilitate the addition of records to a KSDS, *free space* can be assigned to both the control areas and the control intervals of the data set. Although the free space increases the size of the data set, it improves the performance of the data set by improving the way file additions are processed.

- When a new record is added to a KSDS, it's inserted into its correct sequential location in the proper control interval, and the records after it are shifted right.

- If there isn't enough free space in the control interval for a record that's being inserted, some of the records in the control interval are moved to one of the free control intervals. This is called a *control interval split*.

- If there isn't a free control interval when a control interval split occurs, a *control area split* occurs. Then, VSAM allocates a new control area, moves about half the control intervals from the original control area to the new one, and performs a control interval split using one of the newly freed control intervals.

How a record in a KSDS is randomly accessed by primary key

As you've already learned, a KSDS consists of a data component and an index component. The primary purpose of the index component is to locate the records in the data component by their key values. To increase the efficiency of this process, the index component consists of an *index set* and a *sequence set* as shown in figure 14-8.

As you can see, the sequence set is the lowest level of the index. It's used to determine which control interval a specific record is stored in. In contrast, the index set consists of records at one or more levels that point to the sequence set records. In this figure, though, the index set has only a top level, which always consists of just one record.

The entries in the index set record in this figure contain the highest key values stored in each of the sequence set records, and the entries in the sequence set records contain the highest key values stored in each of the control intervals. To access a record, VSAM searches from the index set to the sequence set to the control interval that contains the desired record. Then, VSAM reads that control interval into virtual storage and searches the keys of the records until the specific record is found.

The *free pointer* shown in each sequence set record points to free control intervals in the control area. There is also control information within each control interval (not shown) that identifies the free space in the interval. By using the free pointers and control information, VSAM is able to manage the free space as it adds records to a KSDS. VSAM also updates the records in the index and sequence sets as it processes those additions. As a result, the data set can always be used for both sequential and random processing by primary key.

To improve performance, the systems programmer tries to define a production KSDS so all of the index set is brought into internal storage areas called *buffers* when the data set is processed so that the information can be accessed more quickly. This is one of several ways that the performance of a KSDS can be fine-tuned.

How alternate indexes work

Alternate indexing adds another level of index searching when you access a record in a KSDS. To access the base cluster sequentially by alternate key, the alternate index is read sequentially. But then, for each record that an alternate key points to, VSAM has to search the primary index to find the disk location of the record and access it randomly. Similarly, to access the base cluster randomly by an alternate key, VSAM has to search the alternate index to find the primary key, and then search the primary index for the record location. In short, both types of processing have significant overhead, even though they still make sense for some applications.

Keep in mind, too, that updating the alternate indexes whenever a record is added to or deleted from a KSDS can add considerable overhead to a program

How the record for employee 501 is accessed by its primary key

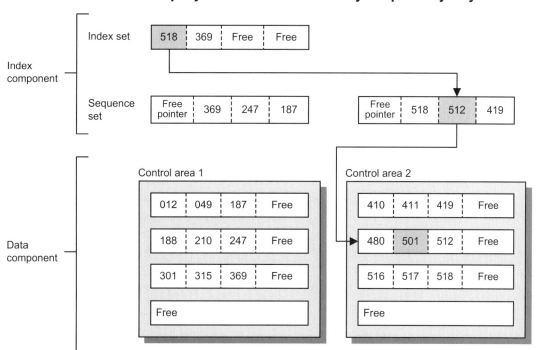

Description

- The index component of a KSDS consists of an *index set* and a *sequence set*. The index set points to records in the sequence set, and the sequence set points to the control intervals in the data component that contain the specific records.

- The index set consists of index records at one or more levels. The highest level of an index set always contains just one record, and the records at the lowest level contain pointers to sequence set records.

- The sequence set contains one record for each control area in the data component. Each of these records contains one entry for each control interval.

- The *free pointer* in each sequence set record points to the free control intervals that can be used for record additions.

- To randomly access a record by a specific key, VSAM searches the index component level by level until it reaches the sequence set record that contains the key. Then, it searches the control interval that the sequence set record points to for the specific record.

- To improve performance, the systems programmer tries to define the KSDS so all of the index set is brought into internal storage areas called *buffers* when the data set is processed.

Figure 14-8   How a record in a KSDS is randomly accessed by primary key

that maintains the records in a KSDS. For that reason, VSAM doesn't require that an alternate index be upgraded every time its base cluster is changed. Instead, the alternate indexes can be rebuilt periodically (at night, for example), and users have to realize that the additions and deletions to their data sets aren't reflected in the alternate indexes until those upgrades are done.

Here again, performance can be improved by bringing as much of the alternate index as possible into internal storage when the data set is processed. But that is the responsibility of the systems programmer.

Perspective

This chapter has presented the concepts and terms that you need for working with any of the three types of VSAM data sets. Although the inner workings of VSAM are more complex than this chapter implies, you don't really need to know any more of the implementation details. If this chapter has succeeded, you should simply realize that VSAM uses some record management techniques that provide for the efficient processing of key-sequenced data sets, even if they require alternate indexes.

With this chapter as background, you're ready to learn how to work with VSAM data sets under OS/390. So in the next chapter, you'll learn how to code JCL to allocate both old and new VSAM data sets. And in chapter 16, you'll learn how to use the AMS utility to define and manage VSAM data sets.

Terms

VSAM	data component	ICF
Virtual Storage Access	primary index	master catalog
Method	primary key	user catalog
AMS	unique key	alias
Access Method Services	duplicate keys	cluster
entry-sequenced data set	alternate index	control area
ESDS	alternate key	control interval
sequential file	non-unique key	spanned record
sequential access	base cluster	free space
key field	relative-record data set	control interval split
key	RRDS	control area split
relative byte address	relative file	index set
RBA	record area	sequence set
key-sequenced data set	relative record number	free pointer
KSDS	randomizing routine	buffer
indexed file	reusable data set	
random access	record management	
index component	Integrated Catalog Facility	

15

How to use JCL for VSAM data sets

In this chapter, you'll learn how to use JCL to work with VSAM data sets. First, you'll learn how to code DD statements for existing VSAM data sets, and then you'll learn how to use JCL to create new VSAM data sets. Since both are relatively easy, this is a short chapter.

Note, however, that the Storage Management Subsystem (SMS) needs to be active on your system before you can use JCL to create new data sets. As a result, you may want to read chapter 13 on SMS before you read this chapter. Although that isn't necessary, it does give you a larger perspective on what's happening behind the scenes.

How to use existing VSAM data sets

To define a new VSAM data set, you can either use JCL as shown in this chapter or Access Method Services (AMS) as shown in the next chapter. In either case, all of the characteristics that you define are stored in the catalog, so coding the DD statement for an existing VSAM data set is relatively simple.

The DD statement for existing VSAM data sets

Figure 15-1 presents the four parameters that you may need to code in the DD statement for an existing VSAM data set. In most cases, you just need to provide the data set name and code the DISP parameter as OLD or SHR, as shown by the first example. Then, VSAM gets all of the other information it needs from the catalog entry.

If your shop uses SMS, you can also code the normal and abnormal subparameters of the DISP parameter. Usually, VSAM data sets are retained, which is the default, so you don't need to code the disposition. In some cases, though, it makes sense to delete a VSAM data set as shown in the second example. As you will see in the next chapter, this method of deleting a VSAM data set is easier than using AMS to delete it.

If you want to allocate a dummy VSAM data set, you need to code the AMP parameter with the AMORG option as shown in the third example in this figure. This option simply tells OS/390 that you're allocating a VSAM data set. You don't need this option for a regular VSAM data set because the catalog entry identifies the data set as VSAM. However, OS/390 doesn't search the catalog for a dummy data set, so you have to supply this information directly.

The AMP parameter also lets you code one or more processing options for a VSAM data set. Two of these options, for example, let you specify the number of buffers to use for the data and index components of a KSDS. And another one lets you specify the number of concurrent requests a program may issue against the data set. Although the systems programmer may occasionally need one or more of these options, the application programmer shouldn't need any of them.

The syntax of the DD statement for existing VSAM data sets

```
//ddname    DD    { DSNAME=data-set-name }
                  { DUMMY                }
                  [ ,DISP=(status,normal-disp,abnormal-disp) ]
                  [ ,AMP=(option,option...) ]
```

Explanation

DSNAME   Specifies the data set name. By convention, the high-level qualifier in the name usually identifies the catalog that owns the data set.

DUMMY   Specifies that OS/390 should simulate a VSAM data set, not actually allocate it.

DISP   Specifies the data set's status (OLD or SHR). If your installation uses SMS, you can also code the normal and abnormal dispositions.

AMP   Specifies one or more options that relate to VSAM data sets. One of these options is AMORG, which identifies the data set as a VSAM data set.

Examples of DD statements for existing VSAM data sets

A DD statement that allocates a VSAM data set for shared access

```
//CUSTMAST DD    DSNAME=MM01.CUSTOMER.MASTER,DISP=SHR
```

A DD statement that specifies exclusive access and deletes the data set when the job step completes (SMS only)

```
//PAYTRAN   DD    DSNAME=MM01.PAYMENT.TRANS,DISP=(OLD,DELETE)
```

A DD statement that allocates a dummy VSAM data set

```
//PAYTRAN   DD    DUMMY,AMP=AMORG
```

Description

- With few exceptions, you code the DD statement for an existing VSAM data set the same way you code the DD statement for a non-VSAM data set. Because VSAM data sets are always cataloged, you only need to code a few parameters.

- Because VSAM doesn't support them, you can't use temporary data set names like &&TEST for VSAM data sets.

- You normally don't need to code the AMORG option of the AMP parameter because OS/390 realizes that a data set is a VSAM file when it retrieves the information from the catalog. For a DUMMY data set, though, OS/390 doesn't search the catalog so you need to code the AMORG option.

- If your installation uses SMS, you can code the normal and abnormal dispositions for a data set. Without SMS, VSAM data sets are always retained after they are processed, and you have to use AMS to delete them.

Figure 15-1   The DD statement for existing VSAM data sets

The DD statements for the alternate indexes used in a COBOL program

When you run an application program that accesses a base cluster via an alternate index, you have to let OS/390 know what alternate index you're using and how it should be processed. How you do this varies from one programming language to another. For a COBOL program, you use DD statements as shown in figure 15-2.

As you can see, the ddnames indicate the relationship between the base cluster, its alternate indexes, and the COBOL code. For the first alternate index listed in the COBOL SELECT statement for the base cluster, the ddname is the base cluster ddname with 1 at the end. If the SELECT statement lists additional alternate indexes, their ddnames end with the appropriate digits in sequence.

What if the ddname in the COBOL program uses eight characters, like EMMASTER? You just drop the last character of the ddname for the cluster and replace it with the appropriate digit. This is illustrated in the second example in this figure.

In the DSNAME parameter for an alternate index, you specify the data set name for the path that's used to process the alternate index. You'll learn about paths and how to define them in the next chapter. For an existing file, though, the paths should already be established, so you just have to check with your supervisor to find out what data set names to use.

The COBOL SELECT statement for a KSDS that's processed by two alternate keys

```
SELECT EMPMAST ASSIGN TO EMPMAST
               ORGANIZATION IS INDEXED
               ACCESS IS RANDOM
               RECORD-KEY IS ER-EMPLOYEE-NUMBER
               ALTERNATE RECORD KEY IS ER-SOCIAL-SECURITY-NO
               ALTERNATE RECORD KEY IS ER-DEPT-NO
                   WITH DUPLICATES.
```

The DD statements for the EMPMAST file

```
//EMPMAST    DD    DSNAME=MMA2.EMPLOYEE.MASTER,DISP=SHR
//EMPMAST1   DD    DSNAME=MMA2.EMPLOYEE.MASTER.SSN.PATH,DISP=SHR
//EMPMAST2   DD    DSNAME=MMA2.EMPLOYEE.MASTER.DEPT.PATH,DISP=SHR
```

The DD statements for a KSDS with a ddname that's 8 characters long

```
//EMMASTER   DD    DSNAME=MMA2.EMPLOYEE.MASTER,DISP=SHR
//EMMASTE1   DD    DSNAME=MMA2.EMPLOYEE.MASTER.SSN.PATH,DISP=SHR
//EMMASTE2   DD    DSNAME=MMA2.EMPLOYEE.MASTER.DEPT.PATH,DISP=SHR
```

Description

- When you run a COBOL program that processes a file by alternate indexes, you have to code a DD statement for each alternate index that's listed in the COBOL SELECT statement for the base cluster.

- In the DSNAME parameter, you specify the data set name of the path that controls the alternate index processing (you'll learn about paths and how to set them up in the next chapter).

- The ddname for an alternate index consists of the base cluster ddname plus a sequence number: 1 for the first alternate index specified in the COBOL SELECT statement, 2 for the second one, and so on.

- If the ddname for the base cluster consists of eight characters, you drop the last character and replace it with the appropriate digit to create the alternate index ddname.

Figure 15-2   The DD statements for the alternate indexes used in a COBOL program

How to create VSAM data sets

If SMS is active at your installation, you can use JCL to create VSAM data sets without using AMS. In fact, you'll probably find that's the easiest way to define data sets that don't have any special requirements. Keep in mind, though, that you can't set all of the VSAM data set options through JCL. For some options, you still need to use AMS.

The DD statement for new VSAM data sets

Figure 15-3 presents the syntax of the DD statement that you use to create new VSAM data sets. As you can see, it combines parameters that you already know with new parameters that supply the information that VSAM requires for a new data set. In particular, the RECORG parameter supplies the file organization, and the KEYLEN and KEYOFF parameters provide the length and offset for the key of a KSDS.

The AVGREC parameter and the last four parameters in this summary are ones that became available with SMS. So if you've read chapter 13, you should already know how to use them. Otherwise, you should read that chapter later on.

The syntax of the DD statement for new VSAM data sets (SMS only)

```
//ddname    DD    DSNAME=data-set-name
                  ,DISP=(NEW,normal-disp,abnormal-disp)
                  [ ,UNIT=unit ]
                  [ ,VOL=SER=vol-ser ]
                  [ ,SPACE=(unit,(primary,secondary)) ]
                  [ ,AVGREC= U | K | M ]
                  [ ,RECORG= KS | ES | RR ]
                  [ ,LRECL=length ]
                  [ ,KEYLEN=length ]
                  [ ,KEYOFF=offset ]
                  [ ,LIKE=data-set-name ]
                  [ ,STORCLAS=storage-class ]
                  [ ,DATACLAS=data-class ]
                  [ ,MGMTCLAS=management-class ]
```

Explanation

DSNAME	Specifies the data set name.
DISP	Specifies the data set's status and normal and abnormal dispositions. Usually coded as (NEW,CATLG) to create and catalog a new data set.
UNIT	Specifies the type of device on which the data set will reside. Usually coded as SYSDA.
VOL=SER	Specifies the six-character vol-ser of the volume where the data set is to be created. If omitted, SMS will select a volume.
SPACE	Specifies the space to be allocated for the data set. Unit indicates the unit of measure: CYL for cylinders, TRK for tracks, or record size for records. If the unit is records, you must include the AVGREC parameter.
AVGREC	Indicates that the allocation unit specified in the SPACE parameter is records; also specifies whether the values for the primary and secondary space allocations represent units (U), thousands of records (K), or millions of records (M).
RECORG	Specifies the type of file organization: KSDS (KS), ESDS (ES), or RRDS (RR).
LRECL	Specifies the record length.
KEYLEN	Specifies the length of the primary key for a KSDS.
KEYOFF	Specifies the position of the first byte of the primary key for a KSDS.
LIKE	Copies data set characteristics from the specified data set.
STORCLAS	Establishes the SMS storage class for the data set.
DATACLAS	Establishes the SMS data class for the data set.
MGMTCLAS	Establishes the SMS management class for the data set.

Description

- If SMS is active at your installation, you can create VSAM data sets in JCL using the parameters shown above. Otherwise, you have to use AMS to create VSAM data sets.

- Because AMS provides parameters that go beyond those that are offered through JCL, you still need to use AMS to create some VSAM data sets.

Figure 15-3   The DD statement for new VSAM data sets

Examples of DD statements for new VSAM data sets

To show you how easy it is to create VSAM data sets with JCL, figure 15-4 presents provides three examples of DD statements that create key-sequenced data sets. Here, the first example uses a specific volume request to create a KSDS with 120-byte records and a 7-byte key that starts in byte 5 of each record.

In contrast, the second example omits the VOL parameter, so it uses a non-specific volume request to create the same data set. In that case, OS/390 decides which volume to place the data set on. Curiously, you can't use a non-specific volume request when you use AMS to define a file, so this is one of the benefits of using JCL.

The third example in this figure uses SMS classes to create a new KSDS. Because the JCL specifies the storage, data, and management classes, it doesn't have to specify most of the other parameters that are normally coded for a new data set. Those specifications are provided by the classes instead. Note, however, that the last three parameters in this example override the parameters that are provided by the data class to make sure that the record length, key length, and key offset are specified correctly.

A DD statement that creates a new KSDS using a specific volume request

```
//DUNNING   DD   DSNAME=MM01.DUNNING.MASTER,DISP=(NEW,CATLG),
//               UNIT=SYSDA,VOL=SER=MPS800,
//               SPACE=(CYL,(200,50)),
//               RECORG=KS,LRECL=120,
//               KEYLEN=7,KEYOFF=5
```

A DD statement that creates a new KSDS using a non-specific volume request

```
//DUNNING   DD   DSNAME=MM01.DUNNING.MASTER,DISP=(NEW,CATLG),
//               UNIT=SYSDA,
//               SPACE=(CYL,(200,50)),
//               RECORG=KS,LRECL=120,
//               KEYLEN=7,KEYOFF=5
```

A DD statement that creates a new KSDS by using SMS classes

```
//DUNNING   DD   DSNAME=MM01.DUNNING.MASTER,DISP=(NEW,CATLG),
//               STORCLAS=MVPS100,
//               DATACLAS=MVPD050,
//               MGMTCLAS=MVPM010,
//               LRECL=120,
//               KEYLEN=7,KEYOFF=5
```

Description

- Because all VSAM data sets must be cataloged, you code the DISP parameter for a new data set as NEW,CATLG.

- With JCL, you can use a non-specific volume request when you create a new VSAM data set. With AMS, you can't use a non-specific volume request.

- When you create a new VSAM data set by using SMS classes, you can override some of the characteristics specified in the classes by using the JCL parameters.

- The SMS data class specifies whether the file has VSAM organization.

Figure 15-4   Examples of DD statements for new VSAM data sets

Perspective

I hope this chapter has illustrated that it's easy to use JCL for working with both old and new VSAM data sets. Remember, though, that you can't set all of the options for a new VSAM data set through JCL. You also can't define an alternate index for a KSDS through JCL. For those tasks and more, you need to use AMS, which is presented in detail in the next chapter.

Terms

None

16

How to use Access Method Services (AMS)

In this chapter, you'll learn how to use the VSAM utility program called Access Method Services, or AMS. As you will see, it lets you define VSAM data sets with all of the possible options. It lets you define and build alternate indexes. It lets you print and modify catalog entries. And it lets you perform other useful functions like deleting, printing, and copying data sets. In short, AMS is a valuable program that every programmer should know how to use.

How to code AMS jobs

To start, this chapter introduces you to the AMS commands you're most likely to come across in your shop. Then, it shows you how to code the JCL for a job that uses AMS, and it shows you how to code the AMS commands within the job stream.

Some commonly-used AMS commands

Figure 16-1 summarizes the AMS commands that are most commonly used in an OS/390 shop. In this chapter, you'll learn how to use all of the commands listed for the application programmer. These are the commands that every application programmer is likely to need at one time or another, so you should be familiar with all of them. As you can see, these include commands for defining all three types of VSAM data sets, for defining and building alternate indexes for key-sequenced data sets, and for listing catalog information.

The other commands that are listed in this figure are for functions that are usually handled by the systems programmer. These include commands for defining the master catalog and user catalogs, for defining aliases for user catalogs, and for backing up and restoring data sets. Although this chapter doesn't present their coding details, you should be able to master these and other AMS commands on your own once you complete this chapter, just by consulting the appropriate reference manual.

Please note that the commands listed in this figure are all *functional commands*. In addition, AMS provides *modal commands* that you can use for conditional processing of functional commands. Here again, the modal commands aren't presented in this chapter, but you should be able to master them on your own without much difficulty.

As you read the rest of this chapter, you'll see that more detail is presented for each command than you can possibly remember. However, all of the information in the figures is presented in an efficient reference format. As a result, you can do a first reading of this chapter with the goal of understanding what each command can do. Then, when you need to use one of the commands, you can refer back to the appropriate figures.

AMS commands for the application programmer

AMS command	Function
DEFINE CLUSTER	Defines a VSAM data set, whether it's key-sequenced, entry-sequenced, or relative-record.
LISTCAT	Lists information about data sets.
ALTER	Changes the information that has been specified for a catalog, cluster, alternate index, or path.
DELETE	Removes a catalog entry for a catalog, cluster, alternate index, or path.
PRINT	Prints the contents of a VSAM or non-VSAM data set.
REPRO	Copies records from one VSAM or non-VSAM data set to another VSAM or non-VSAM data set.
DEFINE ALTERNATEINDEX	Defines an alternate index.
DEFINE PATH	Defines the path that relates an alternate index to its base cluster.
BLDINDEX	Builds an alternate index.

AMS commands for the systems programmer

AMS command	Function
DEFINE MASTERCATALOG	Defines a master catalog.
DEFINE USERCATALOG	Defines a user catalog.
DEFINE ALIAS	Assigns an alternate name to a user catalog.
EXPORT	Produces a backup or transportable copy of a data set.
IMPORT	Restores an exported copy of a data set.

Description

- The commands listed for the application programmer are the ones that are presented in this chapter. These are the *functional commands* that most application programmers will need to use.

- The commands listed for the systems programmer are the main functional commands that they need to use. In addition, there are *modal commands* like IF and SET commands that provide for conditional processing of functional commands.

Figure 16-1   Some commonly-used AMS commands

The JCL requirements for using AMS commands

Figure 16-2 presents the JCL requirements for using AMS commands. To start, you need to code an EXEC statement for the program named *IDCAMS* (you'll hear it pronounced I-D-cams or *id*-cams). Because IDC is the standard prefix for VSAM programs, this is simply the name of the AMS program. Then, you must code a SYSPRINT DD statement for the printed output produced by the program, and a SYSIN DD statement for the AMS commands that are submitted to the program.

Usually, you can code the SYSPRINT and SYSIN DD statements as shown in the two examples. Here, the SYSPRINT statement says that the output class is the same as the message class in the JOB statement. And the SYSIN statement says that the input will follow as an instream data set. Then, the data that follows (one or more AMS commands) is ended by either a /* statement or the next JCL statement.

In some cases, you may also have to code DD statements for the data sets that are going to be processed by an AMS command, but that's relatively uncommon. You'll see how that works later in this chapter.

The syntax requirements for AMS commands

Figure 16-2 also presents the syntax requirements for the AMS commands that you include in the SYSIN data set. If you study these requirements and the examples, you should be able to quickly master the syntax. Just be careful to start every command line in column 2 or later (not column 1) and to end every continued line with a hyphen (-).

If you want to use comments within your commands, you can code them as shown in the second example in this figure. Note that the hyphen for a continued line that ends with a comment must go after the comment.

The JCL for an AMS job that runs a LISTCAT command

```
//MM01LC1   JOB  (36512),'R MENENDEZ',NOTIFY=&SYSUID
//          EXEC PGM=IDCAMS
//SYSPRINT DD   SYSOUT=*
//SYSIN    DD   *
 LISTCAT ENTRIES(MM01.CUSTOMER.MASTER) -
        VOLUME
/*
```

The JCL for an AMS job with comments that runs an ALTER command

```
//MM01LC2   JOB  (36512),'R MENENDEZ',NOTIFY=&SYSUID
//          EXEC PGM=IDCAMS
//SYSPRINT DD   SYSOUT=*
//SYSIN    DD   *
 /* THIS JOB CHANGES BOTH THE NAME AND FREESPACE ALLOCATION */
 ALTER MM01.CUSTOMER.MASTER -
       NEWNAME(MM01.CUSTMAST)    /* CHANGE NAME */ -
       FREESPACE(10 10)          /* CHANGE FREESPACE ALLOCATION */
/*
```

The JCL requirements for an AMS job

* The program name for Access Method Services (AMS) is *IDCAMS*.

* A SYSPRINT DD statement is required for the printed output produced by IDCAMS.

* A SYSIN DD statement is required for the commands that are submitted to IDCAMS. Usually, this data set is an instream data set.

* If you run a command that causes a data set to be processed, you may also have to include a DD statement for that data set. Often, though, the data set is identified by the command so this isn't necessary.

The AMS syntax requirements

* AMS commands must be coded within columns 2 through 72, so don't start a command in column 1.

* To continue a command on the next line, end the current line with one or more spaces followed by a hyphen, then continue coding on the next line.

* To separate parameters and subparameters, you can use spaces or commas. In this book, spaces are used as the separators.

* To code a comment, start it with /* and end it with */. Comments can be coded on separate lines or to the right of a command line. When they are coded on the right, the hyphen for a continuation comes after the comment.

* Although you can code more than one parameter on each line, we recommend that you code one parameter per line so it's easier to read and modify the command.

Figure 16-2   The JCL and AMS syntax requirements for an AMS job

How to use the DEFINE CLUSTER command to define a data set

To create a VSAM data set when you're using AMS, you use the DEFINE CLUSTER command. To make this command more manageable, the syntax summary in figure 16-3 presents just the parameters that the application programmer is likely to need. Other parameters that can affect performance are omitted because they are normally used by the systems programmer when a data set is put into production.

If you study the syntax for this command, you can see that some of its parameters can be coded at three different levels. The cluster level applies to the entire data set. The data level applies to the data component of a data set. And the index level applies to the index component of a KSDS. As you read about these parameters in the pages that follow, you'll learn what parameters should be coded at what levels.

The good news is that this is the most complicated of the AMS commands, so the rest of this chapter should be relatively easy once you understand how this command works. To make the many parameters easier to understand, they are grouped by function in the next five figures. As you read about the individual parameters, you can refer back to this syntax summary to see where they fit.

The syntax of the DEFINE CLUSTER command

```
DEFINE CLUSTER (    NAME(entry-name)
                    [ OWNER(owner-id) ]
                    [ FOR(days) | TO(date) ]
                    [ INDEXED | NONINDEXED | NUMBERED | LINEAR]
                    [ RECORDSIZE(avg max) ]
                    [ KEYS(length offset) ]
                    [ SPANNED | NONSPANNED ]
                    [ CISZ(size) ]
                    [ FREESPACE(ci ca) ]
                    [ VOLUMES(vol-ser...) ]
                    [ FILE(ddname) ]
                    [ {CYLINDERS(primary [secondary])}
                      {KILOBYTES(primary [secondary])}
                      {MEGABYTES(primary [secondary])}
                      {TRACKS(primary [secondary])    }
                      {RECORDS(primary [secondary])   } ]
                    [ REUSE | NOREUSE ]
                    [ SHAREOPTIONS(a b) ]
                    [ IMBED | NOIMBED ]       )
                    [ STORAGECLASS(storage-class) ]
                    [ DATACLASS(data-class) ]
                    [ MANAGEMENTCLASS(management-class) ] )
   [ DATA       ( [ NAME(entry-name) ]
                    [ VOLUMES(vol-ser...) ]
                    [ FILE(ddname) ]
                    [ CISZ(size) ]
                    [ {CYLINDERS(primary [secondary])}
                      {KILOBYTES(primary [secondary])}
                      {MEGABYTES(primary [secondary])}
                      {TRACKS(primary [secondary])    }
                      {RECORDS(primary [secondary])   } ] ) ]
   [ INDEX      ( [ NAME(entry-name) ]
                    [ VOLUMES(vol-ser...) ]
                    [ {CYLINDERS(primary [secondary])}
                      {KILOBYTES(primary [secondary])}
                      {MEGABYTES(primary [secondary])}
                      {TRACKS(primary [secondary])    }
                      {RECORDS(primary [secondary])   } ] ) ]
   [ CATALOG(name) ]
```

Description

- The DEFINE CLUSTER command is used to define a KSDS, ESDS, or RRDS. The parameters above are the ones the application programmer is most likely to use.

- Parameters at the CLUSTER level apply to the entire cluster. Parameters at the DATA or INDEX level apply only to the data or index component.

Figure 16-3   The syntax of the DEFINE CLUSTER command

Parameters that identify a data set

Figure 16-4 summarizes three parameters that identify a data set. Of these, the most important one is the NAME parameter. If you refer back to figure 16-3, you can see that it can be coded at the cluster, data, and index level. Because VSAM creates cryptic names for the data and index components if you only code the NAME parameter at the cluster level, I recommend that you also code this parameter at the lower levels.

In the examples, you can see a simple naming convention for the three levels. At the cluster level, you name the data set using the standard OS/390 naming rules. Then, at the data and index levels, you add DATA and INDEX to the cluster name. That makes it easy for you to identify the components of a data set when you list catalog entries later on.

In contrast, the OWNER parameter is used for documentation only, so it doesn't affect the function of this or subsequent AMS commands. In the second example, you can see that this parameter is coded so MM01 will be used as the owner-id instead of the TSO user-id.

If you refer back to figure 16-3, you can see that the CATALOG parameter is the only one that isn't coded at the cluster, data, or index level. So if you use it, you always code it as the last parameter of the command. Normally, though, you don't need to code it because the high-level qualifier of the cluster name is used to identify the catalog that owns it.

Note, however, that if the high-level qualifier isn't defined as a user catalog or an alias, OS/390 uses the step catalog, the job catalog, or the master catalog as the catalog for the data set. This is the standard search sequence that is used for identifying the catalog to be used. If that isn't what you want, you do need to code the CATALOG parameter. In the second example in this figure, though, the CATALOG parameter isn't necessary because MM01 is also the high-level qualifier of the cluster name.

The parameters for data set identification

Parameter	Explanation
`NAME(entry-name)`	Specifies the name of the cluster or component.
`OWNER(owner-id)`	Specifies a one- to eight-character owner-id. This is for documentation only. If you omit it when you issue a DEFINE CLUSTER command from a TSO terminal, VSAM uses your TSO user-id as the owner-id.
`CATALOG(name)`	Specifies the name of the catalog that will own the cluster. If omitted, OS/390 uses its standard search sequence to identify the catalog.

OS/390's standard search sequence for a catalog entry

Catalog with matching high-level qualifier → Step catalog → Job catalog → Master catalog

A command that defines a KSDS

```
DEFINE CLUSTER     ( NAME(MM01.CUSTOMER.MASTER)          -
                     INDEXED                             -
                     RECORDSIZE(200 200)                 -
                     KEYS(6 0)                           -
                     VOLUMES(TSO001) )                   -
         DATA      ( NAME(MM01.CUSTOMER.MASTER.DATA)     -
                     CYLINDERS(50 5)                     -
                     CISZ(4096) )                        -
         INDEX     ( NAME(MM01.CUSTOMER.MASTER.INDEX) )
```

A command that defines an ESDS

```
DEFINE CLUSTER     ( NAME(MM01.AR.TRAN)                  -
                     OWNER(MM01)                         -
                     NONINDEXED                          -
                     RECORDSIZE(190 280)                 -
                     CISZ(4096)                          -
                     VOLUMES(TSO001) )                   -
         DATA      ( NAME(MM01.AR.TRAN.DATA)             -
                     CYLINDERS(10 1) )                   -
         CATALOG(MM01)
```

Description

- When you code a value for the NAME parameter at the cluster level but not at the DATA or INDEX level, VSAM creates cryptic names for the data and index components. That's why we recommend that you code your own names at all three levels.

- The CATALOG parameter is the only one that isn't coded at the CLUSTER, DATA, or INDEX level. If you code it, it should be the last parameter for the command, but it usually isn't necessary because the standard search sequence identifies the appropriate catalog.

Figure 16-4   Parameters that identify a data set

Parameters that describe the data set's characteristics

Figure 16-5 summarizes the parameters that describe a data set's characteristics. For instance, the first parameter indicates what type of file organization is used for the data set: KSDS, ESDS, or RRDS. The KEYS parameter gives the length and starting position of the primary key for a KSDS. And the SPANNED parameter indicates whether a record can flow from one control interval into the next one, which usually isn't allowed.

The other three parameters set the record size, the control interval size, and the amount of free space for each control interval and control area. If you omit them, VSAM will set default values for them, but that's usually not what you want. Since these parameters can have a significant effect on performance, they should be given special attention.

In the RECORDSIZE parameter, you code the average and maximum record sizes. For fixed-length records, you code the same value for both as shown in the first example. For variable-length records, you code an estimate for the average record length and the maximum record size as shown in the second example. The only time the average record size really matters is when you specify the space allocation in records.

In the CISZ parameter, you code the size of the control intervals for the data set. As this figure says, 4096 will work for most data sets. But if the maximum record size is larger than that, you can adjust the control interval size to the next multiple of 2K that is larger than the maximum record size to avoid the need for spanned records. These simple rules will work for test data sets, and the systems programmer can adjust this size for improved performance when the data set is put into production.

For an ESDS or RRDS, you can code the CISZ parameter at the cluster or the data level. For a KSDS, though, you should code this parameter at the data level, and let VSAM set an efficient control interval size for the index component. If you code this parameter at the cluster level for a KSDS, VSAM uses that control interval size for both the data and the index components.

In the FREESPACE parameter, you code the percentage of free space that you want left in each control interval and each control area when the file is created. So the free space allocation in the first example provides that 30% of each control interval and 20% of each control area be left empty. Since the default is no free space, this is an important parameter for the performance of any data set that receives file additions. When a data set is put into production, this parameter should be set based on the frequency of additions and how often the data set is reorganized.

Note that the free space is taken from, not added to, the amount of space that is allocated to the file. So if you provide for 20% free space, you may need to increase the space allocation for the data set accordingly.

The parameters for data set characteristics

Parameter	Explanation
{INDEXED } {NONINDEXED} {NUMBERED }	Specifies that a KSDS is being defined. Specifies that a ESDS is being defined. Specifies that an RRDS is being defined.
RECORDSIZE(avg max)	Specifies the average and maximum record size. If omitted, VSAM sets defaults of 4089 for both average and maximum if the records aren't SPANNED; it sets defaults of 4086 and 32600 if the records are SPANNED.
KEYS(len off)	Specifies the length and offset of the primary key for a KSDS. The default length is 64 bytes with an offset of 0.
SPANNED | NONSPANNED	Specifies whether records can cross control interval boundaries. If the record size is larger than one control interval, you need to code SPANNED.
CISZ(size)	Specifies the size of the control intervals. For most data sets, you can set this at 4096 unless the records are larger than that. For larger records, you can set this at the next multiple of 2K (2048), like 6144 or 8192. If omitted, VSAM sets this size.
FREESPACE(ci ca)	Specifies the percentage of free space to reserve for the control intervals (ci) and control areas (ca) of the data component. If file additions are likely, you should code this parameter because the default is no free space. The free space that you specify is part of the space allocated to the data component.

A command that defines a KSDS with fixed-length records and free space

```
DEFINE CLUSTER   ( NAME(MM01.CUSTOMER.MASTER)        -
                   INDEXED                           -
                   RECORDSIZE(600 600)               -
                   KEYS(6 0)                         -
                   VOLUMES(TSO001)                   -
                   FREESPACE(30 20) )                -
        DATA     ( NAME(MM01.CUSTOMER.MASTER.DATA)   -
                   CYLINDERS(50 5)                   -
                   CISZ(4096) )                      -
        INDEX    ( NAME(MM01.CUSTOMER.MASTER.INDEX) )
```

A command that defines an ESDS with variable-length records

```
DEFINE CLUSTER   ( NAME(MM01.AR.TRAN)                -
                   NONINDEXED                        -
                   RECORDSIZE(400 800)               -
                   CISZ(4096)                        -
                   VOLUMES(TSO001) )                 -
        DATA     ( NAME(MM01.AR.TRAN.DATA)           -
                   CYLINDERS(10 1) )
```

Description

- The control interval size and amount of free space specified for a KSDS can have a significant effect on performance. For production data sets, then, the CISZ and FREESPACE parameters are usually set by a systems programmer.

Figure 16-5   Parameters that describe the data set's characteristics

Parameters that specify the data set's space allocation

Figure 16-6 summarizes the parameters for the space allocation of a data set. Two that you're already familiar with are the VOLUMES and space allocation parameters, so let's start with them and end with IMBED and FILE.

The VOLUMES parameter is required, which means that AMS doesn't provide for a non-specific volume request (although JCL does). When you code this parameter, you can specify more than one volume separated by spaces. In most cases, you code this parameter at the cluster level so the data and index components of a KSDS are on the same volume.

The space allocation parameter for the DEFINE CLUSTER command is coded in much the same way that you code the SPACE parameter in the DD statement for a non-VSAM file. First, you code the allocation unit. Then, you code the primary space allocation for the data set followed by the secondary allocation that is used when the primary allocation is filled up. Up to 122 of these secondary allocations can be used before the data set has to be reorganized.

When you allocate the space in terms of cylinders, the control area for the data set will be one cylinder. Because this leads to an efficient index structure for key-sequenced data sets, you'll use this approach most often. However, if you don't know the size of a cylinder on the device being used, the easiest way to specify the space allocation is in terms of records. Then, VSAM allocates the minimum number of tracks or cylinders that are required for the allocation. You can also allocate the space in terms of megabytes, kilobytes, or tracks. In any case, the systems programmer can adjust the value for production performance.

If you refer back to figure 16-3, you can see that the space allocation can be coded at the cluster, data, or index level. When you define an ESDS or RRDS, it doesn't matter whether you code the space allocation at the cluster or data level. Either way, the entire allocation is given to the data component.

When you define a KSDS, though, there is a slight difference in how the allocations are made. If you code the allocation at the data level, the entire allocation is given to the data component, and an additional allocation that's large enough for the index is given to the index component. But if you code the allocation at the cluster level, VSAM determines how much space to give to the index component and gives the rest to the data component. Either way, VSAM does a good job of calculating how much space is required for the index component, so you don't need to override that calculation by coding a space allocation at the index level.

If you code the IMBED parameter, the sequence set records of the index component are imbedded in the first tracks of the control areas, which can improve performance in some cases. But whether that's coded should probably be left to the systems programmer.

If you code the FILE parameter, it means that you're using an old DASD that has removable disk packs. Then, when you run a job that processes the data set, you need to supply a DD statement with the ddname that's given in the FILE parameter. That DD statement should identify the volumes that are to be used.

The parameters for space allocation

Parameter	Explanation
VOLUMES(vol-ser)	Specifies one or more volumes that will contain the cluster or component. It is required, and it's normally coded at the cluster level of a KSDS so the index and data components are on the same volume.
FILE(ddname)	Specifies a ddname that identifies a DD statement that allocates the volume or volumes when the job is run. This is required only for removable DASD volumes.
unit (primary [secondary])	*Primary* specifies the amount of space to allocate initially, expressed in terms of the *unit* (cylinders, kilobytes, megabytes, tracks, or records). *Secondary* specifies the secondary space allocation. If you specify this allocation in cylinders, the control areas will be one cylinder each.
IMBED	NOIMBED	Specifies whether sequence set records should be imbedded in the data component of a KSDS. When imbedded, the first track of each control area is used to store the sequence set records, which can improve performance.

A command that defines a KSDS with the space allocation at the data level

```
DEFINE CLUSTER   ( NAME(MM01.CUSTOMER.MASTER)        -
                   INDEXED                           -
                   RECORDSIZE(600 600)               -
                   KEYS(6 0)                          -
                   FREESPACE(30 20)                  -
                   VOLUMES(TSO001)                   -
                   IMBED )                           -
        DATA     ( NAME(MM01.CUSTOMER.MASTER.DATA)   -
                   CYLINDERS(50 5)                   -
                   CISZ(4096) )                      -
        INDEX    ( NAME(MM01.CUSTOMER.MASTER.INDEX) )
```

What unit to use for space allocation

- For most data sets, you should allocate space in terms of cylinders so the control areas will be one cylinder each. For a KSDS, that provides for an efficient index structure.

- If you don't know the cylinder size for the device that will be used for a data set, it's usually easiest to specify the space allocation in terms of records. As an alternative, you can figure the total space required and then specify the allocation in terms of kilobytes or megabytes.

Where to code the space allocation for a KSDS

- If you specify the allocation at the cluster level, VSAM determines how much space to allocate for the index component and allocates the rest to the data component.

- If you specify the allocation at the data level, VSAM allocates the full amount to the data component and allocates an additional amount to the index component.

- If you specify an allocation at the index level, you override VSAM's calculation for how much index space is required. Normally, though, you don't need to do that.

Figure 16-6   Parameters that specify the data set's space allocation

Parameters for SMS-managed files

If you've read chapter 13, you know how SMS works and you know about the three DD parameters that you can use to assign classes to SMS-managed files. You can also assign classes to a file when you define a cluster with AMS by using the three parameters in figure 16-7. If you omit one of these parameters, the SMS automatic class selection (ACS) routines assign the appropriate class to the file.

In the first example in this figure, none of the parameters are coded, so the ACS routines select the classes for the file, and the classes set all of the other parameters for the data set. As a result, only the NAME parameter is coded at the cluster, data, and index levels.

In the second example, the parameters for the storage and data classes are coded, so just the management class is assigned by the ACS routines. In addition, other parameters are coded that override some of the parameters that are set by the classes.

Before you can use the SMS classes with confidence, of course, you must find out what parameter values each class assigns. Once you've done that, though, you can use the classes to reduce the number of parameters that you have to code when you define a data set. Note, too, that you can use the DATACLASS parameter to define any data set, not just an SMS-managed data set, as long as SMS is active on your system.

The parameters for SMS-managed files

Parameter	Explanation
STORAGECLASS	Specifies the storage class for SMS-managed data sets only.
DATACLASS	Specifies the data class for any data set as long as SMS is installed and active.
MANAGEMENTCLASS	Specifies the management class for SMS-managed data sets only.

A command that defines a KSDS with the SMS defaults

```
DEFINE CLUSTER  ( NAME(MM01.CUSTOMER.MASTER) )        -
        DATA    ( NAME(MM01.CUSTOMER.MASTER.DATA) )   -
        INDEX   ( NAME(MM01.CUSTOMER.MASTER.INDEX) )
```

A job that overrides two classes, the key location, and the space allocation

```
DEFINE CLUSTER  ( NAME(MM01.CUSTOMER.MASTER)          -
                  STORAGECLASS(MVPS100)               -
                  DATACLASS(MVPD050)                  -
                  KEYS(6 0) )                         -
        DATA    ( NAME(MM01.CUSTOMER.MASTER.DATA)     -
                  CYLINDERS(50 5) )                   -
        INDEX   ( NAME(MM01.CUSTOMER.MASTER.INDEX) )
```

Description

- Chapter 13 shows how to use the SMS facilities with JCL, and you can also use these facilities with the DEFINE CLUSTER command.

- SMS manages files by establishing storage classes, data classes, and management classes for different types of data sets. These classes determine what volume a data set is written to, what the characteristics of the data set are, how long it will reside on the volume before it is archived offline, and how often it should be backed up.

- If you don't use the AMS parameters to specify the storage, data, and management class for a cluster, the Automatic Class Selection (ACS) routines that are set up for a system automatically pick these classes.

- If necessary, you can override the parameters in a class by coding the parameters in the AMS command.

Figure 16-7   Parameters for SMS-managed files

Other DEFINE CLUSTER parameters

Figure 16-8 presents the last set of parameters that an application programmer is likely to code in the DEFINE CLUSTER command. If you code the FOR or TO parameter, you set the *retention period* or *expiration date* that determines how long the data set should be retained before it is deleted. For instance, the first example in this figure specifies a retention period of 30 days.

In general, it's better to use the FOR parameter than the TO parameter because a retention period is easier to code than an expiration date. When you use a retention period, VSAM converts it to an expiration date anyway, so in either case, it's an expiration date that gets stored in the catalog entry for the data set.

As you might guess, the expiration date determines when a data set can be deleted. However, you can override the date using a parameter on the DELETE command, as you'll see later in this chapter. In contrast, if you omit both the FOR and the TO parameters, a data set can be deleted at any time.

If you code the REUSE parameter as shown in the second example in this figure, you create a reusable data set. Then, if the data set is opened for input or for input and output, the data set is processed as usual. But when the data set is opened as output, the old records are ignored, so the new records overwrite them. The alternative to using a reusable data set is to delete the old data set, redefine it, and then recreate it.

The last parameter in this figure is the SHAREOPTIONS parameter. It tells VSAM what level of file sharing should be allowed for the data set. When you code this parameter, the first subparameter provides a value for the *cross-region share option*, which controls how two or more jobs on a single system can share a data set. The second subparameter provides a value for the *cross-system share option*, which controls how jobs on different processors can share a data set.

This figure also summarizes the values that you can use for these options. For most data sets, you'll use 1, 2, or 3 as the cross-region share option and 3 as the cross-system share option because 4 is too restrictive for either option.

Other parameters of the DEFINE CLUSTER command

Parameter	Explanation
FOR(days) | TO(date)	Specifies a retention period (in the format dddd) or an expiration date (in the format yyyyddd).
REUSE|NOREUSE	Specifies whether a data set is reusable.
SHAREOPTIONS(a b)	Specifies the level of file sharing permitted as summarized below. The default level is 1 3.

Share options

Cross-region share options (a)

1   The file can be processed simultaneously by multiple jobs as long as all jobs open the file for input only. If a job opens the file for output, no other job can open the file.

2   The file can be processed simultaneously by multiple jobs as long as only one job opens the file for output; all other jobs must open the file for input only.

3   Any number of jobs can process the file simultaneously for input or output, but VSAM does nothing to insure the integrity of the file.

4   Any number of jobs can process the file simultaneously for input or output, but VSAM imposes these restrictions: (1) direct retrieval always reads data from disk even if the desired index or data records are already in a VSAM buffer; (2) data may not be added to the end of the file; and (3) a control area split is not allowed.

Cross-system share options (b)

3   Any number of jobs on any system can process the file simultaneously for input or output, but VSAM does nothing to insure the integrity of the file.

4   Any number of jobs on any system can process the file simultaneously for input or output, but VSAM imposes the same restrictions as for cross-region share option 4.

A command that defines a KSDS with share options and a retention period

```
DEFINE CLUSTER  ( NAME(MM01.CUSTOMER.MASTER)        -
                  INDEXED                            -
                  RECORDSIZE(800 800)                -
                  KEYS(6 0)                          -
                  VOLUMES(TSO001)                    -
                  SHAREOPTIONS(2 3)                  -
                  FOR(30) )                          -
        DATA    ( NAME(MM01.CUSTOMER.MASTER.DATA)    -
                  CYLINDERS(50 5)                    -
                  CISZ(4096) )                       -
        INDEX   ( NAME(MM01.CUSTOMER.MASTER.INDEX) )
```

A command that defines a reusable ESDS

```
DEFINE CLUSTER  ( NAME(MM01.AR.TRAN)                 -
                  NONINDEXED                         -
                  RECORDSIZE(400 800)                -
                  VOLUMES(TSO001)                    -
                  REUSE )                            -
        DATA    ( NAME(MM01.AR.TRAN.DATA)            -
                  CYLINDERS(10 1) )
```

Figure 16-8   Other DEFINE CLUSTER parameters

How to use the LISTCAT command to print catalog information

The LISTCAT command is the AMS command that lets you get data set information from a user catalog, which is something that you will frequently want to do. The syntax of this command is given in figure 16-9. As you can see, the parameters for this command let you identify the catalog you want to work with, the names of the entries to be listed, the types of entries to be listed, and the amount of information to be listed for each entry.

When you use this command, you want to be sure that you don't get far more information than you need. To do that, you try to restrict the number of entries that are listed, and you try to restrict the amount of information that is listed for each entry. In the example in this figure, the LISTCAT command lists just the NAME information for three named entries. In the next two figures, you'll learn more about specifying the entries and information that is listed.

If necessary, you can code the CATALOG parameter to identify the catalog that you want to work with. If you omit that parameter, though, VSAM uses the standard search sequence to determine the catalog that should be used: the catalog identified by the high-level qualifier of the entries listed, the step catalog, the job catalog, or the master catalog.

The syntax of the LISTCAT command

```
LISTCAT [ CATALOG(name) ]
        [ {ENTRIES(entry-name...)}
          {LEVEL(level)} ]
        [ entry-type... ]
        [ NAME | HISTORY | VOLUME | ALLOCATION | ALL ]
```

Explanation

CATALOG	Specifies the name of the catalog from which entries are to be listed. If omitted, the standard search sequence is used.
ENTRIES	Specifies the names of the entries you want to list.
LEVEL	Specifies one or more levels of qualification. Any data sets whose names match those levels are listed.
entry-type	Specifies the type of entries you want listed (you can code more than one type): ALIAS ALTERNATEINDEX or AIX CLUSTER DATA GENERATIONDATAGROUP or GDG INDEX NONVSAM PAGESPACE PATH USERCATALOG
NAME	Specifies that only the names and types of the specified entries be listed. This is the default.
HISTORY	Specifies that the NAME information plus the history information (such as creation and expiration dates) be listed.
VOLUME	Specifies that the HISTORY information plus the volume locations of the specified entries be listed.
ALLOCATION	Specifies that the VOLUME information plus detailed extent information be listed.
ALL	Specifies that all catalog information be listed.

A LISTCAT command that lists the NAME information for three data sets

```
LISTCAT CATALOG(MM01) -
        ENTRIES(MM01.CUSTOMER.MASTER -
                MM01.EMPLOYEE.MASTER -
                MM01.DAILY.TRANS)     -
        NAME
```

Description

- The LISTCAT output is written to the SYSPRINT file that's included in an AMS job.
- If an ENTRIES or LEVEL parameter isn't coded, VSAM lists *all* of the entries in the catalog. You should avoid that, though, because it may contain hundreds of entries.
- In general, you should try to make your LISTCAT commands as specific as possible by limiting the entry names and types as well as the type of information that's returned.

Figure 16-9   The syntax of the LISTCAT command

How to identify the entries you want to list

Figure 16-10 shows four ways to identify the entries that you want the LISTCAT command to list. In the first example, a *generic entry name* is used in the ENTRIES parameter to identify all entries that have MM01 as the high-level qualifier, any characters (*) at the next level, and MASTER at the third level. This will select entries with names like these:

```
MM01.CUSTOMER.MASTER
MM01.EMPLOYEE.MASTER
MM01.VENDOR.MASTER
```

Since you can code the asterisk at more than one level, this is an excellent way to identify the data sets that you want listed.

In the second example, you can see that using the LEVEL parameter is similar to using a generic entry name. In this parameter, you code a partial name that consists of one or more levels. VSAM then lists all of the catalog entries whose names begin with the partial name. This example, then, will list entries like:

```
MM01.CUSTOMER.MASTER
MM01.CUSTOMER.MASTER.DATA
MM01.CUSTOMER.MASTER.INDEX
MM01.CUSTOMER.TRANS
```

In other words, VSAM prints all entries with names that start with the levels specified in the LEVEL parameter, no matter how many levels the names contain.

In the third example, you can see how the entry-type parameter is used to restrict the entries that are listed. Here, just entries that are part of a generation data group (see chapter 12) are listed. But note that the LEVEL command also specifies that the high-level qualifier must be MM01.

Finally, in the fourth example, you can see that two (or more) entry-type parameters can be coded in a single command. In this case, entries for both data and index components will be listed.

Keep in mind that you should always limit the number of entries for a LISTCAT command by coding one of the three parameters in this figure. If you don't, the command will list all of the entries in the catalog, and there could be hundreds of them.

A LISTCAT command that uses a generic entry name

```
LISTCAT CATALOG(MM01)              -
        ENTRIES(MM01.*.MASTER)     -
        NAME
```

A LISTCAT command that uses the LEVEL parameter

```
LISTCAT LEVEL(MM01.CUSTOMER)       -
        NAME
```

A LISTCAT command that uses the LEVEL and entry-type parameters

```
LISTCAT LEVEL(MM01)                -
        GDG                        -
        NAME
```

A LISTCAT command that uses two entry-type parameters

```
LISTCAT CATALOG(MM01)              -
        DATA                       -
        INDEX                      -
        NAME
```

Description

- To code a *generic entry name*, you replace one or more of the levels in a data set name with an asterisk. The asterisk means that any characters will be accepted for that level.

- When you code the LEVEL parameter, you specify a partial data set name consisting of one or more levels. Then, all data set names that begin with those levels will be returned.

- If you don't specify an ENTRIES, LEVEL, or entry-type parameter, AMS lists all of the entries in the catalog.

Figure 16-10   How to identify the entries you want to list

How to limit the information that's listed

Figure 16-11 shows the parameters that determine what information the LISTCAT command lists for each entry. The NAME parameter lists the least information for each entry, while the ALL parameter lists all of the information for each entry.

To give you some idea of what information is included with each parameter, this figure shows some output for the NAME parameter and some for the VOLUME parameter. For the NAME parameter, you can see that the information includes just the type, entry name, and owning catalog. In this case, ICFCAT.VSTOR02 is the actual name of the catalog, while MM01 is the alias.

For the VOLUME parameter, you can see the HISTORY information plus the VOLUME information that is added to the NAME information. Here, the history information includes the owner-id, the VSAM release that the data set was created under, and the creation and expiration dates for the entry. As for the volume information, it includes the volume serial numbers of the volumes used for the data set as well as a hex code for the device type.

If you specify ALLOCATION instead of VOLUME, you get the volume information plus information about the disk extents used for each entry. And if you specify ALL, you get the allocation information plus attribute information and statistics. Although examples aren't included in this book, you can easily make your own by running the LISTCAT command for one of the data sets on your system.

If you've read about generation data groups in chapter 12, you may now be interested to look at the last entry for the NAME output in this figure. Here, you can see the full name of one of the generations of a non-VSAM data set:

    MM01.DAILYEMS.G0930V00

In this case, the name of the data set is MM01.DAILYEMS, and the generation number is G0930V00. So if you want to process one of the generations of a data set and need to know its generation number, using the LISTCAT command is one way to get it.

The five information types

```
NAME      HISTORY     VOLUME     ALLOCATION     ALL
```

Example of NAME output

```
LISTCAT LEVEL(MM01) -
        NAME


CLUSTER ------- MM01.CUSTOMER.MASTER
     IN-CAT --- ICFCAT.VSTOR02

DATA ---------- MM01.CUSTOMER.MASTER.DATA
     IN-CAT --- ICFCAT.VSTOR02

INDEX --------- MM01.CUSTOMER.MASTER.INDEX
     IN-CAT --- ICFCAT.VSTOR02

GDG BASE ------ MM01.DAILYEMS
     IN-CAT --- ICFCAT.VSTOR02

NONVSAM ------- MM01.DAILYEMS.G0930V00
     IN-CAT --- ICFCAT.VSTOR02
```

Example of VOLUME output

```
LISTCAT ENTRIES(MM01.CUSTOMER.MASTER) -
        VOLUME


CLUSTER ------- MM01.CUSTOMER.MASTER
     IN-CAT --- ICFCAT.VSTOR02
     HISTORY
         OWNER-IDENT--------MM01        CREATION--------2002.129
         RELEASE---------------2        EXPIRATION------2002.365

  DATA ------- MM01.CUSTOMER.MASTER.DATA
     IN-CAT --- ICFCAT.VSTOR02
     HISTORY
         OWNER-IDENT-------(NULL)       CREATION--------2002.129
         RELEASE---------------2        EXPIRATION------2002.365
     VOLUMES
         VOLSER-----------TSO001        DEVTYPE------X'3010200F'

  INDEX ------- MM01.CUSTOMER.MASTER.INDEX
     IN-CAT --- ICFCAT.VSTOR02
     HISTORY
         OWNER-IDENT-------(NULL)       CREATION--------2002.129
         RELEASE---------------2        EXPIRATION------2002.365
     VOLUMES
         VOLSER-----------TSO001        DEVTYPE------X'3010200F'
```

Description

- The ALLOCATION listing is like the VOLUME listing with additional information about the extents used for each file.

- The ALL listing is like the ALLOCATION listing with additional information that includes attribute information.

Figure 16-11   How to limit the information that's listed

How to use the ALTER and DELETE commands

The ALTER and DELETE commands are used to modify a catalog entry or to delete a data set. Since you will probably need to do both at one time or another, these commands are presented next.

How to use the ALTER command to modify a catalog entry

You can use the ALTER command to modify a catalog entry as shown in figure 16-12. The parameters in the syntax for this command let you change an entry's name or its volume allocations.

In the first example, this command is used to change an entry's name to MM01.CUSTMAST. This type of command can be used for a cluster, data component, index component, alternate index, path, or catalog.

In the second example, this command is used to remove two volumes that have been allocated for a data set and to add two volumes to the allocation. In this case, you need to use the data component as the entry to be altered, not the cluster. Note, however, that you can't remove a volume for a data set if space on that volume has already been allocated to the data set. To see what volumes have already been allocated, you can use the LISTCAT command with the ALLOCATION parameter.

Besides the parameters shown in this figure, you can use other DEFINE CLUSTER parameters to alter the catalog entry for a data set. For instance, the third example shows how the SHAREOPTIONS parameter can be used to change the share options for a data set. Note, however, that there are many restrictions on what parameters you can alter once a data set has been created. So you need to consult the appropriate AMS manual or check with a systems programmer at your installation if you absolutely have to change one of the parameters. The alternative is to redefine the data set with the changed parameters and create it anew from the current version of the data set.

The syntax of the ALTER command

```
ALTER    entry-name
      [ CATALOG(name) ]
      [ NEWNAME(entry-name) ]
      [ ADDVOLUMES(vol-ser...) ]
      [ REMOVEVOLUMES(vol-ser...) ]
```

Explanation

entry-name	Specifies the name of the object whose catalog entry is to be altered.
CATALOG	Identifies the catalog that contains the object to be altered. Required only if the catalog can't be located by the standard search sequence.
NEWNAME	Specifies a new entry name for the entry.
ADDVOLUMES	Adds the specified volumes to the list of volumes where space may be allocated to the data component. Can't be used with a cluster.
REMOVEVOLUMES	Removes the specified volumes from the list of volumes where space may be allocated to the data component. Ignored if space has already been allocated on the specified volumes. Can't be used with a cluster.

A command that changes that name of a data set

```
ALTER MM01.CUSTOMER.MASTER      -
      NEWNAME(MM01.CUSTMAST)
```

A command that adds two volumes and removes two other volumes

```
ALTER MM01.CUSTOMER.MASTER.DATA    -
      ADDVOLUMES(VOL291 VOL292)    -
      REMOVEVOLUMES(VOL281 VOL282)
```

A command that changes the share options

```
ALTER MM01.CUSTOMER.MASTER.DATA   -
      SHAREOPTIONS(3 3)
```

Description

- You can use the ALTER command to change a VSAM object's name, volume allocation, and other characteristics. This command can be used for a cluster, data component, index component, alternate index, path, or catalog.

- Besides the parameters shown in the syntax above, you can code many of the DEFINE CLUSTER parameters like the FREESPACE or SHAREOPTIONS parameters. However, there are restrictions to the use of some of these, so be sure to consult your systems programmer or the appropriate AMS reference manual to see what these restrictions are.

Figure 16-12   How to use the ALTER command to modify a catalog entry

How to use the DELETE command to delete a data set

You use the DELETE command to delete a data set as shown in figure 16-13. To identify the data sets that you want to delete, you can list their names as shown in the first two examples. Or, you can use a generic entry name or an entry type to identify the data sets to be deleted as shown in the third example. If you want to delete the data sets even if their expiration dates haven't yet been reached, you can code the PURGE parameter.

Normally, when a data set is deleted, its name is removed from the catalog, but the data set itself remains on the DASD. For most data sets, that's all that's needed because there's no way to access the data set once it's removed from the catalog. Eventually, then, it gets overwritten by other data sets. If that isn't enough for sensitive data sets, though, you can code the ERASE parameter so the data set itself is overwritten by binary zeros. But keep in mind that this is an unnecessary waste of computer time for most data sets.

The syntax of the DELETE command

```
DELETE    (entry-name...)
        [ CATALOG(name)   ]
        [ entry-type... ]
        [ PURGE  |  NOPURGE ]
        [ ERASE  |  NOERASE ]
```

Explanation

entry-name	Specifies the name of the entry or entries to be deleted. If you specify more than one entry name, you must enclose the list in parentheses.
CATALOG	Specifies the name of the catalog that owns the entries to be deleted. Required only if the correct catalog can't be found using the standard search sequence.
entry-type	Specifies that only entries of the listed types should be deleted. The valid entry types are the same as for the LISTCAT command.
PURGE | NOPURGE	PURGE means that an object should be deleted even if its retention period has not expired. NOPURGE means to delete entries only if their expiration dates have passed (the default).
ERASE | NOERASE	ERASE means that the data component of a cluster or alternate index should be erased (overwritten with binary zeros). NOERASE means that the data component should not be erased (the default).

A command that deletes a data set whether or not it has expired

```
DELETE MM01.CUSTOMER.MASTER -
       PURGE
```

A command that deletes three named data sets

```
DELETE (MM01.CUSTOMER.MASTER        -
        MM01.CUSTMAST.DISTRICT.AIX   -
        MM01.CUSTMAST.DISTRICT.PATH)
```

A command that deletes all alternate indexes for data sets that match a generic entry name

```
DELETE MM01.CUSTMAST.*.AIX  -
       ALTERNATEINDEX
```

Description

- You can use the DELETE command to remove the entries for one or more data sets from a VSAM catalog.
- You can use generic entry names to identify the data sets that you want removed.
- Although the DELETE command removes the catalog entry for a data set, the data set remains on the disk until it's overwritten by another data set.
- Although you can use the ERASE parameter to overwrite a data set when it is deleted, that can be time-consuming and it usually isn't necessary.

Figure 16-13   How to use the DELETE command to delete a data set

How to print and copy data sets

To print and copy data sets, you can use the AMS PRINT and REPRO commands. As you will see, these are useful commands that work for both VSAM and non-VSAM data sets.

How to use the PRINT command to print a data set

Figure 16-14 presents the syntax of the PRINT command with the parameters separated into four groups. You use one of the parameters in the first group to identify the data set to be printed. You can use the parameters in the second group to control how the printed output is handled. Then, if you don't want to print all of the records, you can use the parameters in the third and fourth groups to identify the records to be printed.

If you look at the examples in this figure, you can see how this works. In the first example, the INDATASET parameter identifies the data set to be printed, and CHARACTER identifies the printing format. Then, the SKIP parameter says to skip the first 28 records before starting and the COUNT parameter says to print just 3 records.

In the second example, a KSDS is printed in hex format starting with the record that has a key value of 1000 and ending with the record that has a key value of 1200. If the key in either parameter contains commas, semicolons, blanks, parentheses, or slashes, you must code the key between apostrophes, but normally that isn't necessary.

To give you some idea of what the printing formats look like, two lines of character and two lines of hex output are shown at the bottom of this figure. As you can see, the output for each record starts with its key. Although the character format works fine when each byte contains one character, numeric formats like packed-decimal are unreadable in this format. In that case, you need to use hex format, which presumes that you know how to decode the hex values. The dump format prints the data set in both character and hex format.

If you experiment with this command, you'll quickly see that it's easy to use. Remember too that it can be used with both VSAM and non-VSAM data sets, so it's a versatile command.

The syntax of the PRINT command

```
PRINT { INDATASET(entry-name) }
      { INFILE(ddname)         }

      [ CHARACTER | HEX | DUMP ]
      [ OUTFILE(ddname) ]

      [ {SKIP(count)}
        {FROMKEY(key)}
        {FROMNUMBER(number)}
        {FROMADDRESS(address)} ]

      [ {COUNT(count)}
        {TOKEY(key)}
        {TONUMBER(number)}
        {TOADDRESS(address)} ]
```

Explanation

INDATASET	Specifies the name of the data set to be printed.
INFILE	Specifies the name of a DD statement that identifies the data set to be printed.
CHARACTER	Specifies that the data should be printed in character format.
HEX	Specifies that the data should be printed in hexadecimal format.
DUMP	Specifies that the data should be printed in both character and hex format.
OUTFILE	Specifies an output file other than the default SYSPRINT.
SKIP	Specifies the number of records to be skipped before the records are printed.
FROM...	Specifies the key (KSDS), number (RRDS), or relative-byte address (ESDS) of the first record to be printed.
COUNT	Specifies the number of records to be printed.
TO...	Specifies the key (KSDS), number (RRDS), or relative byte address (ESDS) of the last record to be printed.

A command that prints records 29, 30, and 31 in character format

```
PRINT INDATASET(MM01.CUSTOMER.MASTER)   -
      CHARACTER                         -
      SKIP(28)                          -
      COUNT(3)
```

A command that prints the records from key 1000 to key 1200 in hex format

```
PRINT INDATASET(MM01.CUSTOMER.MASTER)   -
      HEX                               -
      FROMKEY(1000)                     -
      TOKEY(1200)
```

The start of a listing in character format

```
KEY OF RECORD - 287760
287760JOHN WARDS AND ASSOC5600 N CLARKE          CHICAGO     IL603002027   0102
```

The start of the same listing in hex format

```
KEY OF RECORD - F2F8F7F7F6F0
F2F8F7F7F6F0D1D6C8D540E6C1D9C4E240C1D5C440C1E2E2D6C3F5F6F0F040D540C3D3C1D9D2
```

Figure 16-14   How to use the PRINT command to print a data set

How to use the REPRO command to copy a data set

Figure 16-15 shows how to use the REPRO command to copy a data set. As you can see, its syntax is similar to the syntax of the PRINT command, but this time the parameters are separated into five groups.

To start, you use one of the parameters in the first group to identify the input data set and one of the parameters in the second group to identify the output data set. Then, if you don't want to copy all of the records in the input data set, you can use the parameters in the third and fourth groups to identify the records to be copied. This works just like it does in the PRINT command. In the example in this figure, the first 1000 records of the input data set are copied to the output data set.

You can use this command with both VSAM and non-VSAM data sets, and the input files can have different organizations. For instance, you can copy a non-VSAM sequential file into a VSAM KSDS. The only restriction is that you can't use a non-VSAM ISAM file as the output data set, but you shouldn't want to do that.

When you use this command, you must remember that the output data set must already exist. Then, if the output data set is empty, VSAM copies the input data set into the output data set. However, if the output data set contains records, VSAM merges the input records with the output records. For an ESDS, the input records are added at the end of the output data set. For a KSDS or RRDS, the records are added in their correct positions based on their key values or relative record numbers.

With that in mind, you can understand how the parameters in the last group work. If you code REUSE for a reusable data set, the input records overwrite the records that were in the output data set. If you code NOREUSE, the input records are merged with the existing records in the reusable data set.

Regardless of whether or not the data set is reusable, when the records are merged, the REPLACE and NOREPLACE parameters take effect. If you code REPLACE, records with duplicate keys or relative record numbers replace the corresponding records in the output data set. If you code NOREPLACE, the duplicate records in the output data set are retained and the duplicate input records are discarded.

The syntax of the REPRO command

```
REPRO { INDATASET(entry-name) }
      { INFILE(ddname)         }

      { OUTDATASET(entry-name) }
      { OUTFILE(ddname)        }

      [ {SKIP(count)}
        {FROMKEY(key)}
        {FROMNUMBER(number)}
        {FROMADDRESS(address)} ]

      [ {COUNT(count)}
        {TOKEY(key)}
        {TONUMBER(number)}
        {TOADDRESS(address)} ]

      [ REUSE | NOREUSE ]
      [ REPLACE | NOREPLACE ]
```

Explanation

INDATASET	Specifies the name of the data set to be copied.
INFILE	Specifies the name of a DD statement that identifies the data set to be copied.
OUTDATASET	Specifies the name of the output data set.
OUTFILE	Specifies the name of a DD statement that identifies the output data set.
SKIP	Specifies the number of records to be skipped before copying begins.
FROM...	Specifies the key (KSDS), number (RRDS), or relative byte address (ESDS) of the first record to be copied.
COUNT	Specifies the number of records to be copied.
TO...	Specifies the key (KSDS), number (RRDS), or relative byte address (ESDS) of the last record to be copied.
REUSE	NOREUSE	Specifies whether or not a reusable output file should be reset. If not, the new records are merged with the existing ones in the file.
REPLACE	NOREPLACE	Specifies whether or not duplicate records should be replaced.

A command that copies the first 1000 records in a data set

```
REPRO INDATASET(MMA2.CUSTOMER.MASTER)        -
      OUTDATASET(MMA2.CUSTOMER.MASTER.COPY)  -
      COUNT(1000)
```

Description

- You can use the REPRO command to copy non-VSAM or VSAM data sets with any file organization, and the input and output files can have different organizations.

- The output data set in a REPRO command must exist when the job is run. If the output data set is empty, the records are copied from the input data set to the output data set. If the output data set contains records, the records from the input file are merged with the records in the output file depending on the data set's organization.

Figure 16-15   How to use the REPRO command to copy a data set

How to define and build an alternate index

To define and build an alternate index for a KSDS requires three different AMS commands. First, you use the DEFINE ALTERNATEINDEX command to define the alternate index. Next, you use the DEFINE PATH command to define a path that lets you process a base cluster via its alternate index. Then, you use the BLDINDEX command to create the alternate index from data that's derived from the base cluster.

How to use the DEFINE ALTERNATEINDEX command

Figure 16-16 gives the syntax of the DEFINE ALTERNATEINDEX (or AIX) command. As you can see, its syntax is similar to the syntax for the DEFINE CLUSTER command. That's because an alternate index is actually a KSDS. As a result, you should already know how to code most of the parameters for this command. Note, however, that there are also six new parameters that are summarized in this figure.

To name an alternate index, I suggest that you use a combination of the base cluster name, the name of the alternate key, and the letters AIX. I also suggest that you name the data and index components by adding DATA and INDEX to the name of the cluster. If, for example, social security number is going to be used as an alternate index for an employee master file, the index can be defined with names like these:

```
MM2.EMPMAST.SSN.AIX
MM2.EMPMAST.SSN.AIX.DATA
MM2.EMPMAST.SSN.AIX.INDEX
```

That way, you can easily identify the names when you list the catalog entries.

When you code the RELATE parameter, you supply the name of the base cluster that the index will apply to. Then, the KEYS parameter gives the length and offset of the alternate key in the base cluster. And the UNIQUEKEY and NONUNIQUEKEY parameters determine whether duplicate keys are allowed.

As for the UPGRADE and NOUPGRADE parameters, they determine whether an alternate index is part of the base cluster's *upgrade set*. If it is, the alternate index is updated whenever the base cluster is processed by primary key. Otherwise, the index must be upgraded as a separate function.

Because alternate indexes are frequently rebuilt as a separate function, I suggest that you define each alternate index with the REUSE parameter. Then, you can use the BLDINDEX command to rebuild the records of the alternate index without deleting and redefining the index.

The syntax of the DEFINE ALTERNATEINDEX command

```
DEFINE ALTERNATEINDEX (    NAME(entry-name)
                           RELATE(cluster-name)
                         [ OWNER(owner-id) ]
                         [ FOR(days) | TO(date) ]
                         [ KEYS(length offset) ]
                         [ UNIQUEKEY | NONUNIQUEKEY ]
                         [ UPGRADE | NOUPGRADE ]
                         [ VOLUMES(vol-ser...) ]
                         [ FILE(ddname) ]
                         [ {CYLINDERS(primary [secondary])}
                           {KILOBYTES(primary [secondary])}
                           {MEGABYTES(primary [secondary])}
                           {TRACKS(primary [secondary])   }
                           {RECORDS(primary [secondary])  } ]
                         [ REUSE | NOREUSE ]
                         [ SHAREOPTIONS(a b) ]
                         [ MODEL(entry-name [cat-name]) ] )
            [ DATA      ( [ NAME(entry-name) ]
                         [ VOLUMES(vol-ser...) ]
                         [ {CYLINDERS(primary [secondary])}
                           {KILOBYTES(primary [secondary])}
                           {MEGABYTES(primary [secondary])}
                           {TRACKS(primary [secondary])   }
                           {RECORDS(primary [secondary])  } ] ) ]
            [ INDEX     ( [ NAME(entry-name) ]
                         [ VOLUMES(vol-ser...) ]
                         [ {CYLINDERS(primary [secondary])}
                           {KILOBYTES(primary [secondary])}
                           {MEGABYTES(primary [secondary])}
                           {TRACKS(primary [secondary])   }
                           {RECORDS(primary [secondary])  } ] ) ]
            [ CATALOG(name) ]
```

Explanation of the parameters that aren't in the DEFINE CLUSTER command

RELATE	Specifies the name of the base cluster to which this alternate index applies.
UNIQUEKEY	Duplicate keys aren't allowed.
NONUNIQUEKEY	Duplicate keys are allowed.
UPGRADE	The alternate index is part of the base cluster's upgrade set.
NOUPGRADE	The alternate index isn't part of the base cluster's upgrade set.
MODEL	Specifies the name of an existing alternate index to use as a model.

Description

- Because an alternate index is actually a KSDS, the DEFINE ALTERNATEINDEX or DEFINE AIX command is similar to the DEFINE CLUSTER command.

Figure 16-16   The syntax of the DEFINE ALTERNATEINDEX command

How to use the DEFINE PATH command

To process the records of a base cluster via an alternate index, you need to define another catalog entry called a *path*. To do that, you use the DEFINE PATH command that's summarized in figure 16-17. Here, the first three parameters are the critical ones.

To start, you use the NAME parameter to provide a name for the path. As a naming convention, I suggest that you use the cluster name for the alternate index with PATH instead of AIX at the end of the name. Then, you use the RELATE parameter to supply the name of the alternate index. In other words, the DEFINE PATH command relates the path to the alternate index, and the DEFINE AIX command relates the alternate index to the base cluster.

The UPDATE or NOUPDATE parameter tells AMS whether or not you want the base cluster's upgrade set to be updated when you process the cluster via the path. If you specify UPDATE, all of the alternate indexes in the upgrade set are updated when you open the path. If you specify NOUPDATE, the upgrade set isn't updated when you process the file via the path.

The example in this figure shows how the DEFINE AIX and DEFINE PATH commands are related. Here, you can see the naming conventions used for the index and path. You can see that the alternate index has a unique key that's added to the upgrade set for the base cluster. And you can see that the DEFINE PATH command tells AMS to update the upgrade set when the base cluster is processed via the path.

You can also see that the alternate index is defined as a reusable data set. That way, the alternate index can be rebuilt whenever needed without having to be redefined.

The syntax of the DEFINE PATH command

```
DEFINE PATH  (    NAME(entry-name)
                  PATHENTRY(aix-name)
             [ UPDATE | NOUPDATE ]
             [ FOR(days) | TO(date) ]
             [ MODEL(entry-name [cat-name]) ]
             [ RECATALOG | NORECATALOG ] )
  [ CATALOG(name) ]
```

Explanation

NAME	Specifies the name of the path.
PATHENTRY	Specifies the name of the alternate index to which this path is related.
UPDATE	The upgrade set should be updated when this path is processed.
NOUPDATE	The upgrade set shouldn't be updated when this path is processed.
MODEL	Specifies the name of an existing path to use as a model.
RECATALOG	Specifies that a path entry is to be recataloged. The NAME and PATHENTRY parameters must be specified as they were when the path was originally defined.
NORECATALOG	Specifies that a new path entry should be created in a catalog.
CATALOG	Specifies the name of the catalog that contains the alternate index. Required only if the correct catalog can't be found using the standard search sequence.

Two commands that define an alternate index and its path

```
DEFINE AIX   ( NAME(MMA2.EMPMAST.SSN.AIX)              -
               RELATE(MMA2.EMPMAST)                    -
               KEYS(9 12)                              -
               UNIQUEKEY                               -
               UPGRADE                                 -
               REUSE                                   -
               VOLUMES(MPS800) )                       -
        DATA ( NAME(MMA2.EMPMAST.SSN.AIX.DATA)         -
               CYLINDERS(1 1) )                        -
       INDEX ( NAME(MMA2.EMPMAST.SSN.AIX.INDEX) )
DEFINE PATH  ( NAME(MMA2.EMPMAST.SSN.PATH)             -
               PATHENTRY(MMA2.EMPMAST.SSN.AIX)         -
               UPDATE )
```

Description

- A *path* lets you access base cluster records via an alternate index.

- You don't have to supply the name of the base cluster in the DEFINE PATH command because it is identified in the RELATE parameter of the DEFINE AIX command.

- A base cluster's *upgrade set* is all of its upgradeable alternate indexes. You add an alternate index to the upgrade set by coding the UPGRADE parameter in the DEFINE AIX command.

- The upgrade set is always updated when the base cluster is processed by its primary key. To update the upgrade set when the base cluster is processed by an alternate key (via a path), you code the UPDATE parameter in the DEFINE PATH command.

Figure 16-17   How the DEFINE AIX and the DEFINE PATH commands work together

How to use the BLDINDEX command

Before you can process a base cluster via an alternate index, of course, you need to build the index. To do that, you use the BLDINDEX command that's summarized in figure 16-18. In this case, the base cluster is the input data set that you identify by one of the parameters in the first group, and the alternate index is the output data set that you identify by one of the parameters in the second group. However, you can use either the index name or the path name for the output data set.

When the BLDINDEX command is executed, it reads all the records in the base cluster and extracts the alternate key and primary key from each one. Next, it sorts these pairs of keys into ascending sequence by alternate key. Then, it writes the alternate index records to the alternate index. Along the way, if AMS finds duplicate keys for a UNIQUEKEY index, it flags the duplicates as errors.

Whenever possible, VSAM should do the sort as an internal sort because that's faster than an external sort. As a result, you usually shouldn't code the EXTERNALSORT parameter. If VSAM can't do an internal sort, though, it looks for two sort work files and does an external sort.

For that reason, you usually should provide DD statements for those work files. To do that, you can use the WORKFILES parameter to give the ddnames for the two work files. But it's easier to use the default ddnames (IDCUT1 and IDCUT2). In the example in this figure, you can see how the DD statements for those ddnames are coded.

Remember that you will not only use the BLDINDEX command to build an alternate index for the first time, but also to rebuild an index when it isn't part of the base cluster's upgrade set or when its path isn't defined for update. That's common practice because maintaining all of the alternate indexes as a KSDS is processed requires considerable overhead.

The syntax of the BLDINDEX command

```
BLDINDEX { INDATASET(cluster-name) }
         { INFILE(ddname)           }

         { OUTDATASET(aix-or-path-name) }
         { OUTFILE(ddname)              }

         [ EXTERNALSORT | INTERNALSORT ]

         [ WORKFILES(ddname ddname) ]

         [ CATALOG(name) ]
```

Explanation

INTERNALSORT — Specifies that the index records should be sorted in virtual storage. This is the default. Then, if VSAM can't find enough virtual storage for an internal sort, it automatically does an external sort.

EXTERNALSORT — Specifies that the index records should be sorted by an external sort program that uses disk work files. It's faster, though, to use the internal sort.

WORKFILES — Supplies the ddnames for the work files that are used by an external sort. If omitted, OS/390 uses IDCUT1 and IDCUT2 as the ddnames for these files, and you must provide DD statements for them.

CATALOG — Specifies the name of the catalog that will own the sort work files. If omitted, the standard search sequence is used.

A job that builds an alternate index

```
//MM01LC3  JOB  (36512),'R MENENDEZ',NOTIFY=&SYSUID
//         EXEC PGM=IDCAMS
//SYSPRINT DD   SYSOUT=*
//IDCUT1   DD   UNIT=SYSDA,VOL=SER=MPS800,DISP=OLD
//IDCUT2   DD   UNIT=SYSDA,VOL=SER=MPS800,DISP=OLD
//SYSIN    DD   *
 BLDINDEX INDATASET(MMA2.EMPMAST)          -
          OUTDATASET(MMA2.EMPMAST.SSN.AIX) -
          CATALOG(MMA2)
/*
```

Description

- You use the BLDINDEX command to build an alternate index for the first time. You also use it to rebuild the index whenever that's necessary.

- To build an alternate index, VSAM first reads all the records in the base cluster and extracts the primary and alternate keys for each record. Then, it sorts the key pairs into ascending sequence by alternate key and writes the alternate index to its KSDS. If an alternate index allows nonunique keys, VSAM combines the duplicate primary keys for each alternate key into a single alternate index record.

- Unless you code the EXTERNALSORT parameter, VSAM tries to do the sort internally. If it can't, it does an external sort using two work files that you must provide DD statements for.

Figure 16-18   How to use the BLDINDEX command to build an alternate index

Perspective

The goal of this chapter has been to show you how to use the AMS commands that most application programmers need. If this chapter has succeeded, you should now know what these commands can do. Then, when you need to use one of them later on, you can refer back to this chapter for the specific coding details.

Keep in mind, though, that there's more to AMS than this chapter shows. In particular, there are other parameters and considerations for improving the performance of production data sets. Most shops, however, have a systems programmer or VSAM expert who specializes in fine-tuning the performance of VSAM data sets when they are put into production. As a result, the application programmer doesn't need that level of VSAM mastery.

Terms

functional command
modal command
IDCAMS
retention period
expiration date
cross-region share option
cross-system share option
generic entry name
upgrade set
path

Section 5

OS/390 tools for the application programmer

The five chapters in this section show you how to use the main OS/390 tools that are available to application programmers. In chapter 17, you'll learn how to use the IBM procedures for compiling and testing the programs that you develop. In chapter 18, you'll learn how to use the OS/390 utility programs that make it easy for you to work with data sets and to generate test data. And in chapter 19, you'll learn how to use the sort/merge utility that lets you sort the records in a data set or merge the records from two or more data sets. These are tools that every application programmer should know how to use.

Then, chapter 20 introduces you to the use of TSO commands, CLIST procedures, and REXX procedures. And chapter 21 shows you how to use the UNIX system services that make it possible for you to work with UNIX files that are stored on a mainframe. Although you may never need the facilities that are presented in these two chapters, you should at least be aware that they're available.

17

How to use JCL procedures to compile and test programs

In chapter 9, you learned how to create and use your own JCL procedures. Now, you'll learn how to use the program development procedures that are supplied by IBM. These are the procedures that let you compile and test the programs that you develop.

As you read this chapter, you'll see that the focus is on the procedures that apply to COBOL and CICS program development. We took that approach because most mainframe development is still being done with those languages. Once you learn how to use the procedures for those languages, though, you should be able to apply those skills to the procedures for any other language.

Program development concepts

When you develop a program for an IBM mainframe with a language like COBOL or assembler language, you run a procedure that converts your source program into a machine language program that can be run by the system. Within that procedure, two or more job steps are run. In the topics that follow, you'll learn more about some of the common procedures that are used for program development.

A compile-link-and-go procedure

Usually, it takes three steps to compile and test a program on an IBM mainframe system. This is illustrated by the system flowchart in figure 17-1, which presents the three steps that are required for a COBOL program. This is commonly referred to as a *compile-link-and-go procedure*.

In the first step, the COBOL *compiler* reads the program you've written, called the *source program*, and converts it to an *object module* that is stored on disk in an *object library*. If the source program uses *copy members* (pieces of source code that are copied into the program), they're retrieved from a *copy library* and inserted into the program during this step.

Typically, the compiler also produces printed output as part of this step. Among other things, this output can include a *compiler listing* that shows the COBOL statements in the program, including any copy members. The listing also includes a description of any coding errors that make it impossible for the compiler to create the object program.

If the program compiles without any errors, the second step is performed. In this step, a program called a *linkage editor* (or *link editor*) links the object module with any subprograms that it requires. These can be system subprograms or subprograms written by you or another programmer. Either way, the subprograms must be compiled into object modules that are stored in object libraries before the linkage editor can link them.

The output of the link-edit step is a *load module* that is stored on disk. This is your program in a form that can be executed. The linkage editor can also create printed output that identifies the programs included in the load module.

In the third step, the load module is run. The input to this program is whatever data sets the program calls for, and the output is whatever data sets the program produces. Throughout this book, you've learned how to allocate the data sets for a program and execute its load module.

This procedure is the same for other languages too, although some of the terms may differ. If you're using assembler language, for example, the compiler is usually referred to as an *assembler* and compiling is referred to as *assembling* (although many people use the terms *compiler* and *compile* for both compilers and assemblers). Also, the copy library is referred to as the *source statement library*.

The system flowchart for a COBOL compile-link-and-go procedure

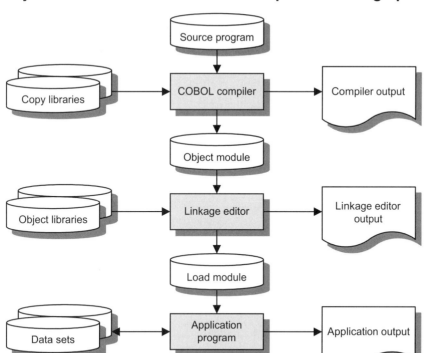

Description

- In step 1, the COBOL *compiler* compiles the *source program* into an *object module*. If necessary, it gets groups of source statements called *copy members* from the *copy library*. When you use other programming languages, the copy library is called the *source statement library*.

- In step 2, the *linkage editor* links edits the object module with any other object modules that it needs. These can be IBM-supplied object modules or object modules for subprograms that have been written by application programmers. The result is an executable program called a *load module*.

- In step 3, the load module is executed. The program then processes its input data sets and produces its output data sets, which can include printed output.

- When you develop a program with assembler language, the compiler is often called an *assembler* and compiling is called *assembling*. Otherwise, this procedure works the same way for an assembly as it does for a compilation.

- A procedure like this can be referred to as a *compile-link-and-go procedure*.

Figure 17-1   A compile-link-and-go procedure

A compile-load-and-go procedure

A *compile-load-and-go procedure* (or just *compile-and-go*) is similar to the procedure you've just seen. However, it only requires two steps. In the second step, a program called the *loader* link edits the object modules, loads your executable program into storage, and runs it...without saving a load module. This is illustrated by the system flowchart in figure 17-2.

You can use this type of procedure when you're testing a program, and you're making changes to the source program after each test run. If you want to test the same version of the program more than once, though, you should use a *compile-and-link procedure* to create a load module. Then, you can run that load module repeatedly with separate JCL as you test your program. This is also the way production programs are run.

The system flowchart for a COBOL compile-load-and-go procedure

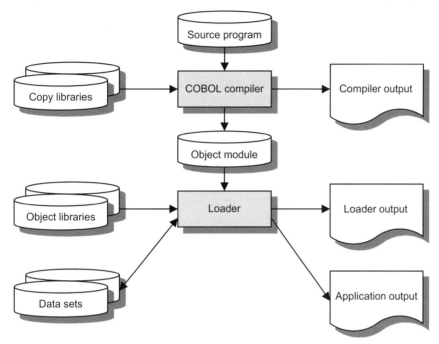

Description

- Like the linkage editor, the *loader* links the object modules for a program. However, it doesn't actually create a load module on DASD. Instead, it links the object modules, loads the executable program into storage, and executes it...all in one step.

- A procedure like this can be referred to as a *compile-load-and-go* or just a *compile-and-go procedure*. It is only used for testing, because production programs are run from load modules.

Figure 17-2   A compile-load-and-go procedure

A translate-compile-and-link procedure

When you use some programming subsystems like CICS, DB2, or IMS, you embed their commands within a language like COBOL, PL/I, or assembler language. For instance, most CICS programs are developed by embedding CICS commands within COBOL programs. Then, the CICS commands need to be translated into COBOL before the COBOL program can be compiled and link edited into a load module.

This is illustrated by the procedure in figure 17-3. Here, the source program is first processed by the CICS *translator*, which converts the CICS code into COBOL. Then, the COBOL compiler compiles the source code into an object module, and the linkage editor links the object modules into a load module. The load module can then be run under the CICS subsystem.

Because CICS programs can only be run under the CICS subsystem, you can't run CICS load modules as JCL batch jobs. As a result, you can't use a link-and-go or load-and-go procedure for CICS programs. Instead, you set up the appropriate CICS tables for running the load modules, which you can learn how to do in our CICS book, *Murach's CICS for the COBOL Programmer*.

The system flowchart for a CICS translate-compile-and-link procedure

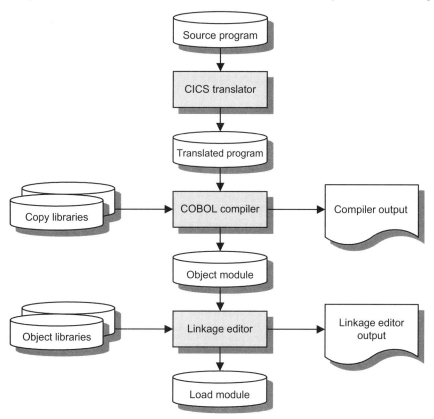

Description

- When you develop a CICS program, you embed CICS commands within another programming language like COBOL, PL/I, or assembler language.

- Before a CICS program can be compiled, it must be translated into the base programming language. This is done by the *CICS translator.*

- For a CICS/COBOL program, the CICS translator converts CICS commands to COBOL Move and Call statements that can be compiled by the COBOL compiler.

- After a CICS program is translated, it is compiled and link edited just like any other source program.

- CICS programs run under the CICS subsystem, not as OS/390 batch jobs. As a result, you can't run CICS load modules with JCL.

Figure 17-3   A translate-compile-and-link procedure

The IBM procedures for program development

To make it easier for you to develop programs, IBM provides JCL procedures for common program-development jobs. In the topics that follow, you'll learn more about them.

A summary of the IBM procedures

Figure 17-4 summarizes the procedures for six of the programming languages that IBM supports. As you can see, there are four procedures for each of these languages. You can use the *compile-only procedure* when you want to create an object module for a subprogram. You can use the *compile-and-link procedure* when you want to create a load module that you can repeatedly execute as a batch JCL job. And you can use the other two procedures when you want to compile, link, and run a program.

Besides these procedures for programming languages, IBM provides other procedures for program development. Later in this chapter, for example, you'll see the translate-compile-and-link procedure for CICS/COBOL programs. You'll also see a procedure for creating CICS mapsets.

IBM procedures for six programming languages

Language	Compile only	Compile & link	Compile, link & go	Compile & go
COBOL for OS/390	IGYWC	IGYWCL	IGYWCLG	IGYWCG
VS COBOL II	COB2UC	COB2UCL	COB2UCLG	COB2UCG
High Level Assembler	ASMAC	ASMACL	ASMACLG	ASMACG
PL/I for OS/390	IBMZC	IBMZCPL	IBMZCPLG	IBMZCPG
VS Fortran 2	VSF2C	VSF2CL	VSF2CLG	VSF2CG
C for OS/390	EDCC	EDCCL	(n/a)	EDCCBG
C++ for OS/390	CBCC	CBCCL	CBCCLG	CBCCBG

The four types of procedures

* A *compile-only procedure* compiles the source program and usually creates an object module. The name for this type of procedure ends with a C for compile (even if you're using assembler langauge).

* A *compile-and-link procedure* compiles the source program and link edits it. The name for this type of procedure usually ends with CL.

* A *compile-link-and-go procedure* compiles, link edits, and runs the resulting load module. The name for this type of procedure usually ends with CLG.

* A *compile-and-go procedure* compiles the source program and then uses the loader to link and run the program without creating a load module. The name for this type of procedure usually ends with CG.

Description

* For each programming language that is offered with OS/390, IBM supplies the four types of cataloged JCL procedures that are summarized above.

* Besides the procedures for programming languages, IBM supplies other procedures for program development. These include procedures for developing programs for the CICS, DB2, and IMS subsystems as well as for developing CICS mapsets.

* Often, the IBM procedures are modified within a shop to meet its specific requirements.

Figure 17-4   A summary of the IBM procedures for program development

The step names and data sets for COBOL procedures

To use one of the IBM procedures, you need to know the names of the job steps within the procedure. You also need to know what ddnames you may have to provide DD statements for, depending on your system and program requirements. For instance, figure 17-5 shows the step names and ddnames that are used for the COBOL procedures.

If you're familiar with COBOL program development on IBM mainframes, you know that two different COBOL compilers are available. The older one is called VS COBOL II. The newer one is called COBOL for OS/390. For each of these compilers, four different procedures are available as shown in the last figure. The step names in these procedures are the same, though, except for the compile step, which is either COB2 or COBOL. The ddnames that can be used for the steps in these procedures are the same for both compilers.

To code the JCL for running one of these IBM procedures, you need to provide DD statements for any ddnames required by the job that are not provided for by the IBM procedure. For the compile step, for example, you always need to provide a SYSIN DD statement that allocates the source program (normally, a member of a source library). If your program uses copy members, you also need to provide a SYSLIB DD statement that allocates the copy library.

For the link-edit step, you need to override the SYSLMOD DD statement in the procedure so the load module for your program gets stored in a user library. If your program calls subprograms, you may also need to concatenate a user object library to the system object library by coding a SYSLIB DD statement.

Finally, for the go step, you need to code DD statements for the data sets used by your program. You may also want to allocate data sets for any of the ddnames listed for the GO step in this figure.

To introduce you to the JCL for running a COBOL program-development procedure, this figure provides an example. As you can see, this JCL starts by executing the procedure named IGYWCLG, which is the compile-link-and-go procedure for COBOL for OS/390. This assumes that the procedure is in SYS1.PROCLIB. Otherwise, you need to code a JCLLIB statement that identifies the procedure library.

Next, the JCL provides SYSIN and SYSLIB DD statements for the COBOL step of the procedure. Then, it provides SYSLMOD and SYSLIB DD statements for the LKED step of the procedure. Note here that the SYSLIB statement concatenates a user library with the library that's provided by the IBM procedure because the COBOL program uses object modules from both libraries. Last, the JCL provides for two data sets in the GO step that are required by the application program.

If you remember what you learned in chapter 9 about using procedures, you should understand how this JCL works right now. If not, you may want to review that chapter to refresh your memory. In a moment, though, you'll actually review some of the IBM procedures so you'll get a better idea of what's going on.

Step names for the COBOL procedures

Step	VS COBOL II	COBOL for OS/390
Compile	COB2	COBOL
Link	LKED	LKED
Go	GO	GO

DD statements used with the cataloged procedures

Step	ddname	Description
COB2/COBOL	SYSIN	Source program input for the COBOL compiler.
	SYSLIB	The copy library or libraries.
	SYSLIN	Object module output.
LKED	SYSLIB	The subprogram library or libraries.
	SYSLIN	Object module input.
	SYSIN	Additional object module input.
	SYSLMOD	Load module output.
GO	SYSOUT	Output from DISPLAY statements.
	SYSIN	Input for ACCEPT statements.
	SYSDBOUT	Symbolic debugging output.
	SYSUDUMP SYSABEND	Abnormal termination (or storage dump) output.

JCL that invokes the compile-link-and go procedure for OS/390 COBOL

```
//MM01CLG       JOB  (36512),'R MENENDEZ',NOTIFY=MM01
//STEP1         EXEC PROC=IGYWCLG
//COBOL.SYSIN   DD   DSN=MM01.PAYROLL.SOURCE(PAY4000),DISP=SHR
//COBOL.SYSLIB  DD   DSN=MM01.PAYROLL.COPYLIB,DISP=SHR
//*-----------------------------------------------------------------*
//LKED.SYSLMOD  DD   DSN=MM01.PAYROLL.LOADLIB(PAY4000),DISP=SHR
//LKED.SYSLIB   DD
//              DD   DSN=MM01.PAYROLL.OBJLIB,DISP=SHR
//*-----------------------------------------------------------------*
//GO.PAYTRAN    DD   DSN=MM01.PAYROLL.TRANS,DISP=SHR
//GO.PAYRPT     DD   SYSOUT=A
```

Description

* To use a cataloged procedure, you need to know the step names used in the procedure. You also need to know what the ddname requirements are.

* You use these step names and ddnames to supply the members, libraries, or data sets needed by a procedure.

* To find out the names of the procedures that are available for a specific compiler, you need to refer to the appropriate reference manual. It will also tell you what the step names and ddname requirements are for each procedure.

Figure 17-5   The step names and data sets for COBOL procedures

The translation and compiler options for CICS and COBOL procedures

When a translator or compiler is installed on an IBM mainframe, various options are set. These are the default options. Some of the IBM procedures, however, override these default options. Then, when you code the JCL for using one of these procedures, you can override the options set by the procedure or the original system defaults.

Some of the CICS and COBOL options are listed in figure 17-6. Most of these are usually set the way you want them, but you may want to override some of them on occasion. In most IBM shops, for example, apostrophes (') are used as delimiters instead of quotation marks ("), even though the COBOL standard is quotation marks. If you want to change this setting, you can set the QUOTE option to specify quotation marks or the APOST option to specify apostrophes.

If you want the compiler to write the object module to the data set identified by the SYSLIN DD statement, the OBJECT option needs to be on. If your program uses copy members, the LIB option also needs to be on. Normally, both of these options are on, but if you discover that one has been set to NOOBJECT or NOLIB, you can reset it to OBJECT or LIB. (Another option that can be used for object modules is DECK, but that option is rarely used today, even though you'll still see the NODECK option on compiler listings.)

If you want to change some of the options for the compiler listing, you can set the compiler options in the fourth group in this figure. If, for example, the compiler prints a cross-reference listing that you never use, you can set the NOXREF option. Or, if the compiler isn't printing the cross-reference listing and you want one, you can set the XREF option.

Keep in mind, though, that this figure presents only a few of the translator and compiler options. If you want to review the many options that are provided for an IBM software product, you need to check its reference manual.

When you use an IBM procedure for program development, you can change an option by coding the PARM parameter on the EXEC statement for the procedure. This is illustrated by the example in this figure. Here, three options for the COBOL step within the procedure are changed. Two are turned on, and one is turned off.

When you override any of the options for a procedure step, though, all of the procedure step options are overridden. As a result, you need to include any of the procedure options that you want to keep. To find out what those procedure options are, you can review the procedures, as you'll see in a moment.

You may also want to find out what the default options of the COBOL compiler are. Then, if they're set the way you want them, you don't have to worry about overriding them. To find out what the default options are, you can run a procedure with the PARM parameter set to no options, like this:

```
PARM.COBOL=''
```

This overrides any procedure options so you can review the compiler listing to see what the default options are.

Translator options for CICS

Option	Function
QUOTE	Use the ANSI standard quotation mark (").
APOST	Use the apostrophe (').
EDF	The Execution Diagnostic Facility is to apply to the program.
EXCI	The translator is to process EXCI commands.
FLAG	Print the severity of error messages produced by the translator.
LENGTH	Generate a default length if the LENGTH option is omitted from a CICS command.
OOCOBOL	Instructs the translator to accept object-oriented COBOL syntax.
COBOL3	Specifies that the translator is to translate programs compiled by COBOL for OS/390.

Compiler options for VS COBOL II and COBOL for OS/390

Category	Option	Function
Object module	OBJECT	Write object module output to SYSLIN.
	DECK	Write object module output to SYSPUNCH.
Delimiter	QUOTE	Use the ANSI standard quotation mark (").
	APOST	Use the apostrophe (').
Source library	LIB	Allow Copy statements.
Compiler listing	SOURCE	Print source listing.
	OFFSET	Print offset of each Procedure Division verb.
	LIST	Print assembler listing of object module.
	MAP	Print offset of each Data Division field.
	XREF	Print sorted cross reference of data and procedure names.
Testing	TEST	Allow interactive debugging.
	FDUMP	Provide formatted dump at abend.

An EXEC statement that turns two compiler options on and one off

```
//STEP1        EXEC PROC=IGYWCLG,PARM.COBOL='APOST,OBJECT,NOXREF'
```

Description

* Translator and compiler options can be set at three levels. First, the default options are set when the software is installed. Second, the IBM procedures can override the default options. Third, your JCL can override the IBM procedure options or the system defaults.

* To turn an option on or off, you code the PARM parameter for a job step. To turn an option on, you code one of the option names shown above. To turn an option off, you precede the name by NO as in NOXREF (QUOTE and APOST are exceptions).

* When you use the PARM parameter to set options, they override all of the options set by the procedure you're using. So if you want to retain any options set in the procedure, you must code them in the PARM parameter too.

* To find out what the default settings are for the compiler options, you can code a PARM parameter with no settings so all the procedure options are overridden. Then, you can see the default settings by reviewing the compiler listing.

Figure 17-6   The translation and compiler options for CICS and COBOL procedures

How to use some of the IBM procedures

To give you a better idea of how the IBM procedures for program development work, the rest of this chapter presents five procedures and the JCL for using them. Three are COBOL procedures, and two are CICS procedures.

The compile-only procedure for OS/390 COBOL

Figure 17-7 presents the IBM compile-only procedure for COBOL for OS/390 along with the JCL for running it. If you remember what you learned about procedures in chapter 9, you should be able to understand what this procedure is doing.

After the PROC statement sets the values for the symbolic parameters, you'll find three comments. The second one tells you that you must always supply a DD statement for the SYSIN data set. That's the one that contains the source program that's going to be compiled.

After the comments, you can see the single job step for this procedure, which is named COBOL. For this step, the EXEC statement runs a program named IGYCRCTL, which is the COBOL compiler. Note that a PARM parameter isn't coded, so no compiler options are set.

In the DD statements that follow, you can see that the SYSLIN DD statement allocates a temporary data set named &&LOADSET. That's the data set that's used for the object module that is created by the compiler. Because this is a temporary data set, though, it isn't saved when the procedure ends. If you want to save it so it can be used as a subprogram, you need to code a SYSLIN DD statement when you run this program to override the procedure's DD statement.

Because this procedure doesn't include a SYSLIB DD statement, it doesn't provide for the use of copy members. If your program uses them, you also need to provide a SYSLIB DD statement in the JCL that runs this procedure.

The job in the middle of this figure shows you how to run the procedure. In this case, the JCLLIB statement identifies the library that the procedure is stored in when the compiler is installed: SYS1.IGY.SIGYPROC. That way, OS/390 can find the procedure when the job is run. Note, however, that procedures like this are often moved to the SYS1.PROCLIB or another installation-specific library that is automatically searched when a procedure is run. If that's the case in your shop, you don't have to code a JCLLIB statement in your job.

In the EXEC statement for this job, you can see that the IGYWC procedure is executed and the APOST and OBJECT options are set. Since the procedure doesn't set any options, these options will override the default options for the compiler in case that's necessary. Then, the SYSIN DD statement identifies the member of the source library that contains the program to be compiled. The SYSLIB DD statement identifies the copy library that's used. And the SYSLIN DD statement overrides the SYSLIN DD statement in the procedure so the object module is saved in an object library.

The IBM compile-only procedure for OS/390 COBOL

```
//IGYWC   PROC  LNGPRFX='SYS1.IGY',SYSLBLK=3200
//*  COMPILE A COBOL PROGRAM
//*  CALLER MUST SUPPLY //COBOL.SYSIN DD ...
//*
//COBOL   EXEC PGM=IGYCRCTL,REGION=2048K
//STEPLIB  DD   DSNAME=&LNGPRFX..SIGYCOMP,
//              DISP=SHR
//SYSPRINT DD   SYSOUT=*
//SYSLIN   DD   DSNAME=&&LOADSET,UNIT=SYSDA,
//              DISP=(MOD,PASS),SPACE=(TRK,(3,3)),
//              DCB=(BLKSIZE=&SYSLBLK)
//SYSUT1   DD   UNIT=SYSDA,SPACE=(CYL,(1,1))
//SYSUT2   DD   UNIT=SYSDA,SPACE=(CYL,(1,1))
//SYSUT3   DD   UNIT=SYSDA,SPACE=(CYL,(1,1))
//SYSUT4   DD   UNIT=SYSDA,SPACE=(CYL,(1,1))
//SYSUT5   DD   UNIT=SYSDA,SPACE=(CYL,(1,1))
//SYSUT6   DD   UNIT=SYSDA,SPACE=(CYL,(1,1))
//SYSUT7   DD   UNIT=SYSDA,SPACE=(CYL,(1,1))
```

The JCL to invoke this procedure

```
//MM01CL      JOB    (36512),'R MENENDEZ',NOTIFY=MM01
//JOBPROC     JCLLIB ORDER=SYS1.IGY.SIGYPROC
//STEP1       EXEC   PROC=IGYWC,PARM.COBOL='APOST,OBJECT'
//COBOL.SYSIN DD     DSN=MM01.PAYROLL.SOURCE(PAY4000),DISP=SHR
//COBOL.SYSLIB DD    DSN=MM01.PAYROLL.COPYLIB,DISP=SHR
//COBOL.SYSLIN DD    DSN=MM01.PAYROLL.OBJLIB(PAY4000),DISP=SHR
```

Where the IBM procedures are located

- Most IBM procedures for program development are initially stored in a procedure library other than SYS1.PROCLIB. If so, you need to use the JCLLIB statement to identify the library that contains the procedure that you want to use.

- Often, commonly-used procedures are moved to SYS1.PROCLIB from the libraries they were initially stored in. In that case, you don't need to specify a procedure library for the job.

Figure 17-7   How to use the compile-only procedure for OS/390 COBOL

The compile-and-link procedure for OS/390 COBOL

Figure 17-8 presents the IBM compile-and-link procedure for COBOL for OS/390 along with the JCL for running it. Here, the PROC statement, the comments, and the COBOL step are similar to what you saw in the compile-only procedure. This means that you need to code a SYSIN DD statement for the source program when you run the procedure. You also need to code a SYSLIB DD statement for the copy library if your program uses one.

You can also code a SYSLIN DD statement that overrides the temporary data set that's used to save the object module produced by the COBOL step. You only need to do that, though, if you want to save the object module after the job has finished. Otherwise, the temporary data set is used as input to the LKED step, which creates the load module.

In the LKED step, however, you can see that the SYSLMOD DD statement for the load module says that it should be saved in a temporary data set named &&GOSET(GO). (You have to substitute the values set by the PROC statement into the symbolic parameters to get this data set name.) Because you want to be able to use this load module after the job has finished, though, that isn't what you want. As a result, you need to override the SYSLMOD DD statement in the JCL for running the procedure.

If your program calls static subprograms, you also need to concatenate your subprogram libraries with the library allocated by the SYSLIB DD statement in the LKED step. (A *static subprogram* is one that's been compiled into an object module and is link edited with the program into a single load module.) You can't just override the SYSLIB statement in the procedure because it identifies the library that contains the system object modules that need to be linked with your COBOL program.

One last point to note is that the LKED step isn't run if 8 is less than the return code for the COBOL step. This means that if the COBOL compiler finds serious errors in the source program, the LKED step isn't run. In that case, you need to correct the errors and try the procedure again.

Here again, the JCL example after the procedure shows you how to run it. To start, the JCLLIB statement identifies the library that the IGYWCL procedure is stored in. Then, for the COBOL step, the SYSIN DD statement identifies the source program member in the source library and the SYSLIB DD statement identifies the copy library.

For the LKED step, the SYSLMOD DD statement identifies the load library that the load module should be stored in. Then, the SYSLIB DD statement concatenates a user object library to the object library that's identified by the procedure (it's SYS1.CEE.SCEELKED when you replace the symbolic parameter with the value set in the PROC statement). That way, the linkage editor can find the system object modules as well as the user object modules.

The IBM compile-and-link procedure for OS/390 COBOL

```
//IGYWCL PROC  LNGPRFX='SYS1.IGY',SYSLBLK=3200,
//             LIBPRFX='SYS1.CEE',
//             PGMLIB='&&GOSET',GOPGM=GO
//*  COMPILE AND LINK EDIT A COBOL PROGRAM
//*  CALLER MUST SUPPLY //COBOL.SYSIN DD ...
//*
//COBOL  EXEC PGM=IGYCRCTL,REGION=2048K
//STEPLIB  DD  DSNAME=&LNGPRFX..SIGYCOMP,
//             DISP=SHR
//SYSPRINT DD  SYSOUT=*
//SYSLIN   DD  DSNAME=&&LOADSET,UNIT=SYSDA,
//             DISP=(MOD,PASS),SPACE=(TRK,(3,3)),
//             DCB=(BLKSIZE=&SYSLBLK)
//SYSUT1   DD  UNIT=SYSDA,SPACE=(CYL,(1,1))
//SYSUT2   DD  UNIT=SYSDA,SPACE=(CYL,(1,1))
//SYSUT3   DD  UNIT=SYSDA,SPACE=(CYL,(1,1))
//SYSUT4   DD  UNIT=SYSDA,SPACE=(CYL,(1,1))
//SYSUT5   DD  UNIT=SYSDA,SPACE=(CYL,(1,1))
//SYSUT6   DD  UNIT=SYSDA,SPACE=(CYL,(1,1))
//SYSUT7   DD  UNIT=SYSDA,SPACE=(CYL,(1,1))
//LKED   EXEC PGM=HEWL,COND=(8,LT,COBOL),REGION=1024K
//SYSLIB   DD  DSNAME=&LIBPRFX..SCEELKED,
//             DISP=SHR
//SYSPRINT DD  SYSOUT=*
//SYSLIN   DD  DSNAME=&&LOADSET,DISP=(OLD,DELETE)
//         DD  DDNAME=SYSIN
//SYSLMOD  DD  DSNAME=&PGMLIB(&GOPGM),
//             SPACE=(TRK,(10,10,1)),
//             UNIT=SYSDA,DISP=(MOD,PASS)
//SYSUT1   DD  UNIT=SYSDA,SPACE=(TRK,(10,10))
```

The JCL to invoke this procedure

```
//MM01CL      JOB    (36512),'R MENENDEZ',NOTIFY=MM01
//JOBPROC     JCLLIB ORDER=SYS1.IGY.SIGYPROC
//STEP1       EXEC   PROC=IGYWCL,PARM.COBOL='APOST,OBJECT'
//COBOL.SYSIN DD     DSN=MM01.PAYROLL.SOURCE(PAY4000),DISP=SHR
//COBOL.SYSLIB DD    DSN=MM01.PAYROLL.COPYLIB,DISP=SHR
//*------------------------------------------------------------------*
//LKED.SYSLMOD DD    DSN=MM01.PAYROLL.LOADLIB(PAY4000),DISP=SHR
//LKED.SYSLIB DD
//          DD     DSN=MM01.PAYROLL.OBJLIB,DISP=SHR
```

Figure 17-8   How to use the compile-and-link procedure for OS/390 COBOL

The compile-link-and-go procedure for OS/390 COBOL

If you understand the first two procedures, the compile-link-and-go procedure in figure 17-9 should be easy for you because the COBOL and LKED steps are similar. As a result, you can focus on the GO step.

The GO step starts with an EXEC statement that executes a program identified by a backward reference to the SYSLMOD data set in the LKED step. But that's the load module that was created by the LKED step. This means that the GO step runs the load module for your source program.

Why is a backward reference needed? So this procedure works even if you override the SYSLMOD DD statement when you run the procedure. In fact, that's what the JCL example in this figure does. As a result, the backward reference actually identifies the load module named PAY4000 in the load library named MM01.PAYROLL.LOADLIB.

In the COND parameter for the EXEC statement, you can see that the program won't be run if 8 is less than the return code of the COBOL step, which means that the source program had serious errors. The program also won't be run if 4 is less than the return code for the LKED step, which usually means that the linkage editor couldn't link edit the user subprograms with the main program.

In the JCL for running this procedure, you can see that the DD statements for the COBOL and LKED steps are the same as they were for the last procedure. In the DD statements for the GO step, though, you need to allocate all of the data sets used by the program.

In this example, the DD statements allocate data sets for the PAYTRAN and PAYRPT ddnames that are defined by the program. The SYSOUT DD statement also allocates a SYSOUT data set, which will receive the output from any Display statements that are used in the program. In the GO step of the procedure, you can see a SYSUDUMP DD statement, which means that a storage dump will be printed if the program has an abnormal termination.

The IBM compile-link-and-go procedure for OS/390 COBOL

```
//IGYWCLG PROC LNGPRFX='SYS1.IGY',SYSLBLK=3200,
//              LIBPRFX='SYS1.CEE',GOPGM=GO
//*  COMPILE, LINK EDIT AND RUN A COBOL PROGRAM
//*  CALLER MUST SUPPLY //COBOL.SYSIN DD ...
//*
//COBOL  EXEC PGM=IGYCRCTL,REGION=2048K
//STEPLIB  DD  DSNAME=&LNGPRFX..SIGYCOMP,
//             DISP=SHR
//SYSPRINT DD  SYSOUT=*
//SYSLIN   DD  DSNAME=&&LOADSET,UNIT=SYSDA,
//             DISP=(MOD,PASS),SPACE=(TRK,(3,3)),
//             DCB=(BLKSIZE=&SYSLBLK)
//SYSUT1   DD  UNIT=SYSDA,SPACE=(CYL,(1,1))
//SYSUT2   DD  UNIT=SYSDA,SPACE=(CYL,(1,1))
//SYSUT3   DD  UNIT=SYSDA,SPACE=(CYL,(1,1))
//SYSUT4   DD  UNIT=SYSDA,SPACE=(CYL,(1,1))
//SYSUT5   DD  UNIT=SYSDA,SPACE=(CYL,(1,1))
//SYSUT6   DD  UNIT=SYSDA,SPACE=(CYL,(1,1))
//SYSUT7   DD  UNIT=SYSDA,SPACE=(CYL,(1,1))
//LKED   EXEC PGM=HEWL,COND=(8,LT,COBOL),REGION=1024K
//SYSLIB   DD  DSNAME=&LIBPRFX..SCEELKED,
//             DISP=SHR
//SYSPRINT DD  SYSOUT=*
//SYSLIN   DD  DSNAME=&&LOADSET,DISP=(OLD,DELETE)
//         DD  DDNAME=SYSIN
//SYSLMOD  DD  DSNAME=&&GOSET(&GOPGM),SPACE=(TRK,(10,10,1)),
//             UNIT=SYSDA,DISP=(MOD,PASS)
//SYSUT1   DD  UNIT=SYSDA,SPACE=(TRK,(10,10))
//GO     EXEC PGM=*.LKED.SYSLMOD,COND=((8,LT,COBOL),(4,LT,LKED)),
//             REGION=2048K
//STEPLIB  DD  DSNAME=&LIBPRFX..SCEERUN,
//             DISP=SHR
//SYSPRINT DD  SYSOUT=*
//CEEDUMP  DD  SYSOUT=*
//SYSUDUMP DD  SYSOUT=*
```

The JCL to invoke this procedure

```
//MM01CL        JOB     (36512),'R MENENDEZ',NOTIFY=MM01
//JOBPROC       JCLLIB  ORDER=SYS1.IGY.SIGYPROC
//STEP1         EXEC    PROC=IGYWCLG,PARM.COBOL='APOST,OBJECT'
//COBOL.SYSIN  DD      DSN=MM01.PAYROLL.SOURCE(PAY4000),DISP=SHR
//COBOL.SYSLIB DD      DSN=MM01.PAYROLL.COPYLIB,DISP=SHR
//*-------------------------------------------------------------------*
//LKED.SYSLMOD DD      DSN=MM01.PAYROLL.LOADLIB(PAY4000),DISP=SHR
//LKED.SYSLIB  DD
//             DD      DSN=MM01.PAYROLL.OBJLIB,DISP=SHR
//*-------------------------------------------------------------------*
//GO.SYSOUT    DD      SYSOUT=A
//GO.PAYTRAN   DD      DSN=MM01.PAYROLL.TRANS,DISP=SHR
//GO.PAYRPT    DD      SYSOUT=A
```

Figure 17-9   How to use the compile-link-and-go procedure for OS/390 COBOL

The translate-compile-and-link procedure for CICS/COBOL

If you're a CICS/COBOL programmer, you may be interested in the procedure in figure 17-10. It's the translate-compile-and-link procedure for developing CICS load modules. As you can see, this procedure is named DFHYITVL, and it consists of three steps: TRN for the CICS translation, COB for the COBOL compilation, and LKED for the link-editing step. Note, however, that some of the lines have been omitted in this figure as indicated by two vertical dots so the procedure would fit on one page.

The JCL example after this procedure shows how you can use it. In the EXEC statement that invokes this procedure, you need to code a PROGLIB parameter that specifies the load library in which the load module that's created by the link-edit step will be stored. This overrides the value given by the PROC statement in the procedure, which is substituted for a symbolic parameter in the LKED step (not shown in this figure).

If you want to code a PARM parameter that sets options for the TRN and COB steps, you need to make sure that you don't override the options that are set by the procedure. In this case, the COBOL3 option is set in the TRN step and eight options are set in the COB step. As a result, you need to include these options in your PARM parameter if you want to set other options.

For the TRN step of your JCL, you need to code a SYSIN DD statement that identifies the source program. And for the COB step, if your program uses copy members, you need to code a SYSLIB DD statement that identifies the libraries that contain the copy members used by the program. In this case, though, you can't just override the SYSLIB statement in the procedure because its concatenated libraries contain members required by CICS. Instead, you have to code a DD statement with no parameters as a placeholder for the first library in the procedure. Then, you code a second DD statement to concatenate the copy library that you need, overriding the second library in the procedure (if you substitute the symbolic variable values, you'll find that the first and second DD statements in the procedure identify the same library, so it's safe to override the second one).

If your program uses static subprograms, you also need to concatenate any subprogram libraries that your program needs with the ones that are allocated in the procedure. You can do that by coding a SYSLIB DD statement for the LKED step as shown in the JCL example. Here, two DD statements with no parameters are required because the procedure allocates two object libraries, and you shouldn't override either one. In most cases, though, you can omit the LKED.SYSLIB statements because most CICS programs don't use static subprograms.

Finally, in the LKED step, you need to code a SYSIN DD statement that gives a name to the load module that is going to be stored in the load library that you identified with the PROGLIB parameter of the EXEC statement. The SYSIN data set is used to provide additional information to the linkage editor. In this example, it tells the linkage editor that the load module should be named

The IBM translate-compile-and-link procedure for CICS/COBOL

```
//DFHYITVL PROC SUFFIX=1$,              Suffix for translator module
//         INDEX='CICSTS13.CICS', Qualifier(s) for CICS libraries
//         PROGLIB='CICSTS13.CICS.SDFHLOAD', Name of o/p library
//         DSCTLIB='CICSTS13.CICS.SDFHCOB',  Private macro/dsect
//         AD370HLQ='SYS1',           Qualifier(s) for AD/Cycle compiler
//         LE370HLQ='SYS1',           Qualifier(s) for LE/370 libraries
//         OUTC=A,                    Class for print output
//         REG=4M,                    Region size for all steps
//         LNKPARM='LIST,XREF',       Link edit parameters
//         STUB='DFHEILID',           Lked INC. fr DFHELII
//         LIB='SDFHC370',            Library
//         WORK=SYSDA                 Unit for work datasets
//TRN      EXEC PGM=DFHECP&SUFFIX,PARM='COBOL3',REGION=&REG
//STEPLIB  DD DSN=&INDEX..SDFHLOAD,DISP=SHR
//SYSPRINT DD SYSOUT=&OUTC
//SYSPUNCH DD DSN=&&SYSCIN,DISP=(,PASS),
//            UNIT=&WORK,DCB=BLKSIZE=400,
//            SPACE=(400,(400,100))
//COB      EXEC PGM=IGYCRCTL,REGION=&REG,
//         PARM='NODYNAM,LIB,OBJECT,RENT,RES,APOST,MAP,XREF'
//STEPLIB  DD DSN=&AD370HLQ..SIGYCOMP,DISP=SHR
//SYSLIB   DD DSN=&DSCTLIB,DISP=SHR
//         DD DSN=&INDEX..SDFHCOB,DISP=SHR
//         DD DSN=&INDEX..SDFHMAC,DISP=SHR
//         DD DSN=&INDEX..SDFHSAMP,DISP=SHR
//SYSPRINT DD SYSOUT=&OUTC
//SYSIN    DD DSN=&&SYSCIN,DISP=(OLD,DELETE)
//SYSLIN   DD DSN=&&LOADSET,DISP=(MOD,PASS),
//            UNIT=&WORK,SPACE=(80,(250,100))
  .
  .
  .
//LKED     EXEC PGM=IEWL,REGION=&REG,
//            PARM='&LNKPARM',COND=(5,LT,COB)
//SYSLIB   DD DSN=&INDEX..SDFHLOAD,DISP=SHR
//         DD DSN=&LE370HLQ..SCEELKED,DISP=SHR
  .
  .
  .
//SYSLIN   DD DSN=&&COPYLINK,DISP=(OLD,DELETE)
//         DD DSN=&&LOADSET,DISP=(OLD,DELETE)
//         DD DDNAME=SYSIN
```

The JCL to invoke this procedure

```
//MM01CMPL    JOB  (36512),'R.MENENDEZ',NOTIFY=MM01
//CICSCMP     EXEC DFHYITVL,
//            PROGLIB='MM01.CICS.LOADLIB'
//TRN.SYSIN   DD   DSN=MM01.CICS.SOURCE(CUSTMNT1),DISP=SHR
//COB.SYSLIB  DD
//            DD   DSN=MM01.CICS.COPYLIB,DISP=SHR
//LKED.SYSLIB DD
//            DD
//            DD   DSN=MM01.CICS.OBJLIB.DISP=SHR
//LKED.SYSIN  DD   *
   NAME CUSTMNT1(R)
/*
```

Figure 17-10   How to use the translate-compile-and-link procedure for CICS/COBOL

CUSTMNT1. The R in parentheses after the module name tells the linkage editor to replace the module if it already exists.

In practice, most shops have JCL jobs that you can use for running the translate-compile-and-link procedure. Then, you just substitute the names for the load library, the source program, the copy library, the subprogram library, and the load module whenever you run the procedure.

The procedure for assembling a BMS mapset

If you're a CICS/COBOL programmer and you create your own mapsets, you may be interested in the procedure in figure 17-11. It creates a physical map and a symbolic map from a BMS mapset that is written in assembler language. Here again, most shops will have the JCL that you need for running this procedure already set up. As a result, you just have to replace the names in the EXEC and DD statements with names that are appropriate for the mapset you want to assemble.

If you look at the procedure, you can see that it is named DFHMAPS and it consists of four job steps. The COPY step runs the IEBGENER utility that's presented in chapter 18 to create a temporary data set from the source code for the mapset. In this step, you can see a comment that says you need to provide a SYSUT1 DD statement to identify the source code for the mapset.

The temporary data set then becomes input to the ASMMAP step that runs the assembler to create an object module for the physical map. It is followed by a LINKMAP step that runs the linkage editor to create the load module for the physical map. Last, the ASMDSECT step also uses the temporary data set created by the COPY step to create the symbolic map, or DSECT.

In the PROC statement for this procedure, you can see that the MAPLIB parameter gives the name of a library for the physical map, and the DSCTLIB parameter gives the name of a library for the DSECT. So if you want to store the maps in other libraries, you need to code these parameters in the EXEC statement for running the procedure. Similarly, the MAPNAME parameter in the PROC statement doesn't give a value. Its comment says that you must supply the mapset name in this parameter when you run the procedure.

The JCL example after the procedure shows you how to run it. In the EXEC statement for invoking the procedure, you code the MAPLIB parameter to identify the library for the physical map, the DSCTLIB parameter to identify the library for the symbolic map, and the MAPNAME parameter to supply the name that's used for those maps. Then, you code a SYSUT1 DD statement for the COPY step to identify the source member for the mapset. As you can see, the name of the source member and the name given in the MAPNAME parameter should be the same.

An OS/390 procedure for preparing a BMS mapset

```
//DFHMAPS PROC INDEX='CICSTS13.CICS', FOR SDFHMAC
//              MAPLIB='CICSTS13.CICS.SDFHLOAD', TARGET FOR MAP
//              DSCTLIB='CICSTS13.CICS.SDFHMAC', TARGET FOR DSECT
//              MAPNAME=,                      NAME OF MAPSET - REQUIRED
//              A=,                            A=A FOR ALIGNED MAP
//              RMODE=24,                      24/ANY
//              ASMBLR=ASMA90,                 ASSEMBLER PROGRAM NAME
//              REG=2048K,                     REGION FOR ASSEMBLY
//              OUTC=A,                        PRINT SYSOUT CLASS
//              WORK=SYSDA                     WORK FILE UNIT
//COPY     EXEC PGM=IEBGENER
//SYSPRINT DD SYSOUT=&OUTC
//SYSUT2   DD DSN=&&TEMPM,UNIT=&WORK,DISP=(,PASS),
//            DCB=(RECFM=FB,LRECL=80,BLKSIZE=400),
//            SPACE=(400,(50,50))
//SYSIN    DD DUMMY
//* SYSUT1 DD * NEEDED FOR THE MAP SOURCE
//ASMMAP   EXEC PGM=&ASMBLR,REGION=&REG,
//* NOLOAD CHANGED TO NOOBJECT
//   PARM='SYSPARM(&A.MAP),DECK,NOOBJECT'
//SYSPRINT DD SYSOUT=&OUTC
//SYSLIB   DD DSN=&INDEX..SDFHMAC,DISP=SHR
//         DD DSN=SYS1.MACLIB,DISP=SHR
//SYSUT1   DD UNIT=&WORK,SPACE=(CYL,(5,5))
//SYSUT2   DD UNIT=&WORK,SPACE=(CYL,(5,5))
//SYSUT3   DD UNIT=&WORK,SPACE=(CYL,(5,5))
//SYSPUNCH DD DSN=&&MAP,DISP=(,PASS),UNIT=&WORK,
//            DCB=(RECFM=FB,LRECL=80,BLKSIZE=400),
//            SPACE=(400,(50,50))
//SYSIN    DD DSN=&&TEMPM,DISP=(OLD,PASS)
//LINKMAP  EXEC PGM=IEWL,PARM='LIST,LET,XREF,RMODE(&RMODE)'
//SYSPRINT DD SYSOUT=&OUTC
//SYSLMOD  DD DSN=&MAPLIB(&MAPNAME),DISP=SHR
//SYSUT1   DD UNIT=&WORK,SPACE=(1024,(20,20))
//SYSLIN   DD DSN=&&MAP,DISP=(OLD,DELETE)
//* NOLOAD CHANGED TO NOOBJECT
//ASMDSECT EXEC PGM=&ASMBLR,REGION=&REG,
//   PARM='SYSPARM(&A.DSECT),DECK,NOOBJECT'
//SYSPRINT DD SYSOUT=&OUTC
//SYSLIB   DD DSN=&INDEX..SDFHMAC,DISP=SHR
//         DD DSN=SYS1.MACLIB,DISP=SHR
//SYSUT1   DD UNIT=&WORK,SPACE=(CYL,(5,5))
//SYSUT2   DD UNIT=&WORK,SPACE=(CYL,(5,5))
//SYSUT3   DD UNIT=&WORK,SPACE=(CYL,(5,5))
//SYSPUNCH DD DSN=&DSCTLIB(&MAPNAME),DISP=OLD
//SYSIN    DD DSN=&&TEMPM,DISP=(OLD,DELETE)
```

The JCL to invoke this procedure

```
//MM01MAPS JOB  (36512),'R.MENENDEZ',NOTIFY=MM01
//MAPASM   EXEC DFHMAPS,
//              MAPLIB='MM01.CICS.LOADLIB',    TARGET LOADLIB FOR MAP
//              DSCTLIB='MM01.CICS.COPYLIB',   TARGET COPYLIB FOR DSECT
//              MAPNAME=ORDSET1                NAME OF MAPSET (REQUIRED)
//COPY.SYSUT1 DD DSN=MM01.CICS.SOURCE(ORDSET1),DISP=SHR   MAPSET SOURCE
/*
```

Figure 17-11   How to use the procedure for assembling a BMS mapset

Perspective

If this chapter has succeeded, you should now be able to use the IBM procedures for compiling and testing COBOL and CICS/COBOL programs. However, you should also be able to apply the skills that you've learned to any procedure for any language. To do that, you need to use the appropriate IBM manuals to find out what the step names, data set requirements, and options are. You may also want to print the code for the procedure that you're going to use. Once you've done that, though, the principles are the same.

After you set up the JCL for running a procedure, you can use it whenever you need to run the procedure again. Each time you use it, you just substitute the library and member names that the procedure requires. The trick, of course, is setting up the JCL the first time, which you should now be able to do.

Terms

compiler	assembler
source program	assemble
object module	compile-link-and-go procedure
object library	loader
copy member	compile-load-and-go procedure
copy library	compile-and-go procedure
compiler listing	CICS translator
source statement library	compile-only procedure
linkage editor	compile-and-link procedure
link editor	static subprogram
load module	

18

How to use the OS/390 utility programs

Utility programs are programs that can be used for common data processing functions. For example, a copy utility can be used to copy a data set, and a print utility can be used to print the contents of a data set. In this chapter, you'll learn how to use some of the utilities that are known collectively as the *MVS utilities*. This is an older set of utilities that is provided by OS/390, and this chapter presents only the ones that are still useful.

If you've read chapter 16, you are already familiar with the VSAM utility known as IDCAMS or AMS. This is a newer utility that provides some of the same functions that the MVS utilities provide. In this chapter, the REPRO and PRINT commands of this utility are presented so you can compare them with the MVS utilities for the same functions, even though these commands are also presented in chapter 16.

Introduction to OS/390 utilities

Utility programs (or just *utilities*) are programs that can be used for common data processing functions like copying or printing a data set. With OS/390, you get an older set of utilities known as the *MVS utilities*. You get the VSAM utility called AMS that is presented in chapter 16. You get a sort/merge program that's presented in chapter 19. And you get some utilities that can be used with the hierarchical file system that's presented in chapter 21.

A summary of the MVS utilities

In this chapter, you'll learn how to use the seven MVS utilities that are still in common use. These are summarized in figure 18-1. Because they were developed before VSAM, these utilities can only be used with non-VSAM data sets. The other MVS utilities aren't presented in this book because they are no longer needed or because there's a better way to get the functions done.

This figure also summarizes the AMS commands, TSO commands, and ISPF options that you can use to do some of the same functions that the MVS utilities do. Here, you can see that the AMS commands work with both non-VSAM and VSAM files. As you will see, though, the MVS utilities provide functions and processing options that aren't available with the other commands and panels. That's one reason why some MVS utilities are still in use.

Although using ISPF is usually the easiest way to do a utility function, there are times when you want to do a function as part of a batch job. In a testing environment, for example, you may want to repeatedly run a program and then print the contents of one of the output data sets. That's another reason why the MVS utilities are still in use.

The DD statement requirements

When you code the JCL for running a utility you need to know what ddnames you need to provide DD statements for, and you need to know what each of these data sets represents. In figure 18-1, you can see some of the ddnames that are commonly used with the MVS utilities. SYSUT1, for example, commonly represents the primary input file, SYSUT2 represents the primary output file, and SYSPRINT represents either the output messages or printed output that the utility produces.

If you code *control statements* to direct the processing done by a utility, you also need to provide a SYSIN data set. This is normally an instream data set, so you code the control statements right after the SYSIN DD statement. You'll see this illustrated throughout this chapter.

The MVS utilities that are presented in this chapter

Name	Function
IEBGENER	Copies or prints sequential data sets.
IEHMOVE	Copies or moves sequential data sets.
IEBPTPCH	Prints or punches the contents of sequential data sets.
IEBCOPY	Copies, merges, compresses, backs up, or restores partitioned data sets.
IEHLIST	Lists system information for PDS directories or VTOC entries.
IEBCOMPR	Compares the contents of sequential data sets.
IEBDBG	Generates test data.

AMS commands that do similar functions

Name	Function
REPRO	Copies or moves VSAM or non-VSAM data sets.
PRINT	Prints the contents of VSAM or non-VSAM data sets.

TSO commands and ISPF options that do similar functions

Name	ISPF option	Function
COPY	3.3 (Move/Copy utility)	Copies a data set or member.
LIST	1 (Browse)	Displays the contents of a data set or member.
PRINTDS	3.6 (Hardcopy utility)	Prints the contents of a data set or member.
LISTCAT	3.4 (DSLIST utility)	Lists catalog entries.
LISTDS	3.2 or 3.4 (Data set or DSLIST utility)	Lists data set information.

DD statements typically required by an MVS utility

ddname	Use
SYSPRINT	Output messages or printed output.
SYSUT1	The input file.
SYSUT2	The output file.
SYSIN	The control statement file.

Description

- A *utility program* (or just *utility*) is a program that can be used for common data processing functions.

- The *MVS utilities* are older utilities that are provided by OS/390. Some of these utilities have been replaced by newer utilities or ISPF options.

- The JCL for running a utility program has to provide a DD statement for each ddname that's used by the utility.

- The SYSIN data set is normally an instream data set that consists of *control statements* that provide processing specifications.

Figure 18-1   The MVS utilities and the common DD statement requirements

Utilities that copy and move data sets

If you refer back to figure 18-1, you can see that there are three utilities that you can use for copying and moving data sets. Two of these are MVS utilities, and one is the AMS utility. Because the REPRO command of the AMS utility is the most versatile, you'll use that the most for copying data sets. There are times, though, when you'll want to use one of the MVS utilities instead.

The IEBGENER utility

The IEBGENER utility provides an easy way to copy a non-VSAM sequential data set. This utility is summarized in figure 18-2. Here, you can see that this utility uses the common ddnames for its input and output files.

In the examples in part 1 of this figure, you can see that the SYSIN data set isn't used to provide control statements. The SYSIN DD statement is still required, though, so it's coded as a DUMMY data set. Without control statements, this utility copies all of the records in the input data set to the output data set without any modifications.

In the first example, the IEBGENER utility is used to make a backup copy of the customer master file. You'll notice that the SYSUT2 DD statement is missing the DCB information for the output data set. When subparameters such as LRECL, RECFM and BLKSIZE are omitted, IEGENER copies this information from the input file. However, you still need to specify the SPACE parameter for the new data set.

Since a SYSOUT data set is a non-VSAM sequential data set, you can also use this utility without control statements to do a quick printout of the records in a data set. To do that, you just copy the input data set to a SYSOUT data set as shown in the second example. The limitation of this technique is that the output isn't formatted in any way. Instead, one output line is printed for each input record without any regard for page overflow or data formats. That means that (1) the lines print right over page separations, (2) numeric data formats like packed-decimal and binary aren't printed in an intelligible form, and (3) any characters in a record that don't fit on a single 132-character line are truncated. Nevertheless, printing a data set with this utility is occasionally useful for testing.

The DD statements required by the IEBGENER utility

ddname	Use
SYSPRINT	An output message file.
SYSUT1	The input file.
SYSUT2	The output file.
SYSIN	The control statement file.

A job step that uses IEBGENER to copy a sequential file

```
//COPY      EXEC  PGM=IEBGENER
//SYSPRINT  DD    SYSOUT=*
//SYSUT1    DD    DSNAME=MM01.CUSTMAST,DISP=SHR
//SYSUT2    DD    DSNAME=MM01.CUSTMAST.BACKUP,DISP=(NEW,CATLG),
//                UNIT=SYSDA,SPACE=(CYL,(1,1))
//SYSIN     DD    DUMMY
```

A job step that uses IEBGENER to print a sequential file

```
//PRINT     EXEC  PGM=IEBGENER
//SYSPRINT  DD    SYSOUT=*
//SYSUT1    DD    DSNAME=MM01.CUSTMAST,DISP=SHR
//SYSUT2    DD    SYSOUT=*
//SYSIN     DD    DUMMY
```

Description

- The IEBGENER utility can be used to copy non-VSAM sequential data sets to or from tape or DASD. As a result, this utility can be used to back up and restore sequential data sets.

- You can also use this utility to print a non-VSAM sequential data set by copying it to a SYSOUT data set. Although the printed output isn't formatted, this is a quick way to list the contents of the records in a data set.

- You can use the SYSIN data set to provide control statements that can rearrange fields and convert their data formats as shown in part 2 of this figure.

- If you don't use control statements, the SYSIN DD statement is still required so you must code it as a DUMMY data set.

Figure 18-2   How to use the IEBGENER utility to copy a data set (part 1 of 2)

If you want to rearrange or convert data formats as you copy a data set, you can use the GENERATE and RECORD control statements that are summarized in part 2 of figure 18-2. In this case, the GENERATE statement summarizes the specifications that you provide in the RECORD statement, and the RECORD statement provides specifications for the fields of the output records.

This is illustrated by the example in this figure. Here, the first field specification says that the field in bytes 1-5 of each input record should be written in bytes 1-5 of the output record without conversion. Then, the second field specification says that the field in bytes 21-40 of each input record should be written in bytes 6-25 of the output record, again without conversion.

The third field specification in this example says that the field in bytes 61-69 of each input record should be written to the output record starting with byte 26, and the data should be converted to packed-decimal format. That means, however, that a nine-byte zoned-decimal field gets converted to a five-byte packed-decimal field, so the output field gets saved in bytes 26-30 of each output record. Similarly, the fourth field specification converts a nine-byte input field to a five-byte packed-decimal field. And the last field specification says that the literal value TEST should be stored in the four bytes starting with byte 36 of each output record.

After you code the RECORD statement, you can code the GENERATE statement. As you can see in the example, it uses 5 as the MAXFLDS parameter because there are five field specifications in the RECORD statement. And it uses 4 in the MAXLITS parameter because there are four characters in the one literal that is used in the RECORD statement. Note, however, that if you use more than one literal, you code the sum of the characters used in the literals in the MAXLITS parameter.

This example also illustrates some basic coding rules for control statements. First, you start each statement in column 2 or later. Second, you separate parameters and subparameters with commas and no intervening spaces just as you do in JCL statements. Third, to continue a statement on another line, you code a non-blank character in column 72 of the first line and you start the next line in column 16. This applies to all of the MVS utilities.

The syntax of the GENERATE control statement

```
GENERATE   MAXFLDS=n,
         [ ,MAXLITS=n ]
```

Explanation

MAXFLDS   The number of field parameters in RECORD statements.

MAXLITS   The number of bytes of literal data included in the field parameters in RECORD statements.

The syntax of the RECORD control statement

```
RECORD   FIELD=(length,in-loc|'literal',conv,out-loc])
       [ ,FIELD=(length,in-loc|'literal',conv,out-loc) ]...
```

Explanation

length   The length of the field in the input record.

in-loc   The starting position of the field in the input record. The default is 1.

literal   Used instead of in-loc to supply a literal value to the output field.

conv   The conversion operation to be performed on the field. Specify XE to convert to hexadecimal, PZ to convert from packed-decimal to zoned-decimal, and ZP to convert from zoned-decimal to packed-decimal. If omitted, no conversion is done.

out-loc   The starting position of the field in the output record. The default is 1.

A job step that uses IEBGENER to copy a sequential file with reformatting

```
//COPY       EXEC  PGM=IEBGENER
//SYSPRINT  DD     SYSOUT=*
//SYSUT1    DD     DSNAME=MM01.CUSTMAST,DISP=SHR
//SYSUT2    DD     DSNAME=MM01.CUSTMAST.TEST,DISP=(NEW,CATLG),
//                 UNIT=SYSDA,SPACE=(CYL,(1,1)),
//                 DCB=(RECFM=FB,LRECL=40,BLKSIZE=800)
//SYSIN     DD     *
 GENERATE MAXFLDS=5,MAXLITS=4
 RECORD FIELD=(5,1,,1),FIELD=(20,21,,6),FIELD=(9,61,ZP,26),          X
              FIELD=(9,70,ZP,31),FIELD=(4,'TEST',,36)
/*
```

Coding rules for control statements when you're using the MVS utilities

• Start the statement anywhere after column 1.

• Separate parameters and subparameters with commas and no intervening spaces.

• To continue a statement, enter a non-blank character like X in column 72 and start the next line in column 16.

Description

• You can use the GENERATE and RECORD statements to rearrange input fields and convert data formats before each record is copied to the output file.

• If you increase or decrease the size of the output record, you should code the DCB parameter in the DD statement for the output file with the new length in the LRECL subparameter.

Figure 18-2   How to use the IEBGENER utility to copy a data set (part 2 of 2)

The REPRO command of the AMS utility

If you've read chapter 16, you're already familiar with the REPRO command of the AMS utility (IDCAMS) and the three types of VSAM data sets. You can use this command with both VSAM and non-VSAM data sets, and the input files can have different organizations. That's why you'll use this utility for most of your copying operations.

So you don't have to refer back to chapter 16, figure 18-3 repeats the information that's presented there. As you can see, the parameters of this command are divided into five groups.

To start, you use one of the parameters in the first group to identify the input data set and one of the parameters in the second group to identify the output data set. Then, if you don't want to copy all of the records in the input data set, you can use the parameters in the third and fourth groups to identify the records to be copied. In the example in this figure, the first 1000 records of the input data set are copied to an output data set using the INFILE and OUTFILE parameters.

You can also use the INDATASET and OUTDATASET parameters to refer to data sets directly. When you use these parameters, you must remember that the output data set must already exist. Then, if the output data set is empty, the AMS utility copies the input data set into the output data set. However, if the output data set is a VSAM data set that contains records, the AMS utility merges the input records with the output records. For a non-VSAM sequential data set or an ESDS, the input records are added at the end of the output data set. For a KSDS or RRDS, the records are added in their correct positions based on their key values or relative record numbers.

With that in mind, you can understand how the parameters in the last group work. If you code REUSE for a reusable VSAM data set, the input records overwrite the records that were in the output data set. If you code NOREUSE, the input records are merged with the existing records in the reusable data set.

Regardless of whether or not the data set is reusable, when the records are merged, the REPLACE and NOREPLACE parameters take effect. If you code REPLACE, records with duplicate keys or relative record numbers replace the corresponding records in the output data set. If you code NOREPLACE, the duplicate records in the output data set are retained and the duplicate input records are discarded.

If you aren't familiar with the AMS utility, the example in this figure shows you how to copy a data set. In the EXEC statement, you can see that the name of this utility is IDCAMS. Then, the SYSPRINT DD statement defines the data set for messages, and the SYSIN data set provides for an instream data set that contains the REPRO command. The REPRO command itself says that the first 1000 records of a data set identified in the INDD DD statement should be copied to the data set identified in the OUTDD DD statement.

The syntax of the REPRO command

```
REPRO { INDATASET(entry-name) }
      { INFILE(ddname)         }

      { OUTDATASET(entry-name) }
      { OUTFILE(ddname)        }

      [ SKIP(count) | FROMKEY(key) | FROMNUMBER(number) | FROMADDRESS(address) ]

      [ COUNT(count) | TOKEY(key) | TONUMBER(number) | TOADDRESS(address) ]

      [ REUSE | NOREUSE ]
      [ REPLACE | NOREPLACE ]
```

Explanation

INDATASET	Specifies the name of the data set to be copied.
INFILE	Specifies the name of a DD statement that identifies the input data set.
OUTDATASET	Specifies the name of the output data set.
OUTFILE	Specifies the name of a DD statement that identifies the output data set.
SKIP	Specifies the number of records to be skipped before copying begins.
FROM...	Specifies the key (KSDS), number (RRDS), or relative byte address (ESDS) of the first record to be copied.
COUNT	Specifies the number of records to be copied.
TO...	Specifies the key (KSDS), number (RRDS), or relative byte address (ESDS) of the last record to be copied.
REUSE | NOREUSE	Specifies whether or not a reusable output file should be reset. If not, the new records are merged with the existing ones in the file.
REPLACE | NOREPLACE	Specifies whether or not duplicate records should be replaced.

A job step that copies the first 1000 records in a data set

```
//          EXEC PGM=IDCAMS
//SYSPRINT DD   SYSOUT=*
//INDD     DD   DSNAME=MM01.CUSTMAST,DISP=SHR
//OUTDD    DD   DSNAME=MM01.CUSTMAST.TEST,DISP=(NEW,CATLG),
//              UNIT=SYSDA,SPACE=(CYL,(1,1)),
//              DCB=(RECFM=FB,LRECL=40,BLKSIZE=800)
//SYSIN    DD   *
 REPRO INFILE(INDD)      -
       OUTFILE(OUTDD)    -
       COUNT(1000)
/*
```

Description

- You can use the REPRO command of the AMS utility to copy non-VSAM or VSAM data sets with any file organization, and the input and output files can have different organizations.

- To continue an AMS command on the next line, end the current line with one or more spaces followed by a hyphen, then continue coding on the next line.

Figure 18-3   How to use the REPRO command of the AMS utility to copy a data set

The IEHMOVE utility

The IEHMOVE utility has one advantage over the IEBGENER and AMS utilities when it comes to copying data sets. That is, you don't have to specify the space requirements for the output data set. Instead, IEHMOVE automatically determines the space allocation for the output data set based on the allocation for the input data set.

Figure 18-4 shows how to use this utility. As you can see, it can be used to copy or move a data set, depending on whether you use the COPY or MOVE control statement. When you use the MOVE control statement to specify that a move operation be done, the input data set is deleted after it has been copied.

In the example for this utility, you can see that it has some unusual DD statement requirements. First, you use the SYSUT1 DD statement to identify a volume that can be used for the small work file that this utility requires. Second, you may need to code another DD statement that identifies the system residence device. This is an antiquated requirement that can be filled by coding a SYSRES DD statement like the one in the example. It uses the VOL=REF statement to point to a file that is always on the system residence device (the supervisor call library). Note, however, that the ddname you use for this statement doesn't matter.

Beyond that, you need to code one DD statement for the input file and one DD statement for the output file. You can use any ddnames you like for these statements, and you only code the UNIT, VOL, and DISP parameters in them. In other words, these DD statements don't give the names for the input and output data sets; they just identify the volumes that they're on. The file names are derived from the COPY or MOVE statement.

As unusual as the DD statements are, you should be able to use this utility for copying or moving sequential files without much trouble. Then, if you want to use this statement for copying or moving members of a partitioned data set, you can code the SELECT and EXCLUDE statements as shown in part 2 of this figure.

The syntax of the COPY and MOVE control statements

```
COPY | MOVE  { DSNAME=data-set-name }
             { PDS=library-name     }
             { DSGROUP=name         }
             { VOLUME=unit=serial   }
             [ ,FROM=unit=serial ]
               ,TO=unit=serial
             [ ,UNCATLG ]
             [ ,RENAME=new-name ]
             [ ,EXPAND=number ]
```

Explanation

DSNAME	Specifies the input data set name for a sequential data set.
PDS	Specifies the input data set name for a partitioned data set (either a PDS or a PDSE).
DSGROUP	Specifies one or more data set name qualifiers that are used to identify a data set group. All data sets on the volume that have those qualifiers are copied or moved.
VOLUME	Species the device type and the volume serial number of a volume.
FROM	Specifies the input volume if the data set isn't cataloged.
TO	Specifies the output volume.
UNCATLG	Uncatalogs the input file.
RENAME	Specifies the name of the output file if different from the input file.
EXPAND	Specifies a number of additional directory blocks to be inserted into the directory of a partitioned data set.

DD statement requirements

ddname	Use
SYSPRINT	An output message file.
SYSUT1	Identifies a volume for a temporary work file of about 50 tracks of space.
Any	Identifies the volume serial number of the system residence device. Not always required, but it can be coded as shown in the example just to be safe.
Any	One DD statement with UNIT, VOL, and DISP information for each volume processed by the utility. The file names are supplied by the COPY or MOVE control statement.
SYSIN	The control statement file.

A job step that copies and renames a sequential file

```
//COPYSEQ  EXEC PGM=IEHMOVE
//SYSPRINT DD   SYSOUT=*
//SYSUT1   DD   UNIT=SYSDA,VOL=SER=WORK01,DISP=OLD
//SYSRES   DD   UNIT=SYSDA,VOL=REF=SYS1.SVCLIB,DISP=OLD
//DDUT1    DD   UNIT=SYSDA,VOL=SER=TSO001,DISP=OLD
//DDUT2    DD   UNIT=SYSDA,VOL=SER=TSO002,DISP=OLD
//SYSIN    DD   *
 COPY DSNAME=MM01.CUSTMAST,FROM=SYSDA=TSO001,TO=SYSDA=TSO002,       X
            RENAME=MM01.CUSTOMER.MASTER
/*
```

Description

- The IEHMOVE utility can be used to move or copy a non-VSAM data set to or from tape or DASD, without allocating space for the output file (a move deletes the original file).

Figure 18-4   How to use the IEHMOVE utility to copy or move a data set (part 1 of 2)

As part 2 of this figure shows, the SELECT and EXCLUDE statements are used to include or exclude members of a partitioned data set when the PDS is copied or moved. Everything else works the way it does when you copy or move a sequential data set. In the example in this figure, a partitioned data set is moved and renamed, but four of the members in the original data set are not included in the new data set.

The syntax of the SELECT and EXCLUDE control statements

```
SELECT MEMBER=(name[,name...])

EXCLUDE MEMBER=(name)
```

Explanation

MEMBER   Specifies the name of a member to be included or excluded. Although you can
          code only one member in an EXCLUDE statement, you can code as many
          EXCLUDE statements as you need.

A job step that moves and renames a partitioned data set with some exclusions

```
//MOVEPDS   EXEC PGM=IEHMOVE
//SYSPRINT DD   SYSOUT=*
//SYSUT1    DD   UNIT=SYSDA,VOL=SER=WORK01,DISP=OLD
//SYSRES    DD   UNIT=SYSDA,VOL=REF=SYS1.SVCLIB,DISP=OLD
//DDUT1     DD   UNIT=SYSDA,VOL=SER=TSO001,DISP=OLD
//DDUT2     DD   UNIT=SYSDA,VOL=SER=TSO001,DISP=OLD
//SYSIN     DD   *
 MOVE PDS=MM01.COPYLIB.COB,FROM=SYSDA=TSO001,TO=SYSDA=TSO001,        X
              RENAME=MM01.COPYINV.COB
 EXCLUDE MEMBER=PRODMSTR
 EXCLUDE MEMBER=PROMSTR
 EXCLUDE MEMBER=BFREC
 EXCLUDE MEMBER=TRREC
/*
```

Description

- You can use SELECT or EXCLUDE control statements after the MOVE or COPY
  statement to indicate which members of a partitioned data set you want to include or
  exclude from the operation.

- You can't use both SELECT and EXCLUDE statements in the same operation.

Figure 18-4   How to use the IEHMOVE utility to copy or move a data set (part 2 of 2)

Utilities that print data sets

If you refer back to figure 18-1, you can see that there are three utilities that you can use for printing data sets. Two of these are MVS utilities, and one is the AMS utility. Because the PRINT command of the AMS utility is the most versatile, you'll use it the most. There are times, though, when you'll want to use one of the MVS utilities.

The IEBGENER utility

In figure 18-2, you've already seen how you can use the IEBGENER utility to print a listing of a sequential data set. This prints the first 132 characters of each record on one line of the SYSOUT data set with no formatting. Occasionally, that's all you need, but otherwise you can use one of the next two utilities.

The PRINT command of the AMS utility

If you've read chapter 16, you're already familiar with the PRINT command of the AMS utility and the three types of VSAM data sets. You can use this command with both VSAM and non-VSAM data sets, and the input files can have different organizations. That's why you'll use this utility for most of your printing operations.

So you don't have to refer back to chapter 16, figure 18 5 repeats the information that's presented in that chapter. As you can see, the PRINT parameters are separated into four groups. You use one of the parameters in the first group to identify the data set to be printed. You can use the parameters in the second group to control how the output is printed. Then, if you don't want to print all of the records, you can use the parameters in the third and fourth groups to identify the records to be printed.

If you look at the examples in this figure, you can see how this works. In the first example, the INDATASET parameter identifies the data set to be printed, and CHARACTER identifies the printing format. Then, the SKIP parameter says to skip the first 28 records before starting and the COUNT parameter says to print just 3 records.

In the second example, a KSDS is printed in hex format starting with the record that has a key value of 1000 and ending with the record that has a key value of 1200. If the key in either parameter contains commas, semicolons, blanks, parentheses, or slashes, you must code the key between apostrophes, but normally that isn't necessary.

To give you some idea of what the printing formats look like, two lines of character and two lines of hex output are shown at the bottom of this figure. As you can see, the output for each record starts with its key. Although the character format works fine when each byte contains one character, numeric formats like packed-decimal are unreadable in this format. In that case, you need to use hex format.

The syntax of the PRINT command

```
PRINT { INDATASET(entry-name) }
      { INFILE(ddname)         }

      [ CHARACTER | HEX | DUMP ]
      [ OUTFILE(ddname) ]

      [ SKIP(count) | FROMKEY(key) | FROMNUMBER(number) | FROMADDRESS(address) ]

      [ COUNT(count) | TOKEY(key) | TONUMBER(number) | TOADDRESS(address) ]
```

Explanation

INDATASET	Specifies the name of the data set to be printed.
INFILE	Specifies the name of a DD statement that identifies the data set to be printed.
CHARACTER	Specifies that the data should be printed in character format.
HEX	Specifies that the data should be printed in hexadecimal format.
DUMP	Specifies that the data should be printed in both character and hex format.
OUTFILE	Specifies an output file other than the default SYSPRINT.
SKIP	Specifies the number of records to be skipped before the records are printed.
FROM...	Specifies the key (KSDS), number (RRDS), or relative-byte address (ESDS) of the first record to be printed.
COUNT	Specifies the number of records to be printed.
TO...	Specifies the key (KSDS), number (RRDS), or relative byte address (ESDS) of the last record to be printed.

A command that prints records 29, 30, and 31 of a non-VSAM file in character format

```
PRINT INDATASET(MM01.CUSTOMER.MASTER)    -
      CHARACTER                          -
      SKIP(28)                           -
      COUNT(3)
```

A command that prints the records from key 1000 to key 1200 of a VSAM file in hex format

```
PRINT INDATASET(MM01.CUSTOMER.VSAM)    -
      HEX                              -
      FROMKEY(1000)                    -
      TOKEY(1200)
```

The start of a listing in character format

```
RECORD SEQUENCE NUMBER - 29
287760JOHN WARDS AND ASSOC5600 N CLARKE         CHICAGO      IL603002027  0102
```

The start of the same listing in hex format

```
KEY OF RECORD - F2F8F7F7F6F0
F2F8F7F7F6F0D1D6C8D540E6C1D9C4E240C1D5C440C1E2E2D6C3F5F6F0F040D540C3D3C1D9D2
```

Description

- You can use the PRINT command of the AMS utility to print non-VSAM or VSAM data sets with any file organization.

Figure 18-5   How to use the PRINT command of the AMS utility to print a data set

The IEBPTPCH utility

Figure 18-6 shows you how to use the IEBPTPCH utility to print a data set. In the example, you can see how easy it is to use this utility to print the first 100 records in a data set and unpack the packed-decimal fields so they're easy to read. In this case, all you need to code is a PRINT statement. Since most of the fields in a record are in either character or packed-decimal format, this is useful for printing the data in test files, and this capability isn't provided by the PRINT command of the AMS utility.

When you print a data set this way, the data is printed in groups of eight characters. These groups are separated by two blanks so 112 characters can be printed on one line. If the output record requires more than 112 characters, the data is wrapped to additional lines. If you don't like this printing format, though, you can use the RECORD statement shown in part 2 of this figure to provide different formatting.

The syntax of the PRINT control statement

```
PRINT [ PREFORM= A | M ]
      [ ,TYPORG= PS | PO ]
      [ ,TOTCONV= XE | PZ ]
      [ ,CNTRL= 1 | 2 | 3 ]
      [ ,STRTAFT=n ]
      [ ,STOPAFT=n ]
      [ ,SKIP=n ]
      [ ,MAXNAME=n ]
      [ ,MAXFLDS=n ]
      [ ,INITPG=n ]
      [ ,MAXLINE=n ]
```

Explanation

PREFORM	Specifies that the input file already contains printer-control characters in the first byte of each record. A indicates ASA characters; M indicates machine characters. If you specify PREFORM, you can't specify any other PRINT options.
TYPORG	Indicates the input file organization: PS for sequential files, PO for partitioned files.
TOTCONV	Indicates conversion of the entire input record (as opposed to conversion of individual fields specified by the RECORD statement that follows). XE means to convert to hexadecimal; PZ means to unpack packed-decimal fields. If TOTCONV is omitted, no conversion is done.
CNTRL	Specifies the line spacing for the output listing. The default is 1.
STRTAFT	Indicates how many records to skip before printing.
STOPAFT	Indicates the number of records to be printed.
SKIP	Indicates that only every *n*th record is to be printed.
MAXNAME	Specifies the number of MEMBER statements that follow.
MAXFLDS	Specifies the number of FIELD parameters in the RECORD statements that follow.
INITPG	Specifies the starting page number. The default is 1.
MAXLINE	Specifies the number of lines to print on each page. The default is 50.

A job step that prints the first 100 records of a sequential data set

```
//PRINT      EXEC PGM=IEBPTPCH
//SYSPRINT DD   SYSOUT=*
//SYSUT1   DD   DSN=MM01.CUSTOMER.MASTER,DISP=SHR
//SYSUT2   DD   SYSOUT=*
//SYSIN    DD   *
 PRINT TYPORG=PS,TOTCONV=PZ,STOPAFT=100,MAXLINE=60
/*
```

Description

- The IEBPTPCH utility can be used to print the data from a non-VSAM sequential or partitioned data set.

- This utility uses the standard ddnames for the message, input, output, and control statement files.

- This utility requires at least a PRINT control statement, and it can also accept TITLE, MEMBER, and RECORD statements as shown in part 2 of this figure.

Figure 18-6   How to use the IEBPTPCH utility to print a data set (part 1 of 2)

Part 2 of this figure shows how to use the TITLE, MEMBER, and RECORD statements as you print a data set. If you look at the first example, you can see how MEMBER statements are used to identify the two members of a partitioned data set that are to be printed. You can also see how RECORD statements are used to print the first 80 characters in each record without grouping. Each RECORD statement just says to print the first 80 characters as a single field starting in the first position of the output line (the default).

In the second example, you can see how the TITLE statement is used to print a title in the first line of the printout starting in position 20. This example also shows how to use the RECORD statement to reposition and format the input fields in the printed output lines. Here, the first field specification says to print bytes 1-5 of each input record in positions 1-5 of the output line. The second field specification says to print bytes 6-10 of each input record in positions 8-12 of the output line. And the third field specification says to print bytes 11-30 in bytes 15-34 of each output line. This provides spacing between the fields that are printed.

Then, the fourth field specification says to unpack the packed-decimal field in bytes 61-65 of each input record and to print the result starting in position 37 of the output line. Since a five-byte packed-decimal field unpacks into nine bytes, this means the output field is printed in positions 37-45. Similarly, the last field specification says to unpack the data in bytes 66-70 of each input record and print it starting in position 48 of the output record.

Note that when you code MEMBER or RECORD statements, you need to also code the MAXNAME and MAXFLDS parameters in the PRINT statement for this utility. In the first example, then, the MAXNAME parameter is set to 2 because there are two MEMBER statements that follow. Similarly, the MAXFLDS parameter is set to 2 in the first example and to 5 in the second example, because two field specifications are used in the RECORD statements for the first example and five field specifications are used in the second example.

The syntax of the TITLE control statement

```
TITLE ITEM=('literal'[,out-loc])
```

Explanation

literal   The title to be printed.

out-loc   The starting position of the literal in the title line. The default is 1.

The syntax of the MEMBER control statement

```
MEMBER NAME=name
```

Explanation

name   The name of the member to be printed.

The syntax of the RECORD control statement

```
RECORD    FIELD=(length[,in-loc][,conv][,out-loc])
          [,FIELD=(length[,in-loc][,conv][,out-loc])]...
```

Explanation

length   The length of the field.

in-loc   The position of the field in the input record. The default is 1.

conv   The conversion operation to be performed on the field. Specify XE to convert to hexadecimal or PZ to unpack packed-decimal fields. If omitted, no conversion is done.

out-loc   The position where the field should begin in the output line. The default is 1.

A job step that prints two members of a partitioned data set

```
//PRINT     EXEC PGM=IEBPTPCH
//SYSPRINT DD    SYSOUT=*
//SYSUT1    DD    DSN=MM01.COPYLIB.COBOL,DISP=SHR
//SYSUT2    DD    SYSOUT=*
//SYSIN     DD    *
 PRINT MAXNAME=2,MAXFLDS=2,TYPORG=PO
 MEMBER NAME=CUSTMAST
 RECORD FIELD(80)
 MEMBER NAME=ORDTRAN
 RECORD FIELD(80)
/*
```

A job step that prints a sequential data set

```
//PRINT     EXEC PGM=IEBPTPCH
//SYSPRINT DD    SYSOUT=*
//SYSUT1    DD    DSN=MM01.CUSTOMER.MASTER,DISP=SHR
//SYSUT2    DD    SYSOUT=*
//SYSIN     DD    *
 PRINT MAXFLDS=5
 TITLE ITEM=('LISTING OF CUSTOMER MASTER FILE',20)
 RECORD FIELD(5,1,,1),FIELD(5,6,,8),FIELD=(20,11,,15),            X
            FIELD(5,61,PZ,37),FIELD=(5,66,PZ,48)
/*
```

Description

- You can use the TITLE, MEMBER, and RECORD statements to add a title to the printout, to identify the members to be printed, and to format the output lines.

Figure 18-6   How to use the IEBPTPCH utility to print a data set (part 2 of 2)

Utilities for handling partitioned data sets and VTOCs

The next two utilities work with partitioned data sets and VTOCs. The first utility lets you perform functions like copying a partitioned data set or merging two partitioned data sets into one. The second one lets you list the VTOC entries on a volume or the members in a partitioned data set. These functions are not offered by the AMS utility.

The IEBCOPY utility

The IEBCOPY utility can be used to perform five different functions on a partitioned data set (PDS) or, under SMS, on a partitioned data set extended (PDSE): copy, merge, compress, back up, and restore. When you use this utility, you code the COPY control statement shown in figure 18-7 to identify the input and output data sets that are to be used. You can also code either SELECT or EXCLUDE statements to include or exclude members of a PDS while the function is performed.

The utility decides which of its five functions to do based on the types of the input and output data sets. If, for example, the input data set is a partitioned data set and the output data set is a new partitioned data set, the utility copies the original data set. But if the input is one or more partitioned data sets and the output is an existing partitioned data set, the utility merges the members in the input data sets with the members in the output data set.

The JCL and control statements for a merge are illustrated by the first example in this figure. Here, you can see that DD statements need to be coded for SYSUT3 and SYSUT4. These are two work files that the utility requires, and each can be given an initial allocation of just one track. These work files are required no matter what function the utility performs.

The third function of this utility is illustrated by the second example in this figure. Here, the input and output data sets are the same, so the utility *compresses* the partitioned data set. That means that any unused space in the data set is reclaimed. Since a partitioned data set builds up unused space as modifications and deletions are made to its members, this should be done occasionally for most partitioned data sets.

The fourth function is to back up a partitioned data set to a sequential data set in a special *unloaded format*. This is done when the input is a PDS and the output is a sequential data set on tape or DASD. The fifth function is to reload (or restore) an unloaded PDS. It is done when the input is a sequential data set and the output is a PDS.

When you run this utility for any of its functions, the SYSPRINT data set receives messages that you may find useful. These messages include a listing of the members that have been copied. They also tell you how much unused space is in the output data set. And if you haven't allocated enough space for the output data set, these messages tell you that too.

The syntax of the COPY control statement

```
COPY OUTDD=ddname,INDD=ddname[,ddname...]
```

Explanation

OUTDD   Specifies the ddname of the data set to be created.

INDD   Specifies the ddnames of one or more input files.

The syntax of the SELECT and EXCLUDE control statements

```
SELECT  MEMBER=member[,member...]
EXCLUDE MEMBER=member[,member...]
```

Explanation

MEMBER   Specifies the names of one or more members to be included or excluded.

DD statement requirements

ddname	Use
SYSPRINT	An output message file.
SYSUT3	A work file that requires about one track.
SYSUT4	A work file that requires about one track.
Any	One DD statement for each ddname specified by the OUTDD and INDD parameters.
SYSIN	The control statement file.

A job step that merges two partitioned data sets

```
//MERGE     EXEC PGM=IEBCOPY
//SYSPRINT DD    SYSOUT=*
//DDIN      DD    DSN=MM01.COPYLIBX.COB,DISP=OLD
//DDOUT     DD    DSN=MM01.COPYLIB.COB,DISP=OLD
//SYSUT3    DD    UNIT=SYSDA,SPACE=(TRK,(1,1))
//SYSUT4    DD    UNIT=SYSDA,SPACE=(TRK,(1,1))
//SYSIN     DD    *
 COPY OUTDD=DDOUT,INDD=DDIN
/*
```

A job step that compresses a partitioned data set

```
//COMPRESS EXEC PGM=IEBCOPY
//SYSPRINT DD    SYSOUT=*
//COMPFILE DD    DSN=MM01.COPYLIB.COB,DISP=OLD
//SYSUT3    DD    UNIT=SYSDA,SPACE=(TRK,(1,1))
//SYSUT4    DD    UNIT=SYSDA,SPACE=(TRK,(1,1))
//SYSIN     DD    *
 COPY OUTDD=COMPFILE,INDD=COMPFILE
/*
```

Description

- The IEBCOPY utility can be used to copy a partitioned data set, merge two or more partitioned data sets, archive a PDS to a sequential file in a special *unloaded format*, reload an unloaded PDS, or *compress* a PDS to reclaim unused space within the PDS. The operation is determined by the types of input and output data sets that are specified.

- The IEBCOPY utility can perform these functions on a PDS or a PDSE.

Figure 18-7   How to use the IEBCOPY utility to work with partitioned data sets

The IEHLIST utility

Chapter 16 shows you how to use the LISTCAT command of the AMS utility. If you've read that chapter, you know that command can be used to print the detailed catalog information for VSAM data sets. For non-VSAM data sets, however, the detailed information can't be found in a catalog. Instead, that information is stored in the VTOC of the DASD volume that contains the data set.

To list the VTOC information for a volume, you can use the LISTVTOC control statement of the IEHLIST utility that's summarized in figure 18-8. With this utility, you need to code a DD statement that identifies the volume that contains the VTOC to be listed, even though the VOL parameter of the control statement also identifies that volume. Note, however, that you can use whatever ddname you want in the DD statement for the volume.

This is illustrated by the first example in this figure, which lists all of the VTOC entries for the volume with serial number TSO001. If you just want to list the VTOC information for specific data sets, though, you can code their names in the DSNAME parameter. Most of the time, you don't need to code the FORMAT parameter because the information that's supplied by default is all that you need. If you do code this parameter, the list includes all the information in the Data Set Control Blocks for the data sets that are listed.

You can also use the LISTPDS control statement of this utility to list the members in a PDS or PDSE directory. This is illustrated by the second example in this figure. Here, all of the members for a PDS named SYS1.COBLIB are listed.

Because the ISPF utilities perform both of these functions without the bother of coding JCL and control statements, you probably won't use this utility if you just want the name or location of a single file or member. If you want to print a listing of an entire VTOC, PDS, or PDSE directory, though, this utility can come in handy.

The syntax of the LISTVTOC and LISTPDS control statements

```
LISTVTOC   VOL=unit=serial
         [ ,DATE=dddyy|dddyyyy ]
         [ ,DSNAME=(name[,name...]) ]
         [ ,FORMAT ]

LISTPDS    DSNAME=(dsname[,dsname...])
         ,VOL=unit=serial
```

Explanation

VOL	Specifies the unit (such as SYSDA) and serial number for the volume to be processed. The volume must be allocated with a DD statement.
DATE	Specifies an expiration date so the files that are expired by that date are flagged with asterisks.
DSNAME	Specifies one or more data set names. For LISTVTOC, only the VTOC entries for those data sets are listed. For LISTPDS, only the directories of the specified data sets are listed. You can omit the parentheses if code only one name; you can code up to 10 names in a single statement; and you can code more than one statement if you want to list more than 10 data sets.
FORMAT	Specifies that complete VTOC information should be printed.

DD statement requirements

ddname	Use
SYSPRINT	The printed output file.
Any	One DD statement for each volume that contains a VTOC or PDS that you want to list the entries for.
SYSIN	The control statement file.

A job step that lists VTOC entries

```
//LISTVTOC EXEC PGM=IEHLIST
//SYSPRINT DD    SYSOUT=*
//DDVOL1    DD    UNIT=SYSDA,VOL=SER=TSO001,DISP=SHR
//SYSIN     DD    *
 LISTVTOC VOL=SYSDA=TSO001
```

A job step that lists all the members in a partitioned data set

```
//LISTPDS  EXEC PGM=IEHLIST
//SYSPRINT DD    SYSOUT=*
//DDVOL1    DD    UNIT=SYSDA,VOL=SER=TSO001,DISP=SHR
//SYSIN     DD    *
 LISTPDS DSNAME=SYS1.COBLIB,VOL=SYSDA=TSO001
```

Description

- The IEHLIST utility can be used to list VTOC entries or to list the members in a PDS or PDSE.
- If FORMAT isn't coded, VTOC entries are listed with one line per data set that includes name, creation and expiration dates, file type, and number of extents.

Figure 18-8   How to use the IEHLIST utility to list VTOC entries or PDS members

Miscellaneous utilities

The last two utilities in this chapter can be used to compare two data sets and to generate the data for a new data set. These functions can only be done by these MVS utilities.

The IEBCOMPR utility

The IEBCOMPR utility is designed to compare two data sets and produce output that details any differences that are found. This utility is typically used to compare two versions of a file that you think might be equal so you can delete one of them. The files that are compared can be sequential, partitioned, or partitioned extended, but both files must have the same record format and length.

Figure 18-9 shows two examples that use this utility. The first one compares two sequential data sets that are identified by the SYSUT1 and SYSUT2 DD statements. In this case, the SYSIN data set is a DUMMY because no control statements are needed. In the second example, the SYSIN data set consists of one COMPARE statement that tells the utility that two partitioned data sets are being compared.

When you run this utility, the SYSPRINT output tells you whether the data sets are equal. For sequential data sets, this means that both data sets have the same number of records and that the records are the same. If the data sets aren't equal, the SYSPRINT output tells you which data set has extra records and which records aren't equal.

For PDS and PDSE data sets, this is more complicated. To be equal, two conditions have to be met. First, one PDS or PDSE has to be a subset of the other. That means that all of the members of the first PDS or PDSE have to be in the second PDS or PDSE, although the second PDS or PDSE can have members that aren't in the first PDS or PDSE. Second, all of the members of the first PDS or PDSE have to be equal to the members with the same names in the second PDS or PDSE. Here again, if the data sets aren't equal, the SYSPRINT output gives you information that tells you why they aren't.

The syntax of the COMPARE control statement

```
COMPARE [ ,TYPORG= PS | PO ]
```

Explanation

TYPORG   Indicates the input file organization: PS for sequential files, PO for partitioned files.

A job that compares sequential data sets

```
//COMPSEQ   EXEC PGM=IEBCOMPR
//SYSPRINT DD    SYSOUT=*
//SYSUT1    DD    DSN=MM01.CSTMAST1,DISP=SHR
//SYSUT2    DD    DSN=MM01.CSTMAST2,DISP=SHR
//SYSIN     DD    DUMMY
```

A job that compares partitioned data sets

```
//COMPPDS   EXEC PGM=IEBCOMPR
//SYSPRINT DD    SYSOUT=*
//SYSUT1    DD    DSN=MM01.SRCLIB.P42A.COB,DISP=SHR
//SYSUT2    DD    DSN=MM01.SRCLIB.P43A.COB,DISP=SHR
//SYSIN     DD    *
 COMPARE TYPORG=PO
/*
```

Description

- The IEBCOMPR utility can be used to compare two sequential data sets or two partitioned data sets.

- The SYSPRINT output indicates whether the data sets are equal. If they're not equal, the output tells you where they aren't equal.

- Two sequential data sets are equal if both have the same number of records and the records in both data sets are the same.

- Two PDS or PDSE data sets are equal (1) if the members in one are a subset of the members in the other, and (2) if the members with the same names are equal.

- If the data sets are equal, the return code for this utility is zero. Otherwise, the return code is 08.

Figure 18-9   How to use the IEBCOMPR utility to compare data sets

The IEBDG utility

The IEBDG utility can be used to generate test data and write it to a sequential data set. This can be useful when you're developing a program and existing data sets aren't available for testing it. If you're writing a program that uses a KSDS and existing data sets aren't available for it, you can use the AMS REPRO command to copy a sequential data set that you generate with IEBDG into a KSDS.

Figure 18-10 shows you how to use the IEBDG utility. If you review both parts of this figure, you can see how the pieces fit together. After you use the DSD statement to identify the output data set, you use FD statements to define the fields in each record of the data set and the CREATE statement to tell this utility how many records to create. The END statement just tells this utility that there aren't any more control statements.

When you use the FD statement to define one of the fields in the output record, you can use the FORMAT parameter to give the field a specific format and initial value. The codes for this parameter are given in the table at the bottom of part 1 of this figure. Otherwise, you can use the PICTURE parameter followed by a literal value to give the field a length and starting value.

To vary the data in a field, you can use the ACTION or INDEX parameter. If you specify RP in the ACTION parameter, the data is given a rippled effect in each new record. If, for example, you use RP for a five-byte field that has ABCDE stored in it, BCDEA is stored in the second record, CDEAB is stored in the third record, and so on.

In contrast, if you code INDEX for a numeric field, the value is increased by one in each new record, unless the CYCLE parameter is coded. If that parameter is coded, the value is increased by one only after that many records have been written to the data set. If, for example, the CYCLE parameter is 5, the value in the field is increased by one every five records. You can see how both of these parameters are coded in the example in part 2 of this figure.

The syntax of the DSD control statement

```
DSD    OUTPUT=(ddname)
```

Explanation

OUTPUT   Specifies the ddname of the output file.

The syntax of the FD control statement

```
FD    NAME=name
      ,LENGTH=length
   [ ,STARTLOC=starting-position ]
   [ ,FILL= 'character' | X'hex-value' ]
   [ ,FORMAT=pattern | PICTURE=length,[P]'literal' ]
   [ ,SIGN=sign ]
   [ ,ACTION=action ]
   [ ,INDEX=number ]
   [ ,CYCLE=number ]
```

Explanation

NAME   Specifies the user-defined name of the field.

LENGTH   Specifies the length of the field.

STARTLOC   Specifies the starting-position of the field in the output record. If omitted, the next available position is used.

FILL   Specifies a single-character alphanumeric literal or a two-character hexadecimal literal used to fill this field in each output record. If omitted, FILL=X'00' (hex zero) is assumed.

FORMAT   Specifies a data format (see below).

PICTURE   Specifies a user-defined picture where *length* is the number of characters between the quotation marks. For a packed-decimal number, code a P before the first quotation mark.

SIGN   The sign of the field (+ or -).

ACTION   Specifies what action is to be applied to the field as the next record is generated. If omitted, the field stays the same in all records. One of the most useful actions is RP (for rippled), which shifts the data one byte to the left for each successive record.

INDEX   Specifies a number that's added to the field for each record or record cycle.

CYCLE   Used only with INDEX. Specifies the number of records that should pass before the index value is added to the field.

Patterns for the FORMAT parameter of the FD statement

FORMAT	Name	Description	Initial value (5-byte field)
AN	Alphanumeric	Letters A-Z, digits 0-9	ABCDE
AL	Alphabetic	Letters A-Z	ABCDE
ZD	Zoned decimal	Digits 0-9	00001
PD	Packed decimal	Packed number	(Hex) 00 00 00 00 1C
BI	Binary pattern	Binary number	(Hex) 00 00 00 00 01
RA	Random pattern	Random hexadecimal digits	(Hex) 4F 38 2D A5 A0

Figure 18-10   How to use the IEBDG utility to generate a data set (part 1 of 2)

In the example in part 2 of this figure, you can see how all four control statements are used. Here, the DSD statement gives the ddname for the output data set, the FD statements define seven fields, and the CREATE statement says to write a data set with 125 records. Note that the CREATE statement must also list the names for all of the fields that are defined by FD statements.

In this case, the KEY field will have a starting value of 00001 that will be increased by 1 every 5 records. Next, the CUSTNAME and ADDRESS fields will have initial values of the letters A through Z and the CITY field will have an initial value of the letters A through R. All three of these values will be varied with the ripple effect. In contrast, the STATEZIP field will have a constant value of CA93711.

The YTDSALES field will have an initial value of 000123456 that is stored in a five-byte, packed-decimal field. Note here that the LENGTH parameter gives a length of 5 and the PICTURE parameter gives a length of 9 because a nine-byte number gets packed into five bytes. To add a sign to a field like this, you can also code the SIGN parameter.

When you're defining the fields for the output data set, you can continue in this way until all the fields have been defined. If you don't provide for all the fields, though, the value in the FILL parameter of the CREATE statement is used to fill all of the undefined bytes. In this case, the DCB parameter in the DD statement for the output data set specifies that the records are going to be 150 bytes long, so the undefined bytes are filled with hex zeros.

The syntax of the CREATE control statement

```
CREATE    QUANTITY=number
       [ ,FILL= 'character' | X'hex-constant' ]
       [ ,NAME=(name[,name...]) ]
```

Explanation

QUANTITY	Specifies the number of records to be generated.
FILL	Specifies a single-character alphanumeric literal or a two-character hexadecimal literal used to fill undefined character positions in each output record. If omitted, FILL=X'00' (hex zero) is assumed.
NAME	Names one or more fields defined in FD statements that are used to build the output record.

The syntax of the END control statement

```
END
```

A job step that creates a sequential test file

```
//CREATE     EXEC   PGM=IEBDG
//SYSPRINT DD      SYSOUT=*
//DDOUT     DD      DSNAME=MM01.CUSTMAST.TEST,DISP=(NEW,CATLG),
//                  UNIT=SYSDA,SPACE=(CYL,(1,1)),
//                  DCB=(DSORG=PS,RECFM=FB,RECL=150)
//SYSIN      DD      *
 DSD      OUTPUT=(DDOUT)
 FD       NAME=KEY,LENGTH=5,FORMAT=ZD,INDEX=1,CYCLE=5
 FD       NAME=CUSTNAME,LENGTH=26,FORMAT=AN,ACTION=RP
 FD       NAME=ADDRESS,LENGTH=26,FORMAT=AN,ACTION=RP
 FD       NAME=CITY,LENGTH=18,FORMAT=AN,ACTION=RP
 FD       NAME=STATEZIP,LENGTH=7,PICTURE=7,'CA93711'
 FD       NAME=YTDSALES,LENGTH=5,PICTURE=9,P'000123456'
 FD       NAME=FILLER1,LENGTH=61,FILL='X'
 CREATE QUANTITY=125,FILL=X'00',NAME=(KEY,CUSTNAME,ADDRESS,CITY,         X
               STATEZIP,YTDSALES,FILLER1)
 END
/*
```

Description

- You can use the IEBDG utility to generate test data and write it to a non-VSAM sequential data set.

- The DSD (Data Set Definition) statement defines the data set generated by the utility.

- The FD (Field Definition) statement defines the fields that will be put in each record of the output data set.

- The CREATE statement specifies the number of records to be generated and coordinates the use of the FD statements.

- The END statement marks the end of the control statements.

Figure 18-10   How to use the IEBDG utility to generate a data set (part 2 of 2)

Perspective

What this chapter has tried to do is present the MVS utilities that are still useful along with the most useful control statements and parameters for those utilities. It has also tried to show you the capabilities of each so you'll know when it makes sense to use one of these utilities instead of the AMS or ISPF alternatives. If this chapter has succeeded, you should now be able to use these utilities whenever they are appropriate for the tasks you need to do. And you should be able to use them with relative ease.

Terms

utility program
utility
MVS utilities
control statement
compress a PDS
unloaded format of a PDS

19

How to use the sort/merge utility

Sequential files are still commonly used in mainframe shops to store transaction records. Then, before the records in these files can be processed, they often need to be sorted or merged into an appropriate sequence. For instance, sales transactions may need to be sorted into salesperson, customer, or item number sequence before they can be used to prepare reports or update master files.

To do this sorting or merging, you use the sort/merge utility that comes with OS/390. As you will see, you normally use JCL to run this utility as a standalone program. However, you can also use this utility to do an internal sort or internal merge within an application program.

The basics of using the sort/merge utility

The *sort/merge utility* (or *sort/merge program*) can be used to sort the records in one or more files or to merge the records in two or more files. Because sorting is done far more frequently than merging, this type of program can also be called just a *sort program*.

To get you started with the use of this program, this topic presents the JCL requirements for sorting and merging. Then, it shows you how to code the control statements that are required for simple sorts and merges.

The JCL requirements for sorting

To *sort* the records in a file, the sort/merge program reads the records from one or more input files. Then, it sorts those records based on the data in one or more *control fields* (or *sort keys*). If, for example, a transaction file needs to be sorted by customer number, the customer number field is the control field and customer number can be referred to as the sort key. After the records are sorted, the sort/merge program writes them to a single output file.

When you use JCL to run the sort/merge program for a sort, you obviously need to provide DD statements for the input file or files (SORTIN) and the output file (SORTOUT). In addition, though, you need to provide DD statements for the four other files that are summarized in figure 19-1. These include a partitioned data set that contains the sort/merge modules (SORTLIB), a file for the messages that are produced by the program (SYSOUT), one or more work files that are used by the program (SORTWKnn), and an input file that contains the *control statements* for the sort (SYSIN).

To illustrate, this figure shows the JCL for a job step that invokes the sort/merge utility (named SORT) to sort a transaction file into ascending sequence based on the data in bytes 9-13 of each record. The location of this control field is given by the SORT control statement that follows the SYSIN DD statement as an instream data set. In a moment, you'll learn how to code this control statement.

If you want to sort two or more files at the same time, you can concatenate them like this:

```
//SORTIN    DD    DSNAME=MM01.INVOICE.TRANS.APRIL,DISP=SHR
//          DD    DSNAME=MM01.INVOICE.TRANS.MAY,DISP=SHR
//          DD    DSNAME=MM01.INVOICE.TRANS.JUNE,DISP=SHR
```

This assumes of course that the control field is in the same location in all of the files.

Although the JCL for this job step provides for only one work file, you can provide for more than one. Either way, the space allocation for the work files should be about twice the combined sizes of the input files. That extra space lets the sort/merge program work more efficiently while it does the sorting.

A system flowchart for a sort

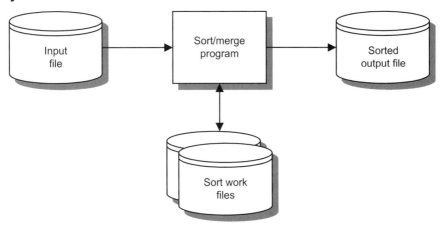

The DD statements required by a sort

ddname	Use
SORTLIB	A partitioned data set that contains the modules required by the sort/merge utility. Normally, SYS1.SORTLIB.
SYSOUT	The messages produced by the sort/merge utility. Normally, a SYSOUT data set.
SORTIN	The input file or files to be sorted. If more than one file is to be sorted, you can concatenate them.
SORTOUT	The sorted output file. It can be a new non-VSAM file with DISP=(NEW,KEEP) or DISP=(NEW,CATLG); an extension of an existing non-VSAM file with DISP=MOD; or an existing VSAM file.
SORTWKnn	The work files that are required by the sort, where *nn* is a consecutive number starting with 01. One or two files are usually adequate, and the total DASD space allocated to the work files should be about twice the input file size. You can specify up to 255 work files.
SYSIN	The sort control statements. Normally, an instream data set.

The JCL for a job step that does a sort

```
//SORT      EXEC  PGM=SORT
//SORTLIB   DD    DSNAME=SYS1.SORTLIB,DISP=SHR
//SYSOUT    DD    SYSOUT=*
//SORTIN    DD    DSNAME=MM01.INVOICE.TRANS,DISP=SHR
//SORTOUT   DD    DSNAME=MM01.INVOICE.TRANS.SORTED,DISP=(NEW,CATLG),
//                UNIT=SYSDA,VOL=SER=MPS8BV,
//                SPACE=(CYL,(10,5))
//SORTWK01 DD     UNIT=SYSDA,SPACE=(CYL,(20,5))
//SYSIN     DD    *
 SORT FIELDS=(9,5,CH,A)
/*
```

Description

- To *sort* the records in a file, the *sort/merge utility* (or *program*) reads the records from one or more input files, sorts them based on the data in one or more *control fields* (or *sort keys*), and writes the sorted records to an output file.

Figure 19-1   The JCL requirements for a sort

The JCL requirements for merging

To *merge* the records from two or more files, the sort/merge program reads the records from the sorted input files and merges them into one output file based on the data in one or more control fields. Unlike a sort, though, a merge doesn't require work files. This is illustrated by the flowchart and example in figure 19-2.

This figure also summarizes the DD statements that are required by a merge. Then, it shows an example of the JCL for running a merge. This time, a MERGE control statement identifies the control fields that are used for the merge, and the records are merged based on the data in bytes 9-13 of each record.

Note that the input files have to be in sequence based on the merge control field before they can be merged. If that means that you have to sort the files before you merge them, though, it is usually more efficient to sort the files together as concatenated files, which has the same effect as a merge. That's why sorting is done far more frequently than merging.

A system flowchart for a merge

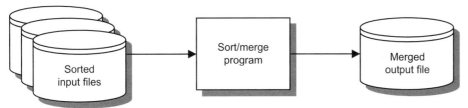

A merge example

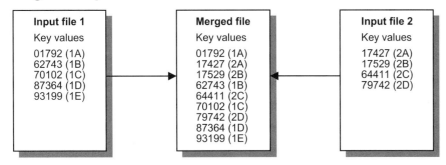

The DD statements required by a merge

ddname	Use
SORTLIB	A partitioned data set that contains the modules required by the sort/merge utility. Normally, SYS1.SORTLIB.
SYSOUT	The messages produced by the sort/merge utility. Normally, a SYSOUT data set.
SORTINnn	The input files to be merged, where *nn* is a consecutive number starting with 01 through 16. These files must already be in the sequence that is used for the merge.
SORTOUT	The merged output file.
SYSIN	The merge control statements. Normally, an instream data set.

The JCL for a job step that does a merge

```
//SORT      EXEC   PGM=SORT
//SORTLIB   DD     DSNAME=SYS1.SORTLIB,DISP=SHR
//SYSOUT    DD     SYSOUT=*
//SORTIN01 DD      DSNAME=MM01.INVOICE.TRANS.APRIL,DISP=SHR
//SORTIN02 DD      DSNAME=MM01.INVOICE.TRANS.MAY,DISP=SHR
//SORTIN03 DD      DSNAME=MM01.INVOICE.TRANS.JUNE,DISP=SHR
//SORTOUT   DD     DSNAME=MM01.INVOICE.TRANS.Q2,DISP=(NEW,CATLG),
//                 UNIT=SYSDA,VOL=SER=MPS8BV,
//                 SPACE=(CYL,(10,5))
//SYSIN     DD     *
 MERGE FIELDS=(9,5,CH,A)
/*
```

Description

- To *merge* the records in two or more files, the sort/merge program reads the records from the input files and merges them into one output file based on the control field values.

Figure 19-2   The JCL requirements for a merge

The SORT and MERGE statements

Figure 19-3 presents the syntax and the coding details for the SORT and MERGE control statements. The purpose of both statements is to identify one or more control fields that the sort or merge is based upon. For each field, you code the starting position, the length, and a code that identifies the format of the field. You also specify whether you want the records sorted or merged in ascending or descending sequence for that field.

For business applications, you normally use the first four codes that are summarized in this figure, especially CH for normal character data and PD for packed-decimal numeric data. If you're sorting a tape that has been created on another platform, though, you may find some of the other codes useful. Before you can code a SORT or MERGE statement, of course, you need to find out the locations and formats of the control fields.

When you need to sort the records based on more than one control field, you code these fields in sequence from most important to least important. If, for example, you want to sort the records into ascending sequence by invoice number within customer number, you code the customer number field first, followed by the invoice number.

To illustrate how this works, suppose the customer numbers and invoice numbers in the first five records are these:

```
44444 1234
33333 1235
44444 1236
22222 1237
33333 1238
```

Then, the sorted control fields are these:

```
22222 1237
33333 1235
33333 1238
44444 1234
44444 1236
```

And if the customer numbers are to be in ascending sequence with the invoice numbers in descending sequence, the sorted control fields are these:

```
22222 1237
33333 1238
33333 1235
44444 1236
44444 1234
```

If you have any difficulty with this, just remember to list the control fields from left to right, from the most important to the least important.

If the control fields for two or more records in a sort can be equal, you can also code the EQUALS parameter in the SORT control statement. This says that the sort/merge program should retain the original sequence of any records with equal sort keys. Since this means extra work for the sort/merge program and since this usually isn't necessary, you probably won't ever code this parameter.

The syntax for the SORT and MERGE statements

```
SORT    { FIELDS=(position,length,format,sequence...)        }
        { FIELDS=(position,length,sequence...),FORMAT=format }

     [ { ,EQUALS   }
       { ,NOEQUALS } ]

MERGE   { FIELDS=(position,length,format,sequence...)        }
        { FIELDS=(position,length,sequence...),FORMAT=format }
```

Explanation

position	The location of the first byte of the control field in the input record.
length	The length in bytes of the control field.
format	A code that identifies the format of the data in the control field (see below).
FORMAT	If all control fields have the same format, you can omit the format subparameters for the individual fields and code the format for all the control fields in this parameter.
sequence	A for ascending sequence, or D for descending sequence.
EQUALS NOEQUALS	Specifies the order of records with matching control fields in the sorted output file. EQUALS means that the order of the records in the input files should be preserved in the output file; NOEQUALS means the input order isn't preserved.

Format codes

CH	Character	AQ	Character with alternate collating sequence
ZD	Signed zoned decimal	CSF	Numeric with optional leading sign
PD	Signed packed decimal	CSL	Numeric with leading separate sign
FI	Signed fixed-point binary	CST	Numeric with trailing separate sign
BI	Unsigned binary	CLO	Numeric with leading overpunch sign
AC	ASCII characters	CTO	Numeric with trailing overpunch sign
		ASL	ASCII numeric with leading separate sign
		AST	ASCII numeric with trailing separate sign

Examples

```
SORT FIELDS=(9,5,CH,A)
```

Sorts the records into ascending sequence by the character data in bytes 9-13.

```
SORT FIELDS=(9,5,CH,A,72,5,PD,D)
```

Sorts the records into ascending sequence by the character data in bytes 9-13 and into descending sequence by the packed-decimal data in bytes 72-76.

```
MERGE FIELDS=(21,20,A,9,5,A),FORMAT=CH
```

Merges the records into ascending sequence by the character data in bytes 21-40 and 9-13.

Description

* Sort/merge control statements are coded in positions 2 through 71. To continue a control statement from one line to the next, end the first line after the comma for one of the parameters, code any character in column 72, and start the next line in column 16.

Figure 19-3   The SORT and MERGE control statements

The RECORD statement

Besides the SORT and MERGE statements, you may have to code the RECORD statement for a sort or merge. This statement is required for VSAM input files, and it can improve the processing efficiency for files that contain variable-length records. It is summarized in figure 19-4.

If you read through this figure, you shouldn't have any trouble using this statement. In the first example, you can see how it is used for a VSAM file. In the second example, you can see how it is used for a file of variable-length records. Although the sequence of the control statements doesn't matter, this statement is typically coded after the SORT statement, as shown in both these examples.

The syntax for the RECORD statement

```
RECORD TYPE=type
    [ ,LENGTH=(in-length,E15-length,out-length,min-length,avg-length) ]
```

Explanation

TYPE   Specifies the format of the file's records: F for fixed-length, V for variable-length, or D for ASCII variable-length.

in-length   The length of the input records. Required for VSAM files.

E15-length   Used only if an E15 sort exit is used to change the input length (see figure 19-7 for information on sort exits).

out-length   The length of the output records. Used only when the SORTOUT DD statement is omitted.

min-length   When variable-length records are used, specifies the minimum record length.

avg-length   When variable-length records are used, specifies the average record length.

Examples

```
SORT FIELDS=(9,5,CH,A)
RECORD TYPE=F,LENGTH=(400)
```

Identifies a file with fixed-length, 400-byte records.

```
SORT FIELDS=(9,5,CH,A)
RECORD TYPE=V,LENGTH=(,,,200,400)
```

Identifies a file with variable-length records that have a minimum length of 200 and an average length of 400 bytes.

Description

- You only need to use the RECORD statement when the input file or files for a sort or merge are VSAM files.

- You can also use the RECORD statement to specify the characteristics of a non-VSAM file with variable-length records. Although that isn't required, this can help the sort/merge program optimize its performance.

Figure 19-4   The RECORD control statement

Other sort/merge control statements

Besides the SORT, MERGE, and RECORD statements, you can code six other control statements for sorts and merges. These statements can help make your sorts and merges more efficient, and they provide some additional processing capabilities.

The INCLUDE and OMIT statements

The best way to improve the efficiency of a sort or a merge is to reduce the number of records that are sorted or merged. To do that, you can use the INCLUDE and OMIT statements to identify the records that should be included or omitted from the sort or merge. These statements are summarized in figure 19-5.

As you can see, you code a condition in these statements that tells the sort/merge program what records to include or omit. For instance, the first example says to include only those records that have an A in position 1, and the second example says to omit those records that have an A in position 1. The third example uses the GE operator to tell the sort/merge program that it should only include records that have a packed-decimal value in bytes 72-76 that is greater than or equal to 1000.

To select records on the basis of more than one condition, you can use the AND or OR operator within the COND parameter. When you use AND, a record is selected if all the conditions are true. When you use OR, a record is selected if any of the conditions is true. In the fourth example, then, a record will be included in the sort/merge if the packed-decimal value in bytes 72-76 is less than 10 or greater than or equal to 1000.

The syntax of the INCLUDE and OMIT statements

```
INCLUDE COND=(field,comparison,{field   }, [ {AND}, ]...)
                               {constant}   {OR }
OMIT    COND=(field,comparison,{field   }, [ {AND}, ]...)
                               {constant}   {OR }
```

Explanation

field	A field to be used in a comparison. The field is specified as in the SORT or MERGE statement: position, length, format.
comparison	One of these comparison operators:

EQ	Equal	GE	Greater than or equal to
NE	Not equal	LT	Less than
GT	Greater than	LE	Less than or equal to

constant   A literal value in one of these formats:

Decimal	`5`	`+104`	`-39`
Character	`C'CA'`	`C'JONES'`	`C'X24'`
Hexadecimal	`X'00'`	`X'F9F9'`	`X'40404040'`

AND	Indicates another condition follows. All conditions must be true for the field to be selected.
OR	Indicates another condition follows. One of the conditions must be true for the field to be selected.

Examples

```
INCLUDE COND=(1,1,CH,EQ,C'A')
```
Include only the records that have an A in byte 1.

```
OMIT COND=(1,1,CH,EQ,C'A')
```
Omit the records that have an A in byte 1.

```
INCLUDE COND=(72,5,PD,GE,1000)
```
Include only the records with a packed-decimal value in bytes 72-76 that's greater than or equal to 1000.

```
INCLUDE COND=(72,5,PD,GE,1000,OR,
              72,5,PD,LT,10)
```
Include only the records with a packed-decimal value in bytes 72-76 that's greater than or equal to 1000 or less than 10.

Description

- The INCLUDE and OMIT statements let you improve sort/merge efficiency by letting you sort or merge just the records that need to be processed.

Figure 19-5   The INCLUDE and OMIT control statements

The INREC and OUTREC statements

Another way to improve sort/merge efficiency is to sort or merge only the fields of the input records that need to be included in the output file. To do that, you can use the INREC statement that is summarized in figure 19-6. For instance, the first example includes only the first 50 bytes of each input record, and the second example includes only three portions of each input record (but not the entire record).

You can use the OUTREC statement in the same way to write only certain fields to the sorted output file, as shown in the third example. However, the OUTREC processing isn't done until the sorting or merging is finished. So while it still improves I/O operations by limiting the amount of output that's written, it doesn't have as big an effect on processing efficiency as using the INREC statement does.

You can also use the INREC and OUTREC statements to reformat the sort/ merge records. For instance, the fourth example writes bytes 1-80 and bytes 100-124 of each input record to each record of the output file, but it rearranges these bytes in the process.

As for the fifth example, it does even more extensive formatting by inserting constant values (or *separation fields*) into each output record. Here, the first subparameter says to insert the character E in byte 5. Since the first four bytes are unaccounted for in this OUTREC statement, OS/390 inserts blanks in them. Then, the second subparameter says to insert bytes 1-80 from the input record into the output record starting in byte 7. Again, since byte 6 is unaccounted for, it will contain a blank. Finally, the last subparameter says to insert blanks in the 10 bytes immediately after the 80-byte field. But even though the INREC and OUTREC statements allow for extensive data manipulation like this, in general, the most you'll want to do is select input fields and perhaps rearrange them in the output file.

The syntax of the INREC and OUTREC statements

```
INREC  FIELDS=([c:][separation-fld,]position,length[,align,]...)

OUTREC FIELDS=([c:][separation-fld,]position,length[,align,]...)
```

Explanation

c: Specifies the column (byte) in which a data field or separation field should be placed, relative to the start of the record. If the column settings that are coded skip over any bytes, those bytes are filled with spaces.

separation-fld Tells the sort/merge utility to insert a constant value into the record. The constant can be specified in one of these forms:

nX Inserts *n* repetitions of spaces

nZ Inserts *n* repetitions of binary zeros

nC'text' Inserts *n* repetitions of the specified text

nX'hex' Inserts *n* repetitions of the specified hex value

If *n* is omitted, one repetition of the specified constant is inserted.

position The location of the first byte of the field.

length The length of the field in bytes.

align Tells the sort/merge utility to align the field on a halfword (H), fullword (F), or doubleword (D) boundary, but this shouldn't be necessary on a modern system.

Examples

```
INREC FIELDS=(1,50)
```
Just use the data in bytes 1-50 of the input records.

```
INREC FIELDS=(1,50,75,25,125,50)
```
Just use the data in bytes 1-50, 75-99, and 125-174 of the input records.

```
OUTREC FIELDS=(1,80,100,25)
```
The output records contain only the data in bytes 1-80 and bytes 100-124 of the input records.

```
OUTREC FIELDS=(100,25,1,80)
```
The output records start with the data in bytes 100-124 of the input records, followed by the data in bytes 1-80.

```
OUTREC FIELDS=(5:C'E',7:1,80,10X)
```
The output records start with four blank spaces followed by the character E in byte 5, followed by another blank space, then the data from bytes 1-80 of the input records starting in byte 7, and finally, ten blank spaces.

Description

- The INREC and OUTREC statements let you change the format of the records before or after they are sorted. You can select only certain fields to be included in the sort/merge records, rearrange the fields, or add *separation fields* (literal values) to the records.

- Using INREC to limit the fields that are used in the sort/merge improves efficiency more than using OUTREC to limit the fields that are written after the sort/merge.

Figure 19-6   The INREC and OUTREC control statements

The SUM statement

The SUM statement can be used to summarize numeric data for each group of records that have the same sort key value, and then write just one summary record for each group to the output file. This, of course, improves efficiency by reducing the number of records that are written to the output file.

In figure 19-7, you can see how the SUM statement is coded. Then, in the first example, you can see how this statement can be used to write one summary record for each group of records that has the same value in bytes 9-13 of the input records. If, for example, there are five records for customer number 12345, which is stored in those bytes, just one output record is written for that customer number. However, that record will include the totals of the numeric values in bytes 72-76 and 77-83 for the five records. If an overflow occurs in either summed field, the job step will terminate.

A statement like this can be useful when you're going to use the output file to prepare a sales report. By letting the sort/merge program summarize the data, your application program has less work to do. And by reducing the number of records that your application has to process, efficiency is improved.

The SUM statement can also be used to eliminate duplicate records from a file. In the second example, records that have the same value in bytes 9-13 on the input file are sorted. Because SUM FIELDS=NONE is specified, only one record from each key is kept and no summing is performed.

The MODS statement

The MOD statement that's summarized in figure 19-7 lets you call *exit routines* from various processing points in the sort/merge program. Two of the *exits* most commonly used are E15, which occurs right after an input record is read, and E35, which occurs right before an output record is written. Then, the exit routines can do processing that's similar to what's done by the INREC and OUTREC control statements. Of course, the exit routines have no limitations as to what they can do.

Unless your shop is already using some special exit routines, you probably won't ever have to use the MODS statement. Today, you can get the same result by using an application program that does an internal sort or merge, as explained in the next topic.

The SUM statement

```
SUM { FIELDS=(position,length,format...) }
    { FIELDS=NONE                         }
```

Explanation

position	The location of the first byte of the field to be summarized.
length	The length in bytes of the field to be summarized.
format	A numeric field format code: BI, FI, PD, or ZD.
NONE	Specifies that no sum is to be calculated. If more than one record with the same sort key is present in the input, only the last one will be written to the output file.

The MODS statement

```
MODS exit=(routine,bytes,ddname[,C])
```

Explanation

exit	The sort exit to be taken, such as E15 (before sort) or E35 (after sort).
routine	The name of the routine to process the exit.
bytes	The size of the exit routine.
ddname	The ddname of the data set that contains the routine.
C	Used to indicate a COBOL routine.

Examples

```
SORT FIELDS=(9,5,CH,A)
SUM FIELDS=(72,5,PD,77,7,PD)
```

Sorts the records by the sort key in bytes 9-13, and sums the packed-decimal data in bytes 72-76 and bytes 77-83 for each group of records with the same sort key. The data for the rest of each output record is copied from the last record in the group.

```
SORT FIELDS=(9,5,CH,A)
SUM FIELDS=NONE
```

Sorts the records by the sort key in bytes 9-13 and deletes any duplicate records.

```
MODS E15=(SPLEXIT,2000,EXITLIB)
```

Tells the sort/merge program that the E15 exit should be processed by a routine called SPLEXIT, that the routine occupies 2000 bytes, and that the routine is in the data set allocated by the EXITLIB DD statement.

Description

- The SUM statement lets you add up numeric data in sorted records that have the same control field values and writes just one output record for each value.

- The MODS statement lets you call an *exit routine* that is executed during the sort or merge. Although the sort/merge program provides 16 different *exits*, the E15 and E35 exits are the ones you're most likely to use. E15 occurs right after each input record is read, and E35 occurs just before each output record is written. An exit routine is usually used to modify the input records before they're sorted or the output records before they're written.

Figure 19-7   The SUM and MODS control statements

Application programs that do internal sorts and merges

When you use a sort program by itself, through JCL, it's referred to as a *standalone sort*. When you use a sort program from within an application program like a COBOL program, it's referred to as an *internal sort*. How this can affect processing is illustrated by the system flowcharts in figure 19-8.

With a standalone sort, the sort/merge program sorts a file in step 1, and an application program prepares a report from the sorted file in step 2. With an internal sort, one application program reads the input records, passes them to the sort/merge program for sorting, and prepares a report from the records that are returned by the sort/merge program.

How internal sorts and merges can improve efficiency

In general, an application program with an internal sort will run more efficiently than the combination of a standalone sort plus an application program. That's because the sort/merge program doesn't have to take the time to write the sorted records to an output file. Instead, it returns the sorted records directly to the application program.

This means that fewer I/O operations are required when you use an internal sort. If, for example, the invoice file in figure 19-8 consists of 500 blocks of records, the system with the standalone sort requires 1000 more I/O operations than the system with the internal sort: 500 extra output operations for the sort program to write the sorted file, and 500 extra input operations for the application program to read the sorted file.

For the same reason, *internal merges* can be more efficient than *standalone merges*. That is, the merged file isn't written to disk when an internal merge is used, so fewer I/O operations are required. Keep in mind, though, that before a merge can be run, the input files have to be in the appropriate sequence. Often, that means that they have to be sorted before they're merged. In that case, it's more efficient to concatenate the files and sort them with an internal sort than it is to first sort the files and then merge them with an internal merge.

When you use an internal sort or merge, you can process the input records before they are released to the sort/merge program and after they are returned by the sort/merge program. For instance, you can check transaction records for validity right after they're read and only release the valid records to the sort. That way, fewer records need to be sorted. And you can prepare a report or update a master file after the transaction records are returned from a sort. This is another benefit that you get from using an internal sort or merge.

How records are sorted with a standalone sort

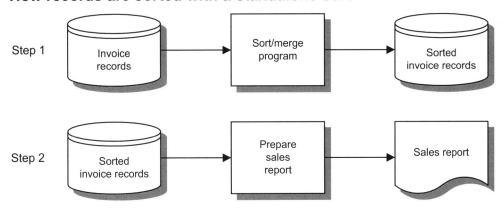

How records are sorted with an internal sort

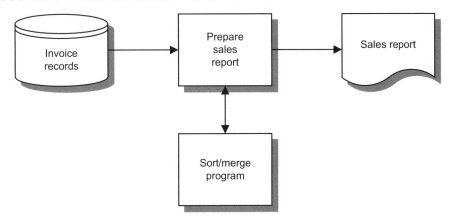

Description

- A sort that you do by invoking the sort/merge program through JCL is called a *standalone sort*. A sort that is invoked from an application program is called an *internal sort*.

- When you use a standalone sort, the sort/merge program reads the input file, sorts the records, and creates an output file of sorted records. Then, the sorted records can be processed by an application program that requires the records in that sequence.

- When you use an internal sort, the sort/merge program can return the sorted records to the application program before creating an output file. That makes the sort more efficient by saving the time it takes to write the sorted file to disk and then read it from disk.

- An *internal merge* can also be more efficient than a *standalone merge* because the merged file is never created, so fewer I/O operations are required.

- When you use an internal sort or merge, your program can process the records before they are released to the sort/merge program and after they are returned from the sort/merge program.

Figure 19-8   How internal sorts and merges can improve efficiency

The JCL requirements for programs with internal sorts and merges

When you code the JCL for running an application that uses an internal sort or merge, you code DD statements for all of the files that the program requires in the usual way. In addition, you need to code a SORTLIB DD statement for the modules that the sort/merge program requires, plus one or more DD statements for the work files that are required by a sort. In some cases, you may also need to provide a DD statement for sort/merge control statements that are designed to improve the performance of the sort or merge.

To show you how this works, figure 19-9 presents an overview of a sequential update program that has been written in COBOL along with the JCL for running this program. As you can see, this program has two input files (RCTTRAN and OLDMAST) and two output files (ERRTRAN and NEWMAST). Because the program uses an internal sort, it also requires a work file.

In the JCL for this program, you can see the five DD statements for these files, plus the SORTLIB DD statement. Although you can use the SORT-CONTROL register in a COBOL program to provide the ddname for a file that provides sort/merge control statements, you shouldn't need any. Instead, the COBOL program provides all the information that the sort/merge program needs for running efficiently.

If you aren't familiar with sequential update programs, you may be surprised to find that sequential master files are still in use in mainframe shops. When a program like this is run, the records in the old master file are updated by transactions that have been sorted into the same sequence as the master file records. Then, the updated records are written to a new sequential master file. For some master files, this works better than random processing of a key-sequenced VSAM file.

The system flowchart for a sequential update program

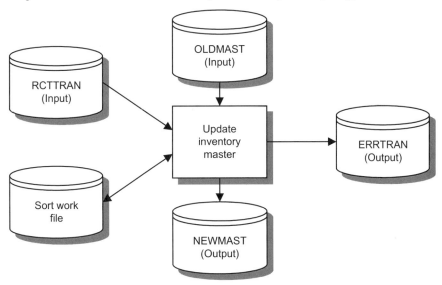

The processing done by the program

- This program validates the data in a file of receipt transactions (RCTTRAN), sorts the valid transactions into item-number sequence, and then uses the sorted transactions to update data in an old master file (OLDMAST) that is in sequence by item number. The output is a new master file that contains the updated records (NEWMAST).

- If a transaction is invalid or if a valid transaction has an item number that doesn't match the item number in a master record, the transaction is written to a file of error transactions (ERRTRAN).

The JCL requirements for a program with an internal sort or merge

- That JCL must include a SORTLIB statement and one or more SORTWK statements that provide information to the sort/merge program.

- In a COBOL program, you can also use the SORT-CONTROL register to provide the ddname of a file that contains sort/merge control statements.

The JCL for the sequential update program when it's written in COBOL

```
//SEQUPDTE JOB     (36512),MENENDEZ,NOTIFY=MM01
//INV2200  EXEC    PGM=INV2200
//RCTTRAN  DD      DSNAME=MM01.INV.TRANS,DISP=SHR
//OLDMAST  DD      DSNAME=MM01.INV.MASTER,DISP=SHR
//NEWMAST  DD      DSNAME=MM01.INV.MASTER.NEW,DISP=(NEW,CATLG),
//                 UNIT=SYSDA,VOL=SER=MPS8BV,
//                 SPACE=(CYL,(10,5))
//ERRTRAN  DD      DSNAME=MM01.INV.TRANS.ERRORS,DISP=(NEW,CATLG),
//                 UNIT=SYSDA,VOL=SER=MPS8BV,
//                 SPACE=(CYL,(1,1))
//SORTLIB  DD      DSNAME=SYS1.SORTLIB,DISP=SHR
//SORTWK01 DD      UNIT=SYSDA,SPACE=(CYL,(20,5))
```

Figure 19-9   The JCL requirements for a program with an internal sort

Perspective

As databases replace files and interactive processing replaces batch processing, the need for sorting and merging is reduced. Today, however, there are still plenty of applications in mainframe shops that require sorting. If this chapter has succeeded, you'll be able to use the sort/merge program to do whatever sorting those applications require. And you'll be able to use this chapter for efficient reference whenever you need to refresh your memory on the JCL or control statement details.

Terms

sort/merge utility
sort/merge program
sort program
sort
control field
sort key
control statement
merge
separation field
exit routine
exit
standalone sort
internal sort
standalone merge
internal merge

20

How to use TSO, CLIST, and REXX

This chapter is designed to introduce you to TSO commands, CLIST procedures, and REXX procedures. As you will see, they provide other ways to do some of the same functions that you can do with JCL. However, they also go well beyond the capabilities of JCL.

When you finish this chapter, you should be able to code and run some TSO commands. You should also be able to code and run some simple CLIST or REXX procedures. Remember, though, that this chapter is just an introduction to these capabilities. It doesn't try to teach you how to use them all in detail. Instead, it gives you an idea of what you can do with TSO commands, CLIST, and REXX so you can decide how much more you want to learn about them.

Introduction to TSO commands

TSO/E (Time Sharing Option/Extended), or just *TSO*, is an OS/390 sub-system that lets terminal users invoke system facilities interactively. As you learned in chapter 2, each TSO/E user is given a unique address space and can allocate data sets and invoke programs just as a batch job can. To do functions like that, the user invokes the commands that TSO provides.

Some commonly-used TSO commands

Figure 20-1 lists some of the *TSO commands* that are commonly used by application programmers, along with the ISPF equivalents for running these commands. This shows that ISPF is just an interface for running some of the TSO commands.

Note, however, that some of the TSO commands in this summary don't have ISPF equivalents. Note too that TSO provides many other commands that aren't included in this list. That's why it's worth knowing how to run TSO commands without using the ISPF options.

If you review the commands in this list, you can see that many of them offer functions that you've learned how to do in other ways in other chapters of this book. For instance, the ALLOCATE command allocates a data set just as a DD statement does in a JCL job. And the LISTCAT and SMCOPY commands list catalog entries and copy data sets just as the LISTCAT and REPRO commands do when you're using the VSAM AMS utility (see chapter 16).

On the other hand, some of the commands in this summary offer functions that aren't presented in other chapters of this book. For instance, the SEND command lets you send a message to another terminal user. The LISTBC command displays the broadcast messages that have been sent to your terminal. And the LISTALC command lists the data sets that are currently allocated to your TSO session.

Some commonly-used TSO commands

Command	ISPF option	Description
Session mangagement		
LOGON	None	Start a terminal session.
LOGOFF	X, then LOGOFF	End a terminal session.
HELP	T (Tutorial) or PF1/13	Display help information.
SEND	None	Send a message to another user.
LISTBC	None	Display broadcast messages.
Data set management		
EDIT	2 (Edit)	Edit the contents of a data set or member.
LISTCAT	3.4 (DSLIST utility)	List catalog entries.
LISTDS	3.2 or 3.4 (Data set or DSLIST utility)	List data set information.
RENAME	3.2 or 3.4 (Data set or DSLIST utility)	Rename a data set.
DELETE	3.2 or 3.4 (Data set or DSLIST utility)	Delete a data set.
SMCOPY	3.3 (Move/Copy utility)	Copy a data set or member.
PRINTDS	3.6 (Hardcopy utility)	Print the contents of a data set or member.
Data set allocation		
ALLOCATE	3.2 (Data set utility, but not quite the same)	Allocate a data set.
FREE	None	Free an allocated data set.
LISTALC	None	List data sets currently allocated.
ALTLIB	None	Activate an alternate procedure library.
Foreground program development		
CALL	None	Execute a load module.
LINK	4.7 (Foreground link-edit)	Link-edit a compiled program.
LOADGO	None	Link-edit and execute a compiled program.
TEST	None	Test a program.
Background jobs		
SUBMIT	5 (Batch processing)	Submit a job for background processing.
STATUS	3.8 (Outlist utility)	Display the current status of submitted jobs.
OUTPUT	3.8 (Outlist utility)	Get the output from background jobs.
CANCEL	3.8 (Outlist utility)	Cancel a submitted job.

Description

- TSO offers dozens of commands, but these are the ones that are commonly used by an application programmer.
- When you use ISPF, you are actually running TSO commands. Note, however, that ISPF doesn't provide for the use of all of the TSO commands.

Figure 20-1   Some commonly-used TSO commands

How to code TSO commands

Figure 20-2 presents the essential information that you need for coding a TSO command. If you look at the examples at the bottom of this figure, you'll get a quick idea of how this works.

Once you know the syntax of a specific command, you code the command name followed by the operands, which are separated by spaces. When parentheses are required, you usually code them the way you do in JCL statements. And to continue a command on the next line, you can code a hyphen or plus sign at the end of the continued line or you can just keep typing until the command runs on to the next line.

When you code a data set name within an operand, TSO automatically adds your user-id to the front of the name, so you shouldn't include that in your entry. If, for example, you enter SOURCE.COBOL as a data set name and your user-id is MM01, TSO interprets the name as MM01.SOURCE.COBOL. However, you can override that by coding the data set name within single quotation marks. In other words, if you enter 'CUSTOMER.DATA' as the data set name, TSO interprets it as CUSTOMER.DATA.

If you look again at the examples, you can see how easy it is to code TSO commands. For instance, the first example shows a LOGON command, which you should already know how to use for your installation. The second example shows an SMCOPY command. The third example shows that the ALLOCATE command has the same operands as the DD statement. And the fourth example shows how you can use the SEND command to send a message to another user when you know the user-id.

Although this chapter doesn't present the syntax for the TSO commands, you can get that information by coding the HELP command as shown in the fifth example. This consists of the word HELP followed by the name of the command that you want information on. For many TSO commands, that's all the help you need.

The general syntax of any TSO command

```
command-name  operand [operand] ...
```

The format of a data set name in a TSO session

```
user-id.name.type
```

Common type qualifiers for data set names in a TSO session

ASM	Assembler language source code	EXEC	REXX procedure
CLIST	CLIST procedure	JCL	JCL job stream
COBOL	COBOL source code	PROCLIB	JCL procedure

Coding rules

* Separate the operands by commas or spaces.
* Code the positional operands first in their proper positions, but code the keyword operands in any sequence.
* In general, use parentheses the way they're used in JCL statements.
* Don't include the user-id when coding data set names that start with the user-id because that's automatically added to your entry.
* If you want to override the TSO conventions for data set names, code the data set name within single quotation marks. Then, the user-id isn't added to the data set name.

Two ways to continue a command on the next line

* When you enter a command in a native TSO/E screen or in the ISPF Command Shell panel, you can type until the line automatically wraps to the next line.
* When you specify a command in a CLIST that doesn't fit on one line, you can type a space followed by a hyphen (-) or plus sign (+) after one of the parameters and continue on the next line. If you use a hyphen, continue coding in the first position of the next line. If you use a plus sign, you can continue coding in any position of the next line.

Examples of TSO commands

```
LOGON MM01/RM ACCT(36512)
```
Logs on a user with user-id MM01, password RM, and account number 36512.

```
SMCOPY FROMDATASET('CUSTMAST.TEST1') TODATASET('CUSTMAST.TEST2')
```
Copies the data set named CUSTMAST.TEST1 to a data set named CUSTMAST.TEST2.

```
ALLOCATE DSNAME(TESTLIB.CLIST) SPACE(10 2) CYLINDERS DIR(10) +
        DSORG(PO) RECFM(FB) LRECL(80) BLKSIZE(6160) RETPD(60)
```
If the user-id for the session is MM01, this allocates a new partitioned data set named MM01.TESTLIB.CLIST where CLIST identifies the type of data stored in the data set. The remaining parameters provide the space allocation and data set characteristics.

```
SEND 'DO YOU HAVE A COPY OF AR2000?' USER(MM02)
```
Sends the message in quotes to the user with user-id MM02.

```
HELP LISTCAT
```
Displays the help information for the LISTCAT command.

Figure 20-2   How to code TSO commands

How to run TSO commands

If you've been using ISPF to develop and run your JCL jobs, you already know how to run the LOGON command in native TSO (that is, outside of ISPF). To do that, you just type the command when TSO shows the READY message and press the Enter key to run the command. That's also how you enter any other TSO command in native TSO. You just type the command and press Enter.

As an application programmer, though, you usually work in ISPF instead of native TSO, so you usually want to run your TSO commands from ISPF. To do that, you can use one of the two methods given in figure 20-3. First, if you select option 6 from the ISPF Primary Option Menu, the ISPF Command Shell panel is displayed. From this panel, you can run TSO commands the same way you do in native TSO, either by entering them from scratch at the command prompt or by selecting a previously executed command that's displayed on the screen. Second, you can run TSO commands from the command area of any other ISPF panel just by preceding the command with TSO and one or more spaces.

As you run TSO commands, three types of TSO messages may be displayed. These are summarized in this figure. When a *prompt* is displayed, you need to enter a required operand that you omitted from the command. Then, as a command runs, you can read the *informational messages* to follow the progress of the command. You can also read the *broadcast messages* to get information about the system, which sometimes includes information about its availability.

With this as background, you should be able to run some TSO commands on your own. If, for example, you want to run a program that requires a master input file and a printed output file, you can allocate the data sets, run the program, and deallocate the data sets by running a series of commands like these:

```
ALLOCATE DDNAME(CUSTMAST) DSNAME(CUSTMAST.DATA)
ALLOCATE DDNAME(SALESRPT) SYSOUT(A)
CALL TEST(MKTG1200) PARM('JANUARY')
FREE DDNAME(CUSTMAST SALESRPT)
```

Here, the ALLOCATE commands allocate the input and output files needed by the program, and the CALL command runs the program named MKTG1200 and passes the parameter JANUARY to it. Then, when the program finishes running, the FREE command deallocates the files because that isn't done automatically when you run TSO commands.

Similarly, you can use TSO commands to change the default allocations for the standard SYSIN and SYSOUT data sets so the input comes from your terminal and the output is sent to your terminal. To do that, you can enter these commands:

```
ALLOCATE DDNAME(SYSIN) DSNAME(*)
ALLOCATE DDNAME(SYSOUT) DSNAME(*)
```

Then, when you run a COBOL program through TSO, any ACCEPT statements will get the information from your terminal, and any DISPLAY statements will display its data on your terminal. This is sometimes useful when you're testing programs.

The ISPF Command Shell panel for entering TSO commands

Access from the ISPF Primary Option Menu: 6 (Command)

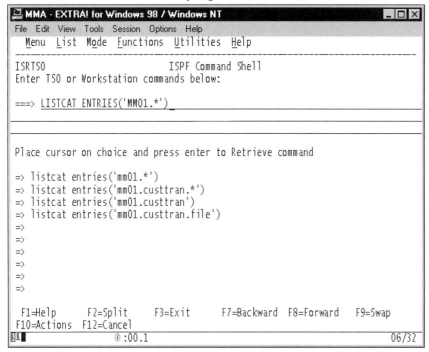

Two ways to run TSO commands from ISPF

- Select option 6 from the Primary Option Menu. Then, use the ISPF Command Shell panel to enter your commands just as you would enter them in native TSO. You can also place the cursor over any previously entered command that's displayed on this panel and press Enter, and the command will appear on the command line.

- Enter TSO followed by the command in the command area of any ISPF panel.

The three types of system messages that you may receive

- *Prompts* are displayed when you enter commands with missing operands. A prompt asks you to supply a missing operand and always ends with a question mark.

- *Informational messages* provide information about the progress of a command's execution.

- *Broadcast messages* are created by a system operator or another TSO user. You usually receive a set of these messages when you log in, and you can list them at any time by using the LISTBC command.

Description

- Although you can run TSO commands from native TSO, you usually don't do that if you're working in ISPF. Instead, you usually use one of the two ways listed above to run TSO commands from ISPF.

Figure 20-3   How to run TSO commands from ISPF

Introduction to CLIST procedures

A *CLIST procedure* (also know as a *command procedure* or *CLIST*) is a series of TSO commands and statements that can be run as a single unit. To illustrate, figure 20-4 illustrates a command procedure for testing a program. It consists of three ALLOCATE commands, a CALL command, and a FREE command that are run in sequence. As you will see, though, a CLIST can also contain procedure statements.

How to create and run a CLIST

Figure 20-4 presents the basic techniques that you need for creating a CLIST. To do that, you enter the commands and statements that you want, and you save them in a member of a partitioned data set with CLIST as the type qualifier. At that point, the CLIST is ready to be run.

To run a CLIST from any ISPF panel, you need to start by allocating and activating your CLIST library, as shown in this figure. Here, the ALLOCATE command assigns your user CLIST library to the SYSUEXEC ddname. This establishes your library as a user procedure library. Then, the ALTLIB command activates the user library so it gets searched before the TSO system procedure library is searched.

Once you've allocated and activated your user library, which you can do at the start of a session, you can run a CLIST from any ISPF panel by entering TSO, a space, and the name of the CLIST. If you code the name without a preceding percent sign, though, the name looks to TSO like the name of a command, so TSO first searches its own command libraries to see whether you've entered a TSO command. However, if you precede the CLIST name with a percent sign, you tell TSO that the name is a CLIST, not a command, so TSO looks first in the active user library. Since this is obviously more efficient, you should always precede your CLIST names with percent signs.

This figure also shows how to use the EXEC command to run a CLIST from native TSO (or from the ISPF Command Shell). When you use the *explicit form* of this command, you identify both the library and the member name. Because this command assumes that the type is CLIST, you don't have to include it in the library name. Then, if your user-id is MM01, an entry of TEST gets expanded into MM01.TEST.CLIST.

When you use the *implicit form* of the EXEC command, you omit the command name and the name of the library. Before you can do that, though, you have to allocate and activate the user library that contains your CLIST procedures. Here again, you use the ALLOCATE and ALTLIB commands, which you can do at the start of a session. Once that's done, you can run a CLIST by entering a percent sign followed by the name of the CLIST.

By the way, depending on your installation's standards and the library names you use, your user CLIST library may be allocated and activated when you log on to TSO. In that case, you don't have to use the ALLOCATE and ALTLIB commands before you run a CLIST.

A CLIST named MKTGTEST that runs a COBOL program

```
ALLOCATE DDNAME(CUSTMAST) DSNAME(CUSTMAST.DATA)
ALLOCATE DDNAME(SYSIN) DSNAME(*)
ALLOCATE DDNAME(SYSOUT) DSNAME(*)
CALL TEST(MKTG1200) PARM('JANUARY')
FREE DDNAME(CUSTMAST SYSIN SYSOUT)
```

How to create a CLIST that consists of TSO commands

- Use the ISPF editor to enter the TSO commands in the sequence in which you want them executed.
- Save the commands as a member of a partitioned data set that has CLIST as the type qualifier.

How to run a CLIST from any ISPF panel

Allocate and activate your user CLIST library when you start a session

```
TSO ALLOCATE DDNAME(SYSUEXEC) DSN(TEST.CLIST) SHR REUSE
TSO ALTLIB ACTIVATE USER(EXEC)
```

Enter % followed by the name of the CLIST to be run

```
TSO %MKTGTEST
```

Two ways to run a CLIST in native TSO

Use the explicit form of the EXEC command to identify the library and member

```
EXEC TEST(MKTGTEST)
```

Allocate your library and then use the implicit form of the EXEC command

```
ALLOCATE DDNAME(SYSUEXEC) DSN(TEST.CLIST) SHR REUSE
ALTLIB ACTIVATE USER(EXEC)
%MKTGTEST
```

Description

- A *CLIST procedure* (or *command procedure* or *CLIST*) is a series of TSO commands and procedure statements that are stored in a member of a partitioned data set.
- To allocate and activate the user library that contains the CLIST procedures that you want to run, you can use the ALLOCATE command for the SYSUEXEC ddname and the ALTLIB command. If you don't activate a user library, TSO looks for a CLIST in its system procedure library (SYSPROC or SYSEXEC).
- To run a CLIST from any ISPF panel, you need to code TSO, a space, and the CLIST name preceded by the percent sign, which helps TSO find your CLIST faster.
- When you use the *explicit form* of the EXEC command to run a CLIST from native TSO or from the ISPF Command Shell, you identify the CLIST library. But when you use the *implicit form*, you don't. Instead, TSO searches the user library and then the TSO system procedure library for the CLIST.

Figure 20-4   How to create and run a CLIST

How to use symbolic variables in a CLIST

When you create a CLIST, you can use *symbolic variables* to hold values that can be changed when the CLIST is invoked. This is illustrated in figure 20-5. If you study this figure, you'll see that this is similar to the use of symbolic parameters when you're creating and using JCL procedures.

The procedure at the top of this figure uses two symbolic variables that are identified by the PROC statement. If you look at the syntax for this statement in the middle of this figure, you can see that the PROC statement in the CLIST consists of one *positional operand* and one *keyword operand* (a keyword operand is followed by a set of parentheses). Then, in the TSO commands that follow the PROC statement, you can see the name of the positional operand in the first and last commands, preceded by an ampersand (&) in each case. And you can see the name of the keyword operand in the CALL command, also preceded by an ampersand. These are the symbolic variables that will change when the CLIST is executed.

To run a CLIST that uses symbolic variables, you enter the CLIST name followed by the values for the symbolic variables. These values must start with the positional operands in their proper sequence, followed by the keyword operands with each value given in parentheses after the keyword. In the example in this figure, then, CUSTMAST will be substituted for the positional operand and MAY will be substituted for the keyword operand. You can see how this works by studying the commands that are executed when the CLIST is run. Note that the two periods that were coded in the first ALLOCATE statement result in a single period remaining when the symbolic variable is replaced by a value. That's because the first period is used as a delimiter to mark the end of the symbolic variable, while the second one is text that's retained.

By using symbolic variables in this way, you make a CLIST more useful. For instance, you can use the CLIST in this figure to vary the data set name and parameter value each time the program is run. This can be useful when testing a program with several combinations of the two. As you will see, though, you can also use symbolic variables to hold values that are changed *as* the CLIST is run.

A CLIST named MKTGTEST that uses symbolic variables

```
PROC 1 MASTERDSN PARM()
ALLOCATE DDNAME(CUSTMAST) DSNAME(&MASTERDSN..DATA)
ALLOCATE DDNAME(SYSIN) DSNAME(*)
ALLOCATE DDNAME(SYSOUT) DSNAME(*)
CALL TEST(MKTG1200) PARM('&PARM')
FREE DDNAME(&MASTERDSN SYSIN SYSOUT)
```

A command for running the CLIST from any ISPF panel

```
TSO %MKTGTEST CUSTMAST PARM(MAY)
```

The commands that are executed when the CLIST is run

```
ALLOCATE DDNAME(CUSTMAST) DSNAME(CUSTMAST.DATA)
ALLOCATE DDNAME(SYSIN) DSNAME(*)
ALLOCATE DDNAME(SYSOUT) DSNAME(*)
CALL TEST(MKTG1200) PARM('MAY')
FREE DDNAME(CUSTMAST SYSIN SYSOUT)
```

The syntax of the PROC statement

```
PROC count [positional-operand] ... [keyword-operand(value)] ...
```

Explanation

count	The number of positional operands. Enter zero if none are coded.
positional-operand	Symbolic variable name for a positional operand without the ampersand.
keyword-operand	Symbolic variable name for a keyword operand without the ampersand.
value	Default value for a keyword operand.

The rules for forming a symbolic variable name

- Each name consists of an ampersand (&) followed by a name.
- The name consists of up to 31 alphabetic or numeric characters, starting with a letter.

Description

- You can use *symbolic variables* to generalize a CLIST. You can also use them in the way that you use variables in application programs.
- To enable a CLIST to receive values that are passed to it when it's invoked, you code a PROC statement at the start of the CLIST and symbolic variable names within the CLIST. Later, when the CLIST is executed, the passed values are substituted for the symbolic variables.
- To run a CLIST that receives passed variables, you supply the name of the CLIST and the values that are passed to it.
- The PROC statement is actually a procedure statement (see the next figure).

Figure 20-5   How to use symbolic variables in a CLIST

Some of the procedure statements that you can use in a CLIST

Besides TSO commands, you can code *procedure statements* within a CLIST. These statements are actually processed by the *procedure interpreter*, not by TSO. The PROC statement, for example, is a procedure statement. To give you some idea of the range of functions that these statements provide, figure 20-6 summarizes some of them.

If you have programming experience, you should be familiar with many of the statements in this summary. As you can see, there is a full set of control statements like DO-WHILE and IF statements that let you vary the processing based on the conditions that occur while a CLIST is running. There are terminal I/O statements that let you display messages on a user's terminal and get data from a user's terminal. And there are file I/O statements that let you read data from and write data to sequential files.

Beyond that, you can use arithmetic expressions and relational expressions in a CLIST. You can nest one CLIST within another. You can use other procedure statements that aren't included in this figure. And you can use built-in functions and control variables as shown in the next figure.

As you work with these statements and features, you should keep in mind that the statements within a CLIST are interpreted, not compiled. This means that a CLIST doesn't have to be compiled and linked before it can be executed. Instead, the procedure interpreter reads, *interprets*, and executes one CLIST statement at a time. This makes it relatively easy to develop simple procedures.

Some of the procedure statements that you can use in CLISTs

Command	Description
Control statements	
DO	Marks the start of a group of statements called a DO group that is ended by an END statement.
DO-UNTIL	Performs a group of statements until a condition becomes true.
DO-WHILE	Performs a group of statements while a condition is true.
DO repetitions	Repeatedly performs a group of statements and increments a variable until the variable reaches the value given in the statement.
END	Marks the end of a group of statements.
EXIT	Terminates the execution of a CLIST.
GOTO	Branches to a statement in the CLIST that is identified by a label.
IF	Performs one statement or DO group if the condition in the statement is true, and another statement or DO group if the condition is false. The condition can include relational expressions as well as logical expressions.
SELECT	Defines a series of conditions and the statement or group of statements that is to be executed when each condition is true. This is the CLIST implementation of the case structure.
SET	Changes the value of a symbolic variable to the value in an expression, which can be an arithmetic expression.
Terminal I/O statements	
READ	Accepts one or more values from the terminal user and stores them in the variables that are specified. If more than one variable is specified, the user must separate the entries with commas.
WRITE	Displays a message at the user's terminal.
WRITENR	Displays a message at the user's terminal, but doesn't move to the next line.
File I/O statements	
OPENFILE	Opens a sequential file that has been allocated by an ALLOCATE statement by giving the ddname for the file followed by the processing mode.
GETFILE	Reads a record from the sequential file that's identified by its ddname and places the data into a symbolic variable named &ddname.
PUTFILE	Adds a record to the end of the sequential file that's identified by its ddname.
CLOSFILE	Closes the file that's identified by its ddname.

Description

- A *procedure statement* is executed by the procedure interpreter. In contrast, a TSO command is executed by TSO.

- The procedure statements provide many of the capabilities of an application programming language including control logic, terminal I/O, and file I/O.

Figure 20-6   Some of the procedure statements that you can use in a CLIST

Built-in functions and control variables that you can use in a CLIST

Figure 20-7 presents seven *built-in functions* (or just *functions*) that you can use in a CLIST. When you use one, you code one or more operands in parentheses after the function name, which starts with an ampersand.

As you can see, six of these functions let you work with string (character) data that has been entered into symbolic variables. For instance, the &SUBSTR function lets you extract a substring from a string by identifying its starting and ending position within the string. This is useful when several values are read into a single symbolic variable from a terminal or a file.

The seventh function in this figure can be used to determine whether a data set exists and is available. This gives you the ability to terminate a CLIST by issuing an EXIT statement if a required data set isn't available. Your CLIST can also issue WRITE statements to tell the terminal user what has happened.

Control variables, which also start with an ampersand, let you get and use system information in a CLIST. For instance, &SYSUID holds the user-id of the user who is running the CLIST, and &LASTCC holds the condition code that was returned by the last TSO command that was executed.

To illustrate the use of these features, this figure presents a short CLIST for entering publication orders. When this procedure is run, the interactive session will look something like this (the user entries are shaded):

```
PLACE YOUR PUBLICATION ORDER

ENTER YOUR EMPLOYEE NUMBER:
1234
ENTER YOUR DEPARTMENT NUMBER:
101

ENTER DOCUMENT-ID AND QUANTITY (LEAVE BLANK TO END):
1-890774-12-X,1
ENTER DOCUMENT-ID AND QUANTITY (LEAVE BLANK TO END):

YOUR ORDER HAS BEEN PLACED
```

If you look at the code in this figure, you can see that this CLIST starts with a TSO ALLOCATE command that allocates the file that the procedure requires, and it ends with a FREE command that deallocates this file. In between are procedure statements that use symbolic variables, the &STR function, and the &SYSUID control variable. For each publication ordered, the program writes one record to the file. Note that a PROC statement isn't needed because all of the symbolic variable values are supplied by user entries as the procedure executes.

If you're a programmer, you can probably understand most of this code right now. But the point of this chapter isn't to teach you how to code CLISTs. It's just to introduce you to their capabilities. At this point, then, you should see that you can combine several program development commands into a generalized CLIST. But you can also use CLIST procedures for small, interactive, special-purpose applications.

Built-in functions that you can use in CLIST procedures

Function	Use
&DATATYPE	Returns the data type of the string: NUM or CHAR.
&LENGTH	Returns the length of the string.
&EVAL	Forces the string to be evaluated when it normally wouldn't be.
&STR	Stops the string from being evaluated.
&SUBSTR	Extracts a substring from a string.
&SYSINDEX	Returns the starting position of a substring within a string.
&SYSDSN	Returns OK if the data set exists and is available. Otherwise, it returns a message.

Some of the control variables that you can use in CLIST procedures

Variable	Use
&SYSUID	The user-id of the current user.
&LASTCC	The condition code returned by the last TSO command or CLIST statement.
&SYSNEST	Contains YES if the procedure is nested, or NO if it isn't.
&SYSTIME	The current time in the form *hh:mm:ss*.
&SYSDATE	The current date in the form *mm/dd/yyyy*.

A CLIST for entering publication orders

```
ALLOCATE DDNAME(ORDER) DSNAME(ORDER.DATA) MOD
OPENFILE ORDER OUTPUT
WRITE PLACE YOUR PUBLICATION ORDER
WRITE
WRITE ENTER YOUR EMPLOYEE NUMBER:
READ EMPNO
WRITE ENTER YOUR DEPARTMENT NUMBER:
READ DEPTCODE
WRITE
SET NULL =
DO UNTIL &STR(&DOCID) = &NULL
    WRITE ENTER DOCUMENT-ID AND QUANTITY (LEAVE BLANK TO END):
    READ DOCID QUANTITY
    IF &STR(&DOCID) ¬= &NULL THEN DO
        SET ORDER = &EMPNO &SYSUID &DEPTCODE &STR(&DOCID) &QUANTITY
        PUTFILE ORDER
        END
    END
WRITE
WRITE YOUR ORDER HAS BEEN PLACED
CLOSFILE ORDER
FREE DDNAME(ORDER)
```

Description

- You can use *built-in functions* to perform some useful operations on strings and to find out whether a data set exists.

- You can use *control variables* to get system information.

Figure 20-7   Built-in functions and control variables that you can use in a CLIST

Introduction to REXX

A *REXX procedure* is a series of TSO commands and REXX statements that can be run as a single unit. To illustrate, figure 20-8 illustrates a REXX procedure for testing a COBOL program. It consists of three ALLOCATE commands, a CALL command, and a FREE command that are run in sequence. As you will see, though, a REXX procedure can also include REXX statements, just as a CLIST can include procedure statements.

How to create and run a REXX procedure

Figure 20-8 presents the basic techniques that you need for creating a REXX procedure. To do that, you enter the commands and statements that you want, and you save them in a member of a partitioned data set with EXEC as the type qualifier. Note, however, that a REXX procedure must start with a comment that includes the word REXX, and any TSO statements in the procedure have to be enclosed in quotation marks.

To run a REXX procedure from any ISPF panel, from native TSO, or from the ISPF Command Shell panel, you use the techniques shown in this figure. Since these are so similar to the ones for running CLIST procedures, I won't describe them in detail again. However, there are two differences that you should note. First, a REXX procedure library has EXEC as the type qualifier, not CLIST. Second, the explicit form of the EXEC statement for running a REXX procedure must end with EXEC. That tells TSO to look for a REXX procedure instead of a CLIST.

A REXX procedure named MKTGTEST that runs a COBOL program

```
/* REXX */
"ALLOCATE DDNAME(CUSTMAST) DSNAME(CUSTMAST.DATA)"
"ALLOCATE DDNAME(SYSIN) DSNAME(*)"
"ALLOCATE DDNAME(SYSOUT) DSNAME(*)"
"CALL TEST(MKTG1200) PARM('JANUARY')"
"FREE DDNAME(CUSTMAST SYSIN SYSOUT)"
```

How to create a REXX procedure that consists of TSO commands

- Use the ISPF editor to enter TSO commands in the sequence in which you want them executed, but code each TSO command within quotation marks.

- Start the procedure with a comment that includes the word REXX.

- Save the commands as a member of a partitioned data set that has EXEC as the type qualifier.

How to run a REXX procedure from any ISPF panel

Allocate and activate your user EXEC library when you start a session

```
TSO ALLOCATE DDNAME(SYSUEXEC) DSN(TEST.EXEC) SHR REUSE
TSO ALTLIB ACTIVATE USER(EXEC)
```

Enter % followed by the name of the REXX procedure to be run

```
TSO %MKTGTEST
```

Two ways to run a REXX procedure in native TSO

Use the explicit form of the EXEC command to identify the library and member

```
EXEC TEST(MKTGTEST) EXEC
```

Allocate your library and then use the implicit form of the EXEC command

```
ALLOCATE DDNAME(SYSUEXEC) DSN(TEST.EXEC) SHR REUSE
ALTLIB ACTIVATE USER(EXEC)
%MKTGTEST
```

Description

- A *REXX procedure* can contain TSO commands that are executed in sequence, but it can also contain the statements, variables, and expressions that make up the REXX language.

- To run a REXX procedure from any ISPF panel, you need to code TSO, a space, and the procedure name preceded by the percent sign, which helps TSO find the procedure faster.

- When you use the *explicit form* of the EXEC command to run a REXX procedure from native TSO or from the ISPF Command Shell, you identify the EXEC library. But when you use the *implicit form*, you don't. Instead, TSO searches the user library and then the TSO system procedure library for the REXX procedure.

Figure 20-8 How to create and run a REXX procedure

How to use variables in a REXX procedure

When you create a REXX procedure, you can use *variables* to hold values that can be changed when the procedure is invoked. This is illustrated in figure 20-9. If you study this figure, you'll see that this is similar to the use of symbolic variables when you're creating and using CLIST procedures.

The procedure at the top of this figure uses two variables that are identified by the ARG statement. This is one of the many REXX statements that you can use in a REXX procedure. When you code any of these statements, you can use uppercase and lowercase letters. In fact, it's a common practice to code statement names as all lowercase letters and to code variable names as a combination of lowercase and uppercase letters. Internally, though, REXX treats all variable names as uppercase.

The ARG statement in this figure says that two variables named MasterDSN and Parm are going to be passed to the procedure when it is executed. Although this is similar to the way the PROC statement is coded for symbolic variables in a CLIST, note that all the variables in a ARG statement are positional. In the statements after the ARG statement, these variables are enclosed in quotation marks. Then, when the procedure is executed, it is these variables that are replaced by the values that are passed to the procedure.

To run a REXX procedure like this from an ISPF panel, you enter the procedure name followed by the values for the variables in the sequence in which they're listed on the ARG statement. In the example in this figure, then, CUSTMAST will be substituted for the first variable and MAY will be substituted for the second one. You can see how this works by studying the commands that are executed when the REXX procedure is run.

By using variables in this way, you make a REXX procedure more useful. For instance, you can use the procedure in this figure to vary the data set name and parameter value each time the program is run. This can be useful when testing a program with several combinations of the two. As you will see, though, you can also use variables to hold values that are changed *as* the procedure is run.

A REXX procedure named MKTGTEST that uses two variables

```
/* REXX */
arg MasterDSN Parm
"ALLOCATE DDNAME(CUSTMAST) DSNAME("MasterDSN".DATA)"
"ALLOCATE DDNAME(SYSIN) DSNAME(*)"
"ALLOCATE DDNAME(SYSOUT) DSNAME(*)"
"CALL TEST(MKTG1200) PARM('"Parm"')"
"FREE DDNAME("MasterDSN" SYSIN SYSOUT)"
```

A command for running the REXX procedure from any ISPF panel

```
TSO %MKTGTEST CUSTMAST MAY
```

The commands that are executed when the REXX procedure is run

```
ALLOCATE DDNAME(CUSTMAST) DSNAME(CUSTMAST.DATA)
ALLOCATE DDNAME(SYSIN) DSNAME(*)
ALLOCATE DDNAME(SYSOUT) DSNAME(*)
CALL TEST(MKTG1200) PARM('MAY')
FREE DDNAME(CUSTMAST SYSIN SYSOUT)
```

The syntax of the ARG statement

```
ARG variable ...
```

Explanation

variable   The name of a variable that is going to be passed to the procedure when it is executed.

The rules for forming a variable name

- Each name must begin with a letter or one of these special characters: _ @ # $! ?
- Each name can be up to 250 characters long and can include uppercase and lowercase letters, digits, and these special characters: _ @ # $! ?
- REXX treats all variable names as uppercase, but it's a common practice to name variables with a combination of uppercase and lowercase letters.

Description

- You can use *variables* in REXX procedures to generalize a procedure. You can also use them in the way that you use variables in application programs.
- To enable a REXX procedure to receive the values that are passed to it when it's invoked, you code an ARG statement at the start of the procedure that identifies the variables that should receive the values. Within the REXX procedure, you code the variable names within quotation marks. Later, when the REXX procedure is executed, the passed values are substituted for the variables.
- To run a REXX procedure that receives passed variables, you supply the name of the REXX procedure and the passed values that are substituted for the variables. The variables must be passed in the order in which the procedure is expecting them.
- REXX treats the data in all variables as string data. However, it provides built-in functions for working with this data both as character and numeric data.

Figure 20-9   How to use variables in a REXX procedure

Some typical REXX statements and commands

Besides TSO commands, you can code *statements* within a REXX procedure. To give you an idea of what these statements can do, figure 20-10 summarizes some of them. As you can see, these provide many of the same capabilities as the CLIST procedure statements.

Here again, if you're an application programmer or have programming experience, you should be familiar with many of the statements in this summary. However, the parsing and stacking statements may be new to you because most other languages don't have them. The PARSE statement, for example, makes it easy for you to extract substrings (or fields) from a larger string or from terminal input.

In contrast, the PUSH, QUEUE, and PULL statements are unique because they work with a *data stack*, which you can think of as a stack of records. To add a record to the top of the stack, you use the PUSH command. To add a record to the bottom of the stack, you use the QUEUE command. And to remove a record from the top of the stack, you use the PULL command.

The EXECIO command is also unique because it's a file I/O command that works with data stacks. For instance, this command can be used to read one or more of the records in a sequential file onto a data stack, and it can be used to write one or more of the records in a data stack to a sequential file. In combination, the EXECIO command and the three stacking statements provide a powerful programming feature.

Please note that the EXECIO command is actually a TSO command, not a REXX statement, so it must be enclosed in quotation marks when you code it. It also has an unusual syntax because it was originally designed for the Conversational Monitor System, or CMS, that is used with the VM operating system.

Incidentally, REXX doesn't refer to the statements in this figure as *statements*. Instead, REXX has its own terminology, which includes terms like *clause*, *keyword instruction* (like ARG), and *host command* (a TSO command). Using this terminology, the statements in this figure are clauses. To keep it simple, though, we've used the term *statement*, which is the term that is used by most other programming languages.

Like the statements for a CLIST, REXX statements are interpreted by the *REXX interpreter* so they don't need to be compiled before they can be executed. This makes it relatively easy to develop REXX procedures.

Some typical REXX statements and commands

Command	Description
Control statements	
DO	Marks the start of a group of statements that is ended by the END statement.
DO-UNTIL	Performs a group of statements until a condition becomes true.
DO-WHILE	Performs a group of statements while a condition is true.
DO repeat	Repeatedly performs a group of statements and increments a variable until the variable reaches the value given in the statement.
END	Marks the end of a group of statements.
EXIT	Terminates the execution of a REXX procedure.
IF	Performs one statement or DO group if the condition in the statement is true, and another statement or DO group if the condition is false. The condition can include relational expressions as well as logical expressions.
SELECT	Defines a series of conditions and the statement or group of statements that are to be executed when each condition is true. This is the REXX procedure implementation of the case structure.
Terminal I/O statements	
SAY	Displays a message at the user's terminal.
PULL	Accepts one or more values from the terminal user and stores them in the variables that are specified. If more than one variable is entered, the user must separate the entries with one or more spaces.
Parsing and stacking statements	
PARSE	Provides a variety of ways to copy portions of a string into variables. Can also be used to parse the terminal data that a user enters.
PUSH	Adds data from a variable to the top of a data stack.
QUEUE	Adds data from a variable to the bottom of a data stack.
PULL	Pulls data from the top of a data stack and stores it in a variable.
File I/O command	
EXECIO	A TSO command that can only be used in REXX procedures. It can read data from a sequential file onto a data stack and write data from a data stack to a sequential file.

Description

- REXX provides many statements that give it the capabilities of a full-blown programming language.

- The PARSE statement is a powerful statement that can be used to extract substrings from strings and from terminal input.

- A *data stack* can be thought of as a stack of records. You can use the EXECIO command to read records into a data stack and to write records from a data stack. And you can use the PUSH, QUEUE, and PULL statements to add records to and pull records from a data stack.

Figure 20-10   Some typical REXX statements and commands

Other REXX features

Figure 20-11 presents some of the other REXX features you may be interested in. It also presents a REXX procedure for entering publication orders that uses some of the REXX features and statements. When this procedure is run, the interactive session will look something like this (the user entries are shaded):

```
Place your publication order

Enter your employee number:
1234
Enter your department number:
101

Enter document-id and quantity (leave blank to end):
1-890774-12-X 1
Enter document-id and quantity (leave blank to end):
1-890774-14-6 2
Enter document-id and quantity (leave blank to end):

Your order has been placed
```

If you look at the code in this figure, you can see that this procedure uses the PARSE instruction to move the user entries into variables, and it uses the QUEUE statement to add each order record to the data stack. Then, when the user indicates that all items have been ordered by pressing the Enter key without entering a document-id, the procedure uses the EXECIO command to write all of the records in the data stack to a sequential file. But if this command fails so the RC built-in variable isn't zero, the procedure displays an error message. Note that an ARG statement isn't needed in this procedure because all of the variable values are supplied by user entries as the procedure executes.

If you're a programmer, you can probably understand most of this code. But here again, the point of this chapter isn't to teach you how to code REXX procedures. It is just to introduce you to their capabilities so you can decide whether you want to learn how to use them. At this point, then, you should see that REXX is a powerful language that can be used to develop small, interactive, special-purpose applications.

Some other REXX features

- A complete set of built-in functions that perform arithmetic calculations, format data, manipulate strings, and return system information such as user-id and the current date and time.

- A built-in variable named RC that holds the return code for the last TSO command that was executed.

- Compound variables for building tables and arrays

- User-defined functions

- Subroutines and nested subroutines

- Interactive tracing that makes it easier for you to debug a REXX procedure

A REXX procedure for entering publication orders

```
/* REXX */
say "Place your publication order"
say
say "Enter your employee number:"
parse external EmpNo
say "Enter your department number:"
parse external DeptCode
say
do until Document=""
    say "Enter document-id and quantity (leave blank to end):"
    parse external Document Quantity
    if Document<>"" then
        queue EmpNo DeptCode Document Quantity
        end
    end
queue ""
"ALLOCATE DDNAME(ORDER) DSNAME(ORDER.DATA) MOD"
"EXECIO * DISKW ORDER (FINIS)"
if rc=0 then
    say "Your order has been placed"
else do
    say "Your order could not be placed"
    say "EXECIO error code " rc
    end
"FREE DDNAME(ORDER)"
```

Description

- The REXX language provides for a full range of programming capabilities that go well beyond those of CLIST.

- The *interactive tracing* feature can be used to trace the execution of each statement or command in a REXX procedure. This makes is easier to debug an extensive REXX procedure.

Figure 20-11   Other REXX features

Perspective

The goal of this chapter has been to give you some insight into what you can do with TSO commands, CLIST procedures, and REXX procedures and when you would want to use one of these facilities. Now, if you would like to learn more about these facilities, you can do that by using the IBM manuals. An easier way to do that, though, is to get our book on these subjects, which is called *MVS TSO, Part 2: Commands and Procedures.*

One question you may have at this point is which is the better procedure language to learn: CLIST or REXX? Because CLIST is the older procedure language, it is more widely used, which is a point in its favor. But REXX is significantly more powerful than CLIST in many ways. In addition, REXX is the "official procedure language" of IBM's System Application Architecture (SAA), which means that it is available on several platforms. In fact, IBM has even created an object-oriented version of REXX called *Object REXX.* In practice, though, the decision often comes down to which language is used in your shop.

Terms

TSO/E	procedure statement
Time Sharing Option/Extended	procedure interpreter
TSO	interpret
TSO command	built-in function
prompt	function
informational message	control variable
broadcast message	REXX procedure
CLIST procedure	variable
command procedure	REXX statement
CLIST	data stack
explicit form (of EXEC command)	REXX interpreter
implicit form (of EXEC command)	interactive tracing
symbolic variable	clause
positional operand	keyword instruction
keyword operand	host command

21

How to use UNIX System Services

UNIX is a multi-user, multitasking operating system like OS/390. Unlike OS/390, which is a proprietary operating system that's designed for IBM mainframes, UNIX is a standardized operating system that can run on many different types of computer systems.

Today, UNIX is one of the most popular operating systems used on web servers and a key component in web-based processing. As a result, many businesses need to work with UNIX-based programs and files, even though UNIX isn't their primary operating system. To make that possible on a mainframe, OS/390 includes a facility called UNIX System Services. With this facility, you can run UNIX programs on a mainframe. That includes standard application programs as well as web applications and other utilities commonly found on UNIX systems. You can also access, process, and create UNIX files on the mainframe.

As an OS/390 application programmer, you're more likely to work with UNIX files than with other aspects of UNIX, so that's the focus of this chapter. However, you'll also be introduced to working within the UNIX environment, so you'll have a basis for adding to your skills as you need to.

The file structure in a UNIX system

A UNIX system consists of three basic parts. The *kernel* is the operating system base. The file system provides for creating, accessing, and managing UNIX-based files. And the command interface, or *shell*, lets you perform UNIX functions by entering UNIX commands at your terminal. OS/390 provides for these elements through its *UNIX System Services (USS)*.

Before you can do much of anything in UNIX, you have to understand how the files in a UNIX environment are organized, so that's what this chapter describes first. Once you know about the file structure, you'll learn how to access UNIX files and functions interactively (through TSO commands and the UNIX shell) or in batch (through JCL and utility programs).

Files in a hierarchical file system

Files in a UNIX environment are organized into a hierarchical structure, as shown in the diagram in figure 21-1. If this looks familiar to you, that's because both the DOS and Windows operating systems use a hierarchical file organization too. As you can see, all files within a *hierarchical file system (HFS)* are members of a *directory*. Each directory is, in turn, a member of another directory at a higher level in the hierarchy. At the highest level is the *root directory*. The root directory can be considered analogous to the master catalog in OS/390 and will typically contain only other directories (also called *subdirectories*).

Directories and their subordinate files can be considered analogous to partitioned data sets and their members. That's because each directory contains information about itself as well as the files it holds, including their names, their size, the date they were created or modified, and other relevant information. However, unlike PDS data sets, directories are not considered files themselves. So whereas a PDS can be treated as a sequential file in some cases, directories do not have the same capabilities.

In fact, the entire HFS structure, from the root directory on down, is stored as a single data set on an IBM mainframe. OS/390 then manages the hierarchical files through its own HFS facility. As a result, *HFS files* can be used in both the UNIX System Services and OS/390 environments. This makes it possible for application programs that are designed to run in a UNIX environment to handle files as they normally would under OS/390. For example, Websphere Application Server for OS/390 uses HFS files to store and retrieve information for web applications. It also means that HFS files can be copied to and from sequential, partitioned, or partitioned extended data sets.

Although most HFS files store data, some can be executable modules and still others can consist of UNIX shell scripts. Executable modules, or programs, are similar to the compiled and linked programs found in OS/390 load libraries. *UNIX shell scripts* are similar to procedures. They consist of a series of UNIX commands (and, optionally, scripting commands) that are executed in order whenever the file is invoked.

A hierarchical file system

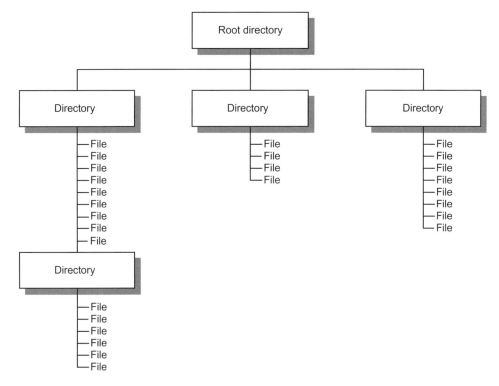

Description

- The *UNIX* operating environment consists of the *kernel* (operating system base), the file system, and the *shell* (command interface). *OS/390 UNIX System Services (USS)* simulates the UNIX operating environment on an IBM mainframe.

- OS/390 UNIX files are organized into a hierarchy as in a UNIX, DOS, or Windows system.

- All files within a *hierarchical file system* (*HFS*) are members of a *directory*. Each directory is in turn a member of another directory at a higher level in the hierarchy. At the highest level of the hierarchy is the *root directory*.

- Each directory includes information about the files it holds, such as their names and other relevant information.

- The entire HFS file structure, from the root directory on down, is stored as a single data set on an IBM mainframe, and OS/390 manages access to specific directories and files.

- The terms *hierarchical file system* and *HFS* are used both for the UNIX file structure in general and for the specific facility that OS/390 uses to manage the files on an IBM mainframe.

- HFS files can contain data, executable modules, or *UNIX shell scripts* that consist of UNIX commands and scripting commands (similar to a procedure). They can also be copied to and from OS/390 sequential, partitioned, or partitioned extended data sets.

Figure 21-1   OS/390 simulates a hierarchical file system for UNIX files

How to name and identify HFS files and directories

There are three rules you should keep in mind when naming HFS files and directories. First, HFS names can be up to 255 characters long and consist of a combination of upper- and lowercase letters, numbers, periods, underscores, and hyphens. Second, nulls and slashes are invalid. And third, uppercase letters and lowercase letters have different values in a UNIX environment. That means that the characters "A" and "a" are not interpreted as the same letter in UNIX. Figure 21-2 illustrates this point by showing three file names that use different combinations of upper- and lowercase letters and therefore identify three unique files even though they're all spelled the same.

Since HFS files are organized within directories and subdirectories, it's necessary to identify a file by its *path*. To do that, you use a *pathname* that gives the names of the directories and subdirectories that lead to the file you want, with the names delimited by slashes. In most cases, the pathname also includes a file name, as shown in this figure. A pathname can be up to 1023 characters long, including all directory names, file names, and separating slashes.

A pathname can be specified as an *absolute pathname* or a *relative pathname*. The first example in this figure uses an absolute pathname to identify a file. It starts at the root directory (identified by the first slash) and continues five directories deep before it names the master file. The relative pathname, shown right below it, assumes that the user is already in directory va5001, so it only names the directory immediately below it (LP) before naming the master file. As you work interactively, you'll use both absolute and relative pathnames regularly. Most programs, though, use absolute pathnames to identify HFS files because that ensures that each file is found no matter what directory the program may be in at the time.

An HFS file name or directory name can contain...

- Up to 255 characters
- Uppercase and lowercase A-Z
- Digits 0 to 9
- Periods (.), underscores (_), and hyphens (-)
- No nulls or slashes

HFS file and directory names are case-sensitive

Three different files

Trans.dat   TRANS.dat   tRans.dat

The elements of a pathname

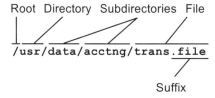

Absolute and relative pathnames

A file with an absolute pathname

```
/usr/data/r1/va5001/LP/master.file
```

The same file with a relative pathname for a user in directory va5001

```
LP/master.file
```

Description

- The set of names required to identify a particular file in a hierarchical file system is called the *path* of the file. You use a *pathname* to identify the file you want.
- A pathname consists of directory and subdirectory names delimited by forward slashes (/). In most cases, it includes a file name as well.
- A pathname can be up to 1023 characters long including all directory names, file names, and separating slashes.
- An *absolute pathname* identifies a file starting from the root directory. It begins with a slash for the root directory, followed by one or more directory names followed by slashes, and ends with a directory name or a file name.
- A *relative pathname* identifies a file starting from the directory that the user is currently working in. It doesn't include a beginning slash but rather starts with the name of a subdirectory within the current directory.

Figure 21-2   How to name and identify HFS files and directories

How to work with HFS files using TSO commands

Although HFS files are designed for the OS/390 UNIX environment, it's perhaps more realistic to assume that you'll be working with the data files in a standard OS/390 environment. So that's what you'll learn to do first. Fortunately, there are several TSO/E commands (or just TSO commands) that enable you to work with HFS files in ISPF. If you've already read chapter 20, you're familiar with TSO commands and how to enter them in ISPF. If not, you'll get a brief introduction in this topic.

TSO commands that operate on HFS files

Figure 21-3 lists some of the TSO commands that you can use to handle HFS files. You can execute any one of these commands from the ISPF Command Shell panel by choosing option 6 on the ISPF Primary Option Menu, entering the command at the command prompt (===>), and then pressing the Enter key. Or, you can execute these commands from any other ISPF panel by preceding the command with the characters TSO.

As you can see, the commands shown in this figure let you create HFS files and directories. They let you edit or browse (look at the contents of) an HFS file. And they let you convert an HFS file to or from a standard OS/390 data set. Because this last function is the one you're most likely to use, the next figure covers the OGET and OPUT commands in more detail.

Some TSO commands for working with HFS files and directories

TSO command	Description
MKDIR	Creates an HFS directory. Any intermediate directories in the pathname you specify must already exist.
OBROWSE	Browses an HFS file using the ISPF browse facility.
OEDIT	Creates or edits an HFS file using the ISPF editor.
OGET	Copies an HFS file to an OS/390 sequential data set or to a PDS or PDSE member. You can specify text or binary data and select EBCDIC/ASCII code conversion.
OGETX	Copies one or more HFS files from a directory to a PDS, a PDSE, or a sequential data set. You can specify binary or text data, select EBCDIC/ASCII code conversion, allow a copy from lowercase filenames, and delete one or all suffixes from the filenames when they become PDS or PDSE members.
OPUT	Copies an OS/390 sequential file or a PDS or PDSE member to an HFS file. You can specify text or binary data, and select EBCDIC/ASCII code conversion.
OPUTX	Copies one or more members from a PDS, a PDSE, or a sequential data set to a directory. You can specify binary or text data, select EBCDIC/ASCII code conversion, specify a copy to lowercase filenames, and append a suffix to the member names when they become filenames.

Two ways to enter TSO commands from ISPF

- Select option 6 from the Primary Option Panel to access the ISPF Command Shell panel shown in the next figure, and enter the command at the command prompt.

- Enter TSO followed by the command in the command area of any ISPF panel.

Description

- If you work regularly in ISPF, you'll find it's easy to use TSO commands like the ones shown above to handle HFS files.

- To see the syntax for any TSO command, you can enter the HELP command from any ISPF panel, like this:

```
TSO HELP command-name
```

- For more information on how to code TSO commands for HFS files, refer to IBM's *OS/390 UNIX System Services Command Reference* manual.

Figure 21-3   TSO commands that operate on HFS files

How to copy files to or from the HFS format

To copy files to or from the HFS format using TSO commands, you use the OPUT and OGET commands shown in figure 21-4. The OPUT command lets you copy a sequential file, PDS member, or PDSE member to an HFS file. If an HFS file by the name you specify doesn't already exist, the system creates it for you. However, the pathname you use must be valid. In other words, any directories you name must already exist. The OGET command lets you copy an HFS file to a sequential file, PDS member, or PDSE member.

The options that you can code on these commands have to do with data storage. Binary and text are two ways of storing data on a UNIX system. Occasionally, you'll transfer HFS files that contain binary data, particularly object modules, in which case you must code the BINARY option. Usually, though, you'll transfer files using the TEXT option. It's the default, so you don't need to code it unless you want to. However, since text data is stored in the EBCDIC format in OS/390 and in the ASCII format in UNIX, you do need to include the CONVERT parameter whenever you transfer text data to or from an HFS file.

The two examples at the bottom of this figure show how the OGET and OPUT commands are typically coded. In the first example, a transaction file called TR.file is copied to a library member called TRDATA. Since the file is stored in text format, the TEXT parameter is specified (although it's optional), and since it's necessary to translate the data from ASCII to EBCDIC, CONVERT(YES) is also specified. In the second example, a compiled program called TRPRG in the PDS library MM01.LOADLIB is copied to an HFS file called trprg in the bin directory. Since this is a compiled program, the BINARY parameter is specified.

These examples also illustrate one of the coding rules for TSO commands. If you don't enclose a data set name in single quotes, TSO adds your TSO user-id as the high-level qualifier to the name. So assuming the user-id is MM01, the TRDATA member shown in the OGET command is created in the MM01.WORK.DATA library. On the other hand, if you code a data set name in single quotes as shown in the OPUT example, the name is used as is.

The ISPF command shell panel for entering TSO commands

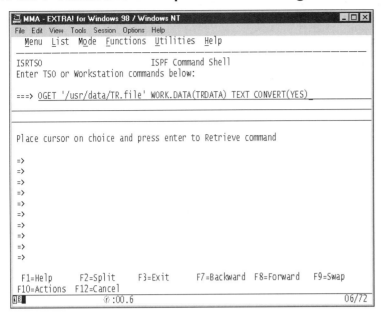

The syntax for the OGET and OPUT commands

```
OGET 'pathname' data-set-name [BINARY|TEXT] [CONVERT(YES|NO)]
OPUT data-set-name 'pathname' [BINARY|TEXT] [CONVERT(YES|NO)]
```

Explanation

pathname	The pathname of the HFS file being copied to or from a data set.
data-set-name	The sequential file or partitioned data set member being copied to or from an HFS file.
BINARY	Specifies that the file being copied contains binary data.
TEXT	Specifies that the file being copied contains text data (the default).
CONVERT	For OGET, converts data from ASCII to EBCDIC. For OPUT, converts data from EBCDIC to ASCII. Specify YES or NO.

An OGET command that copies an HFS file to a PDS member

```
OGET '/usr/data/TR.file' WORK.DATA(TRDATA) TEXT CONVERT(YES)
```

An OPUT command that copies a PDS member to an HFS file

```
OPUT 'MM01.LOADLIB(TRPRG)' '/bin/trprg' BINARY
```

Description

- The easiest way to create an HFS file is to use the ISPF editor as shown in chapter 3 (option 2 on the Primary Option Menu) and then copy the PDS member to an HFS file using the OPUT command.

- If a data set name includes lowercase letters or special characters besides the period, hyphen, and parentheses, it must be enclosed in single quotes. Also, if a standard data set name isn't enclosed in single quotes, TSO will add the user-id to it as the first qualifier.

Figure 21-4   How to copy files to or from the HFS format using TSO commands

How to invoke OS/390 UNIX System Services

Although you can readily access HFS files from within the standard OS/390 environment, you may occasionally need to access files or execute programs from within a UNIX environment. To do that, you use the UNIX shell provided by OS/390 UNIX System Services. The shell is *POSIX*-compatible (*Portable Operating System Interface for UNIX*), which means it uses a standard that allows files created in other UNIX environments to run within it. It also allows other UNIX programs to run within it, as long as they adhere to the POSIX standard. And it's capable of interpreting all of the standard UNIX commands that are common to any version of UNIX.

The OS/390 UNIX command shell

There are several shells available for use in a standard UNIX system. The *Bourne shell* is the original shell created for UNIX operating systems, and it's still the default for most. Two other popular shells are the *C shell* and the *Korn shell*. The OS/390 UNIX command shell is based on the Korn shell, perhaps the most popular and commonly used of the three. It includes all the UNIX commands available in the Bourne shell, plus several additional commands or extensions to existing commands.

Accessing the OS/390 UNIX command shell is fairly easy. First, you need to make sure that the systems programmer who is in charge of security and system access at your installation has set you up so that you can properly access the shell. This involves making modifications to your RACF (security) profile and creating a *home directory* within the UNIX shell. The home directory is where you always start off when you begin a UNIX session. Within this directory, you keep any *environmental variable files* you may need to execute programs. These files contain information that's required in certain languages, like the location of the Java classes that are used in Java programs. You can also use the home directory as the main directory for keeping your work data.

To start a UNIX session, you type the TSO command OMVS from the ISPF Command Shell or TSO OMVS from any other ISPF panel. There are other ways to access the command shell that are more direct. But none of them offers the same flexibility and access to ISPF and TSO services.

Once the UNIX session has started, the system displays a screen similar to the one shown in figure 21-5. As you can see, it starts off by listing software and copyright information. About halfway down the screen, you'll notice a pound sign (#). This is what's known as the UNIX *command prompt*. Depending on how your systems programmer sets you up, you may see a dollar sign ($) instead. If you see a pound sign when you sign on, then you have *super-user*, or *administrator*, *access*, which means that you can access any file or directory you want. Towards the bottom of the screen is the command line where you enter

The OS/390 UNIX command shell

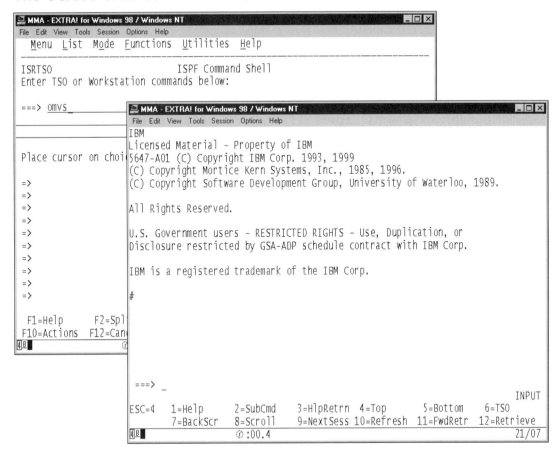

Description

- *POSIX*, or *Portable Operating System Interface for UNIX*, is a standard that defines the language interface between application programs and the UNIX operating system.
- The OS/390 UNIX command shell is based on the *Korn shell* that's popular on most other UNIX systems. This shell conforms to the POSIX standard.
- To access the OS/390 UNIX command shell, enter the TSO command OMVS at the ISPF Command Shell or TSO OMVS from any other ISPF panel.
- Once you're in the UNIX shell, a command prompt (usually a dollar ($) or pound (#) sign) indicates that the system is ready to accept input. You can then type a command at the command line (===>).
- To exit the UNIX command shell, enter *exit* on the command line.

Figure 21-5   How to invoke the OS/390 UNIX command shell

the commands you want the UNIX session to execute. The screen also includes a set of function keys at the bottom, although you'll find that you won't need to use them often.

The OS/390 UNIX command shell differs from standard UNIX systems in that the command line where you enter UNIX commands is separate from the command prompt. On standard UNIX systems, the cursor is always next to the command prompt. When you enter a UNIX command in the OS/390 UNIX shell, you'll see the word INPUT at the lower right corner of the screen change to RUNNING and the command you just entered will appear next to the command prompt on the screen. This means that OS/390 is processing your request. When it finishes, the system displays the result (if any), RUNNING changes back to INPUT, and a new command prompt appears on the screen letting you know that the shell is ready for the next command.

To exit from the OS/390 UNIX command shell, you type *exit* on the command line. This will end the UNIX session and return you to whichever ISPF screen you were on when you invoked OMVS.

Working with OS/390 UNIX shell commands

Figure 21-6 lists some of the more common UNIX commands you're likely to use in a UNIX environment. Since the OS/390 UNIX shell conforms to POSIX standards, the commands shown can be used in any UNIX system. Note that the commands are case-sensitive, so they must be entered in lowercase characters as shown. As you can see from the examples, you can operate on files in the current directory you're working in just by supplying the file name. Or you can enter a pathname to operate on other directories or the files in them.

Of particular interest is the *ls* command. When entered, it returns a listing of the files and directories in the current working directory or in the directory you specify. If you include the *-l* parameter, the listing will display additional information about the files, like when they were created or last modified, who created them, what size they are, and what type of access is allowed. This figure includes an example of a long format listing for the /mm01/data directory. Here, the last column lists the file names, and the first column lists the access permissions for the files, which you'll learn more about in figure 21-10.

The learning curve for working in a UNIX environment is fairly steep. That's because the shell provides over 600 commands that you can use to manipulate data and text in just about every way conceivable. The commands are also cryptic and most include several parameters that can be used to further clarify their function. In those respects, then, UNIX commands and JCL statements are similar.

Some common OS/390 UNIX shell commands

Command	Description
grep	Searches a file for occurrences of a specified word.
ls	Lists the files in a directory.
mkdir	Creates a directory. Any intermediate directories in the pathname you specify must already exist.
rmdir	Deletes a directory.
pwd	Displays the full pathname of the current directory.
whoami	Displays your username.
wc	Counts the number of words or lines in a file.

Examples

grep smith master.file	Searches the file named master.file in the current directory for occurrences of *smith*.
ls	Lists files in the current directory.
ls -l /mm01/data	Produces a detail (long) listing of the files in /mm01/data (see sample output below).
mkdir /usr/data	Creates a new directory named data subordinate to the usr directory, assuming the usr directory already exists.
rmdir /usr/data	Deletes the directory named /usr/data.
wc -w book.report	Gives a count of the number of words in the file named book.report in the current directory.
wc -l master.file	Gives a count of the number of lines in the file named master.file.

A long file listing for directory /mm01/data

```
-rwx--r---   1 ALL      AS            972 Nov 19 07:58 customer.master
-rwx--r---   1 ALL      AS            162 Nov 19 07:27 order.file
-rwx------   1 ALL      AS             41 Nov 20 06:08 stdone.err
-rwx------   1 ALL      AS              0 Nov 20 06:13 stdone.err2
-rwx------   1 ALL      AS              0 Nov 20 06:08 stdone.out
-rwx------   1 ALL      AS            541 Nov 20 06:11 stdone.out2
-rwxr-rr-x   1 ALL      AS            162 Nov 20 07:12 trans.backup
-rwxr-rr-x   1 ALL      AS            162 Nov 19 07:18 trans.data
-rwx--r---   1 ALL      AS            162 Nov 19 07:18 trans.data.copy
```

Description

- The OS/390 UNIX shell is a command line based tool, similar to the DOS operating system on PCs. As a result, you enter commands one at a time to do the desired processing.

- UNIX shell commands are case-sensitive and must be entered in lowercase.

- The UNIX shell contains over 600 commands that are used to control various aspects of the environment and the HFS files contained within it.

- Most commands include additional parameters. For a complete listing of commands and parameters, refer to the *OS/390 UNIX System Services Command Reference* manual.

Figure 21-6   Working with OS/390 UNIX shell commands

How to manage HFS files from the OS/390 UNIX shell

Figure 21-7 shows four of the UNIX shell commands that you're likely to use to manage HFS files. To start, the *cd* command allows you to change the directory you're currently in. There are several ways to use this command. One way is to enter an absolute pathname for the directory you want to go to, as shown in the first *cd* example in this figure. If you simply want to move to a subdirectory of the directory you're currently in, you can enter a relative pathname as in the second example. And a shorthand way to move up one level in the directory structure is to enter the *cd* command followed by two periods.

The *cp* and *mv* commands work in the same way. The *cp* (copy) command copies data from one file into a new file, and the *mv* (move) command moves a file to a new directory or renames it. This figure includes examples of both commands. As you can see, you can use a combination of relative and absolute pathnames to identify the files.

To delete a file, you specify the *rm* (remove) command, followed by the pathname of the file you want to delete. The last example in this figure uses an asterisk (*) as a *wildcard* to delete all files with a file suffix of .data in the data subdirectory. You can use an asterisk wildcard for the cp, mv, and rm commands whenever you want to affect more than one file.

OS/390 UNIX shell commands for managing HFS files

Command	Description
cd	Changes the working directory you are currently in.
cp	Copies the contents of one file to another file. If the file doesn't already exist, the system will create it.
mv	Moves a file to another directory or renames it.
rm	Deletes a file.

How to change the current working directory

cd /mm01/data   Changes the current working directory to /mm01/data.

cd data   Changes the current working directory to /mm01/data, assuming the current directory is /mm01 when the command is entered.

cd ..   Moves up one level in the directory structure.

How to copy files

cp trans.data trans.backup   Copies the contents of trans.data to a new file named trans.backup.

cp /usr/data/master.file mymaster.file   Copies the contents of master.file to a new file named mymaster.file in the current directory.

How to move and rename files

mv acct.data /usr/data/r1/Acct   Moves acct.data to a new directory (Acct) and keeps the same file name.

mv acct.data acct.data.old   Renames acct.data to acct.data.old.

How to delete files

rm MyTestProg.java   Deletes the specified file.

rm /usr/data/r1/va0033/LN/Loan.file   Deletes Loan.file in the specified directory.

rm /usr/data/*.data   Deletes all files with the file suffix .data in the specified directory.

Description

- To change the directory you're currently working in within the OS/390 UNIX shell, you enter the *cd* command followed by an absolute or relative pathname.

- To copy an HFS file, you enter the *cp* command followed by the names of the file you want to copy and the file you want to create. If either file isn't in the current directory, include the entire pathname.

- To move an HFS file to a new directory or to rename it, you enter the *mv* command followed by the file name and then the file's new directory or name.

- To delete an HFS file, you enter the *rm* command followed by the file name.

- You can use the * *wildcard* to specify more than one file for the *cp*, *mv*, and *rm* commands. It means that any characters in that position meet the specification.

Figure 21-7   How to manage HFS files from the OS/390 UNIX shell

How to work with HFS files through JCL

Although HFS files are designed to run in a UNIX environment, you can still access them through a batch job. The JCL you use is a little different, though, than for standard data sets. OS/390 provides some additional parameters for the DD statement that allow you to create, access, and delete HFS files.

How to use the PATH parameter

Figure 21-8 shows the syntax for the PATH parameter on a DD statement. As you can see, this parameter gives the pathname for an HFS file. As a result, you omit the DSN, or DSNAME, parameter from the DD statement since PATH takes care of identifying the file.

When specifying a pathname in the PATH parameter, it's important to include all the directory and subdirectory names associated with the file, starting with the root directory. In other words, you have to specify an absolute pathname. In addition, since file names in a UNIX environment are case-sensitive, you need to make sure that you use the correct case in the PATH parameter. If lowercase letters are used for any part of a pathname, the entire pathname must be enclosed in single quotes. The first example in this figure reflects this.

Pathnames tend to be long, so OS/390 allows you to specify pathnames of up to 255 characters. If a pathname doesn't fit on one line, you can continue it on the next line as shown in the second example. Here, you can see that the entire pathname must be enclosed in single quotes when it's continued, even though it doesn't contain any lowercase characters.

The PATH parameter can be used to identify HFS files for just about any application you use. However, this figure lists some of the DD statements where the PATH parameter is not allowed. Basically, these DD statements reflect OS/390 system files or libraries, areas in which you need to use standard OS/390 data sets.

As in a standard DD statement, symbolic parameters can be used to identify HFS files in the PATH parameter. You don't have to enclose the symbolic parameter in single quotes in this case, but you do have to include the quotes as part of the value within the symbolic parameter if any lowercase letters are used. On the other hand, backward references to DD statements with a PATH parameter aren't allowed and are treated as errors.

The syntax for the PATH parameter of the DD statement

```
PATH=pathname
```

Explanation

pathname   Identifies an HFS file. The pathname includes the directory and subdirectory names
(beginning at the root) and the name of the file.

The format for the pathname

```
PATH={['] /directory[/directory...]/filename[']}
     {&symbolic-name                           }
```

A pathname must...

*   Begin with a slash.
*   Include all directory and subdirectory names that lead to the file itself.
*   Be from 1 to 255 characters long.
*   Be enclosed in single quotes if it contains any lowercase letters.
*   Be enclosed in single quotes if it is continued on more than one line.

A PATH parameter that's used to access a master file in HFS format

```
//DD1  DD  PATH='/usr/data/r1/CA0020/MASTER.file'
```

A PATH parameter with a long file name

```
//DD1  DD  PATH='/USR/DATA/R1/CA0020/ACCOUNTING/REP
              ORTS/FEB01/INVENTORY.RPT'
```

Do not code the PATH parameter on any of the following DD statements

JOBCAT   STEPCAT   SYSABEND   SYSUDUMP
JOBLIB   STEPLIB   SYSMDUMP

Description

*   The PATH parameter on a DD statement is used in place of a DSN or DSNAME parameter to identify a file in HFS format.
*   Symbolic parameters can be used within the PATH parameter.
*   Backward references to a DD statement with a PATH parameter are not allowed and are treated as errors.
*   In some cases, you also need to include the PATHOPTS parameter in order to successfully access an HFS file. You'll learn more about PATHOPTS in the next figure.

Figure 21-8   How to use the PATH parameter

How to use the PATHDISP and PATHOPTS parameters

The PATHDISP parameter specifies the disposition of an HFS file. Like the DISP parameter, PATHDISP includes two positional subparameters that specify the normal and abnormal dispositions for the file. Normal disposition specifies what the system should do with the HFS file if the job step ends normally, and abnormal disposition specifies what to do if the program fails.

Figure 21-9 shows the syntax for the PATHDISP parameter as well as the values (KEEP or DELETE) you can select for each subparameter. You can only code the PATHDISP parameter if the PATH parameter is also present. If you omit it, the default for both normal and abnormal dispositions is KEEP.

Unlike the DISP parameter, the PATHDISP parameter doesn't include a subparameter for the HFS file's status at the start of the job step. Instead, the initial status is specified in the PATHOPTS parameter, also shown in this figure. In addition, the PATHOPTS parameter determines how the file can be accessed. Like the PATHDISP parameter, PATHOPTS can only be coded if the PATH parameter is also present on the DD statement. If you omit it, the system assumes that the HFS file coded in the PATH parameter already exists.

The file options, or subparameters, you specify for the PATHOPTS parameter are divided into two categories: *access* and *status*. Up to seven file options can be coded for each HFS file and they can be in any order you want. However, you can only code one of the three file options shown in this figure for the access group. If more than one access option is coded, the system defaults to ORDWR as the file's access.

In contrast, you can code up to six file options from the status group. This figure includes a list of the most commonly used status options. For a complete list, check the IBM manual entitled *OS/390 MVS JCL Reference*. The status options listed here primarily affect new files or those that are being updated.

To illustrate the use of the file options, this figure includes a DD statement that creates an HFS file (don't worry about the PATHMODE parameter for now, as it will be explained in the next figure). In the PATHOPTS parameter, I specified OWRONLY to limit the file to write-only access, OCREAT to create the file if it doesn't already exist, and OEXCL so that the job step will terminate if a file by the name of TRANS.out does exist. Two alternatives to OEXCL are the OAPPEND and OTRUNC options. The OAPPEND option allows additional records to be added to the end of an existing file, and the OTRUNC option deletes all existing records from the file before new records are written to it.

The syntax for the PATHDISP parameter of the DD statement

```
PATHDISP=(normal-disposition,abnormal-disposition)
```

Normal and abnormal disposition

KEEP   The file is retained. This is the default.

DELETE   The file is deleted.

The syntax for the PATHOPTS parameter of the DD statement

```
PATHOPTS={file-option                         }
         {(file-option[,file-option]...)}
```

Explanation

file-option   Specifies an access or status group option for the file named in the PATH parameter.

Access group options

ORDONLY   Specifies that the program can open the file in read-only mode.

OWRONLY   Specifies that the program can open the file in write-only mode.

ORDWR   Specifies that the program can open the file for both reading and writing.

Status group options

OAPPEND   Sets the file offset to the end of the file before each write. This allows additional data to be written to an existing file.

OCREAT   Specifies that the system is to create the file if it doesn't already exist.

OEXCL   When coded with OCREAT, specifies that the system is to terminate the job step if the file already exists.

OTRUNC   Specifies that the system is to truncate the file length to zero if the file already exists and it was successfully opened with ORDWR or OWRONLY (in other words, the file is reusable).

A DD statement that creates an HFS file

```
//DD1       DD    PATH='/usr/data/TRANS.out',PATHDISP=(KEEP,DELETE),
                  PATHOPTS=(OWRONLY,OCREAT,OEXCL),PATHMODE=(SIRWXU,SIRGRP)
```

Description

- The PATHDISP parameter specifies the disposition of an HFS file when the job step ends normally or abnormally.

- If the PATHDISP parameter is not coded, the default value for both normal and abnormal dispositions is KEEP.

- The PATHOPTS parameter specifies how an HFS file can be accessed and, depending on whether it's new or existing, how it should be processed.

- You can specify up to seven file options for the PATHOPTS parameter, and they can be in any order. However, you can only code one file option from the access group. If more than one is coded, the system defaults to ORDWR.

- If the PATHOPTS parameter isn't coded, the system assumes that the HFS file already exists. If the file isn't found, the job step terminates.

Figure 21-9   How to use the PATHDISP and PATHOPTS parameters

How to use the PATHMODE parameter

Figure 21-10 shows the syntax for the PATHMODE parameter on a DD statement. You can use the PATHMODE parameter to specify the access attributes for an HFS file at the time it is created. These attributes then limit who can access the file later on. The PATHMODE parameter can only be coded on a DD statement that includes a PATH parameter, and it's only recognized if the OCREAT file option is included in the PATHOPTS parameter.

There are four different types of *file access attributes*, or permissions, you can assign to a file: read-only, write-only, execute-only, and read-write-execute. The first two types are self-explanatory. The third, execute-only, signifies that the file is an executable module, like a program or a script file. The last type of permission can be considered all-inclusive, meaning that users can access the file any way they want.

File permissions are in turn divided into three levels. The highest level is the *file owner class*. It determines the types of access that are allowed to the user who creates the file. The next level down is the *file group class*. It determines what types of access are allowed to other users who are in the same file group as the creator of the file (file groups are set up and maintained by the systems administrator). The lowest level is the *file other class*. It determines the file access permission for any other user wanting to access the file. System administrators, or *super-users* as they're called in a UNIX environment, have access to all files regardless of the file access attributes specified in the PATHMODE parameter.

To find out what permissions have been assigned to a file, you can look at the long format listing generated by the *ls* command in the OS/390 UNIX shell. This figure includes the listing for a file named datatst. In this case, read, write, and execute permissions are granted to all users for this file. That means that when this file was created, the PATHMODE parameter looked like this:

```
PATHMODE=(SIRWXU,SIRWXG,SIRWXO)
```

You don't always have to specify all three permission levels in your JCL, though. You only have to specify the file access attributes that are needed to access the file appropriately once it's created. Just remember that if you omit the PATHMODE parameter from the DD statement completely, the system will set the file permissions to prevent access by all users except super-users.

The syntax for the PATHMODE parameter of the DD statement

```
PATHMODE={file-access-attribute                               }
         {(file-access-attribute[,file-access-attribute]...)}
```

Explanation

file-access-attribute   Specifies an access option for the HFS file named in the PATH parameter. Acceptable options are listed below.

File owner class options

SIRUSR   Specifies permission for a file owner to read the file.

SIWUSR   Specifies permission for the owner to write to the file.

SIXUSR   Specifies permission for the owner to execute a program in the file.

SIRWXU   Specifies permission for the owner to read, write, or execute the file.

File group class options

SIRGRP   Specifies permission for users in the file group class to read the file.

SIWGRP   Specifies permission for users in the file group class to write to the file.

SIXGRP   Specifies permission for users in the file group class to execute a program in the file.

SIRWXG   Specifies permission for users in the file group class to read, write, or execute the file.

File other class options

SIROTH   Specifies permission for all users to read the file.

SIWOTH   Specifies permission for all users to write to the file.

SIXOTH   Specifies permission for all users to execute a program in the file.

SIRWXO   Specifies permission for all users to read, write, or execute the file.

Identifying owner, group, and other class values in an HFS file listing

Description

- You use the PATHMODE parameter to specify the access attributes for an HFS file when it is created. These attributes then limit who can later access the file.

- The PATHMODE parameter is only recognized by the system if OCREAT is specified on the PATHOPTS parameter and the file doesn't already exist.

- If you omit the PATHMODE parameter when an HFS file is created, the system will set the file permissions to prevent access by all users except super-users.

- File groups are set up by the systems administrator, and the system recognizes the members of each group by their user logins.

Figure 21-10   How to use the PATHMODE parameter

How to work with HFS files in a batch processing environment

To give you a better idea of how to use the DD statement parameters you just learned about, figure 21-11 includes four jobs that show you how to access existing HFS files or create new ones. Three of the jobs execute a utility called IKJEFT01, which is the name of the TSO/E *Terminal Monitor Program* (*TMP*). Although IKJEFT01 is typically used to execute programs that access DB2 databases, it can also be used for some basic file copy functions. I chose this utility over some of the others you've already learned about because it is one of the easiest and most reliable ways to work with HFS files.

The first example copies one HFS file to another. The OCOPY command in the instream data set (SYSTSIN DD) identifies the ddnames of the input and output files. As you can see in the PATH parameters for these ddnames, the trans.data file is copied to a trans.data.copy file in the same directory. The PATHOPTS parameter for the new file specifies that the file is to be opened for write-only access (OWRONLY) and that if it already exists, the data in the file is to be written over (OTRUNC). In the second example, data is copied from a PDS member called ORDER to an HFS file called order.file. In the third example, the content of the HFS file called trans.data is copied to a sequential file called MM01.TRANS.DATA. All three examples provide an alternative to using the TSO OPUT and OGET commands as well as an automated way of copying data on a regular basis by incorporating the tasks in a batch job.

The last example in this figure shows how an HFS file can be used by an application program. Here, the customer master file is read by a report program called RPT3000. The output is sent to a SYSOUT data set. When HFS files are used in application programs like this, you need to make sure that any necessary DCB information is taken care of by the program itself.

An IKJEFT01 job that copies one HFS file to another

```
//MM01HC   JOB  (36512),'R MENENDEZ',NOTIFY=&SYSUID
//STEP1    EXEC PGM=IKJEFT01
//SYSTSPRT DD   SYSOUT=*
//HFSCP    DD   PATH='/mm01/data/trans.data',PATHOPTS=ORDONLY
//STDOUTL  DD   PATH='/mm01/data/trans.data.copy',
//              PATHOPTS=(OWRONLY,OCREAT,OTRUNC),
//              PATHMODE=(SIRWXU,SIXGRP)
//SYSPRINT DD   SYSOUT=*
//SYSTSIN  DD   DATA
 ocopy indd(HFSCP) outdd(STDOUTL)
 /*
```

An IKJEFT01 job that copies a PDS member to an HFS file

```
//MM01MC   JOB  (36512),'R MENENDEZ',NOTIFY=&SYSUID
//STEP1    EXEC PGM=IKJEFT01
//SYSTSPRT DD   SYSOUT=*
//MEMDATA  DD   DSN=MM01.WORK.DATA(ORDER),DISP=SHR
//HFSOUTL  DD   PATH='/mm01/data/order.file',
//              PATHOPTS=(OWRONLY,OCREAT,OTRUNC),
//              PATHMODE=(SIRWXU,SIXGRP)
//SYSPRINT DD   SYSOUT=*
//SYSTSIN  DD   DATA
 ocopy indd(MEMDATA) outdd(HFSOUTL)
 /*
```

An IKJEFT01 job that copies an HFS file to a sequential data set

```
//MM01HS   JOB  (36512),'R MENENDEZ',NOTIFY=&SYSUID
//STEP1    EXEC PGM=IKJEFT01
//SYSTSPRT DD   SYSOUT=*
//HFSCP    DD   PATH='/mm01/data/trans.data',PATHOPTS=ORDONLY
//DTAOUTL  DD   DSN=MM01.TRANS.DATA,DISP=(,CATLG,DELETE),
//              UNIT=SYSDA,SPACE=(TRK,(1,1)),
//              RECFM=FB,LRECL=80
//SYSPRINT DD   SYSOUT=*
//SYSTSIN  DD   DATA
 ocopy indd(HFSCP) outdd(DTAOUTL)
 /*
```

A report program that accesses an HFS customer master file

```
//MM01RN   JOB  (36512),'R MENENDEZ',NOTIFY=&SYSUID
//STEP1    EXEC PGM=RPT3000
//STEPLIB  DD   DSN=MM01.TEST.LOADLIB,DISP=SHR
//CUSTMAST DD   PATH='/mm01/data/customer.master',PATHOPTS=ORDONLY
//SALESRPT DD   SYSOUT=*
//SYSOUT   DD   SYSOUT=*
//
```

Description

- The IKJEFT01 utility program is a simple and convenient way to copy data to and from an HFS file.
- HFS files can be used as both input and output data sets for most programs.

Figure 21-11   How to work with HFS files in a batch processing environment

How to invoke OS/390 UNIX System Services through JCL

Batch processing offers several benefits to installations with a large number of users and many applications. Mainly, it offsets much of the data processing to business off-hours when the demand on system resources isn't as high. Although you can set up some automated "batch" processes in a UNIX environment, they fall short of the capabilities offered in an OS/390 batch environment. So OS/390 provides a utility that allows you to execute UNIX shell commands, as well as programs designed to run in a UNIX environment, directly in a batch job.

The BPXBATCH utility

BPXBATCH is an OS/390 utility that can be used to run UNIX shell commands, shell scripts, or executable HFS files through an OS/390 batch environment. With this utility, UNIX processes can be executed seamlessly as normal job steps in a nightly, weekly, or monthly job process.

The top of figure 21-12 shows how to code the BPXBATCH utility on an EXEC statement. Of particular importance is the DD statement's PARM parameter. That's because this is where you specify what UNIX shell command, script file, runtime program (like a Java program or a REXX procedure), or load module you want to run. To run a UNIX shell command, a UNIX script file, or a runtime program, you precede the UNIX command or HFS file name with the SH subparameter. SH tells the BPXBATCH utility to execute the command or program specified as though it were entered directly from the UNIX command line prompt. On the other hand, if you want to execute a compiled program, you have to specify PGM in front of the HFS program file. Whenever the PARM parameter includes an HFS file name, make sure that you include the correct pathname. Otherwise, the system won't be able to locate the file and the BPXBATCH utility will terminate.

This figure also gives a list of the ddnames the BPXBATCH utility uses for its standard input and output. STDIN allows you to specify an input file that contains the command, script, or runtime program you want to run or the load module named in the PARM PGM parameter. STDOUT provides a standard output file for any data produced. Typically, STDOUT is equivalent to a standard SYSOUT DD statement, but you can also specify an HFS file. STDERR captures any system messages produced by BPXBATCH as the job step executes. And STDENV can specify an environmental HFS file or data set (some UNIX utilities, like the Java runtime, require that you set environmental variables before you execute a Java program). You don't have to code any of these files, though, if the command or program you're executing via BPXBATCH doesn't need them. If omitted, the system defaults each file to /dev/null, which is equivalent to the DUMMY DD statement.

The syntax for the BPXBATCH utility program

```
//stepname  EXEC  PGM=BPXBATCH[,PARM='SH|PGM  shell-command|program-name']
```

Explanation

SH Names a shell command or an HFS file that contains a shell script or a runtime program. This option is primarily used to perform UNIX commands.

PGM Names a load module that's stored in an HFS file

DD statements used by BPXBATCH

ddname	Description
STDIN	The input HFS file. If not specified, defaults to /dev/null, the equivalent of a DUMMY data set.
STDOUT	The output HFS file. If not specified, defaults to /dev/null.
STDERR	The HFS file for error output. If not specified, any resulting error output is sent to the file specified in STDOUT.
STDENV	An environmental HFS file or data set. It can include environmental options that are used by such programs as the Java runtime. Usually defaults to /dev/null.

BPXBATCH can be executed from

- JCL
- The TSO/E ready prompt
- CLIST and REXX procedures
- A program

Description

- BPXBATCH is an OS/390 utility that can be used to run UNIX shell commands, shell scripts, or executable HFS files (programs) through the OS/390 batch environment.
- You can specify a path of /dev/null for STDIN, STDOUT, STDERR, and STDENV. This is the same as using a DUMMY data set.
- Although the BPXBATCH utility can be run in several different environments, you'll probably only use it in a job.

Figure 21-12   The BPXBATCH utility

Incidentally, in addition to using BPXBATCH in a batch job, you can also invoke it directly through TSO, CLIST and REXX procedures, and even through a program. But although these additional options are available to you, you're most likely to use the BPXBATCH utility in a batch environment.

How to use the BPXBATCH utility in a job

Figure 21-13 shows three examples of how you might use the BPXBATCH utility in a job step. The job in the first example contains a job step that executes a UNIX shell command; the job in the second example contains a job step that executes a script file; and the job in the third example contains a job step that executes a Java program.

The first example executes a UNIX shell command that produces a file listing for the /mm01/data directory. The output listing is stored in the HFS file named in the STDOUT DD statement. As you can see, I specified the SH subparameter before the *ls* command in the EXEC statement's PARM parameter. SH lets BPXBATCH know that it's executing a UNIX shell command rather than a compiled program.

The second example executes the script file named in the STDIN DD statement. Then, the UNIX shell commands and any scripting commands within the script file are executed sequentially. You may have noticed that the EXEC statement in this example does not include a PARM parameter. That's because the contents of the file named in STDIN will be automatically executed by the BPXBATCH utility as UNIX shell commands. If any output is produced, it is stored in the file named in the STDOUT DD statement.

You can also use the BPXBATCH utility to compile and run Java programs. In the third example, the Java runtime is executed for the program called BookOrderApp. Any output produced by the Java System.out class is sent to the HFS file specified in the STDOUT DD statement. Because Java programs require environmental variables, this job also includes an STDENV statement that references the HFS file where the variables are stored.

A BPXBATCH job that executes a UNIX shell command

```
//MM01BP1 JOB (36512),'R MENENDEZ',NOTIFY=&SYSUID
//STEP1    EXEC PGM=BPXBATCH,PARM='SH ls -l /mm01/data'
//STDOUT  DD PATH='/mm01/output/mm01bp1.out',
//           PATHOPTS=(OWRONLY,OCREAT,OTRUNC),
//           PATHMODE=(SIRWXU,SIXGRP)
//STDERR  DD PATH='/mm01/output/mm01bp1.err',
//           PATHOPTS=(OWRONLY,OCREAT,OTRUNC),
//           PATHMODE=(SIRWXU,SIXGRP)
//
```

A BPXBATCH job that executes a UNIX shell script

```
//MM01BP2 JOB (36512),'R MENENDEZ',NOTIFY=&SYSUID
//STEP1    EXEC PGM=BPXBATCH
//STDIN   DD PATH='/mm01/scripts/jcl.script',
//           PATHOPTS=ORDONLY
//STDOUT  DD PATH='/mm01/output/mm01bp2.out',
//           PATHOPTS=(OWRONLY,OCREAT,OTRUNC),
//           PATHMODE=(SIRWXU,SIXGRP)
//STDERR  DD PATH='/mm01/output/mm01bp2.err',
//           PATHOPTS=(OWRONLY,OCREAT,OTRUNC),
//           PATHMODE=(SIRWXU,SIXGRP)
//
```

A BPXBATCH job that executes a Java program

```
//MM01BP3 JOB (36512),'R MENENDEZ',NOTIFY=&SYSUID
//STEP1    EXEC PGM=BPXBATCH,PARM='SH java /mm01/BookOrderApp'
//STDOUT  DD PATH='/mm01/output/mm01bp3.out',
//           PATHOPTS=(OWRONLY,OCREAT,OTRUNC),
//           PATHMODE=(SIRWXU,SIXGRP)
//STDERR  DD PATH='/mm01/output/mm01bp3.err',
//           PATHOPTS=(OWRONLY,OCREAT,OTRUNC),
//           PATHMODE=(SIRWXU,SIXGRP)
//STDENV  DD PATH='/mm01/envfil',
//           PATHOPTS=ORDONLY
//
```

Description

- To execute a UNIX shell command with the BPXBATCH utility, include the shell command in the PARM parameter for the EXEC statement. Be sure to include the SH specification before any command.

- To run a shell script with the BPXBATCH utility, include the STDIN DD statement to allocate the HFS file that contains the script. The UNIX shell commands within the shell script will be executed when the job step runs.

- If you use a shell script with BPXBATCH, you don't have to include a PARM parameter on the EXEC statement.

- The BPXBATCH utility can also be used to compile and execute Java programs. When a Java program is executed, any output produced by the Java System.out class is sent to the HFS file specified in the STDOUT DD statement.

Figure 21-13   How to use the BPXBATCH utility in a job

Perspective

Chances are that you'll have to deal with HFS files sometime in your career, and probably sooner rather than later. The good news is that in most cases, it's likely to be through a batch process. Occasionally, though, you will need to access these files through the OS/390 UNIX shell. Either way, the principles you've learned in this chapter should give you a good basis to perform any file-handling function you need to do.

Terms

UNIX	Bourne shell
kernel	C shell
shell	Korn shell
UNIX System Services (USS)	home directory
hierarchical file system	environmental variable file
HFS	command prompt
directory	super-user access
root directory	administrator access
subdirectory	wildcard
HFS file	access option
UNIX shell script	status option
path	file access attribute
pathname	file owner class
absolute pathname	file group class
relative pathname	file other class
POSIX	super-user
Portable Operating System	Terminal Monitor Program
Interface for UNIX	(TMP)

Appendix A

JCL and JES syntax summary

This appendix presents the formats of the OS/390 and z/OS JCL statements as well as the JES2/JES3 control statements presented in this book. Each statement contains one or more figure references so you can look back to the complete figure if you need a description of the statement's parameters. The figures listed underneath the statement title are the main ones that describe the statement. Any figures listed to the right of a parameter are those that give a separate description of that parameter.

The formats follow the standard syntax rules:

[ ]   The elements within brackets are optional.

{ }   Choose one of the elements listed within braces.

| Choose one of the elements separated by vertical lines.

__   Underlined values are the defaults.

...   An ellipsis indicates that the preceding option may be repeated multiple times.

Uppercase elements are coded as shown. Lowercase elements are provided by the programmer.

Job control statements

The JOB statement
(Figures 4-5 and 5-1)

```
//jobname   JOB  [ accounting-information ] [ ,programmer-name ]    Fig 4-6, 4-7
                 [ ,ADDRSPC= {VIRT} ]                               Fig 5-10
                            {REAL}
                 [ ,BYTES=(value[,action])]                         Fig 5-12
                 [ ,CARDS=(value[,action])]                         Fig 5-12
                 [ ,CLASS=jobclass ]                                Fig 5-6
                 [ ,COND=((value,operator)...)]                     Fig 10-3
                 [ ,MSGCLASS=class ]                                Fig 4-8, 8-13
                 [ ,MSGLEVEL=(stmt,msg) ]                           Fig 4-8, 8-13
                 [ ,NOTIFY=user-id ]                                Fig 4-7
                 [ ,RESTART= ({*                } [,checkid] ) ]    Fig 11-2
                            {stepname             }
                            {stepname.procstepname}
                 [ ,LINES=(value[,action])]                         Fig 5-12
                 [ ,PAGES=(value[,action])]                         Fig 5-12
                 [ ,PERFORM=group ]                                 Fig 11-5
                 [ ,PRTY=priority ]                                 Fig 5-7
                 [ ,RD= R|RNC|NR|NC ]                               Fig 11-3
                 [ ,REGION= {valueK} ]                              Fig 5-9
                            {valueM}
                 [ ,TIME= {([minutes][,seconds])}  ]               Fig 5-11
                          {1440}
                          {NOLIMIT}
                          {MAXIMUM}
                 [ ,TYPRUN= {COPY}      ]                           Fig 5-8
                            {HOLD}
                            {JCLHOLD}
                            {SCAN}
```

The EXEC statement
(Figures 4-9 and 5-2)

```
//stepname EXEC   {PGM=program-name      }                         Fig 4-9
                  {[PROC=]procedure-name}                           Fig 9-1
                  [ ,ADDRSPC= {VIRT} ]                              Fig 5-10
                             {REAL}
                  [ ,COND=([(value,operator[,stepname])...]         Fig 10-4
                         [ ,EVEN|ONLY ]) ]
                  [ ,PARM=information ]                             Fig 4-9
                  [ ,PERFORM=group ]                               Fig 11-5
                  [ ,REGION= {valueK} ]                            Fig 5-9
                             {valueM}
                  [ ,RD= R|RNC|NR|NC ]                             Fig 11-3
                  [ ,TIME= {([minutes][,seconds])} ]               Fig 5-11
                           {1440}
                           {NOLIMIT}
                           {MAXIMUM}
                           {0}
```

The DD statement for non-VSAM DASD data sets

(Figure 4-10)

```
//ddname    DD {DSNAME|DSN=data-set-name}                        Fig 4-11
               {DUMMY                    }                        Fig 6-4
               ,DISP=(status,normal-disp,abnormal-disp)          Fig 4-12
            [ ,AVGREC= U|K|M ]                                    Fig 13-7
            [ ,DATACLAS=data-class-name ]                         Fig 13-4
            [ ,DCB=(option,option...) ]                           Fig 4-15
            [ ,DDNAME=ddname ]                                    Fig 9-8
            [ ,DSNTYPE= LIBRARY|PDS ]                             Fig 13-6
            [ ,LIKE=model-dataset-name ]                          Fig 13-8
            [ ,MGMTCLAS=management-class-name ]                   Fig 13-5
            [ ,REFDD=*.stepname.ddname ]                          Fig 13-8
            [ ,SPACE=(unit,(primary[,secondary][,dir])            Fig 4-14, 6-7, 6-8, 6-9
                     [,RLSE][,CONTIG|MXIG|ALX][,ROUND])
            [ ,STORCLAS=storage-class-name ]                      Fig 13-3
            [ ,UNIT=unit ]                                        Fig 4-13
            [ ,VOL=SER=serial-number ]                            Fig 4-13
```

The DD statement for existing VSAM data sets

(Figure 15-1)

```
//ddname    DD  { DSNAME|DSN=data-set-name }
                { DUMMY                    }
                [ ,DISP=(status,normal-disp,abnormal-disp) ]
                [ ,AMP=(option,option...) ]
```

The DD statement for new VSAM data sets (SMS only)

(Figure 15-3)

```
//ddname    DD  DSNAME|DSN=data-set-name
                ,DISP=(NEW,normal-disp,abnormal-disp)
             [ ,AVGREC= U|K|M ]
             [ ,DATACLAS=data-class-name ]
             [ ,KEYLEN=length ]
             [ ,KEYOFF=offset ]
             [ ,LIKE=data-set-name ]
             [ ,LRECL=length ]
             [ ,MGMTCLAS=management-class-name ]
             [ ,RECORG= KS|ES|RR ]
             [ ,SPACE=(unit,(primary,secondary)) ]
             [ ,STORCLAS=storage-class-name ]
             [ ,UNIT=unit ]
             [ ,VOL=SER=serial-number ]
```

The DD statement for a tape data set
(Figure 7-3)

```
//ddname    DD DSNAME|DSN=data-set-name
               ,DISP=(status,normal-disp,abnormal-disp)
               [ ,CHKPT=EOV ]                                        Fig 11-1
               [ ,DCB=(option,option...) ]                           Fig 7-9
               [ ,LABEL=([data-set-sequence][,label-type]) ]         Fig 7-7, 7-8
               [ ,RETPD=nnnn|EXPDT=date ]                            Fig 7-6
               [ ,{UNIT=(unit[,count][,DEFER])} ]                    Fig 7-4
                  {UNIT=AFF=ddname           }
               [ ,VOL=([PRIVATE][,RETAIN][,volume-sequence]          Fig 7-5
                      [,volume-count][,SER=(serial,...)]) ]
```

The DD statement for instream data sets
(Figure 4-16)

```
//ddname   DD    {*}      [ ,DLM=xx ]
                 {DATA}
```

The DD statement for SYSOUT data sets
(Figures 4-17, 8-4)

```
//ddname    DD [ SYSOUT=(class[,writer][, {form-name} ]) ]           Fig 8-5
                                          {code-name}
               [ ,COPIES=nnn(,(group-value[,group-value])) ]         Fig 8-9
               [ ,DEST=destination ]                                 Fig 8-7
               [ ,FCB=fcb-name ]                                     Fig 8-12
               [ ,FLASH=overlay-name ]                               Fig 8-12
               [ ,FREE= END|CLOSE ]                                  Fig 8-6
               [ ,HOLD= YES|NO ]                                     Fig 8-8
               [ ,OUTLIM=number ]                                    Fig 8-10
               [ ,OUTPUT= {reference                     } ]         Fig 8-3
                          {(,reference[,reference]...)}
               [ ,SEGMENT=page-count ]                               Fig 8-6
               [ ,SPIN= UNALLOC|NO ]                                 Fig 8-6
```

The OUTPUT statement
(Figure 8-1)

```
//name      OUTPUT [ ,CLASS=class ]                                    Fig 8-5
                   [ ,CONTROL= {PROGRAM} ]                             Fig 8-11
                              {SINGLE }
                              {DOUBLE }
                              {TRIPLE }
                   [ ,COPIES= {nnn                                } ]   Fig 8-9
                             {(,(group-value[,group-value...]))}
                   [ ,DEFAULT= YES|NO ]                                Fig 8-2
                   [ ,DEST=destination ]                              Fig 8-7
                   [ ,FCB=fcb-name ]                                  Fig 8-12
                   [ ,FLASH=overlay-name ]                            Fig 8-12
                   [ ,FORMS=form-name ]                               Fig 8-12
                   [ ,JESDS= {ALL} ]                                  Fig 8-13
                            {JCL}
                            {LOG}
                            {MSG}
                   [ ,LINECT=nnn ]                                    Fig 8-11
                   [ ,OUTDISP=(normal-disp[,abnormal-disp]) ]        Fig 8-8
                   [ ,PRTY=nnn ]                                      Fig 8-5
```

The PROC and PEND statements
(Figures 9-1 and 9-2)

```
//name      PROC [ parameter...]

//name      PEND
```

The JCLLIB statement
(Figure 9-3)

```
//[name] JCLLIB ORDER=(library[,library]...)
```

The INCLUDE statement
(Figure 9-5)

```
//[name]    INCLUDE MEMBER=name
```

The SET statement
(Figure 9-12)

```
//[name]    SET symbolic-parameter=value[,symbolic-parameter=value]...
```

The IF/THEN, ELSE, and ENDIF statements
(Figure 10-5)

```
//[name] IF (relational-expression) THEN
.
    statements-executed-if-true
.
//[name] ELSE
.
    statements-executed-if-not-true
.
//[name] ENDIF
```

The COMMAND statement
(Figure 11-6)

```
//[name]   COMMAND  'command command-operand'
```

JES statements

The JES2 /*PRIORITY statement
(Figure 5-4)

```
/*PRIORITY priority                                        Fig 5-7
```

The JES2 /*JOBPARM statement
(Figure 5-4)

```
/*JOBPARM   [ ,BYTES=value ]                               Fig 5-12
            [ ,CARDS=value ]                               Fig 5-12
            [ ,LINES=value ]                               Fig 5-12
            [ ,PAGES=value ]                               Fig 5-12
            [ ,RESTART= Y|N ]                              Fig 11-4
            [ ,SYSAFF=(system[,IND]) ]                     Fig 11-7
```

The JES2 /*OUTPUT statement
(Figure 8-14)

```
/*OUTPUT   code [,parameter][,parameter]...
```

The JES2 /*MESSAGE statement
(Figure 11-6)

```
/*MESSAGE message
```

The JES3 //*MAIN statement
(Figure 5-5)

```
//*MAIN    [ ,BYTES=(value[,action]) ]                     Fig 5-12
           [ ,CARDS=(value[,action]) ]                     Fig 5-12
           [ ,CLASS=job-class ]                            Fig 5-6
           [ ,FAILURE=recovery-option ]                    Fig 11-4
           [ ,HOLD= YES|NO ]                               Fig 5-8
           [ ,LINES=(value[,action]) ]                     Fig 5-12
           [ ,LREGION=valueK ]                             Fig 5-10
           [ ,PAGES=(value[,action]) ]                     Fig 5-12
           [ ,SYSTEM=system ]                              Fig 11-7
```

The JES3 //*FORMAT PR statement
(Figure 8-14)

```
//*FORMAT  PR,DDNAME=[ddname-specification] [,parameter][,parameter]...
```

The JES3 //*OPERATOR statement
(Figure 11-6)

```
//*OPERATOR message
```

Appendix B

IBM reference manuals

This appendix lists the IBM manuals for the JCL and related facilities that are presented in this book. Except for the DFSORT manual, the actual title of each manual is preceded by the operating system and its release number (for example, z/OS V1R1.0.) Although you're not likely to use these manuals on a regular basis, you may need to check them occasionally to verify the syntax of a JCL statement or to learn about a particular feature in a more detail.

You can download these manuals for free from the IBM website. To view them, though, you'll need a current copy of Adobe Acrobat Reader, available at www.adobe.com/products/acrobat. You can also buy printed copies of the manuals from IBM.

> For OS/390 system manuals, the current URL is:
>   www-1.ibm.com/servers/s390/os390/bkserv

> For z/OS system manuals, the current URL is:
>   www-1.ibm.com/servers/eserver/zseries/zos/bkserv

You'll then have to click on the link for the release of the operating system you're using to find the manuals you're looking for.

MVS JCL manuals
- MVS JCL User's Guide
- MVS JCL Reference
- MVS System Codes

TSO/E and ISPF manuals
- TSO/E User's Guide
- TSO/E Command Reference
- TSO/E REXX User's Guide
- TSO/E REXX Reference
- TSO/E CLISTs
- ISPF User's Guide Vol I
- ISPF User's Guide Vol II
- ISPF Reference Summary
- SDSF Guide and Reference

UNIX System Services
- UNIX System Services User's Guide
- UNIX System Services Command Reference

Utility and SMS manuals
- DFSMSdfp Utilities
- DFSMSdfp Checkpoint/Restart
- DFSMS Using Data Sets
- DFSMS Access Method Services for Catalogs
- DFSORT Application Programming Guide

Index

VSAM (continued)
  concatenating data sets, 180, 181
  control area, 350-353
  control area split, 353, 353
  control interval, 350-353
  control interval split, 352, 353
  data component, 45, 342, 343
  data management, 348-356
  data set organization, 44, 45, 340-347
  and dummy data sets, 179, 358, 359
  duplicate keys, 344, 345
  ESDS, 46, 340, 341, 376, 377
  free space, 352, 353
  index component, 45, 342, 343
  index set, 354, 355
  key field, 340, 341
  KSDS, 44, 45, 342, 343, 354, 355, 376-379
  non-unique keys, 344, 345
  random access, 342, 343, 354, 355
  RBA, 340, 341
  relative record number, 346, 347
  reusable data set, 346, 347
  RRDS, 46, 346, 347, 376, 377
  sequence set, 354, 355
  sequential access, 340, 341
  and SMS, 358, 359, 362, 363, 364, 365
  spanned records, 350, 351
VSE, 26, 27
VSE/ESA, 26, 27
VSF2C procedure, 415
VSF2CG procedure, 415
VSF2CL procedure, 415
VSF2CLG procedure, 415
VTAM, 65
VTOC, 42, 43, 48, 49, 452, 453

W

WAN, 10, 11
wc command (UNIX), 517
Websphere Application Server, 65, 506
whoami command (UNIX), 517
Wide area network (WAN), 10,11
WLM, 29, 65, 296, 297
WLM compatibility mode, 296, 297
WLM goal mode, 296, 297
Work file, 172, 173
WORKFILES parameter (BLDINDEX), 402, 403
Workload Manager, *see WLM*
WORM, 16, 17
WRITE statement (CLIST), 493

WRITENR statement (CLIST), 493
Write-Once, Read-Many (WORM), 16, 17

X

/*XEQ statement (JES2), 149
/*XMIT statement (JES2), 149
XREF compiler option, 418, 419

Z

z/Architecture, 6, 7
z/OS, 4, 26, 27
z/VM, 26, 27
z900 server, 15
zSeries server, 4, 5, 7, 32, 33

For more on Murach products, visit us at
www.murach.com

For enterprise programmers

Murach's OS/390 and z/OS JCL	$62.50
MVS TSO, Part 1: Concepts and ISPF (Second Edition)	42.50
MVS TSO, Part 2: Commands, CLIST, and REXX (Second Edition)	42.50
Murach's Structured COBOL	$62.50
Micro Focus Personal COBOL (compiler and Animator on CD ROM)	50.00
Murach's CICS for the COBOL Programmer	$54.00
The CICS Programmer's Desk Reference (Second Edition)	49.50
DB2 for the COBOL Programmer, Part 1 (Second Edition)	$45.00
DB2 for the COBOL Programmer, Part 2 (Second Edition)	45.00
Murach's Beginning Java 2	$49.50
Murach's Visual Basic 6	45.00

Coming soon

Murach's Beginning Visual Basic .NET
Murach's SQL for SQL Server

*Prices and availability are subject to change. Please visit our web site or call for current information.

Our unlimited guarantee...when you order directly from us

You must be satisfied with our books. If they aren't better than any other programming books you've ever used...both for training and reference....you can send them back for a full refund. No questions asked!

Your opinions count

If you have any comments on this book, I'm eager to get them. Thanks for your feedback!

Mike Murach

To comment by

E-mail: murachbooks@murach.com
Web: www.murach.com
Postal mail: Mike Murach & Associates, Inc.
            2560 West Shaw Lane, Suite 101
            Fresno, California 93711-2765

To order now,

 Web: www.murach.com

 Call toll-free:
1-800-221-5528
(Weekdays, 8 am to 5 pm Pacific Time)

 Fax: 1-559-440-0963

 Mike Murach & Associates, Inc.
Practical computer books since 1974